T0329647

AGRARIAN STUDIES 3

Dalit Households in Village Economies

AGRARIAN STUDIES 3

Dalit Households
in Village Economies

Edited by
V.K. RAMACHANDRAN and
MADHURA SWAMINATHAN

 Tulika Books

Published by
Tulika Books
35 A/1 (ground floor), Shahpur Jat, New Delhi 110 049, India
tulikabooks.wordpress.com

First edition (hardback) 2014

ISBN: 978-93-82381-30-3

Printed at Chaman Offset, New Delhi 110 002

Contents

Acknowledgements

Most of the papers in this book were first presented at two conferences held at the Indian Statistical Institute, Kolkata. These conferences and related research for this book were supported by the Indian Statistical Institute, the University Grants Commission, the Indian Council for Social Science Research and the Foundation for Agrarian Studies. We are grateful to Professors Bimal Roy and Sukhadeo Thorat for their personal support for this research effort, and to the participants at the conferences for their papers, comments and contributions to the final content of this book.

K. Varadha Rajan insisted that particular attention be paid to the subject of the economic conditions of Dalit households in the schedules of the Project on Agrarian Relations in India (PARI). Sukhadeo Thorat first suggested that we use our village studies data for a larger work on Dalit households in village economies. We are grateful to both of them.

The articles were edited and the introduction written when one of the editors (VKR) was at Hitotsubashi University and Yokohama National University as a Visiting Professor, and the other editor (MS) was Visiting Professor at Fudan University. We are grateful to our hosts in these universities for the facilities and research environment that were provided us. We thank Professor N.S.N. Sastry, Head of the Indian Statistical Institute, Bangalore Centre, for facilitating the work on the manuscript in its final stages.

Aditi Dixit coordinated the production of this book.

We are grateful to all members of the team at the Foundation for Agrarian Studies who worked on the data for this book, and to the Research Fellows of the Indian Statistical Institute who have worked with us. We are grateful to Indira Chandrasekhar, Managing Editor of Tulika Books, for her work on the manuscript.

1 January 2014   V.K. RAMACHANDRAN
                                                     MADHURA SWAMINATHAN
                                                       Economic Analysis Unit
                                         Indian Statistical Institute, Bangalore Centre

Introduction

Introduction

V.K. Ramachandran

Caste is an institution of oppression and social discrimination specific to South Asia, more so to India. Central to the caste system were the status assigned to the Dalit people and the now-criminal practice of untouchability. Caste is a creation of, intrinsic to and inseparable from the religion of Hinduism.

Caste is hostile to individual and collective freedom: where there is caste, there can be no democracy. In *Annihilation of Caste*, Dr Ambedkar wrote that democracy is 'primarily a mode of associated living, of conjoint communicated experience. It is essentially an attitude of respect and reverence towards fellow men' (Ambedkar 1944). 'No matter what the Hindus say,' Ambedkar wrote in his classic denunciation of the concept of Hindu Rashtra, 'Hinduism is a menace to liberty, equality and fraternity. On that account it is incompatible with democracy' (Ambedkar 1945).

Caste is embedded in production relations. It is an impediment to the growth of the productive forces, and a bulwark against the revolutionary overthrow of the ruling classes. In so far as it has gripped the minds of people, caste has served as a material force. Its main ideological function in the contemporary world is to create, by means of coercion or internalization, an acceptance of social hierarchy based on ascribed status, and to prevent revolutionary action against the cruel and abhorrent forms of oppression and degradation that characterize Indian society today.

In recent years, there have been new scholarship and new attempts to understand the socio-economic conditions of life of Dalit people and households in India, particularly rural India, where oppression is sharpest.

In an important 2004 article, Sukhadeo Thorat wrote that there is now 'a massive literature on the practice of untouchability and atrocities' against the Dalit people (Thorat 2004). The literature to which he refers is one to which a wide range of concerned citizens – academics, political and social activists, and journalists – have contributed. There has been more detailed and concurrent coverage than before in the print, audio-visual and new media, of specific attacks: for all the problems of contemporary journalism, there is really no comparison between the coverage of, for instance, Khairlanji in 2006 and Venmani in 1968.

Thorat (2004) refers also to new 'studies based on village surveys [that] bring out the actual magnitude of the practice of untouchability and atrocities'. The first efforts in this direction were to document direct discrimination; among the most important in this regard was a study published in Shah *et al.* (2006). This study presented the results of a major survey, conducted over eighteen months in 2001–02, in 565 villages in eleven Sates of India (Andhra Pradesh, Karnataka, Kerala, Tamil Nadu, Maharashtra, Rajasthan, Punjab, Uttar Pradesh, Orissa and Bihar).[1] The survey was not a household survey; one questionnaire was canvassed in each village. The summary results give an extraordinary picture of practices of direct discrimination against Dalits in contemporary rural India (Table 1).

TABLE 1   *Overview of the forms in which untouchability is practised in rural India, by degree of prevalence, from a survey conducted in 2001–02, and reported in Shah, Mander, Thorat, Deshpande and Baviskar (2006)*

More than 50% of villages
Denied entry into non-Dalit houses
Bar against sharing food
Denied entry into places of worship

45–50% of villages
Denied cremation and burial grounds
Denied access to water facilities
Ban on marriage processions
Not allowed to sell milk to cooperatives
Denied hair-cutting services
Denied laundry services
Ill-treatment of women by non-Dalit men

30–40% of villages
Schools: separate seating
Payment of wages: no touching
Denied entry into village shops
Denied work as agricultural labour
Cannot sell things in local markets
Denied visits by health workers
Separate seating in eating-places
Denied access to irrigation facilities
Separate utensils in eating-places
Discriminatory treatment in police stations
Separate seating in self-help groups

---

[1] The combined Dalit population of these States accounted for 77 per cent of India's Dalit population.

25–30% of villages
Separate seating in panchayats
Schools: Dalits and non-Dalit students sit separately
Not employed in house construction
Cannot make purchases from milk cooperatives
Denied entry into police station
Denied carpenters' services
Denied entry into shops that are run as part of the public distribution system (PDS)
Denied access to restaurants and hotels
Forced to stand before 'upper'-caste men

20–25% of villages
Paid lower wages for the same work
Ban on festival processions on roads
Denied home delivery of letters
Segregated seating in schools
Denied entry into private health clinics
No access to grazing or fishing grounds
Tailor refuses to take measurements
No buying of pots from potter
Separate drinking water in schools

15–20% of villages
Discriminatory treatment in post offices
Bar on wearing new or bright clothes
Shops: no touching in transactions
Denied access to public roads or passages
Denied entry into Primary Health Centres

10–15% of villages
Denied entry into panchayat offices
Ban on wearing dark glasses, smoking, etc.
Public transport: no seats or last entry
Separate lines at polling booths
Denied entry into polling booth
Discriminatory treatment in Primary Health Centres (PHCs)

Less than 10% of villages
Denied access or entry to public transport
Separate times for voting at polling booths
Discriminatory treatment in private clinics
Forced to seek marriage blessings from 'upper' castes
Forced to seek 'upper' castes' permission for marriages
Bar on using cycles on public roads
Denied entry or seating in cinema halls

There have also been new efforts by mass organizations of Dalits, and of peasants and rural workers, to understand and document issues related to caste oppression. I wrote to two organizations that are based in Andhra Pradesh and Tamil Nadu (both are associated with the All India Kisan Sabha and All India Agricultural Workers Union). These are the anti-untouchability organizations Theendamai Ozhippu Iyakkam (Movement for the Destruction of Untouchability) in Tamil Nadu, and Kulavivaksha Vyathireka Porata Sangham (Struggle Committee Against Caste Discrimination) in Andhra Pradesh. Each has conducted extensive village surveys in their States. The method was to canvas a village-level questionnaire and record every form in which untouchability or direct discrimination was practised in the village. The presentation of the data was not in the more statistically satisfactory form of the material in Shah *et al.* (2006), since there was no attempt as in the latter to record the degree of prevalence of a particular practice (in other words, whether a practice occurred in one village or many, it was given equal weightage in a single final list). Despite this shortcoming, the work and the lists are invaluable, carrying as they do the marks and smell of ugly reality (Tables 2 and 3).

TABLE 2 *Extract from the list of discriminatory practices recorded by the Kulavivaksha Vyathireka Porata Sangham in Andhra Pradesh, 1998*

Separate glasses for Dalits in eating-places. Separate plates and spoons. Dalits have to clean the glasses they use.

Separate seating in eating-places.

Dalits forced to sit on the floor in eating-places.

Other Castes served in plates, Dalits on pieces of newspaper.

Bar on temple entry.

Processions of the village temple deity not permitted to enter Dalit areas.

Other Caste barbers do not cut hair, shave Dalits.

Separate seating in panchayat offices.

Dalits forced to sit on the floor in panchayat offices.

Bar on playing *halai* at Moharram.

Other Caste washermen not permitted to wash Dalits' clothes.

Bar on drawing water from village wells, bore-wells, tanks.

Water for drinking given in separate hand-bowls; food served in Dalits' towels.

Bar on serving in glasses in arrack and toddy shops; served in earthen pots.

Forced to sit on the ground in bus-stands.

Prevented from voting in elections.

Brahman priests do not perform Dalit weddings.

Separate seating at school mid-day meal centres.

Bar on riding bicycles in Other Caste residential streets.

Discrimination in renting out houses.

Separate seating for food at weddings and other functions; Dalits served last.

Use of insulting, casteist language against employees.

Use of insulting, casteist language in educational institutions.

Bar on sitting on chairs or cots in the presence of Other Castes.

Bar on workers, including women domestic workers, working inside the houses of Other Castes.

Untouchability in shops: purchased items not given in the hand.

Bar on wearing slippers in Other Caste areas. Slippers have to be carried in the hand.

Bar on entering Other Caste streets.

Dalit Ganesh processions are not allowed in the residential streets of Other Castes, and Dalits have to perform immersion separately.

Food served to Other Castes at Dalit wedding ceremonies has to be cooked by Other Castes in Other Caste streets.

Dalit homes are away from the main village.

Bar on wearing full *dhotis* and on wearing a towel on the shoulder.

Bar on wearing white clothes.

Other Caste schoolchildren do not eat food cooked by Dalit women in mid-day meal centres.

Bar on funeral processions passing through Other Caste streets.

Separate cemetery.

Separate drinking water supply at *anganwadi* centres.

Bar on participation of Dalit-owned bulls in bull-processions during the Ugadi festival.

Bar on using umbrellas in Other Caste streets.

Bar on touching anything in an Other Caste house.

Bar on musical bands at Dalit weddings.

Dalits have to sit on the floor in the houses of Other Castes.

Dalit worshippers of the deity Ayyappan not allowed to participate equally in rituals.

Bar on participation by Dalit sportsmen and women in village sports and games.

Bar on the erection of Ambedkar statues in village centres.

Dalits not invited to weddings in the families of Other Castes.

Village beggars accept money, paddy and pulses, but do not take any cooked food from Dalits.

Dalit construction workers are not invited for the house-inauguration ceremonies of houses of Other Castes that they have built for Other Castes.

Bar on collecting and presenting *jammi* leaves on the day of the Vijayadasami festival. (The *jammi* is regarded as a sacred tree; it is believed that the Pandavas placed their weapons on the branches of the *jammi* tree and took them back on Vijayadasami. The tree is symbolic of success, and it is customary to offer the leaves of the tree to others as a symbol of wishing them a happy future.)

Dalit performing artists are not permitted to perform on temple stages. (In Andhra Pradesh villages, temples have a stage for performing artists.)

Other Castes do not sell milk to the Dalits – they say that if they do, their cattle will not give milk as they should. Other Castes do not buy milk from Dalit households.

Bar on the participation of Dalit women in the annual Batukamma festival. (In some parts of Andhra Pradesh, women decorate images of the goddess with flowers in large plates and bowls. They dance together, and immerse the decorated image in rivers, canals and tanks.)

Annual wage-labourers, called *paleru*, are served food on stone surfaces. Landlords employ Dalit workers for an annual payment in cash or paddy and cooked food every day. The normal tasks of the workers include taking care of cattle, cleaning them and taking them to the fields, and all sorts of other tasks around the landlord's house and in the fields. The landlords keep flat, smooth stones in their backyards. Dalit workers are served food – generally leftovers from the previous day – on these stones. The workers are expected to clean these stones after they eat.

Source: Communication from Kulavivaksha Vyatirekha Porata Samiti, Hyderabad.

TABLE 3   *Extract from the list of discriminatory practices recorded by the Theendamai Ozhippu Munnani (Front for the Destruction of Untouchability) in Tamil Nadu, 2007*

Bar on using public paths and roads.

Bar on wearing slippers.

Bar on riding bicycles.

Bar on carrying a towel-cloth on the shoulder.

Bar on walking about with *dhoti* folded up.

Bar on wearing a polyester *dhoti*.

Bar on wearing a head-cloth.

Launderers refuse to wash Dalits' clothes.

Launderers keep separate almirahs for Dalits' clothes.

Bar on haircuts in Other Caste barber-shops.

Separate chairs in barber-shops.

Separate glasses in tea-shops. Separate glasses for each Dalit sub-caste in tea-shops.

Dalits have to sit on the floor in eating-places.

Bar on sitting on benches in tea-shops. Dalits have to squat on the floor in tea-shops.

Dalits served tea in coconut-shells. When a Dalit asks for water to drink, it is poured into their hands.

Bar on taking water from public taps.

Setting special times for Dalits to take water from public taps.

Bar on lighting firecrackers at festivals.

Boycotting meetings in the village that are organized or chaired by Dalit government officials.

Bar on bathing in public tanks.

Separate steps for Dalits at public tanks.

Temple entry barred.

Temple processions do not enter Dalit streets.

Dalits barred from climbing temple steps.

Temple offerings of Dalits sprinkled with water before being accepted.

Separate areas in temples (and churches) for Dalits to worship.

Access to public crematoria barred.

Separate funeral pyres in public crematoria.

Separate crematoria for Dalits.

Even where there is a separate crematorium, Dalits are barred access to the crematorium by public road.

Dalits barred from watching television in the panchayat office.

Separate ration shops.

Separate times for Dalits at general ration shops.

Bar on raising livestock.

Dalit speakers, performing artistes barred from using public stages built in villages.

Postmen do not deliver letters to Dalit households; they send messages to recipients to come and collect their mail.

At temple festivals, Dalits are compelled to give goats free to the heads of the traditional dominant caste.

At the village temple festival, after the traditional *kappu* is tied to the wrists of the Other Castes, it is considered inauspicious for them to look at the face of a Dalit.

Ban on raising (male) dogs, in case they mate with bitches belonging to Other Castes.

Dalits compelled to dispose all animal carcasses.

Dalits compelled to prepare all corpses for funerals.

Dalits compelled to play the drums at all village events.

Bar on sitting on benches at bus-stands.

When there is a death in a Other Caste family, Dalits are compelled to take news of the death to others in the village and elsewhere: no payment.

Free labour; unwaged labour services.

Bar on eating in the general wedding-tent (*pandal*) at wedding feasts.

Private wedding halls do not rent out premises for Dalit weddings.

House owners in town and village refuse to lease out houses to Dalits.

Other Castes abbreviate Dalit personal names in an insulting way.

Calling Dalit elders by children's names; using disrespectful and insulting forms of address.

Dalits compelled to clean and carry away night soil.

Barred from some schools.

Walls constructed to bar access to Dalits to streets passing through the Other Caste sections of a village (as in Uthapuram).

In villages (and some towns), Dalits are not permitted to go to the Dalit quarter by the shortest public road; they are compelled to take circuitous routes that circumvent Other Caste habitations.

Government employs only Dalits as sanitation workers.

Schoolteachers discriminate against Dalit pupils.

Encroachment by Other Castes on Dalit agricultural land.

Preventing elected Dalit panchayat members from functioning.

Not giving Dalits a share in common funds of the village.

Source: Communication from Theendamai Ozhippu Munnani.

These are cases of outright violations of civil liberties and rights. They represent *direct* discrimination, that is, the denial of universal rights and liberties to members of a group (or perceived group) because of their membership or perceived membership in that group. Each line in each of the tables above represents a crime – not only in a moral and civilizational sense, but also with respect to the law in India.

As the foregoing suggests, there is now important new descriptive and analytical writing on direct socio-economic discrimination. It has also been pointed out that while there is a body of literature that documents discrimination and the denial of civil liberties, there are few studies by economists of market and non-market forms of discrimination and socio-economic exclusion. There is clearly a need for rigorous micro-studies of the access of the victims of sectional deprivation to land, employment, credit and other inputs in the contemporary context.[2] Indeed, one of the observations in Thorat (2004)

[2] 'Since in a private economy markets are the place where people get access to factors of productions, employment, consumer goods and service,' Sukhadeo Thorat writes, 'the exclusion and discrimination of some groups in market transactions on the basis of group characteristic is a serious case of market failure' (Thorat 2005).

was that 'very few empirical studies have tried to study the phenomenon of economic discrimination'.

Situation Analyses from the Project on Agrarian Relations in India

In 2005–06, the Foundation for Agrarian Studies began a programme of village studies, the Project on Agrarian Relations in India (PARI).[3] The broad objectives of PARI are:

- to analyse village-level production, production systems and livelihoods, and the socio-economic characteristics of different strata of the rural population;
- to conduct specific studies of sectional deprivation in rural India, particularly with regard to the Dalit and Scheduled Tribe (ST) populations, women, specific minorities, and the income-poor; and
- to report on the state of basic village amenities and the access of rural people to the facilities of modern life.

In response to a suggestion made directly to us by Sukhadeo Thorat, we selected certain key economic variables from our data, and processed the data separately for Dalits and Other Castes. We define the latter here as non-Dalit, non-Adivasi, non-Muslim social groups in the villages. In most villages, this coincides with what are called 'caste Hindus', although in some villages the term Other Castes also includes Jat Sikhs (these villages include 25 F Gulabewala, Sri Ganganagar district, Rajasthan; Gharsondi, Gwalior district, Madhya Pradesh; and Tehang, Jalandhar district and Hakamwala, Mansa district, both in Punjab) and Jains (in Nimshirgaon, Kolhapur district, Maharashtra).

PARI surveys now cover twenty-two villages in nine States of India (see Annexure Table 1). The analysis in each of the essays that follow which derive from PARI data do not cover all the villages. Different authors have used data from different villages, generally from the villages for which the data they have used have been cleaned.

The data here represent only a small section of the material that has been collected as part of the PARI surveys. The articles here do not directly deal with policy, but represent a report on the conditions of life of Dalit households in villages that were surveyed during the years that saw the highest rates of growth of GDP in the post-liberalization period. If any policy conclusion emerges, it is that changing the basic conditions of life requires public action and more direct intervention by the state on behalf of victims of group deprivation.

The results from the surveys, as discussed here and will be evident from the essays in the book, are compelling.

---

[3] The project was conducted under my overall direction.

Literacy and Schooling

Literacy and schooling continue be areas where historical discrimination is reflected in persistent, stubborn social disparities (Tables 4, 5 and 6).

The picture is one of very poor aggregate achievement, characterized further by abysmal levels of literacy and schooling among Dalits, rural Muslims and Adivasis (in ascending order of deprivation).

In the great majority of survey villages, 50 per cent or more Adivasi, Muslim and Dalit women are unable to read and write. In the great majority of survey villages, the median number of years of schooling among Dalit, Adivasi and Muslim women above the age of 16 was zero; in fact, in many villages, more than 80 per cent of women belonging to these socially excluded

TABLE 4   *Proportion of population aged 7 years and above who can read and write, by social group and by sex, PARI villages* in per cent

Social Group	Proportion of literate people	
	Male	Female
Scheduled Caste	61	45
Scheduled Tribe	35	20
Muslim	65	46
Other Caste	75	56
All	67	51

TABLE 5   *Proportion of persons aged 16 years and above with ten years or more of schooling, by sex and social group, PARI villages* in per cent

Social group	Proportion of people in group	
	Male	Female
Scheduled Caste	20	12
Scheduled Tribe	5	2
Muslim	21	8
Other Caste	37	22
All	29	17

TABLE 6   *Proportion of persons aged 16 years and above with no schooling, by sex and social group, study villages* in per cent

Social group	Proportion of people in group	
	Male	Female
Scheduled Caste	37	57
Scheduled Tribe	58	83
Muslim	39	60
Other Caste	21	44
All	28	50

groups had not completed even a year of school. At the same time, only 12 per cent of Dalit women, 2 per cent of Adivasi women and 8 per cent of Muslim women in the study villages had completed ten years of schooling. The data for men and women in this regard are appalling evidence on a massive scale that the people of rural India have been robbed of the right to even basic formal education.

Land and Other Household Assets

The results of the village surveys as reported in the articles in this section of the book provide further evidence of the vast economic chasms separating social groups in rural India.

With respect to ownership holdings of land, for instance, in sixteen out of twenty-two villages for which data were processed, 70 per cent of Dalit households had no ownership holdings of land; the corresponding figure for Other Castes was 30 per cent.

The average landlessness ratio for Dalits was pushed up substan-

TABLE 7   *Households with no ownership holdings of land as a proportion of all households (initial computations), selected villages* in per cent

Village	District	State	Households with no ownership ownership holdings of land as a proportion of all households	
			Dalit	Other Castes
Ananthavaram	Guntur	Andhra Pradesh	67	25
Bukkacherla	Ananthapur	Andhra Pradesh	69	70
Kothapalle	Karimnagar	Andhra Pradesh	82	83
Katkuian	West Champaran	Bihar	90	45
Nayanagar	Samastipur	Bihar	89	45
Zhapur	Gulbarga	Karnataka	54	31
Siresandra	Kolar	Karnataka	21	8
Alabujanahalli	Mandya	Karnataka	31	15
Gharsondi	Gwalior	Madhya Pradesh	22	18
Nimshirgaon	Kolhapur	Maharashtra	69	29
Warwat Khanderao	Buldhana	Maharashtra	44	19
Hakamwala	Mansa	Punjab	65	9
Tehang	Jalandhar	Punjab	98	37
Gulabewala	Sri Ganganagar	Rajasthan	98	15
Rewasi	Sikar	Rajasthan	14	3
Harevli	Bijnor	Uttar Pradesh	51	20
Mahatwar	Ballia	Uttar Pradesh	30	6
Amarsinghi	Malda	West Bengal	54	20
Kalmandasguri	Koch Bihar	West Bengal	8	33
Panahar	Bankura	West Bengal	64	17
Weighted average of all villages			70	30

tially by three villages in which Jat Sikh farmers were dominant (Tehang in Jalandhar district and Hakamwala in Mansa district in Punjab, and 25 F Gulabewala in Sri Ganganagar district in Rajasthan), and in Nimshirgaon, Kolhapur district, Maharashtra. Punjab (more specifically, village economies dominated by Jat Sikh landlords) and the Marathwada region represent, of course, very different historical trajectories of social exclusion; they are both, however, characterized by widespread landlessness among the Dalit masses.

The descriptive statistics in the article by Vikas Rawal show sharp and systematic disparity in the ownership of assets, for every type of asset, between Dalit households and households belonging to other social groups (other than Adivasi and Muslim households). With respect to ownership of the means of production, Dalit households had much lower access to productive assets – land, livestock, agricultural machinery, irrigation equipment – than Other Caste households. A stark example comes from the data on ownership of the means of production: only one Dalit household owned a tractor in all fifteen villages for which data are presented in the article. Inequality in owner-ship of assets was highest in 25 F Gulabewala village, Sri Ganganagar district, Rajasthan, where Dalit households comprised 60 per cent of all households but owned less than 1 per cent of all assets. The average asset-holding of an Other Caste household was 131 times the average asset-holding of a Dalit household.

Partha Saha analyses data from PARI surveys of Harveli village, Bijnor district, and Mahatwar village, Ballia district (both in Uttar Pradesh), to examine patterns of ownership of assets by social group. His conclusion is stark: the ownership of assets is concentrated among caste Hindu house-holds. The implications of not owning means of production are, of course, far-reaching, with implications for incomes and vulnerability to different forms of economic adversity and risk.

Household Incomes

When the main means of production are so unequally distributed, and given the exhaustion of new sources of manual employment (other than by means of state-driven programmes) in the countryside, there are great inequalities in income-earning capabilities as well. Provisional figures from pooled data collected from ten survey villages indicate that per capita house-hold incomes among Other Caste households were greater than among Dalit households by a factor of more than 6.[4]

The essay by Vikas Rawal and Madhura Swaminathan deals with the persistent disadvantage experienced by Dalit households in Indian vil-lages in respect of incomes (a theme also discussed in the article by V. Surjit). The essay examines absolute and relative income deprivation among Dalit

---

[4] The villages were Ananthavaram, Bukkacherla, Kothapalle, Harevli, Mahatwar, Warwat Khanderao, Nimshirgaon, 25 F Gulabewala, Rewasi and Gharsondi (see Appendix Table).

households in eight villages. In every village, the average household and per capita income among Dalit households was lower than the average among non-Dalit, non-Adivasi households of the same village. In terms of distribution of incomes, Dalit households were under-represented in the top quintile and over-represented in the lower quintiles. A decomposition of income inequality by caste group showed that inequality on account of between-group differences was large in several villages, particularly in villages characterized by canal-irrigated, high-productivity agriculture.

Manual workers usually constitute the single largest class in a village. Data from the Rural Labour Enquiries and village surveys establish that Dalit households predominate among the class of manual workers, and that manual work is the predominant occupation among Dalits. Dalit workers – women workers in particular – predominated among agricultural workers.

Housing and Household Amenities

Adequate housing, sanitation and access to safe water are universal basic needs, and recognized as basic human rights. In our work at the Foundation for Agrarian Studies, we have proposed a simple criterion to test, from PARI data, the quality of actually existing housing in rural India. The test is the following: does the household live in a house that has two rooms; a pucca roof, walls and floor; a source of water for domestic needs inside or immediately outside the premises; a source of electricity for domestic use; and a working latrine? Although this set of criteria falls well below the international norms for adequate housing to which India is committed, data from the PARI surveys show that these requirements are far from being achieved. In pooled data from fourteen PARI villages, not a single Adivasi household lived in a house that met these criteria; only 4 per cent of Muslim households and 6 per cent of Dalit households lived in housing that met the criteria. Even among Other Caste households, only 22 per cent achieved this very limited target. (See also Singh, Swaminathan and Ramachandran 2013.)

The article by Madhura Swaminathan and Shamsher Singh shows that deprivation among Dalit households with respect to certain simple household amenities is not on account of low incomes alone, but relates to the persistence of various forms of social discrimination. The separation of Dalit hamlets from the main village settlement and the lack of public infrastructure in Dalit settlements is one such form of discrimination.

Dalit Households in Village Economies: Overview

The book is divided into four sections. Sukhadeo Thorat, Nidhi Sadana, and Amit Thorat begin their essay with an important discussion of theories of social exclusion applied to the specific context of India, where 'social exclusion revolves around societal institutions that exclude, discriminate, isolate and deprive some groups on the basis of group identities such as caste, ethnicity, religion, gender, physical disability, regional identity and other identities, in different magnitudes and forms.' The empirical sections of their paper show how problems of income poverty are compounded for those members of society who are victims of group-specific discrimination. They use National Sample Survey (NSS) data from 2004–05 to examine problems of poverty among Dalit households and others in selected income-poor States (that is, in Jharkhand, Orissa, Madhya Pradesh, West Bengal, Bihar and Uttar Pradesh).

Historical Essays

The second section has three papers, each dealing with historical aspects of land, caste and social exclusion.

In Kerala, as is well known, the Left movement brought together three great socio-political struggles: the struggle for freedom from British rule, the struggle against landlordism, and the struggle against caste discrimination. R. Ramakumar tracks the course that the movement took – particularly its anti-caste-discrimination aspect – in one village, Morazha, in Kannur district in the Malabar region of the State. In 1955, Morazha was the site of a detailed socio-economic study by the scholar Thomas Shea. Ramakumar resurveyed the village in 2000. The article combines survey-based material from the village with a discussion of the broader political movements in the village and Malabar. The analysis deals with the role of public action – land reform, in particular – in transforming the living conditions of Dalit agricultural workers. Specific changes in the condition of agricultural workers in Morazha included access to homestead land, to subsidised food from the public distribution system, to government-funded pensions and to (non-usurious) credit from cooperatives. Land reform and the Left-led social reform movement together ended old-style landlordism and old forms of upper-caste domination.

G. Ramakrishnan's essay is on agrarian struggle and its impact on the lives of Dalit workers in the eastern tracts of the former Thanjavur district (roughly speaking, the present districts of Nagapattinam and Thiruvarur). Thanjavur was, historically, the major rice-growing region of Tamil Nadu – its 'granary' – and was where some of the largest landlord holdings of wet land in the State were located. Society in Thanjavur was characterized by large-scale landlordism, and the class and caste oppression of agricultural workers, particularly Dalit agricultural workers. The specific feature of Ramakrishnan's essay is that it draws on documents in Tamil and interviews with participants in the militant struggles that were conducted in the region by the Kisan Sabha and the Communist Party. These movements were waged against big landlords on issues of the eradication of untouchability and different forms of extra-economic coercion of tenants and agricultural workers, and for the right to form class organizations of peasants and agricultural workers.

Aparajita Bakshi examines the impact of land reform in West Bengal on access to land among Dalit and Adivasi households. Data from the Land and Livestock Holding survey of 2003 conducted by the National Sample

Survey Organization (NSSO) show that the index of access to land among Dalit households of West Bengal was twice as high as the national average. The essay presents data from seven village surveys on patterns of ownership by caste group; they indicate clearly that Dalit and Adivasi households were major beneficiaries of land reform. Like Ramakumar and Ramakrishnan, Bakshi uses material from interviews with participants in agrarian movements to build the context in which her essay is located. An important observation of her respondents is that, while the struggles of the peasantry from the 1940s in Bengal did not take up demands that concentrated explicitly and mainly on issues of caste discrimination, Dalits, Adivasis and Muslims, who constituted the major section of peasants and workers in rural Bengal, participated in these struggles in large numbers and became important beneficiaries of agrarian reform in the State.

The third section of the book deals with economic problems confronting Dalits in contemporary rural India. Three articles are based on village-level work, and the fourth on secondary data.

Judith Heyer's study derives from outstanding long-term fieldwork conducted in Coimbatore (now Tiruppur) district from 1981–82 through 2010. The villages are located in a fast-industrializing area, and the industrial transformation that has taken place has had a differentiated impact on Dalits and others in the village. Although Dalit households gained house-site land over this period, they continued to be landless with respect to the ownership of agricultural land. In so far as they remained workers in agriculture, Dalit workers remained landless workers; those who worked in the non-agricultural sector also worked mainly as manual workers, rather than as self-employed entrepreneurs or non-manual workers. Heyer also documents the continuation of practices of untouchability, although she notes that these practices were less severe than during her first fieldwork in 1981–82.

V. Surjit worked in another part of Tamil Nadu – the area about which, in fact, G. Ramakrishnan writes in the preceding section. As a result of long years of agrarian struggle, sections of the Dalit population in the eastern tracts of the old Thanjavur district gained access – as tenants of independent farmers and of temple trusts – to operational holdings of agricultural land. Surjit's main fieldwork was conducted during a year of unprecedented water shortage and farming failure in the Cauvery delta, and he records, in his contribution to this volume, the specific features of economic distress (including huge income losses) among Dalit tenants in the region. While a majority of all cultivators experienced losses during the reference agricultural year, Dalit cultivators were worse off because the costs of cultivation were higher – and incomes lower – for them. Surjit argues that the differences in costs and incomes were made more acute by the fact that Dalit cultivators did not own the instruments or means of agricultural production.

The essay by R. Ramakumar and Tushar Kamble is a vivid and important contemporary case study of the caste Hindu fury that is ignited when a Dalit household in a Maharashtra village begins to acquire land and higher education.

Pallavi Chavan's unique study of how the system of rural bank credit in India serves Dalit borrowers is exemplary with respect to its rigorous and imaginative use of secondary data (from the Reserve Bank of India and National Sample Surveys), and the social concerns of its content. Chavan demonstrates that banks marginalized Dalit borrowers in the period of liberalization. Her analysis shows that, in the 1990s and the first decade of the 2000s, banks did not meet the official targets that had been set for advances to the 'weaker sections' of society; that the number of small borrowal accounts held by Dalit households fell in absolute terms; and that Dalit borrowers had to turn to moneylenders because of poor access to finance from banks. She shows that, in 2008, for every 100 rupees worth of bank credit received by a non-Dalit, non-Adivasi, male borrower, a Dalit woman received less than a single rupee! For Dalit borrowers, financial *inclusion* is a mirage; the evidence presented by Chavan shows the *exclusion* of rural Dalits from the formal banking system.

The third section of the book has papers that use data from the village surveys that comprise the Project on Agrarian Relations in India (PARI); the papers and PARI have been discussed in a previous section of this essay.

This book is an introduction to some of the issues that require study in the field of economic deprivation and exclusion among Dalits in rural India. The articles in the book are evidence, in some cases, of direct discrimination (discussed above), and in others of what has been described as *differential impact* discrimination (for instance, when an employment practice is neutral on the surface, but has a differential impact across social groups in practice). Most of all, they reflect *cumulative* discrimination and disadvantage, that is, differences in human functionings and ownership of the means of production that are the outcome of discrimination and disadvantage over generations.[5]

Each form of discrimination, or aspect of cumulative deprivation, can have a myriad of consequences for the freedom and livelihoods of its victims. The nature of property rights, for instance, determines not only the ownership of land and other assets, but has consequences for incomes, livelihoods and other aspects of social standing and well-being. Village-level patterns of land sales, mortgage and other forms of the transfer of property are nowhere in India entirely free of non-market forms of exclusion and discrimination. A division of labour and a distribution of assets that is determined outside the market determines access also, for example, to quality housing and sanitation, and, consequently, to safe and healthy environments and lives. To take

---

[5] These are terms taken from National Research Council (2004: 50–52, 223 ff), a research report on the United States that has very interesting lessons for the study of social discrimination in India.

yet another example, cumulative deprivation and active discrimination with respect to education and mobility jeopardize freedom in a basic way, and also have an immediate instrumental effect on wages, occupational mobility and occupational status.

While the experiences and studies here can be multiplied, and while each theme we have discussed needs careful and detailed further empirical research in different parts of the country, a crucial generalization from the evidence can and must be made: the system of socio-economic class in rural India does not exist independently of caste discrimination and other forms of sectional deprivation.

There can be no end to poverty and deprivation in India without resolution of the agrarian question, and there is no agrarian question in India to which the issues of caste, tribe, gender, and other forms of social exclusion and discrimination based on hierarchies of status are not intrinsic. It is in rural India that such discrimination has its source, and where deprivation and social exclusion are most acute. One of the necessary conditions for the resolution of the agrarian question, thus, is the creation of conditions for the liberation of the Dalit and Adivasi people (and other victims of sectional deprivation and social exclusion).

References

Ambedkar, B.R. (1944), *Annihilation of Caste, with a Reply to Mahatma Gandhi*, third edition, available at http://www.ambedkar.org/ambcd/02.Annihilation%20of%20Caste.htm, viewed on 15 October 2013.

Ambedkar, B.R. (1945), *Pakistan, or the Partition of India*, second edition, available at www.ambedkar.org/pakistan/pakistan.pdf, viewed on 15 October 2013.

National Research Council (2004), *Measuring Racial Discrimination*, Panel on Methods for Assessing Discrimination, Blank, Rebecca M., Dabady, Marilyn and Citro, Constance F., eds, Committee on National Statistics, Division of Behavioral and Social Sciences and Education, The National Academies Press, Washington, D.C.

Shah, G., Mander, H., Thorat, S., Deshpande, S. and Baviskar, A. (2006), *Untouchability in Rural India*, Sage, New Delhi.

Singh, Shamsher, Swaminathan, Madhura and Ramachandran, V.K. (2013), 'Housing Shortages in Rural India', *Review of Agrarian Studies,* vol. 3, no. 2, available at http://ras.org.in/housing_shortages_in_rural_india, viewed on 25 December 2013.

Thorat, Sukhadeo (2004), 'Hindu Social Order and the Human Rights of Dalits', *Combat Law*, vol. 1, no. 4, available at http://www.indiatogether.org/combatlaw/issue4/hinduorder.htm, viewed on 19 September 2013.

APPENDIX TABLE 1 *List of villages studied as part of the Project on Agrarian Relations in India (PARI), 2005–12*

Village	District	State	Year of survey	Agro-ecological zone	Kharif crop/s	Rabi crop/s	Other crops
Ananthavaram	Guntur	Andhra Pradesh	2005, 2006	East Coast Plains and Hills	Paddy	Maize, pulses	
Bukkacherla	Anantapur	Andhra Pradesh	2005, 2006	Southern Plateau and Hills	Intercropped groundnut	Paddy	
Kothapalle	Karimnagar	Andhra Pradesh	2005, 2006	Southern Plateau and Hills	Paddy, maize, cotton	Paddy, maize	
Harevli	Bijnor	Uttar Pradesh	2006	Upper Gangetic Plains	Paddy	Wheat	Sugarcane
Mahatwar	Ballia	Uttar Pradesh	2006	Middle Gangetic Plains	Maize, red gram	Wheat	
Warwat Khanderao	Buldhana	Maharashtra	2007	Western Plateau and Hills	Cotton intercropped with green gram and red gram	Wheat	
Nimshirgaon	Kolhapur	Maharashtra	2007	Western Plateau and Hills	Soyabean		Sugarcane, grape, vegetables
Dungariya	Udaipur	Rajasthan	2007	Central Plateau and Hills	Maize, red gram, black gram	Wheat	
25 F Gulabewala	Sri Ganganagar	Rajasthan	2007	Trans-Gangetic Plains	Cotton, cluster beans, fodder crops	Wheat, rapeseed	
Rewasi	Sikar	Rajasthan	2010	Central Plateau and Hills	Wheat, mustard, gram	Wheat, mustard, onions, fenugreek	
Gharsondi	Gwalior	Madhya Pradesh	2008	Central Plateau and Hills	Paddy	Wheat, rapeseed, chickpea, lucerne grass	
Badhar	Anuppur	Madhya Pradesh	2008	Central Plateau and Hills	Paddy, wheat, millets, pulses		

(Appendix Table 1 continued on next page)

APPENDIX TABLE 1 *(continued)*

Village	District	State	Year of survey	Agro-ecological zone	Kharif crop/s	Rabi crop/s	Other crops
Alabujanahalli	Mandya	Karnataka	2009	Southern Plateau and Hills	Paddy, ragi	Paddy, finger millet	Sugarcane
Siresandra	Kolar	Karnataka	2009	Southern Plateau and Hills	Ragi, often inter-cropped with jowar, red gram and sesamum		Potato, tomato, carrot, cauli-flower, beetroot, radish, fodder maize and fodder grass, and other vegetables, condiments and tree crops
Zhapur	Gulbarga	Karnataka	2009	Southern Plateau and Hills	Red gram inter-cropped with maize, sesamum, bajra, green gram		
Panahar	Bankura	West Bengal	2010	Lower Gangetic Plains	Paddy	Potato, mustard, rapeseed and wheat, boro paddy or sesame	
Amarsinghi	Malda	West Bengal	2010	Lower Gangetic Plains	Paddy, jute	Paddy	
Kalmandasguri	Koch Bihar	West Bengal	2010	Lower Gangetic Plains	Paddy, jute	Vegetables, sugarcane, potato	
Tehang	Phillaur	Punjab	2011	Trans-Gangetic Plains	Paddy	Wheat	
Hakamwala	Budhlada	Punjab	2011	Trans-Gangetic Plains	Cotton, paddy	Wheat	
Katkuian	West Champaran	Bihar	2012	Middle Gangetic Plains	Paddy	Wheat and pulses	Sugarcane
Nayanagar	Samastipur	Bihar	2012	Middle Gangetic Plains	Paddy	Maize	

APPENDIX TABLE 2 *Proportion of population (7 years and above) who can read and write, by social group and by sex, selected villages*

Name of village	State	Proportion of literate people									
		Scheduled Caste		Scheduled Tribe		Muslim		Other Caste		All	
		Female	Male	Female	Male	Female	Male	Female	Male	Female	Male
Ananthavaram	Andhra Pradesh	43	61	24	44	22	54	68	76	54	60
Bukkacherla	Andhra Pradesh	28	43			67	71	47	71	43	66
Kothapalle	Andhra Pradesh	46	57	25	33	40	73	45	72	45	67
Harevli	Uttar Pradesh	40	46			41	48	58	78	50	65
Mahatwar	Uttar Pradesh	37	68					48	68	43	70
Dungariya	Rajasthan			9	26	50	88	100	100	10	29
25 F Gulabewala	Rajasthan	32	40					66	83	48	60
Rewasi	Rajasthan	45	82	55	76			46	79	46	79
Warwat Khanderao	Maharashtra	55	76			66	80	71	87		
Nimshirgaon	Maharashtra	55	84			44	85	73	90	66	87
Gharsondi	Madhya Pradesh	38	70	10	12	17	46	45	69	40	63
Badhar	Madhya Pradesh	0	40	23	35			10	31	20	34
Alabujanahalli	Karnataka	50	61					58	71	56	69
Siresandra	Karnataka	49	58					56	76	54	71
Zhapur	Karnataka	25	36	22	33	71	80	43	57	33	46
Panahar	West Bengal	30	46	35	39	62	87	69	81	49	62
Amarsinghi	West Bengal	40	59	na	50			63	79	52	70
Kalmandasguri	West Bengal	60	73	36	55	43	52	48	76	50	63
Tehang	Punjab	60	69	0	67	73	50	77	79	68	73
Hakamwala	Punjab	41	48					52	65	47	58

ANNEXURE TABLE 3 *Proportion of persons aged 16 years and above with 10 years or more of schooling, by sex and social group, study villages in per cent*

Name of village	District	State	Proportion of persons aged 16 years and above with 10 years and above schooling							
			Dalit		Adivasi		Muslim		Other	
			Men	Women	Men	Women	Men	Women	Men	Women
Ananthavaram	Guntur	Andhra Pradesh	22	11	6	3	22	0	42	24
Bukkacherla	Anantapur	Andhra Pradesh	11	5	n. a.	n. a.	38	23	35	15
Kothapalle	Karimnagar	Andhra Pradesh	25	22	0	7	38	25	40	16
Gharsondi	Gwalior	Madhya Pradesh	21	2	2.0	3	n. a.	n. a.	36	13
Badhar	Anuppur	Madhya Pradesh	n. a.	n. a.	2.3	2	n. a.	n. a.	5	0
Warwat Khanderao	Buldhana	Maharashtra	22	8	n. a.	n. a.	34	5	36	25
Nimshirgaon	Kolhapur	Maharashtra	35	11	n. a.	n. a.	23	9	56	30
25F Gulabewala	Sri Ganganagar	Rajasthan	3	2	n. a.	n. a.	n. a.	n. a.	41	29
Rewasi	Sikar	Rajasthan	47	5	24.32	7	n. a.	n. a.	34	11
Dungariya	Udaipur	Rajasthan	n. a.	n. a.	0.6	0	29	0	n. a.	n. a.
Mahatwar	Ballia	Uttar Pradesh	42	7	n. a.	n. a.	n. a.	n. a.	49	25
Harevli	Bijnor	Uttar Pradesh	30	2	n. a.	n. a.	n. a.	n. a.	44	19
Kalmandasguri	Koch Bihar	West Bengal	26	15	20	9	9	10	27	5
Panahar	Bankura	West Bengal	7	2	0	5	57	33	45	21
Amarsinghi	Malda	West Bengal	7	3	n. a.	n. a.	n. a.	n. a.	23	13
Alabujanahalli	Mandya	Karnataka	35	24	n. a.	n. a.	n. a.	n. a.	42	33
Siresandra	Kolar	Karnataka	18	17	n. a.	n. a.	n. a.	n. a.	43	32
Zhapur	Gulbarga	Karnataka	17	1	12	3	n. a.	n. a.	25	15
Tehang	Jalandhar	Punjab	23	24	n. a.	n. a.	n. a.	n. a.	43	45
Hakamwala	Mansa	Punjab	12	6	n. a.	n. a.	n. a.	n. a.	22	16
Katkuian	West Champaran	Bihar	0	0	7	0	9	4	20	8
Nayanagar	Samastipur	Bihar	19	7	n. a.	n. a.	n. a.	n. a.	51	30
Pooled data for all villages			20	12	5	2	21	8	37	22

APPENDIX TABLE 4 *Proportion of persons aged 16 years and above with no schooling, by sex and social group, study villages* in per cent

| Name of village | District | Proportion of persons aged 16 years and above with no schooling | | | | | | | |
| | | Dalit | | Adivasi | | Muslim | | Other | |
		Men	Women	Men	Women	Men	Women	Men	Women
Ananthavaram	Guntur	36	54	52	71	22	62	20	28
Bukkacherla	Anantapur	58	76	0	0	15	39	29	59
Kothapalle	Karimnagar	51	69	70	86	38	75	26	61
Gharsondi	Gwalior	22	70	82	88	54	81	20	55
Badhar	Anuppur	100	100	49	81	n. a.	n. a.	43	89
Warwat Khanderao	Buldhana	19	54	n. a.	n. a.	16	40	10	32
Nimshirgaon	Kolhapur	18	51	n. a.	n. a.	15	64	10	28
25F Gulabewala	Sri Ganganagar	65	79	n. a.	n. a.	n. a.	n. a.	13	33
Rewasi	Sikar	19	65	30	66	n. a.	n. a.	23	64
Dungariya	Udaipur	n. a.	n. a.	74	95	14	50	n. a.	n. a.
Mahatwar	Ballia	33	80	n. a.	n. a.	n. a.	n. a.	20	54
Harevli	Bijnor	56	80	n. a.	n. a.	63	78	16	44
Kalmandasguri	Koch Bihar	15	34	25	73	30	52	14	37
Panahar	Bankura	75	71	63	86	20	42	50	28
Amarsinghi	Malda	31	59	0	100	n. a.	n. a.	7	30
Alabujanahalli	Mandya	30	42	0	100	n. a.	n. a.	19	36
Siresandra	Kolar	33	38	n. a.	n. a.	n. a.	n. a.	16	44
Zhapur	Gulbarga	43	77	36	55	20	50	35	59
Tehang	Jalandhar	19	36	0	100	100	100	12	17
Hakamwala	Mansa	45	53	n. a.	n. a.	n. a.	n. a.	28	42
Katkuian	West Champaran	65	88	37	79	38	75	35	71
Nayanagar	Samastipur	49	80	n. a.	n. a.	n. a.	n. a.	17	42
Pooled data for all villages		37	57	58	83	39	60	21	44

The Role of Social Exclusion in Explaining Poverty in Income-Poor States of India

Sukhadeo Thorat, Nidhi Sadana Sabharwal, Amit Thorat

One of the features of the measurement of poverty in India is that the overall ratio of the population below the poverty line to the entire population (i.e. the head-count ratio), though high, does not capture the prevalence and intensity of poverty among specific caste, tribe, ethnic and religious groups. Within the latter, again, the incidence and intensity of poverty are particularly high among persons engaged in wage labour and self-employment. Thus, while certain common factors are associated with poverty among all households, there are group-specific factors (in addition to general factors) that aggravate the poverty of specific groups. At a general level, factors that aggravate poverty include lack of access to income-earning assets (agricultural land and business), to employment, education and skills, and health facilities, as well as an absence of participation in governance. These are factors associated with poverty among all poor households, including those from groups that are discriminated against. For instance, lack of access to income-earning assets such as agricultural land and business reduces access to income. Lack of access to education and skills reduces the employability of poor persons. Similarly, lack of access to health facilities affects health, which in turn reduces productivity as well as levels of employment.

However, in the case of socially excluded groups such as Scheduled Castes (SCs), Scheduled Tribes (STs) and Muslims, additional factors related to their caste, ethnic or religious background, or what we term 'group-specific factors', are associated with poverty among them. Group-specific factors from which socially excluded groups suffer relate to social exclusion and discrimination in varied forms. These involve the denial of equal rights and entitlements due to unfair exclusion and/or (unfair) inclusion combined with discriminatory or differential treatment (Sen 2000). Discriminatory practices can lead to a failure of entitlements, and result in low income and poverty. Unless the constraints posed by social exclusion and discriminatory access are weakened, poverty among discriminated groups may not be reduced appreciably.

Certain groups in society are selectively excluded from opportunities that are open to others because they are discriminated against on the basis of their caste, ethnic background, religion, gender, physical disability, or other type of social identity (DFID 2005).

> The people who are excluded like this are not 'just like' the rest of the poor. They are also disadvantaged by *who they are or where they live* and, as a result, are locked out of the benefits of development. Social exclusion deprives people of choices and opportunities to escape from poverty and denies them a voice to claim their rights and induces more poverty. (Ibid.)

Therefore, addressing the problem of poverty among various discriminated groups in Indian society requires a specific approach, similar to that towards the rest of the poor in some respects but necessarily different in other respects.

In Indian society there are multiple social groups that suffer from exclusion and discrimination in varied forms because of factors associated with their group identity, such as caste, ethnic background, religion, gender, colour, regional identity and physical disability. Communities that have faced discrimination and exclusion constitute the majority of the poor in the country.

In this essay, first, we deal with some theoretical issues on the meaning of social exclusion in general and its application to the Indian context. Secondly, we discuss the processes through which social exclusion can cause poverty among socially excluded groups. Thirdly, we study the incidence of poverty at the all-India level and for seven low-income States of India, namely, Madhya Pradesh, West Bengal, Orissa, Bihar, Jharkhand, Chhattisgarh and Uttar Pradesh. For each State, we estimate the incidence of poverty among the Scheduled Castes (SCs) and Scheduled Tribes (STs) in relation to 'Others' (other than SCs and STs). Data for this analysis come from the National Sample Survey Organization's (NSSO's) Consumer Expenditure Survey of 2004–05. Fourthly, we examine a set of economic factors that affect poverty (such as the ownership of land and nature of employment) and then examine inter-group differences with reference to each factor. Fifthly, we briefly review some indicators of health and malnutrition, and the differences in these across social groups. Lastly, we suggest inclusive policies to provide equal or non-discriminatory access to livelihoods, education and health facilities to discriminated groups – policies that are crucial to the alleviation of poverty.

Social Exclusion and Poverty Reduction

In the current social sciences literature, there is general agreement on the core features of social exclusion, its principal indicators and its consequences with respect to human poverty. Social exclusion is conceived as 'the inability of an individual to participate in the basic political, economic, and social functioning of society' (Buvinic 2005). This results in denial of equal access to opportunities for some groups because of the imposition of certain conditions or restrictions by other groups in society.

The concept of social exclusion has three distinguishable features. First, it affects culturally defined groups. Secondly, it is embedded in social relations, and it is through the network of social relations that groups are wholly or partially excluded from full participation in the society in which they live. Thirdly, social exclusion has adverse consequences on entitlements and on the basic needs that are necessary for good living (Sen 2000). Thus the outcomes of social exclusion in terms of low income and high poverty among excluded groups depend crucially on the functioning of the society, economy and polity through a network of social relations, and the degree to which these relations are exclusionary and discriminatory. The group focus (as against individual focus) in social exclusion recognizes that people are excluded because of ascribed rather than achieved features, which are beyond individual agency or responsibility (Buvinic 2005).

Theoretically speaking, in the case of group exclusion, all persons belonging to a particular social or cultural group are excluded because of their cultural (group) identity, and not due to their individual attributes or qualities. The exclusion of an individual is fundamentally different from the exclusion of a group. Individuals (from both excluded and non-excluded groups) often get excluded from access to economic and social opportunities for various reasons specific to them (and not because of their socio-cultural group identity). For instance, individuals may be excluded from employment because of a lack of requisite education and skills. Individuals may face exclusion in access to education due to a lack of minimum qualifications or because of their inability to pay for an expensive education. Individuals may also be excluded from access to input and consumer markets because of a lack of income and purchasing power. On the other hand, in the case of group exclusion, social and cultural identities become a reference point for exclusion and discrimination.

The economic discrimination that directly results in lack of ownership of income-earning assets and employment, as well as human capabilities such as education, operates through the discriminatory functioning of various market and non-market transactions. Market discrimination operates through restrictions on entry to markets and/or through selective inclusion. Discrimination also arises from unequal treatment in market and non-market transactions, including transactions in agricultural land and various inputs and services necessary for business, in the employment and credit markets, and with education and health institutions.

Social Exclusion and Caste, Ethnicity, Religion, and Other Forms of Identity

In India, social exclusion revolves around societal institutions that exclude, discriminate, isolate and deprive some groups on the basis of group identities such as caste, ethnicity, religion, gender, physical disability, regional identity and other identities, in different magnitudes and forms.

Social exclusion of SCs and Other Backward Classes (OBCs) is closely associated with the institution of caste. The fundamental feature of predetermined and fixed social and economic rights for each caste with restrictions on change implied forced exclusion of one or more castes from the civil, economic and educational rights that other castes enjoyed. Exclusion in the civil, educational and economic spheres is thus internal to the caste system, and a necessary outcome of its governing principles. The core governing principle of the caste system, however, is not inequality alone, but also graded inequality, which implies an unequal entitlement of rights to various castes. With the entitlement to rights being hierarchically unequal, every caste (other than 'Other Castes') suffers from a degree of denial and exclusion. But all suffering castes do not suffer equally. Some suffer more and some less. Loss of rights is not uniform across caste groups. As one moves down the caste hierarchy, rights and privileges also get reduced. By implication, castes located at the bottom of the hierarchy, such as the former 'Untouchables', suffered the most. OBCs did not suffer from the practice of untouchability, or from residential and social isolation, as much as the SCs, but historically, they too have faced exclusion in education, employment and certain other spheres.

Untouchables and OBCs that converted to Islam, Christianity, Sikhism and Buddhism also suffered some forms of discrimination, as some elements of the Hindu caste system were carried forward in the case of these low-caste converts. The problems of former Untouchables who converted to Sikhism and Buddhism, and of OBCs that converted to Islam have been recognized in India, and policies of reservation have been extended in a selective manner to converts to Sikhism and Buddhism. The problems of former Untouchables who converted to Christianity and Islam have not yet been addressed.

Coming to the religious minorities, some among them, particularly Muslims, face discrimination as a religious group in a number of spheres, and this is reflected in their poorer performance with respect to human development indicators (although there are very few empirical studies on discrimination against religious groups in various spheres). Similarly, women face gender discrimination, though the extent of discrimination varies with caste, class and religious background. Another prominent group is that of the STs, semi-nomadic tribes and denotified tribes, all of whom suffer from physical and social isolation and exclusion.

It is apparent that there are multiple groups in Indian society that have suffered from social exclusion in different forms. The basis of their exclusion also varies, as does the nature of discrimination. Due to variations in the forms and spheres of discrimination, the consequences for deprivation and poverty also vary.

Forms and Channels of Discrimination

Exclusion based on caste, ethnicity, gender and religion is reflected in the inability of individuals from the groups discriminated against to interact freely and productively with others. This also inhibits their full participation in the economic, social and political life of the community. Incomplete citizenship or denial of civil rights (freedom of expression, rule of law, right to justice), of political rights (the right and means to participate in the exercise of political power) and of socio-economic rights (rights to property, employment and education) are key dimensions of an impoverished life (World Bank 2006). Viewed from this perspective, the concept of social exclusion based on caste, ethnicity, religion or gender through market and non-market channels can be conceptualized and defined in a particular way. Theoretically, social exclusion can be defined as follows (Thorat and Sabharwal 2010).

(i) Complete exclusion (unfair exclusion or denial) from specific spheres of certain social groups, such as the 'lower' castes by 'higher' castes, tribals by non-tribals, or religious minorities by the majority. Complete exclusion of certain social groups may occur in employment (private or public), in the sale and purchase of factors of production (like agricultural land and non-land capital assets required for businesses) and various services and inputs required in the production process, in the sale and purchase of consumer goods, and so on. Complete exclusion can also occur in the case of social needs such as education, housing, health services and other services transacted through non-market channels (government or government-approved agencies).

(ii) Selective inclusion (or unfair inclusion) but with differential treatment to excluded groups, reflected in differential prices charged or received for goods and services. This covers the price of inputs and consumer goods, the price of factors of production such as wages to human labour, price of land or rent on land, interest on capital, and rent on residential houses. This may also include the prices or fees charged by public institutions for services such as water, electricity, and other goods and services.

(iii) Unfavourable inclusion (often forced) determined by caste and ethnic obligations and duties, reflected, firstly, in over-work, loss of freedom leading to bondage or attachment, and secondly, in differential treatment at the place of work.

(iv) Exclusion in certain categories of jobs and services of former Untouchables or SCs involved in so-called 'unclean' or 'polluting' occupations (such as scavenging, sanitary jobs, leather processing, etc.). This is in addition to the general exclusion or discrimination that persons from these castes face on account of being Untouchables.

(v) Exclusion from decision-making in village panchayats and thereby in the allocation of funds.

How Does Social Exclusion Cause Poverty?

After having brought some clarity to the concept of social exclusion and discrimination, we now discuss the effects of market and non-market discrimination on poverty. Discrimination in labour markets and other markets involves denial of equal economic rights and opportunities to persons from discriminated groups. Such economic discrimination not only negates the provisions of equal opportunity and principles of non-discrimination, but also has fairly serious consequences for access to income-earning assets like agricultural land and non-land assets, employment, and social needs such as education, health and housing, all of which result in lower incomes and higher poverty among discriminated groups.

The adverse consequences of labour market discrimination are fairly obvious. The denial and exclusion of employment in general, and in certain categories of work in particular, result in higher unemployment and underemployment among discriminated groups. Lower wages reduce wage earnings, and compulsory involvement in work due to traditional caste obligations is often characterized by exploitation and unpaid labour.

The consequences of discrimination in other markets through a denial of access to land, credit, factor inputs, and producer and consumer goods, through restrictions on the sale of products, consumer goods and services, and through differential treatment in terms of prices paid in the purchase of capital goods, inputs and services, are equally adverse. Further, various types of restrictions on the purchase of income-earning capital assets and non-land assets reduce the possibility of ownership of these assets and increase the incidence of assetless persons among the discriminated groups.

Restrictions on the purchase of inputs and services as well as price discrimination affect the scale, viability and profit of firms and businesses owned or operated by discriminated groups. The most adversely affected businesses are likely to be those dealing in consumer goods, in which the restrictions on purchases by higher castes from the 'lower' castes may be more pronounced and pervasive due to notions of purity and pollution. At the same time, discrimination in terms of selective restrictions on the purchase of consumer goods by SC consumers from 'higher' caste businesses affects the consumption level of the discriminated group.

Finally, discriminatory access to social needs such as education, health services, food security schemes, housing, etc., leads to lower education levels, lower access to food and public housing, and so on.

These consequences need to be measured in quantitative terms in order to capture the magnitude of exclusion-induced deprivation and poverty.

Income Poverty by Social Group

In this section, subject to the availability of data, we compare the incidence of income poverty among SC and ST groups with income poverty among non-SC and non-ST households in seven low-income States of India (Chhattisgarh, Jharkhand, Orissa, Madhya Pradesh, West Bengal, Bihar and Uttar Pradesh). Further, in order to isolate the economic factors contributing to income poverty from social or group-related factors, we disaggregate the incidence of poverty for each economic category by social group.

We start this section with a description of comparative differences in general socio-economic characteristics across social groups (SCs, STs and Muslims). The empirical evidence on economic, social and health characteristics presented here is based on data for 2004–05, and the analysis is carried out at the all-India level. The rest of the analysis pertains to the seven high poverty States.

Distribution of Population by Social Group: India and Seven Income-Poor States

According to the NSSO's (National Sample Survey Organization's) Employment and Unemployment Survey of 2004–05, about 8 per cent, 20 per cent, 41 per cent and 31 per cent of the Indian population belonged to the categories of ST, SC, OBC and Others, respectively. The proportions of persons in rural areas belonging to ST, SC, OBC and Other groups were 10 per cent, 21 per cent, 43 per cent and 26 per cent, respectively.

Among the seven low-income States, the proportion of SCs was the highest in West Bengal (at 25 per cent), followed by Uttar Pradesh (23 per cent), Bihar (23 per cent), Orissa (19 per cent), Madhya Pradesh and Chhattisgarh (close to 17 per cent), and Jharkhand (15 per cent) (Table 1). The pattern of distribution of the ST population was as follows among the seven States: 32 per cent in Chhattisgarh, 25 per cent in Jharkhand, 23 per cent in Orissa, 20 per cent in Madhya Pradesh, 6 per cent in West Bengal, 0.8 per cent in Uttar Pradesh, and 0.6 per cent in Bihar. A summary is provided in Table 1. The pattern is similar for rural areas.

TABLE 1 *Population composition of seven selected States, by social group*

Per cent of population	SC	ST	Non-SC/ST
> 20 per cent	West Bengal, Uttar Pradesh, Bihar	Chhattisgarh, Jharkhand, Orissa, Madhya Pradesh	West Bengal, Uttar Pradesh, Orissa, Madhya Pradesh Jharkhand, Bihar
19–10 per cent	Orissa, Chhattisgarh, Madhya Pradesh, Jharkhand		
< 10 per cent		West Bengal, Uttar Pradesh, Bihar	Chhattisgarh

Source: See Appendix Table A1.

Incidence of Rural Poverty: India and Seven Low-Income States

The incidence of poverty or head-count ratio is an estimate of the proportion of persons not meeting a level of consumption expenditure sufficient to meet a minimum level of calorie intake. According to the official sources, in the rural areas of India in 2004–05, 28.2 per cent of the population was poor. At the same time, the incidence of poverty was close to 37 per cent for SCs and 48 per cent for STs, and 23 per cent for Others (Table 2).

Among the seven low-income States (see Figure 1), the poverty rate was the highest in Orissa, followed closely by Jharkhand, Bihar and Chhattisgarh (all above 40 per cent). The incidence of poverty was 37 per cent in Madhya Pradesh, 33 per cent in Uttar Pradesh and 28 per cent in West Bengal.

TABLE 2   *Poverty rates across seven selected States, by social group, rural* in per cent

States	SC	ST	Others	All
Uttar Pradesh	44.80	23.60	29.40	33.30
West Bengal	28.90	42.60		28.30
Jharkhand	57.50	54.00	39.40	46.10
Orissa	49.90	75.80	33.00	46.90
Chhattisgarh	32.00	54.80	33.50	40.80
Madhya Pradesh	43.30	58.40	24.80	36.80
Bihar	64.20	56.20	35.90	42.60
All-India	36.80	47.64	22.69	28.28

Source: Thorat, Amit (2009).

We now examine the incidence of poverty among social groups. Among SCs, the incidence of poverty was highest in Bihar (64.2 per cent), followed by Jharkhand (58 per cent) and Orissa (50 per cent). (See Figure 2.) The proportion of income-poor households in the population among the SC social group was 45 per cent in Uttar Pradesh, 43 per cent in Madhya Pradesh and 32 per cent in Chhattisgarh. In West Bengal, 29 per cent of the SC population was poor – this was the lowest incidence of SC income poverty among these seven low-income States.

Among STs, the data show that the incidence of income poverty was highest in Orissa (76 per cent), followed by Madhya Pradesh (58.4 per cent), Bihar (56.2 per cent), Chhattisgarh (55 per cent) and Jharkhand (54 per cent). The incidence of income poverty among STs in West Bengal was 43 per cent and in Uttar Pradesh, 24 per cent. These two States, however, had a very low proportion of STs in their population – 6 per cent in West Bengal and 0.4 per cent in Uttar Pradesh.

Lastly, with respect to 'Other Castes', NSS data indicate that the highest incidence of income poverty was in Jharkhand (39 per cent), followed by Bihar (36 per cent), Chhattisgarh (34 per cent) and Orissa (33 per cent). In the States of Uttar Pradesh, West Bengal and Madhya Pradesh, the incidence of income poverty stood at 29 per cent, 26 per cent and 25 per cent, respectively.

To sum up, among the seven low-income States, as Figure 5 indicates, the incidence of rural poverty among the Scheduled Tribes population was particularly high in Orissa, Madhya Pradesh, Bihar, and Chhattisgarh. The incidence of rural poverty among Scheduled Castes was highest in Bihar, followed by Jharkhand, Orissa, and Uttar Pradesh. In the case of Other Castes, Jharkhand, Bihar, Orissa and Madhya Pradesh showed a high incidence of rural poverty.

Additionally, Figure 5 highlights the fact that in all but one of these seven States, the poverty rate among the SC and ST social groups was higher than among Others. It follows that the SC and ST social groups formed the core of the poor. The only exception was West Bengal, where the poverty rates were higher only for the STs.

FIGURE 1 *Percentage of poor across seven selected States: SC, rural, 2004–05*

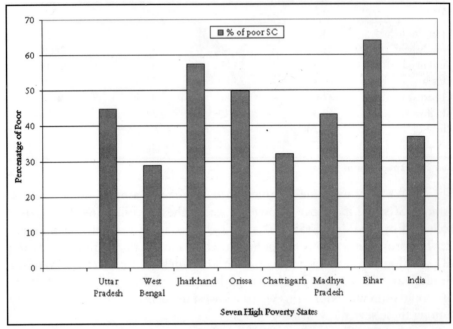

Source: Based on NSSO, Consumer Expenditure Survey, 2004–05, unit-level data.

FIGURE 2 *Percentage of poor across seven selected States: all, rural, 2004–05*

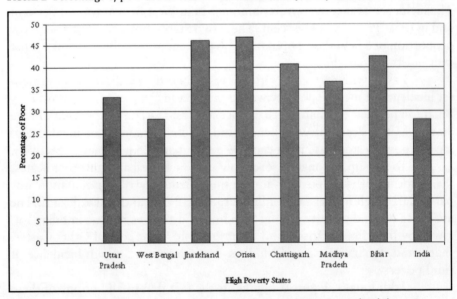

Source: Based on NSSO, Consumer Expenditure Survey, 2004–05, unit-level data.

FIGURE 3 *Incidence of poverty across seven selected States: ST, rural, 2004–05*

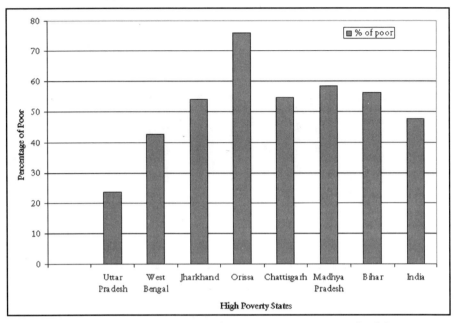

Source: Based on NSSO, Consumer Expenditure Survey, 2004–05, unit-level data.

FIGURE 4 *Incidence of poverty across seven selected States: Others, rural, 2004–05*

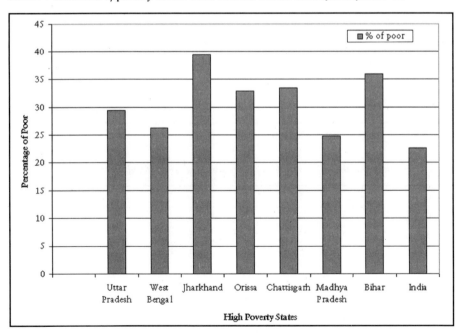

Source: Based on NSSO, Consumer Expenditure Survey, 2004–05, unit-level data.

FIGURE 5 *Percentage of poor across seven selected States, by social group, 2004–05*

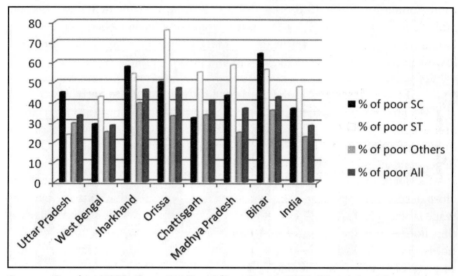

Source: Based on NSSO, Consumer Expenditure Survey, 2004–05, unit-level data.

TABLE 2a *Ranking on the basis of population composition across seven selected States: rural*

States	SC	ST	Non-SC/ST
Uttar Pradesh	2	Negligible	2
West Bengal	1	5	1
Jharkhand	6	2	5
Orissa	4	4	3
Chhattisgarh	7	1	6
Madhya Pradesh	5	3	4
Bihar	3	Negligible	4

Source: Computed from NSSO (2006a).

TABLE 2b *Ranking on the basis of poverty rates across seven selected States: rural*

States	SC	ST	Non-SC/ST
Uttar Pradesh	4	6	6
West Bengal	7	5	7
Jharkhand	2	4	1
Orissa	3	1	4
Chhattisgarh	6	4	3
Madhya Pradesh	5	2	5
Bihar	1	3	2

Source: Computed from NSSO (2006a).

Based on these numbers, we ranked these seven States by share in total population and social group (Table 2a), and by incidence of poverty and social group (Table 2b). One of the interesting findings here is that West Bengal ranked highest in terms of the share of SCs in total population, but lowest in terms of the incidence of income poverty among SCs.

Factors Associated with Poverty and Differences across Social Groups

The specific factors associated with poverty examined in this section are: access to (i.e. ownership of) land and non-land assets, the nature and quality of employment (measured in terms of the proportion of households dependent on wage labour), illiteracy, and mortality rates.

Data on rural households in the seven States in Table 3 indicate a close association between the incidence of income poverty, dependence on wage labour and rate of illiteracy. The incidence of poverty among households dependent on wage labour was 46 per cent and among non-literate households, 39.3 per cent. It is also quite clear from the data that the incidence of poverty among households dependent on wage labour in agriculture was higher (46 per cent) than among those self-employed in agriculture (21.5 per cent), at the national level. The same pattern was observed in all the seven low-income States. The incidence of poverty was thus significantly lower in households that had greater access to resources such as land and capital, and that were self-employed in the agricultural and non-agricultural sectors, than among wage labourers.

Table 3 shows the incidence of poverty for households in selected economic categories. It shows, for example, that in Uttar Pradesh, of all households owning less than 1 hectare of land, 28 per cent were below the poverty line; of all households engaged in wage labour in agriculture, 55 per cent were below the poverty line; and so on. In the following sections, we examine the incidence of poverty taking each economic factor listed in Table

TABLE 3 *Incidence of poverty across seven high poverty States, by economic factors, 2004–05* in per cent

States	Ownership of land (less than 1 ha.)	Self-employed in agriculture	Self-employed in non-agriculture	Wage labour in agriculture	Illiteracy
Uttar Pradesh	28	26	34	55	39
West Bengal	17	18	23	46	40
Jharkhand	47	44	42	75	53
Orissa	49	46	33	65	61
Chhattisgarh	48	32	44	56	49
Madhya Pradesh	43	27	33	57	45
Bihar	31	26	37	67	53
All India	27	22	23	46	39

Source: NSSO (2006b).

3 as a categorizing variable, and examine variations across social groups.

Economic Factors: Access to Land

Using data on land owned by households, we examine two categories of households: those with marginal landholdings (i.e. less than 1 hectare) and those with small landholdings (i.e. 1 to 2 hectares).

Poverty Rates among Households Owning Marginal Landholdings

In 2004–05, the incidence of poverty at the all-India level among those with marginal landholdings was high, close to 35 per cent (Table 4). Among the seven low-income States, the incidence of poverty in this size-class of ownership holding of land was highest in Bihar and Jharkhand (53 per cent). In Madhya Pradesh the corresponding proportion was 51 per cent, followed by Chhattisgarh, Orissa and Uttar Pradesh (Figure 6).

Turning now to the SC population, it is observed that the incidence of poverty among households with marginal landholdings was 40 per cent at the all-India level (Table 4). With respect to the seven low-income States, it was the highest in Bihar (63 per cent) and Jharkhand (60 per cent). In Madhya Pradesh, Orissa and Chhattisgarh the incidence of poverty was 56 per cent, 48 per cent and 42 per cent respectively. In West Bengal it was lower than the other States (32 per cent).

FIGURE 6 *Incidence of poverty among marginal landholding households across seven selected States: all social groups*

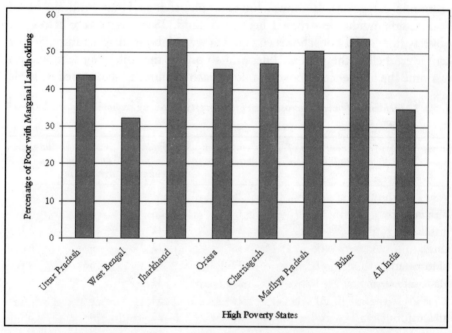

Source: Based on NSSO, Consumer Expenditure Survey, 2004–05, unit-level data.

TABLE 4 *Incidence of poverty among marginal landholding households across seven selected States, by social group, 2004–05* in per cent

States	SC	ST	Others (Non-SC/ST)	All
Uttar Pradesh	50.3	12.9	28.40	43.89
West Bengal	32.4	46.0	30.90	32.39
Jharkhand	60.0	59.5	52.70	53.40
Orissa	48.3	74.9	29.60	45.47
Chhattisgarh	42.0	67.1	40.70	47.03
Madhya Pradesh	55.8	72.9	15.90	50.57
Bihar	62.7	72.2	35.50	53.74
All India	40.1	51.0	28.96	34.76

Source: Thorat, Amit (2009).

FIGURE 7 *Incidence of poverty among marginal landholding classes across seven selected States, by social group, 2004–05*

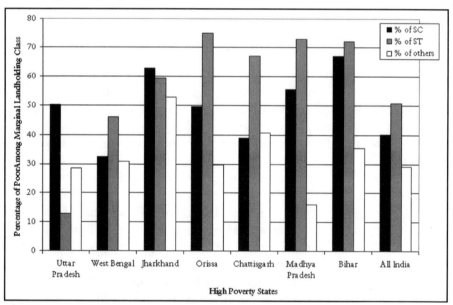

Source: Based on NSSO, Consumer Expenditure Survey, 2004–05, unit-level data.

Among STs, at the all-India level, the incidence of poverty among those with marginal landholdings was 51 per cent. Among the seven low-income States, the highest incidence of poverty occurred in Orissa (a shocking 75 per cent), followed by Madhya Pradesh (73 per cent) and Bihar (72 per cent). As mentioned earlier, the proportion of ST population to the total population was quite low in West Bengal, Uttar Pradesh and Bihar.

At the all-India level, the incidence of poverty among the marginal landholding class was lowest for non-SC/ST households among all social groups (29 per cent). Table 4 indicates that among the seven low-income

States, this ratio was the highest in Jharkhand (52.7 per cent), followed by Bihar (35.5 per cent).

Figure 7 and Table 4 show that, according to NSS data, among households with marginal landholdings, the incidence of poverty was highest for STs, followed by SCs, and lowest for Others. At the all-India level, the poverty rate among STs was twice as much as among Others. Similarly, the incidence of poverty in the SC social group (40 per cent) was higher than in the Others social group (35 per cent). In Uttar Pradesh, Orissa, Madhya Pradesh and Bihar, the gap in the incidence of poverty as between SCs and Others was large. As mentioned earlier, this gap was very small in West Bengal. In Chhattisgarh, Orissa and Madhya Pradesh, the gap in the incidence of poverty between STs and Others was shockingly wide.

To sum up, while the overall incidence of poverty among households with marginal landholdings was high, the magnitude of poverty was significantly higher among SC and ST households within this category in most of the low-income States and at the all-India level. This indicates that besides economic factors, there are additional social constraints associated with caste and ethnicity that intensify the poverty of SC and ST households.

Poverty Rates among Households Owning Small Landholdings

In 2004–05, the incidence of poverty at the all-India level among households with small landholdings (i.e. 1 to 2 hectares) was lower (27 per cent) than the poverty rate among households with marginal landholdings. This indicates that an increase in land ownership contributes to lower poverty rates.

Among the seven low-income States, the incidence of poverty for households in the small landholding class was the highest in Orissa (49 per cent), Chhattisgarh (48 per cent) and Jharkhand (47 per cent). In Madhya Pradesh the poverty incidence was 43 per cent, followed by Bihar and Uttar Pradesh (Table 5). For the SC population in this land category, the all-India poverty rate was 32 per cent, but the incidence of poverty was as high at 56 per cent in Jharkhand and 51 per cent in Orissa. In West Bengal, the poverty rate was not only lower than in the other six low-income States, at 12.5 per cent, but also lower than the poverty rate for Other Castes in the State.

Among small landholding STs, the all-India poverty rate was 59 per cent. Among the low-income States, the incidence of poverty among STs was a shocking 79 per cent in Orissa, 72 per cent in Chhattisgarh and 63 per cent in Madhya Pradesh (Table 5).

Lastly, among the non-SC/ST or Other Caste populations in the small landholding category, the all-India poverty rate was 21 per cent. In the low-income States, the incidence of poverty ranged from 17.5 per cent in West Bengal (lowest) to 32.6 per cent in Jharkhand (highest).

Differences in poverty rates across social groups within the small farmer category are shown graphically in Figure 8. In general, the incidence

TABLE 5 *Incidence of poverty among small landholding households across seven selected States, by social group, 2004–05*

States	SC	ST	Others	All
Uttar Pradesh	34.8	53.40	21.5	28.06
West Bengal	12.5	35.40	17.5	17.27
Jharkhand	55.8	54.80	32.6	47.18
Orissa	51.4	79.10	18.2	48.77
Chhattisgarh	22.9	72.10	20.9	48.29
Madhya Pradesh	33.0	63.00	18.8	43.09
Bihar	40.3	23.70	30.5	31.20
All India	31.7	59.39	20.8	27.43

Source: Thorat, Amit (2009).

FIGURE 8 *Incidence of poverty among small landholding households across seven selected States, by social group, 2004–05*

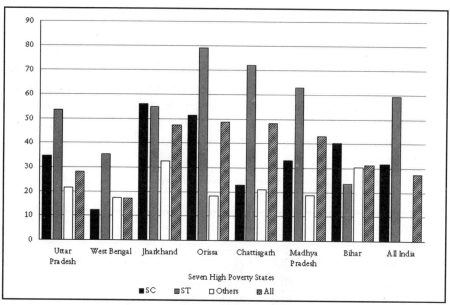

Source: Based on NSSO, Consumer Expenditure Survey, 2004–05, unit-level data.

of poverty was highest for the STs, followed closely by the SCs, and was lowest among Other Castes. In Orissa, Chhattisgarh, Madhya Pradesh and Jharkhand, the gap in the incidence of poverty between STs and Other Castes was very wide. Comparing the incidence of poverty among small farmers from the SC group and the ST group, it is interesting to note that the incidence was higher among the latter group in all States other than Jharkhand. To recapitulate, the magnitude of poverty among small farmers belonging to SCs and STs was significantly higher than the magnitude of poverty among Other Caste small farmers (with the exception of SCs in West Bengal).

To sum up our discussion on the ownership of land and poverty, at the aggregate level, the incidence of poverty was high among those with small and marginal landholdings. At the same time, within each category of ownership holding of land, the incidence of poverty was invariably higher among SCs and STs than among Others. This indicates that, other than economic factors, there are social constraints associated with caste and ethnicity that aggravate poverty among SC and ST populations.

Economic Factors: Access to Capital and Land

In this section, we estimate the incidence of poverty for households in three different livelihood categories (as defined in the NSS): self-employed in agriculture, self-employed in non-agricultural activities and wage labour households. In each category, we disaggregate the population by social group.

Self-Employment in Agriculture

At the all-India level, NSS data indicate that the incidence of poverty among households that were self-employed in agriculture was 21.5 per cent in 2004–05 (Table 6). In Orissa and Jharkhand, more than 40 per cent of the households that were self-employed in agriculture were below the poverty line. In Uttar Pradesh, Madhya Pradesh and Bihar, one-fourth of the households engaged in self-employment in agriculture were income-poor. West Bengal had the lowest incidence of poverty among households self-employed in agricultural activities.

Among SC people in the seven States, according to the NSS, the inci-

FIGURE 9 *Incidence of poverty among households self-employed in agriculture across seven selected States: all social groups, 2004–05*

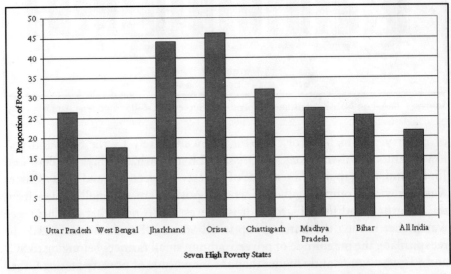

Source: Based on NSSO, Consumer Expenditure Survey, 2004–05, unit-level data.

TABLE 6 *Incidence of poverty among households self-employed in agriculture across seven selected States, by social group, 2004–05*

States	SC	ST	Others	All
Uttar Pradesh	36	27	25	26.4
West Bengal	16.3	35.3	17	17.6
Jharkhand	47	55.7	34	44.0
Orissa	45	79.7	32	46.1
Chhattisgarh	18.1	48.2	19.0	32.0
Madhya Pradesh	21.7	55.3	18.0	27.3
Bihar	45	n.a	24	25.5
All India	23	39	14	21.5

Source: Thorat, Amit (2009).

FIGURE 10 *Incidence of poverty among households self-employed in agriculture across seven selected States, by social group, 2004–05*

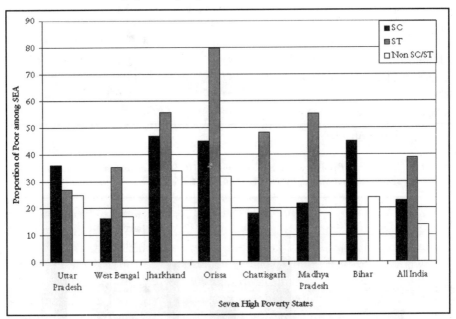

Source: Based on NSSO, Consumer Expenditure Survey, 2004–05, unit-level data.

dence of rural poverty was highest in Jharkhand, followed by Bihar, Orissa and Uttar Pradesh. The incidence of rural poverty among STs was high in Orissa, Jharkhand, Madhya Pradesh and Chhattisgarh, while the incidence of poverty among Other Castes was particularly high in Jharkhand, Orissa, Uttar Pradesh and Bihar. Figure 10 shows very clearly that among households self-employed in agriculture, in four States and at the all-India level, the incidence of poverty was highest among STs, followed by SCs and then Others. The pattern was different in West Bengal and Chhattisgarh (where the poverty rate among SCs was lower than among Others), and in Uttar Pradesh (where the poverty rate among SCs was higher than among STs, although the latter constituted a negligible proportion of the total population).

Self-Employment in Non-Agriculture

At the all-India level, data indicate that the incidence of poverty among households self-employed in non-agriculture was slightly higher (23 per cent) than among those self-employed in agriculture (21.5 per cent). Among the seven selected States, Chhattisgarh and Jharkhand had the highest incidence of poverty with over 40 per cent of households self-employed in non-agriculture

TABLE 7 *Incidence of poverty among households self-employed in non-agricultural activities across seven selected States, by social group, 2004–05*

States	SC	ST	Others	All
Uttar Pradesh	43.0	–	18.3	34.4
West Bengal	18.3	22.3	26.4	23.2
Jharkhand	69.9	61.8	29.6	41.6
Orissa	46.3	55.0	46.3	32.9
Chhattisgarh	59.8	52.6	22.4	44.0
Madhya Pradesh	39.6	52.5	12.4	32.7
Bihar	56.4	72.4	28.1	36.9
All India				23.4

Source: Thorat, Amit (2009).

FIGURE 11 *Incidence of poverty among households self-employed in non-agriculture across seven selected States, by social group, 2004–05*

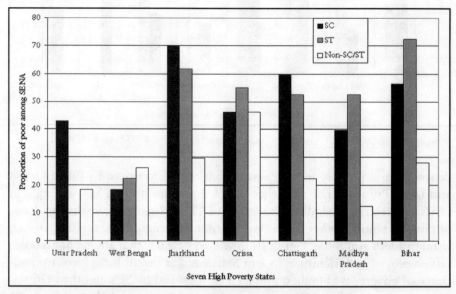

Source: Based on NSSO, Consumer Expenditure Survey, 2004–05, unit-level data.

being below the poverty line. In Bihar, Uttar Pradesh, Madhya Pradesh and Orissa, the incidence of poverty was over 30 per cent, while it was the lowest, at 23 per cent, in West Bengal.

Among rural SCs engaged in non-agricultural self-employment, the incidence of poverty was close to 70 per cent in Jharkhand, and over 40 per cent in all the low-income States other than West Bengal. In the case of rural ST households engaged in non-agricultural self-employment (business, petty trade, etc.), the incidence of poverty was more than 60 per cent in Bihar and Jharkhand. These high rates of poverty indicate that the businesses of these households were small and unproductive, resulting in low incomes.

Figure 11 shows that in four States, the incidence of poverty was higher for STs than for SCs. In Jharkhand and Chhattisgarh, the incidence of poverty among the SCs was higher than among the STs (but the latter constituted a much higher share of the population).

Economic Factors: Dependence on Wage Labour

For those without access to land or capital, the only option was dependence on wage labour. Among households engaged in wage labour in agriculture, in 2004–05, at the all-India level, 46 per cent were poor. Focusing on the low-income States, the corresponding proportions were 75 per cent in Jharkhand, and over 60 per cent in Orissa and Bihar (Table 8, Figure 12).

The estimates of poverty for each social group are plotted in Figure 13. At the national level, the incidence of poverty among agricultural wage labour households belonging to the SCs was close to 54 per cent, but it was as high as 80 per cent in Jharkhand. The poverty rate was above 50 per cent among SC wage labour households in all the low-income States other than West Bengal.

The situation was worse among STs in most States, with a poverty rate of 85 per cent in Orissa, and over 60 per cent in Jharkhand, Chhattisgarh and Madhya Pradesh (all three have significant tribal populations).

TABLE 8 *Incidence of poverty among agricultural labour households across seven selected States, by social group, 2004–05*

States	% of SC	% of ST	% of Others	All
Uttar Pradesh	56.6	82	54	55.3
West Bengal	43.5	50	46	45.5
Jharkhand	79.5	72	75	75.1
Orissa	55.0	85	52	64.5
Chhattisgarh	43.8	69	52	55.5
Madhya Pradesh	54.7	64	50	56.5
Bihar	73.0	70	63	67.4
All India	54.0	39	35	46.4

Source: Thorat, Amit (2009).

FIGURE 12 *Incidence of poverty among agricultural labour households across seven selected States, by social group: all, 2004–05*

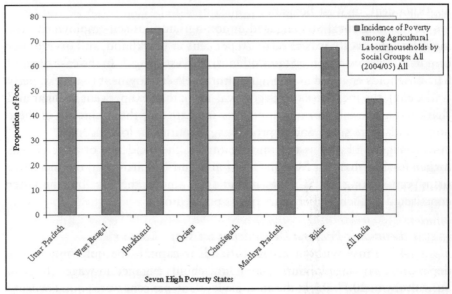

Source: Based on NSSO, Consumer Expenditure Survey, 2004–05, unit-level data.

FIGURE 13 *Incidence of poverty among agricultural labour households across seven selected States, by social group, 2004–05*

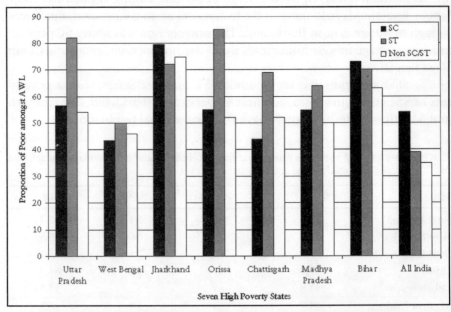

Source: Based on NSSO, Consumer Expenditure Survey, 2004–05, unit-level data.

To recapitulate, the magnitude of poverty (as measured by the poverty rate) among agricultural wage labour households belonging to the SC and ST social groups was significantly higher than among those belonging to Other Castes. This indicates that social constraints tend to intensify poverty among wage workers.

Other Factors: Education and the Incidence of Poverty

The data in Table 9 clearly show a high incidence of poverty among households in which the head of the household was illiterate. Lack of education is an important factor associated with poverty (next only to dependence on wage labour) for all social groups; there are high levels of poverty among households in which the head of the household is illiterate. This is true at the all-India level and across the low-income States.

Among households belonging to the SCs in which the heads of households were illiterate, the poverty rate was over 60 per cent in Bihar and Jharkhand, and in the range of 40 to 50 per cent in Orissa and Madhya Pradesh.

Among ST households whose heads were non-literate, the incidence of poverty was a shocking 81 per cent in Orissa, and over 60 per cent in Chhattisgarh and Madhya Pradesh.

For households headed by non-literate persons in the Other Castes group, the highest incidence of poverty was in Jharkhand (48 per cent), followed by Bihar (46 per cent).

Again, looking at differences across social groups, the data show that at the all-India level, the incidence of poverty was highest among the STs (60 per cent), followed by SCs (48 per cent), and lower among Other Castes (43 per cent).

TABLE 9   *Incidence of poverty among households headed by non-literate persons across seven selected States, by social group, 2004–05*

States	SC	ST	Others	All
Uttar Pradesh	48.3	35.4	35.1	38.78
West Bengal	38.2	49.4	38.4	39.66
Jharkhand	61.5	56.9	47.9	52.97
Orissa	56.3	81.2	45.2	60.93
Chhattisgarh	37.5	62.6	41.9	49.21
Madhya Pradesh	46.6	62.5	· 30.7	44.81
Bihar	67.6	61.6	46.0	52.51
All India	48.0	60.0	43.0	39.30

Source: Thorat, Amit (2009).

Indicators of Deprivation Related to Malnutrition and Health

Indian society is characterized by significant differences in health status between social groups. Children belonging to the SCs and STs have worse nutrition, health and mortality indicators, and poorer access to health and nutrition schemes, than children from 'higher' castes.

In this section, we use data from the National Family Health Survey (NFHS-3) (IIPS 2005–06), supplemented by data from smaller studies, to describe some of these differences, to explore the reasons for such differences, and to discuss some policy measures to improve access to health services and food security schemes for children currently excluded from such schemes.

Mortality

Table 10 shows the infant mortality rate (IMR), defined as the number of infant deaths per 1,000 births, for children from different social groups. The mortality rates were 33 to 100 per cent higher among children from OBC, SC and ST groups than among children from Other social groups.

In States with significant tribal populations – Jharkhand, Orissa and Madhya Pradesh – the gap between infant mortality rates among STs and Other social groups is very large. In Uttar Pradesh and Bihar, the IMR among Dalits (SCs) is significantly higher than among Others. In West Bengal, however, it is of note that the IMR among Dalits (30) is much lower than among Others (58).

TABLE 10 *Infant mortality rates across seven selected States, by social group*

States	Dalit (SC)	Adivasi (ST)	OBC	Others	All
Uttar Pradesh	82	–	71	60	71
West Bengal	30	–	57	58	48
Jharkhand	65	80	60	77	69
Orissa	62	68	71	50	63
Chhattisgarh	35	64	71	94	65
Madhya Pradesh	71	87	62	63	70
Bihar	57	–	60	76	63
All India	66.4	62.1	56.6	48.9	57

Note: – indicates low frequency.
Source: Computed from unit-level data, IIPS and Macro International (2007).

Undernutrition

The data in Table 11 are on malnutrition among children, defined by a weight-for-age criterion (below 3 standard deviations from the median is considered severe malnutrition, and below 2 standard deviations is considered moderate malnutrition). The incidence of severe malnutrition among SC and ST households was approximately 50–100 per cent higher than among Others. This was the case both at the all-India level and in all the low-income States.

TABLE 11 *Underweight children across seven selected States, by social group* in per cent

States	SC	ST	OBC	Others
Uttar Pradesh	47.0	–	44.0	32.0
West Bengal	42.0	–	27.0	35.0
Jharkhand	61.0	64.0	56.0	41.0
Orissa	45.0	54.0	38.0	27.0
Chhattisgarh	47.0	54.0	47.0	29.0
Madhya Pradesh	64.0	71.0	57.0	46.0
Bihar	69.0	–	56.0	47.0
All India	47.9	54.5	43.2	33.7

Note: – indicates low frequency.
Source: Computed from unit-level data, IIPS and Macro International (2007).

Access to Health Services

The above analysis shows that important indicators of health and nutrition were worse for SC and ST children than for Others. Do the children of SC and ST households, who need health services the most, have equal access to them? The data also show that SC mOthers and their children suffered on account of the relatively limited use by them of public health services. For example, access to services other than those of Anganwadi workers was lower for SC and ST children than for other children.

It is clear that economic status, levels of education and access to health services influence the levels of child malnutrition in society (see Thorat and Sabharwal 2009a). Tables 12 and 13, which show levels of malnutrition among different social groups, reveal that nutritional levels among SCs and STs are lower than among Others at similar levels of wealth and mothers' education. Similarly, for those with similar education levels the proportion of underweight children was higher among SCs than Others. This points

TABLE 12 *Access to essential health services of women and children across social groups: rural, 2005–06*

Access to essential health services	SC	ST	OBC	Others
Percentage of children vaccinated	39.7	31.3	40.7	53.8
Percentage distribution of children 0–59 months covered by Anganwadi workers, frequency of weighing	78.1	64.2	83.3	82.7
Place of delivery at home (%)	67.1	82.3	62.5	49.0
Assistance during delivery (%)				
(a) By *dai* (traditional birth attendant)	37.7	50.2	37.1	30.4
(b) By friend/relative	20.7	23.0	15.5	11.3
(c) By skilled provider	40.6	25.4	46.7	57.8
Postnatal check-up: less than 4 hrs (%)	23.7	16.3	26.4	34.5

Source: Computed from unit-level data, IIPS and Macro International (2007).

TABLE 13 *Underweight children across social groups, by 'low' standard of living of households*

States	SC	ST	Non-SC/ST	All
Uttar Pradesh	54	64	41	50
West Bengal	53	54	45	48
Jharkhand	61	69	50	63
Orissa	49	52	39	49
Chhattisgarh	54	51	44	53
Madhya Pradesh	70	76	58	69
Bihar	72	–	61	65

Note: The NFHS categorizes households by 'low', 'medium' and 'high' standards of living, using a score-based aggregation of selected assets and amenities.
Source: Computed from unit-level data, IIPS and Macro International (2007).

TABLE 14 *Underweight children across social groups, by mother's education level (no education), 2005–06*

States	SC	ST	OBC	Others	All
Uttar Pradesh	49	63	49	42	48
West Bengal	52	60	–	43	48
Jharkhand	66	66	62	49	63
Orissa	49	54	48	40	50
Chhattisgarh	49	57	55	44	54
Madhya Pradesh	66	72	61	57	65
Bihar	71	–	59	60	62

Source: Computed from unit-level data, IIPS and Macro International (2007).

strongly towards the possibility of discrimination associated with caste and 'untouchability' influencing observed health outcomes among Dalit children.

The descriptive analysis brings out two important social features of health status and malnourishment. It shows that for all indicators of health status, the situation of SC and ST groups is much worse than that of Other groups. Even among those with similar standards of living and education levels, the health status among Dalits and Adivasis was poorer than Others. This indicates that in addition to poverty and lack of education, Dalits suffer from unequal access to public services, because of caste and untouchability-related discrimination and exclusion.

Discussion and Policy Suggestions
The analysis in this paper has focused on understanding the relative economic position and, specifically, the incidence of poverty among SC and ST households. The analysis is at the all-India level as well as for seven low-income States.

The results, based on analysis of the NSS data for 2004–05, show that in rural areas, in general, poverty was highest among people of STs, followed

by SCs and Others. To separate the role of social exclusion from other factors, we disaggregated the data and estimated the incidence of poverty across
social groups for specific economic categories. For example, we examined the
incidence of poverty among households engaged in wage labour in agriculture, and found that even within this category, the poverty ratio was higher
among SCs than Others in most States (the one exception was West Bengal).

Access to agricultural land is particularly low among SCs because of
the Dalits' traditional exclusion from ownership of property, and Dalits are
thus concentrated among wage workers. Traditionally, ST households have
had better access to land. Nevertheless, even among the small and marginal
landholding categories, the poverty ratio among STs was higher than among
Others, a fact that reflects the low productivity of tribal agriculture. As compared to Dalits and Others, the incidence of poverty among ST households
engaged in non-agricultural activity was high, suggesting that the Adivasi
people suffer from discrimination and disadvantage in the rural non-farm
labour market.

Dalits face unfair exclusion and discrimination. Adivasis, on the other
hand, seem to suffer from what Sen terms 'active and passive exclusion', as
they are affected by development policies of the state and other agents, often
resulting in land alienation and displacement. Adivasis are also often excluded
from participation in the life of the larger community; as Sen observes, this
directly impoverishes a person's life as it additionally reduces the economic
opportunity that comes from social contact. Such exclusion possibly explains
why poverty is highest among STs in rural areas, despite better access than
Dalits and Muslims to agricultural land.

Analysis of the incidence of poverty in seven low-income States shows
that Orissa had the highest poverty rate (47 per cent), followed closely by
Jharkhand, Bihar and Chhattisgarh. Among SCs, the incidence of poverty was
highest in Bihar (64 per cent), followed by Jharkhand (58 per cent) and Orissa
(50 per cent). Among STs, the incidence of poverty was highest in Orissa (76
per cent), followed by Madhya Pradesh (58 per cent), Chhattisgarh (55 per
cent) and Jharkhand (54 per cent).

There are two important findings of our analysis of factors associated with poverty. First, across all social groups, the incidence of poverty was
higher among households engaged in wage labour than among those that were
self-employed, and higher among illiterate households than among literate
households. To put it differently, the incidence of poverty was significantly
lower in households that had greater access to resources such as land and
capital. The second finding is that in a single economic category (such as
marginal cultivator or wage labour) or a single educational category, Dalit
and Adivasi households experienced higher levels of poverty than non-Dalit
and non-Adivasi households. This indicates that besides general causes of
poverty, such as lack of ownership of income-generating assets and education, there are specific causes of poverty linked to group identity based on

caste and ethnicity, factors that worsen the magnitude of poverty among SC and ST households.

The descriptive analysis of health shows that for all indicators of health status, the situation of SCs and STs was much worse than for Others. Again, at a similar standard of living and education, the health status of SCs and STs was lower than the rest of the population. Dalits and Adivasis thus do not have equal access to public services, which can be assumed to be because of caste-related discrimination and exclusion.

Conclusion: Need for Inclusive Policies

This study has documented higher rates of poverty among Scheduled Caste and Scheduled Tribe groups – poverty that is clearly associated with social exclusion and discrimination. While the prevalence of social exclusion is increasingly recognized, a lack of in-depth study has constrained efforts to develop inclusive policies, particularly in the private sector. Inclusive policies that cover various groups that are discriminated against will necessarily have to be guided by the specific nature of exclusion and discrimination faced by each of these social groups in Indian society. It will require study to understand the nature and forms of exclusion and discrimination faced by different social groups. We also need analyses of the consequences of exclusion and discrimination with respect to access to income-earning assets, as well as to social needs such as education, health, housing, and participation in government and administration. Such research will enable us to develop group-specific equal opportunity policies. Research on the theoretical and empirical dimensions of caste, ethnicity and religion-based discrimination is necessary to gain insights into the nature of discrimination and its consequences.

References

Buvinic, Mayra (2005), 'Social Exclusion in Latin America', in Mayra Buvinic and Jacqueline Mazza, with Ruthanne Deutsch, *Social Inclusion and Economic Development in Latin America*, Inter-American Development Bank (distributed by John Hopkins University Press), New York.

Department for International Development (DFID) (2005), 'Reducing Poverty by Tackling Social Exclusion: A DFID Policy Paper', DFID, London.

International Institute for Population Sciences (IIPS) and Macro International (2007), *National Family Health Survey (NFHS-3), India, 2005–06*, IIPS, Mumbai.

National Sample Survey Organization (NSSO) (2006a), *Consumption Expenditure Survey, 2004–05*, National Sample Survey 61st Round (July 2004–June 2005), Government of India, New Delhi.

National Sample Survey Organization (NSSO) (2006b), *Employment and Unemployment Situation Among Social Groups in India, 2004–05*, National Sample Survey 61st Round (July 2004–June 2005), NSS Report no. 516 (61/10/01), Government of India, New Delhi.

Sen, Amartya (2000), 'Social Exclusion: Concept, Application, and Scrutiny', Social Development Papers no. 1, Asian Development Bank, Manila.

Thorat, Amit (2009), 'Study on Data on Poverty across Social and Religious Groups in India: A Report', Indian Institute of Dalit Studies, New Delhi.

Thorat, Sukhadeo (2009), *Dalits in India: A Search for a Common Destiny*, Sage Publications, New Delhi.

Thorat, Sukhadeo and Kumar, Narender, eds (2008a), *B.R. Ambedkar: Perspectives on Social Exclusion and Inclusive Policies*, Oxford University Press, New Delhi.

Thorat, Sukhadeo and Kumar, Narender, eds (2008b), *In Search of Inclusive Policies: Addressing Graded Inequalities*, Rawat Publications, New Delhi.

Thorat, Sukhadeo and Newman, Katherine S., eds (2009), *Blocked By Caste: Economic Discrimination in Modern India*, Oxford University Press, New Delhi.

Thorat, Sukhadeo and Sabharwal, Nidhi Sadana (2009a), 'Discrimination and Children's Nutritional Status in India', *Institute of Development Studies Bulletin,* vol. 40, no. 4, pp. 25–29.

Thorat, Sukhadeo and Sabharwal, Nidhi Sadana (2009b), 'Caste and Ownership of Private Enterprises', *Economic and Political Weekly,* vol. 44, no. 23, June, pp. 13–16.

Thorat, Sukhadeo and Sabharwal, Nidhi Sadana (2010), 'Caste and Social Exclusion: Issues Related to Concept, Indicators and Measurement', Indian Institute of Dalit Studies (IIDS) and UNICEF Working Paper Series, vol. 2, no. 1, pp. 1–43.

World Bank (2006), *World Development Report, 2006: Equity and Development,* World Bank and Oxford University Press, Washington, D.C.

Appendix Tables

TABLE A1 *Shares of selected social groups in the population of seven selected States, 2001* in per cent

States	SC	ST	OBC	Others
Uttar Pradesh	23.0		53.0	23.4
West Bengal	25.2	6.4	6.3	62.0
Jharkhand	14.5	25.3	43.6	16.6
Orissa	19.2	23.0	36.6	21.2
Chhattisgarh	16.4	31.7	41.9	9.9
Madhya Pradesh	16.7	20.0	41.4	21.9
Bihar	22.6	0.6	60.2	16.2

Source: NSSO (2006b).

TABLE A2 *Percentage of rural population across seven selected States, by social group, 2004–05*

States	SC	ST	OBC	Others
Uttar Pradesh	25.7	0.4	54.7	19.1
West Bengal	27.3	8.0	6.5	58.1
Jharkhand	14.3	28.3	44.9	12.5
Orissa	19.7	25.0	37.5	17.7
Chhattisgarh	16.6	35.5	43.0	4.8
Madhya Pradesh	18.1	24.8	42.1	15.0
Bihar	23.7	0.6	60.1	15.2

Source: NSSO (2006b).

Struggles for Land, Labour and Rights:
Some Historical Experiences

Agrarian Change and Changes in the Socio-Economic Conditions of Dalit Households in a Malabar Village

R. Ramakumar

The study of changes in the standard of living of Dalits in Malabar is a theme of special significance in the social sciences. In 1956, when the State of Kerala was formed by merging the regions of Travancore, Cochin and Malabar, there were distinct differences in the state of agrarian relations in the three regions. Malabar, where the agrarian structure was characterized by a most oppressive form of landlordism, was the most backward region. Landlordism in Malabar was built on diverse forms of unfreedom for tenants and landless agricultural workers, who were mostly Dalits.

The transformation in the lives of Dalit agricultural workers in Malabar is the subject of this essay. It deals with changes in the socio-economic conditions of Dalit agricultural workers in Malabar from the nineteenth century through the twentieth century. The essay uses published historical information as well as primary data collected from Morazha village in north Malabar to document these changes. Agrarian relations in Morazha were the subject of a study by economist Thomas W. Shea in 1955, that is, immediately before the formation of the State of Kerala and the first legislative steps towards land reform (Shea 1955a and 1955b). Here, I try to compare selected aspects of the status of Dalits in Morazha in the contemporary period with their conditions as recorded by Shea.

Morazha *desam* (part of a census village) is situated in the Taliparamba taluk of Kannur district in Kerala. The data on Morazha used here were collected as part of a larger study that I undertook, of the socio-economic characteristics of agricultural workers in the village. The data are from a detailed, census-type survey that covered all households in the *desam* that had two characteristics. The first characteristic was the presence of at least one worker in the household who had worked for wages in agriculture in 2000–01. The second was that a major share of the income of the household came from rural manual labour. In other words, the database for this essay covers all households in Morazha *desam* that earned at least a part of their income from agricultural wage work *and* a major part of their income from some form of manual labour. There were 162 such households in the village, of which 25 per cent were Dalit households. I refer to these households in this essay as 'manual labour households involved in agricultural wage work'.[1] The survey was conducted in July–August 2001, and the reference period for the survey was the agricultural year of 2000–01.

Dalits in Malabar: The Historical Context

Agrarian society in the Malabar region in the nineteenth and early twentieth century has been famously described by E.M.S. Namboodiripad as marked by *jati–janmi–naduvazhi medhavitvam* (upper caste–landlord–chieftain hegemony; see Namboodiripad 1948). According to Namboodiripad, Malabar was characterized by the combined domination of landlords in the economic sphere, Brahman-dominated upper castes in social life, and chieftains in the political sphere (Namboodiripad 1994a).

Agricultural workers, most of them Dalits, occupied a special place within this agrarian regime in Malabar. The hegemony of landlords, upper castes and chieftains was built on extreme conditions of unfreedom for the working population. In particular, Dalit agricultural workers were subjected to different types of caste discrimination and economic exploitation.

There was extreme concentration of land ownership in Malabar in the nineteenth century. According to K.N. Panikkar, the 'monopoly of land and big landlordism . . . was a chief characteristic of the agrarian scene in Malabar' (Panikkar 1978: 881). Members of Dalit households, who were almost all agricultural workers, were denied ownership rights to land.[2]

An important feature of the *jati–janmi–naduvazhi* system in the early nineteenth century was the presence of slavery among the Pulaya, Paraya and Cherumar castes. While most slaves were attached to arable lands and transferred along with the land, others were treated as chattel and sold independently of land (Ganesh 1990; Kumar 1965). Buchanan noted in 1801 that the 'slaves are very severely treated; and their diminutive stature

---

[1] There were altogether 1,345 households in Morazha *desam*. In order to identify the agricultural-worker households among them, I conducted two rounds of house-listing surveys, in March and April–May 2001 respectively. Through these house-listing surveys, I collected information on members of household with respect to religion, caste, land ownership, worker status, primary and secondary occupations, place of work, share of irrigated land in total land owned by the household, and modes of irrigation. From the two house-listing surveys, I prepared a complete list of workers in the *desam* who worked for wages in agriculture. In a third round in July 2001, I conducted a detailed, census-type survey on the working and living conditions of all the households (199) to which these workers belonged. From these 199 households, I selected all the households that earned a major share of their income from some form of manual labour. Out of the 199 surveyed households, 162 households earned a major part of their income from manual labour. These are the 'manual labour households involved in agricultural wage work' represented in this essay.

[2] *Janmi*s owned all the agricultural land, forest land and cultivable wasteland in the district. Other categories of the agrarian population – *kanakkar*s, *verumpattakkaran*s and landless labourers – did not generally own land. For a summary description of the major categories in the agrarian population of Malabar during the period of British rule, see Ramachandran (1996: 281).

and squalid appearance show evidently a want of adequate nourishment'
(Buchanan 1870: 371). Abbé J. Dubois, a missionary who lived in Malabar
between 1792 and 1823, noted that the conditions of the 'Parayas and their
state of bondage' were

> at its worst. . . . All children born to Parayas were serfs by birth, just as
> [their] parents were. . . . If one of these Parayas escapes and takes services
> under another, the master can recover him as his own property. . . . It is by
> no means uncommon to see a debtor who is unable to pay his debts in . . .
> cash satisfy his creditors by handing over to them a number of Paraya slaves.
> (Cited in Nair 1986)

In 1843, under pressure from movements for abolition of slavery in
Britain, the colonial state abolished slavery. Yet, for many reasons, the practice
of slavery continued to exist. Hjejle (1967: 98) has argued that legal abolition
'had little to offer the slave population'. The local administrative mechanism
in Malabar was filled with people of the upper castes who themselves were
slave owners and did their best to sabotage the law.

Thus, despite abolition of slavery, traditional forms of unfreedom
and bondage for the backward castes in Malabar survived till the middle of
the twentieth century. New forms of bondage, monetized forms in particular,
also emerged. Debt bondage became common (Hjejle 1967). The burden of
debt forced many workers of the traditional slave castes to attach themselves
to their old landlords. E.J. Edona, a missionary in Kannur in the early twentieth century, noted that even after the abolition of slavery, 'social disabilities
and economic bondage have fettered their freedom', and that 'the perpetual
burden of debt binds them with an iron chain to their masters' (Edona 1940:
133). Debt-bonded workers could not usually work for any landlord other
than their creditor, and were to present themselves for any kind of work at
the landlord's call.[3]

By the middle of the twentieth century, debt-based forms of bondage had declined in importance, while levels of indebtedness remained acute.
As Herring (1983: 162) noted, 'though debt bondage was less prevalent [in
1956–57] than previously, the debt nexus was still important'. Data from
the second Agricultural Labour Enquiry (ALE), 1956–57, show that about
95 per cent of attached agricultural labour households in Malabar, mostly

---

[3] In particular, Edona (1940) discusses certain connections between debt bondage and
gender oppression in Madai and Mattul villages of north Malabar. As a result of low
employment opportunities in the lean season, many agricultural workers were forced
to migrate to Coorg in Karnataka for employment in plantations. The landlords to
whom the workers were attached financed these migrations. The rate of interest on
such loans was about 10 per cent for three months (or 40 per cent per annum). Women
in the workers' families were taken under the landlords' 'protection' while the men
were away. Edona writes, 'how assiduously this protection has been exercised will be
evident from the incidence of venereal disease' that was widespread among women
in Madai and Mattul (ibid.: 131).

Dalits, were in debt. The majority of agricultural workers had taken loans from informal sector sources.

The practice of untouchability against the backward castes was a characteristic feature of social life in Malabar. Untouchability in Malabar was, in practice, a detailed system of distance pollution. Mayer (1952: 26) describes the different gradations of distance pollution prescribed for different caste groups in Malabar. A Nair could not touch a Namboodiri (Brahman), a Tiyya had to keep a distance of at least 32 feet from him, and a Cheruman or Pulaya had to keep at least 64 feet away. Further, a Cheruman or Pulaya had to keep 32 feet away from a Tiyya.

In addition to distance pollution, there were detailed norms on speech usage and behavioural codes for Dalits. A Pulaya worker had to stand in front of the *janmi* with his back bent forward and hands clasped in front, or else he would be severely punished. Pulayas could not wear a *mundu* longer than knee-length, had no right to wrap towels around their forehead, and no right to use footwear.

In the nineteenth and early twentieth century, there was organized resistance from landlords to allowing members of Dalit households to attend school. While there were efforts by the state and Christian missionary groups to improve access to school education for the oppressed castes, the landlords effectively undermined most of these efforts (Edona 1940). When slavery was legally abolished in 1843, the colonial state introduced schools for children from traditional slave-caste households. Hjejle describes how landlords undermined this step:

> A new school was opened in Calicut in July 1844, one at Tellicherry in August and one at Palghat in September. . . . The slave proprietors viewed it with jealousy and apprehension, and immediately after the first school was opened in Calicut, rumours began to circulate that the measure was in reality a scheme by the government to kidnap children for transportation to Mauritius. These rumours had a great effect among the slaves and prevented them from sending their children to school. . . . The experiment was given up altogether in 1849. (Hjejle 1967: 99).

Organized opposition by landlords to schooling of Dalit children continued into the twentieth century. Dalit students who went to enrol at schools were beaten up and thrown out of the school compound by the henchmen of landlords (see Nayanar 1982). Mass literacy among the Dalits of Malabar did not become a reality until the second half of the twentieth century (Ramachandran 1996).

In sum, caste-based discrimination and oppression in Malabar were rooted in the nature of the agrarian relations. Namboodiripad (1981: 19) has argued that 'the origin and development of *janmi* domination was . . . inseparably connected with the existence and development of the caste hierarchy'. As Ronald Herring noted, 'landlordism . . . was inextricably tied to a social system that imposed disabilities and indignities on the lowest orders which were extreme, severe and rigid even by Indian standards' (Herring 1983: 158). Shea (1964) noted that 'caste immobility . . . contributed to the complexity of land tenure patterns; the complexity of tenure relationships . . . further reduced caste mobility'.

After an official visit in 1948, the Congress Agrarian Reforms Committee (headed by J.C. Kumarappa) described the agricultural labourers of north Malabar thus: 'Their frail and bony bodies, their emaciated and worn-out looks, their tattered clothes, all bore testimony to the most extreme form of exploitation' (CARC 1948: 132).

After a detailed study of agrarian relations in Malabar in the same period, Thomas Shea reached a significant conclusion: 'if ever there was a part of India where a positive land reform programme was urgently needed, it is Malabar district' (Shea 1956: 6).

Struggles for Change in the Twentieth Century

Efforts and struggles to transform the conditions of Dalit agricultural workers in Malabar took place over three distinct phases. In the *first phase* (roughly 1917 to 1934), agitations against untouchability were taken up as part of the national movement by members of the Indian National Congress (INC) as well as by religious reform movements. The *second phase* (roughly 1934 to 1957) was a period of elevation of political consciousness among Dalits; this took place through the integration of Dalit struggles against untouchability with the radical struggles of peasant movements for land reform. The *third phase* (1957 and after) witnessed an important shift in the balance of state power in Kerala and the coming to power of governments committed to ending Dalit discrimination. While struggles around land and different forms of discrimination continued into this phase too, the third phase was distinguished by the implementation of land reforms and the institution of a number of social security schemes.

Early Stages of Protest, 1920s to 1934

Organized protests against caste discrimination in Kerala began in Travancore and Cochin earlier than in Malabar. In Travancore, the Ezhava social reform movement under Sree Narayana Guru had evolved into a mass movement in the first decade of the twentieth century itself. The successes of the Sree Narayana Dharma Paripalana Yogam (SNDP Yogam), established in 1903, inspired the organization and struggle of Dalits in Travancore under leaders like Ayyankali and Vellikkara Choti, and in Cochin under leaders like K.P. Vallone (see Saradamoni 1981).[4]

---

[4] In particular, two struggles led by Ayyankali served as important rallying points for larger struggles against caste discrimination in Travancore and Cochin. In 1915, Ayyankali led a successful strike of Dalit agricultural workers in Trivandrum protesting denial of entry to a Pulaya girl in a local school. In 1916, he led another successful

Organized agitation against caste discrimination in Malabar began with the Guruvayur satyagraha of 1932. However, the Guruvayur satyagraha itself was in fact the culmination of a series of smaller agitations and efforts against untouchability. Saradamoni (1981) has noted that inter-caste dining (*mishra-bhojan*) was organized in Calicut in 1917, under Annie Besant's Home Rule League. She also noted that upper-caste leaders of the Congress were 'lukewarm' towards such activities (ibid.: 178).

While Adi Dravida Sanghams, which were local associations of Pulayas and Parayas, had been established in many parts of north Malabar by 1920, their activities were at best muted. The colonial state had introduced Adi Dravida schools for the education of Dalit children; however, resistance from landlords did not allow such schools to succeed. Madakkudiyan Balan, the son of a bonded Dalit worker in Morazha, told me that he was physically evicted from an Adi Dravida school in the 1930s by his father's landlord so that he could start working on the landlord's land (interview with Madak-kudiyan Balan, Morazha, August 2001).

In the 1920s, there were shifts of power within the caste hierarchy of north Malabar. In addition to Nairs, sections of Tiyyas (Ezhavas) and Muslims improved their economic status, and began to assert their positions vis-à-vis Dalits, who were lower in the caste ladder (see Menon 1994). In the absence of any organized resistance against their education, a large number of Tiyyas were able to go to schools and colleges, from where they proceeded for higher studies at the university in Madras. Armed with education, Tiyyas were able to rise to positions of power as 'tehsildars, lawyers, pleaders, sub-judges and up to the rank of deputy collectors' (ibid.: 64). Another section of Tiyyas became rich by accumulating profits from toddy and arrack contracts. Yet another section of them became owners of weaving factories, with active assistance from the Basel Mission. Similarly, a section of Muslims benefited significantly from trading, particularly in spices, paddy and coconut oil, as well as fishing. The process of accumulation among Muslims was aided by the boom in commodity prices and the links that these merchants had with coconut-oil mills in Bombay and Karachi.

Even this narrowly based development of capitalism had an impact on caste relations. Sections of Tiyya and Muslim elites practised untouchability and caste discrimination against the Dalits. For instance, when people of the Tiyya caste opened the Sundareswara temple and Jagannatha temple in Kannur in the 1920s, they denied entry to Pulayas to these (Menon 1994). A feature of the mid- to late 1920s, in addition to upper-caste landlord oppression, was conflict triggered by sections of the rich among Tiyyas and Muslims against the most oppressed sections of the Dalit people, particularly the Pulaya masses.

---

struggle in central Travancore for the rights of Pulaya women to wear bead necklaces (*kallumaala*) and cover their breasts with cloth. Both these struggles involved physical clashes with upper-caste landowners. (See Saradamoni 1981.)

Kerala has been described as a State and society that had two tiers of the outcaste (Ramachandran 1996). Shea (1964: 510) wrote, most tellingly, that the behaviour of the Tiyya elite towards Pulayas was in 'perverse imitation of the behaviour-practices of the elite towards them'. The following excerpts from selected reports in *Mathrubhumi* daily in the late 1920s illustrate incidents of such open aggression against the Dalit people:[5]

> *From a report on 12 December 1929.* On the night of December 8, a group of Tiyyas attacked the houses of Pulayas in Taliparamba. On the night of December 10, a second attack took place in the same region. All Pulaya men fled the village in fear, and Pulaya women, fearing fresh attack, did not go out to work.

> *From an article by K. Kelappan on 14 December 1929.* In Pappinisseri, a Tiyya and a Mappila [Muslim] beat up two Pulaya students. A Pulaya boy, Umitthirian Kanjan, unknowingly touched a Tiyya, Govindan Vaidyar. The boy was chased and beaten; while being chased, the boy jumped into a river and drowned.

> *From a report on 24 December 1929.* A resolution passed at a meeting of Adi Dravidas said that, in Ezhome village, some Muslim people had assaulted Pulayas. The village Adhikari was on the side of the Muslims. On the way to attending the meeting, seven Pulayas from Kuppam were beaten up by some Tiyya people at Pariyaram. A few Pulayas were beaten up on the public road by Tiyya persons in Pappinisseri. On 18 December, two Pulaya organizers of the meeting – Sumukhan and Sekharan – were attacked.

> *From a report on 21 January 1930.* In Valapattanam, a Pulaya boy touched two Mappilas by mistake in the darkness of the night. The Mappilas beat up the boy badly.

> *From a report on 7 October 1931.* On 5 October, A.K. Gopalan [who later became an important mass organizer and mass leader of the Communist Party] organized a procession of Pulayas in Payyannur, demanding the right of entry into the local temple. A group of Tiyyas attacked the *jatha*. Gopalan defended the Pulayas, but was beaten up badly. He was admitted to a hospital; the treatment included six stitches on his head.[6]

> *From an editorial on 10 September 1946.* The Malabar Harijan Seva Sangham passed a resolution documenting atrocities perpetrated on them by caste Hindus and Muslims in Malabar.

Such attacks on Dalits show class aspects of the process of caste dis-

---

[5] These are translations of notes taken by me from the original reports.
[6] Dilip Menon (1994: 109) makes an error when he states that A.K. Gopalan's Payyannur *jatha* of 1931 was for the rights of Tiyyas and untouchables to walk on roads. That *jatha* was for the rights of Pulayas alone, and Tiyya elites had actually attacked the *jatha*.

crimination with the development of capitalism in north Malabar. Writing about this period, Namboodiripad (1981: 18) argued that 'struggles between the two major classes and conflicts between various castes, sub-castes and religious communities were getting mixed up with each other'. He also noted that 'it would . . . be unrealistic to pose the problem as if it is either class struggle or caste conflict. The fact is that there is a certain interpenetration of class and caste' (ibid.).

In the 1920s, a few committed leaders of the Indian National Congress were involved in activities aimed at ending caste discrimination. Saradamoni has argued that non-Dalit leadership of Dalit struggles was historically unavoidable in Kerala due to the absence, unlike among Tiyyas, of 'even a tiny segment among Pulayas who were economically and socially better off.' (Saradamoni 1981: 147). The early activities of Congress leaders took the form of mobilizing Dalits by encouraging temperance, personal hygiene and the wearing of clean clothes among Dalits. Sarojini Naidu's speech at a meeting of 200 Pulayas in Palghat on 8 May 1923 illustrates this emphasis: 'The Pulayas should recognize that their conditions today are hideous. They should shed their bad habits and become well-behaved. They should be clean and hygienic. They should become modern like other classes. They should not eat what others don't eat. *Then all their problems will end*' (*Mathrubhumi*, 10 May 1923; emphasis added).

Over a period of time, Congress leaders also mobilized Dalits in struggles for the right to walk on public roads and to enter Caste-Hindu temples. There is also evidence of active interventions by Congress leaders to improve access to education for Dalits. In Kalliasseri village, in 1928, two Dalit students who went to enrol at a primary school were beaten up and thrown out of the school compound by Nairs and Tiyyas. A Dalit youth – Sumukhan – who tried to stop the attack was beaten up on the public road. After this incident, Congress leaders led efforts to readmit the Dalit students and protect them from casteist attacks. K. Kelappan stayed in Kalliasseri for more than a week and personally accompanied the two students to school every day. E.K. Nayanar, who later became a Communist, told me in an interview that his entry into the national movement in the late 1920s was deeply inspired by this incident. He said: 'I was deeply moved. . . . I did not understand why Dalit children could not sit with other students and study in the school' (interview with E.K. Nayanar, 4 June 2003).

> We started, under the leadership of KPR [Gopalan] and AKG (A.K. Gopalan), and with the instructions of Mahatma Gandhi, to work for the upliftment of Dalits. . . . I, along with a number of young Congress workers, was in the forefront of activities like bathing Dalit children in village ponds, putting clothes on them and taking them to schools to protect them from attacks by upper-caste members. (Ibid.)

The need to abolish landlordism in order that the material basis of caste discrimination be weakened had not yet been appreciated within the national movement in this early phase. By the end of the 1920s, some of the resolutions of meetings of the Pulaya people, organized by radical Congress leaders, began referring to the distribution of wasteland to Pulayas. A meeting of Pulayas in Pappinisseri on 17 January 1930 demanded that wasteland in Kalliasseri, Morazha and Pappinisseri be distributed to the Adi Dravidas (*Mathrubhumi*, 25 January 1930). Similarly, at a special meeting of the Adi Keraliya Maha Sabha held in Pappinisseri on 6 December 1930 with Vishnubharateeyan in the chair, a specific demand raised was distribution of wasteland to Adi Dravidas in Morazha.

The decisive break with the past came with a series of events in the early 1930s: the Salt satyagraha of 1930, the Guruvayur satyagraha of 1931, the Gandhi–Irwin Pact of 1931 and Gandhi's suspension of the Civil Disobedience movement in 1933. According to Namboodiripad (1994b: 13), the Salt satyagraha may be 'considered the beginning of a definite Left trend in the freedom movement in all parts of Kerala, and particularly in Malabar'. The Guruvayur satyagraha was organized to gain for the so-called backward castes, the right to enter the Guruvayur temple in south Malabar. Much hope was built around the satyagraha for the backward castes, especially Pulayas. Kelappan wrote to Nehru in 1931: 'Guruvayur temple is the last refuge of all caste arrogance and prejudice. Once untouchability is dislodged from there, it will have no quarter outside' (quoted in Menon 1994: 87).

For leaders like Gandhi, the Guruvayur satyagraha had to be a nonviolent movement that would not split the 'Hindu community' (Menon 1994). However, as the protest progressed, the limits and fragility of such 'unity' were exposed. When Pulayas broke the tradition and bathed in the temple tank in December 1931, the movement began to face physical attacks from the upper castes. A.K. Gopalan and P. Krishna Pillai tried to enter the sanctum of the temple, reserved for Brahmans. While Gopalan was beaten up by Nairs at the entrance, Krishna Pillai managed to enter and even rang the ceremonial bell. In September 1932, Kelappan began a fast to press for a resolution to the impasse. Gandhi, disturbed by the violent turn of events, wrote an angry letter to Kelappan asking him to withdraw the fast, and Kelappan did so in October 1932. With the withdrawal of the fast, the movement slowly fizzled out. Temple entry in Guruvayur for Dalits became a reality only seventeen years later, when the Madras Temple Entry Authorization (Amendment) Act of 1949 was enacted.

Gandhi's intervention to end the Guruvayur satyagraha in 1932 and his withdrawal of the Civil Disobedience movement in 1934 led to great disenchantment among Congressmen in Malabar.[7] The disillusioned youth of

---

[7] An angry Krishna Pillai wrote: 'Gandhi's organizational ability to lead India is now ending. Gandhi is scared to lead the masses on the correct path' (*Mathrubhumi*, 11 July 1934).

Malabar began to search for alternatives to the Congress, and large sections of Congressmen joined the Congress Socialist Party (CSP), formed in 1934. Krishna Pillai was one of the founders of the CSP – and later, in 1939, of the Communist Party of India (CPI).

The formation of the CSP and the CPI in the 1930s was to lead to a radical redefinition of the caste question in Malabar, and the struggles around it.

The Phase of Politicization of Dalits, 1934–57

The most important shift in addressing the caste question after 1934 was the recognition that abolition of landlordism was central to ending Dalit oppression. In other words, putting an end to caste discrimination was closely linked to weakening the material basis of landlord and upper-caste hegemony.

Under the leadership of the CSP, the All-Malabar Karshaka Sangham (peasants' union) was formed in 1937, to lead the struggles of peasants and agricultural workers in the region. Demands for ownership rights to tenants and distribution of land to Dalits were integrated by the Sangham with the demands to end caste discrimination. N.E. Balaram, a leader of the CPI, described this shift of emphasis in the following words:

> The struggles against untouchability, discrimination, the *janmi* system and unfreedom had begun [even before the CPI was formed]. Some of these struggles had met with success, too. Yet, untouchability, caste discrimination, upper-caste hegemony, the *janmis*, chieftains and British rule survived. The central issue then was how to eliminate these societal evils. Until then, the links between these different societal evils and between economic institutions and societal evils were not appreciated adequately. There was also inadequate appreciation of the links between caste discrimination and the *janmi* system, between the *janmi* system and state power, between upper-caste hegemony and chieftains, and between chieftains and British rule. This ideological gap was filled . . . by the CPI. (Balaram 1973: 44–45).

There were, thus, distinct breaks as well as elements of continuity. In the new understanding, the caste system contained both social oppression *and* class exploitation. Explaining this integration of demands, Namboodiripad noted that 'in the actual social conditions of Kerala, the development of the democratic movement is bound to be linked with the organized struggle against caste-Hindu domination' (Namboodiripad 1981: 15).

In Malabar, tenants-at-will and landless agricultural workers faced the common threat of eviction from landlords. The Karshaka Sangham's slogan of 'land to the tenant and homestead land for landless workers' brought peasants and agricultural workers together. It organized agitations demanding 'security of rights for tenants and hutment dwellers on land, estimation of fair rent, the use of standard measures for measuring rent [in kind], and abolition of non-rent extractions' (George 1992: 19). In his Minute of Dissent to the Malabar Tenancy Committee of 1940, Namboodiripad pointed out that its recommendations ignored the needs of agricultural workers and Dalits (Namboodiripad 1940).

The Karshaka Sangham also led agitations for better conditions of work for agricultural workers. These agitations demanded that landlords raise the wages of workers, prohibit children up to 15 years of age from working in the fields, and institute two months of maternity leave with full pay for female agricultural workers.

While the Sangham focused its energies on attacking *janmi* landlordism, it also continued with earlier agitations to end caste discrimination. The first meeting of the Malabar Karshaka Sangham, held in Parassinikkadavu in 1936, passed two resolutions: first, it demanded the abolition of traditions and customs regarding manner of speech and use of phrases to be used by members of oppressed castes; secondly, it demanded that all illegal levies charged by *janmis* on tenants be abolished immediately (see Vishnubharateeyan 1980). The Sangham frequently organized anti-untouchability days in the districts; in an article announcing one such agitation in Kannur, Krishna Pillai demanded that an ordinance be passed to make untouchability illegal (*Deshabhimani*, 7 August 1947). Significantly, he also noted that efforts to prohibit untouchability were an important part of anti-imperialist struggles.

Citing the instance of one such struggle, Vishnubharateeyan (1980) wrote that the Karshaka Sangham told Ananthan Nambiar, a *janmi* from Kalliattu *amsam*, that he would henceforth be addressed by his name and not as *thampuran* or *yajaman*, the traditional titles of landlords. Further, the peasants and workers decided that they would not get off the road when the Nambiar passed by, and that they would not stand up to honour him on any occasion. Throughout Malabar, the Karshaka Sangham exhorted peasants and workers to not remove their headcloths and not unfold their *mundu*s [*dhoti*s] while talking to the *janmi*. It also asked Dalits to wear *dhoti*s that extended beyond the knees and to grow their moustaches long. Such actions, in an earlier period, would have been crushed by the *janmi*s; however, they were more circumspect when the actions were backed by a powerful political movement.

A feature of the peasant movement in the 1930s and 1940s was that Dalits participated energetically in its activities alongside members of Other Castes. As Radhakrishnan (1989: 93) noted, 'massive inter-caste dinners, for which peasants carried head-loads of vegetables and rice, were a unique and recurrent feature of the conferences organized by the Kisan Sabha, which went a long way in weakening inter-caste barriers and promoting class solidarity'.

Many Dalits died while fighting under the banner of the Sangham. In Payyannur, Pokkan, a Dalit worker, was leading a Sangham demonstration to the *janmi*'s house. The police arrived and opened fire at the demonstrators, killing Pokkan. The first reading room in the Morazha–Kalliasseri region, established in 1934, was called Sree Harshan Reading Room – after a Dalit activist, Harshan, who died while serving a jail sentence with K.P.R. Gopa-lan and other peasant leaders. An incident that generated much interest in Morazha in the 1940s was the marriage of leading Communist leader C.H. Narayanan Nambiar and P. Nani, a Dalit schoolteacher.

In 1957, the first Communist government in Kerala, headed by E.M.S. Namboodiripad, came to power. In the following period when land reforms were officially implemented, the pressure built up by the peasant movement was crucial in freeing Dalit agricultural workers from different kinds of social and economic exploitation.

The Phase of Land Reforms and Social Security: 1957 Onwards

While the achievements in the social sector of Kerala in the second half of the twentieth century had their roots in the State's history, they were also, 'in an important sense, results of public action in post-1957 Kerala' (Ramachandran 1996). The most important public action after 1957 was implementation of land reforms by the Communist government. Land reforms in the State, which have been described as 'the most comprehensive and far-reaching reforms of their kind in contemporary India', represented a historic agrarian transition and a radical shift in the balance of rural power (Herring 1980: A-59). The impact of the reforms went beyond changes in land tenure; land reforms also became the 'centrepiece of the programme for social and economic progress' (CDS 1975: 59), for which Kerala is justly famous.[8] Within the State, the impact of land reforms on agrarian relations, and on the personal freedom and self-dignity of agricultural workers was most dramatic in Malabar, where the erstwhile agrarian system was most backward and oppressive.

Land reforms in Kerala had three basic components. First, security of tenure was provided to tenants. All evictions undertaken after the formation of the State were held to be illegal. The government took ownership of all tenanted land and payment of rent on such land was stopped. Secondly, ceilings were set on ownership holdings of land. Ceiling-surplus land was taken over by the state and redistributed. Thirdly, landless agricultural workers were given ownership rights over homestead plots.

There is a general consensus among scholars that land reform in Kerala was successful with respect to tenancy abolition and the distribution of homestead lands. Between 1957 and 1993, about 2.8 million tenants were conferred ownership rights (or had their rights protected) and about 0.6 million hectares of land accrued to them (Appu 1996). Between 1957 and 1996, about 528,000 agricultural worker households were issued homestead owner-

[8] Land reforms in Kerala were the result of many years of struggle by peasants and agricultural workers. As Richard Franke wrote, 'Kerala's land reform law was the outcome of more than a century of spontaneous rebellion, organizing, petition signing, marching, meetings, strikes, battles with police and landlord goon squads, election campaigns, and parliamentary debates (Franke 1993: 123).

ship certificates (SPB 1997). However, there is also a consensus that Kerala's land reform was not successful with respect to acquiring and distributing ceiling-surplus land to the landless. Only 1.47 per cent of the total operated area was redistributed between 1957 and 1993 (Appu 1996). As a result, the component of land reforms that directly benefited landless agricultural workers was the distribution of homestead land.

The failure in successfully distributing ceiling-surplus land to the landless was mainly due to the significant opposition that the Communist-led State government faced from the Union government, from the judiciary and from landlord-supported political parties in the State. In 1959, before the President of India signed the State's historic land reform Bill, the first Communist ministry was dismissed by the Union government. The non-Communist ministries that followed, with the support of the landlord classes, successfully diluted every radical ceiling provision in the land reform legislation. With the passing of years without any serious implementation, landowners transferred land on a large scale and by different means.

The provision to distribute homestead land to agricultural workers was added to the land reform laws after it became clear that the extent of ceiling-surplus land available would be smaller than expected. This addition was made by the Communist-led government that came to power in 1967. This ministry, led by the Communist Party of India (Marxist), drafted the State's most comprehensive land reform law, which was passed as The Kerala Land Reforms (Amendment) Act, 1970. The Act gave landless agricultural workers the option of purchasing 10 cents of land (0.01 acre), for which they were required to pay only 25 per cent of the market value in normal cases and 12.5 per cent of the market value if the landowner possessed land above the ceiling. Fifty per cent of the amount finally payable was subsidized by the state, with the remaining 50 per cent to be paid in twelve annual instalments (which, in practice, were never paid). Thus, even when some components of land reform were not successfully implemented, most Dalit agricultural worker households in the State received plots of homestead land free of cost.

Even after 1970, non-Communist ministries in the State pushed through amendments in the land reform laws, leading to a reduction of the surplus land that could have been taken over for redistribution. One such amendment was made in 1979, a law that came to be popularly known as the Gift Deeds Act. This Act validated all 'gift' transfers made between 1970 and 1974 by landlords who held ceiling-surplus land to members of their families, and exempted such land from ceiling legislation. Michael Tharakan has noted that the amendment was 'a retrograde step in the field of land reforms in Kerala' (Tharakan 1982: 161). According to his calculations, as a result of this amendment, the extent of land that was rendered unavailable for distribution was about 14,000 acres and about 22,000 potential beneficiary households were denied ownership rights to land. As a result of such amendments, the surplus land declared by the government in 1980 was

44,000 hectares, which accounted for only 6 per cent of the land notified as surplus in 1957 (Kannan 1988).

Critics like Joan Mencher have argued that land reform 'has not benefited the majority of agricultural labourers' in Kerala (Mencher 1980: 1791). Such conclusions follow from not examining the reforms beyond the statistics of redistributed land. Land reforms in Kerala were important both *intrinsically* and *instrumentally* (Ramachandran 2000). They were *intrinsically* important as they weakened the foundations of an oppressive agrarian regime and freed workers from different forms of unfreedom. They were *instrumentally* important as the post-land reform society that emerged made possible advances in the social and economic conditions of the poor. The movement for land reforms in Kerala brought within its ambit a host of social issues that concerned the standards of living of the poor. These issues included access to education, public health systems and food distribution networks, and better working conditions.

Traditional forms of servitude and various forms of caste discrimination, such as untouchability, ceased to be dominant features of Kerala society post-land reforms. The *jati–janmi–naduvazhi* system was the base on which forms of discrimination like untouchability had survived. Land reforms seriously undermined this exploitative system; they undermined not just feudal landlordism, but also the material base of upper-caste domination.[9] Among agricultural workers in post-land reform Palakkad, as Mencher (1980: 1801) herself noted, 'there is certainly a sense of freedom and human dignity that almost all our sample households talked about'.

The instrumental importance of land reforms becomes most evident in advances in the field of education. Historically, in Malabar, educational achievements were determined by a person's caste status, which was closely associated with status in the agrarian economy. While members of Brahman and upper-caste households were the most educated in the population, Dalits and Adivasis were the least educated. In contemporary Malabar, the correlation between achievements in education and a person's position in the agrarian economy has been considerably weakened by land reforms and the spread of public schools. Without land reforms, it would have been impossible to imagine the universal spread of literacy and mass schooling in Malabar.

Further, as a result of the electoral victories of political parties involved in the mass movements for land reform and against social discrimination, a number of social security issues have been brought on to the legislative agenda of the State. Kerala is a State where the government has most effectively intervened for social security for the rural poor, especially agricultural workers. Kerala was the first State in India to attempt to bring agricultural workers out of the informal sector by actually legislating with respect to the conditions of

[9] 'Land reform abolished statutory landlordism and the *janmi* system. It broke the back of Brahman landlordism and weakened substantially upper-caste Hindu landlordism as a whole' (Ramachandran and Ramakumar 2001).

employment of different sections of rural workers. The Kerala Agricultural Workers Act (KAWA) of 1974 was India's first comprehensive legislation for agricultural workers. It sought to give statutory sanction to minimum wages, regulate working hours and working conditions, and establish tripartite mechanisms to settle labour disputes. In 1980, the Act was amended by the CPI(M) ministry to include a scheme to pay pensions to retired agricultural labourers over the age of 60 years.

Results from Morazha[10]
Situation in the 1950s
The socio-economic status of Dalit agricultural workers in Morazha *desam* in the 1950s reflected the general backwardness of standards of living in Malabar. Thomas Shea studied Morazha in 1954–55. His study involved detailed sample surveys of cultivators, primarily tenants, and agricultural labourers. Apart from the surveys, his study also involved detailed documentation of the conditions of life and work of small tenants and agricultural labourers. Shea wrote that the 'economic conditions in Morazha are unusually bad even for Malabar, which is economically one of the worst-off districts in India' (Shea 1955b: 1033).

Food policy during World War II had led to an acute shortage of food in Malabar district in those years. A cholera epidemic in 1943 also took a substantial toll on lives in the district. Morazha itself was badly affected by both the food shortage and the cholera epidemic (see Sivaswamy 1946).[11] When Shea conducted his study in the mid-1950s, the food shortage was still on. He wrote that the worst affected sections of Morazha's population were the agricultural workers, whose lives were characterized by extreme poverty and deprivation. Malnutrition had drastically reduced the length of the working day of an agricultural labourer. Shea noted that while before the war, the working hours of agricultural labourers were from 7 am to 5.30 pm, after the war, physical weakness due to malnutrition reduced their working hours, with labourers working only from 8 am to 12.30 pm (Shea 1955b: 1031). Shea described the living conditions of Morazha's agricultural workers in 1955 as 'wretched in the extreme' (ibid.: 1031).

Land Reforms and Changes in Household Ownership of Land
Prior to land reforms, the distribution of ownership landholdings in Morazha was very unequal. My analysis of the village settlement survey of 1936 shows that about 3 per cent of the landowners (who paid more than Rs 50 as assessment) owned about 52 per cent of the land in the *desam* (Table

---

[10] This section draws on Ramakumar (2006), though I have extended the work further to look at the data disaggregated by caste.

[11] It has been estimated that about 1 per cent of the population died of hunger and epidemic disease during the food crisis of 1942–43 in Malabar. The crisis can therefore be characterized as a famine (Ramachandran 1996).

TABLE 1   *Land assessment details, Morazha desam, 1936*

Annual land revenue paid	Number (total)	Extent (acres)	Assessment (Rs–anas)
Re 1 and less	67	29.10	37.6
Rs 1–10	150	191.90	530.5
Rs 10–30	32	182.90	546.1
Rs 30–50	9	101.70	337.5
Rs 50–100	5	134.30	364.0
Rs 100–250	3	254.80	505.0
Rs 50–500	1	163.40	352.1
Total	267	1058.11	2673.1

Source: Settlement survey of Morazha *desam*, 1936.

1). Kadamberi *devaswam* (a temple management), situated just outside the limits of Morazha revenue village, was the biggest landowner in the village. The *devaswam* was thus a powerful *janmi* (landlord) in Morazha, but the landlord families of the village *de facto* controlled all the land under the *devaswam*'s ownership.

In his analysis of the settlement report for Morazha *desam* of 1936, Thomas Shea found that

> eight *devaswoms*, or temples, hold the *janmam*, or proprietary right, to half of the land in the village. They pay more than 25 per cent of the land revenue, and hold 1/3 of the wet lands. Four of these *devaswoms* are managed by two of the five largest landholders in the village. . . . The five largest *janmies* hold 47.5 per cent of wet lands, 49 per cent of all lands, and pay more than 40 per cent of the total land revenue. (Shea 1955a: 998).

Secondly, there was a strong correlation between the caste status of individuals and land ownership. Either the temple (whose lands were controlled by caste Hindus) or upper-caste cultivators owned most of the land in the *desam*. Data for the constituent parts of Andhur panchayat (which included Morazha *desam*) from the settlement survey of 1936 showed that temples, Brahmans and Nairs (upper castes) together owned about 85 per cent of land (see Table 2). Tiyyas (the intermediate caste) were mainly tenants and owned very little land, while Dalits owned almost no land.

Land reforms in Morazha after 1956–57 put an end to both big landlordism and upper-caste domination in land ownership. My house-listing survey of households in Morazha *desam* in 2001 showed major changes in the distribution of household ownership of land after 1955. First, the extreme concentration of landholdings that Thomas Shea observed in 1955 had disappeared. On the contrary, there was a predominance of small-sized holdings in Morazha in 2001. About 83 per cent of the households owned less than 1 acre of land, and these holdings accounted for about 43 per cent of the total land area (Table 3). There were only two households that owned more than

TABLE 2 *Distribution of land ownership, Andhur panchayat, by social group of landowners, 1936*

Landowners by caste	Area owned (in acres)	Share of area owned (in per cent)
Temple management	1214.7	28.8
Brahman	971.3	23.0
Nair	1392.7	33.0
Tiyya (Ezhava)	176.6	4.2
Muslim	356.6	8.4
Others	112.6	2.6
Total	4224.5	100.0

Source: Andhur Panchayat (1996), Table 1.

TABLE 3 *Distribution of number and area of household ownership holdings, by size-class of landholding, Morazha, 2001*

Land size-class (acres)	Number of households	Share of number (per cent)	Area under holdings (acres)	Share in total area (per cent)
< 0.10	138	10.3	8.5	1.0
0.10–0.24	426	31.7	65.9	7.9
0.25–0.49	289	21.5	100.1	12.0
0.50–0.99	269	20.0	187.0	22.3
1.00–1.49	98	7.3	118.2	14.1
1.50–1.99	42	3.1	72.9	8.7
2.0–3.99	64	4.8	108.8	13.0
4.0–9.99	17	1.3	150.6	18.0
> 9.99	2	0.1	25.1	3.0
All size-classes	1345	100.0	837.1	100.0

Note: Data on number and area of holdings include homesteads.
Source: Survey data, 2001.

10 acres of land; their holdings accounted for just 3 per cent of the total area.

A second finding was of a major shift in the pattern of land ownership across caste groups. By 2001, the monopoly over landholdings by Brahmans and Nairs (and temples) had been weakened (Table 4). Caste Hindus owned only about 39 per cent (as opposed to 85 per cent in 1936) of the total area of land owned by *desam* residents in 2001. The data show that large areas of land were transferred from Brahmans and Nairs to Tiyyas, Pulayas and other oppressed caste groups as a result of land reform. The important point here is that the end of old-type feudal landlordism through land reform in Morazha also meant a *break up of the material basis of upper-caste domination* in the everyday social life of the village.

Among Dalit agricultural workers in Morazha, the shift in the pattern of land ownership came about primarily on account of the distribution of homestead land as part of land reforms. The 113 Dalit households in

TABLE 4   *Distribution of land ownership across residents of Morazha desam, by social group, 2001*

Caste group	Share in population (per cent)	Area owned (acres)	Share in total area (per cent)
Brahman	0.5	12.2	1.6
Nair	25.2	286.5	37.6
Tiyya	34.5	301.5	39.6
Muslim	6.0	24.1	3.2
Pulaya	6.5	24.1	3.2
Others	27.3	113.4	14.9
All castes	100.0	761.8	100.0

Source: Survey data, 2001.

TABLE 5   *Distribution of number and area of homesteads among Dalit households, by size-class of holding, Morazha, 2001*

Land size-class (acres)	No. of Dalit households	Share of Dalit households (per cent)	Area owned by Dalit households (acres)	Share of area owned by Dalit households (per cent)
<0.05	5	4.4	0.2	0.8
0.05–0.09	24	21.2	1.5	6.2
0.10–0.24	56	49.6	8.2	33.4
0.25–0.49	15	13.3	5.2	21.2
0.50–0.99	12	10.6	8.0	32.6
> 1.00	1	0.9	1.5	5.9
All size-classes	113	100.0	24.6	100.0

Source: Survey data, 2001.

Morazha owned a total of about 25 acres of homestead land (Table 5). About 50 per cent of the Dalit households owned homestead plots whose extent was between 0.10 and 0.24 acre. Another 28 per cent of Dalit households owned homestead plots whose extent was above 0.24 acre. The average size of homesteads owned by manual labour households involved in agricultural wage work was 0.217 acre.

Net Revenue from Production in Homestead Plots

Given the importance of homestead land ownership among Dalit agricultural workers, I attempted to estimate the imputed net income from homestead cultivation for the surveyed Dalit households in Morazha. The estimated average imputed net income from homestead plots of Dalits was Rs 798. This average net income from homesteads supplemented the incomes of manual labour households involved in agricultural wage work considerably. As Table 6 shows, on average, the net income from homesteads constituted about 4 per cent of the poverty line for Dalit households, while the correspon-

TABLE 6 *Distribution of households by shares of imputed net income from homesteads on the income poverty line at 2001 prices, Dalit manual labour households involved in agricultural wage work, Morazha, 2001*

Caste category	Net annual revenue per household (Rs) from cultivation in		Net revenue from homesteads as share of poverty line (per cent)
	All types of land	Homestead plots	
Non-Dalit, non-OBC	988.5	733.1	3.9
OBC	1583.1	1297.7	6.0
Dalit	933.9	797.9	3.9
			(6.0)
All castes	1324.1	1079.8	5.7

Note: The figure in parentheses is net revenue as a proportion of the poverty line calculated at average prices prevailing between 1999 and 2003.

Source: Survey data, 2001.

ding share for all castes together was only slightly higher, about 5 per cent.

My estimate above of net income from homesteads is an underestimate, as there was a sharp fall in the prices of agricultural commodities in 2000–01. For instance, the average price of coconut (the most important crop in homesteads) in the market nearest to Morazha in 2001 was about 41 per cent lower than the average price in 1999. The same was true for crops like pepper and arecanut as well. As a result, the average value of production from homestead plots estimated in my study for 2001 was lower than in 1999–2000 or 2001–2. When I replaced the 2001 prices with *the average prices between 1999 and 2003*, the average share of net income from homesteads on the official poverty line registered a significant increase, from 4 per cent to about 6 per cent (Table 6).

Public Action, Land Reform and Advances in Education

In 1951, the literacy rate in Malabar was only 31 per cent, and among women, it was only 22 per cent (Table 7). Among Dalit women in Kerala as a whole (data for Malabar alone are not available for Dalits), the literacy rate was only 17 per cent in 1961. It was after the implementation of land reforms and public investment in school education that literacy rates expanded among Dalits, especially Dalit women. In the absence of land reforms, it would be impossible to imagine the universal spread of literacy and mass schooling in Malabar.

In Morazha in 2001, among the Dalit households I surveyed, more than 50 per cent of household members had entered high school (Table 8). Only about 8 per cent of members of Dalit households had never attended school, and almost all of them belonged to the age-group of 60 years and above. Importantly, educational achievements among Dalit households involved in agricultural wage work were comparable with those of non-Dalit

TABLE 7 *Literacy rates, Malabar, Kerala and Morazha, caste-wise* in per cent

Item	Year	Literacy rate		
		All persons	Male	Female
Malabar, all castes, Census of India	1911	11.1	19.0	3.5
	1951	31.3	41.3	21.7
	1991	74.2	77.8	70.8
Kerala, Dalits, Census of India	1961	–	31.6	17.4
	1991	–	85.2	74.3
Morazha, all castes	2001	84.1	90.1	79.2
Morazha, Dalits	2001	84.3	90.4	78.3

Sources: Census of India, various years; Ramachandran (1996); survey data, 2001.

TABLE 8 *Levels of education among members of manual labour households involved in agricultural work, Morazha, 2001* in number and per cent

Educational level	All households		Dalits	
	Number of members	Share of members	Number of members	Share of members
Never attended school	81	7.8	16	7.6
Up to Class 4	182	17.5	41	19.5
Class 5 to Class 7	229	22.0	40	19.0
Class 8 to Class 10	398	38.2	75	35.7
Class 11 to Class 12	114	11.0	31	14.8
Above Class 12	37	3.6	7	3.3
All	1041	100.0	210	100.0

Source: Survey data, 2001.

households involved in agricultural wage work (see Table 8). Even in the category of members of households educated above Class 12, the achievements of Dalit households were comparable to those of non-Dalit households.

Public Social Security Schemes and Dalit Households

In a survey of social security schemes in India, Mahendra Dev (2002: 228) noted that Kerala 'has the most wide-ranging set of schemes for the benefit of unorganized sector' workers. According to estimates by Duvvury and George (1997), about 51 per cent of Kerala's income-poor population aged 60 and above were recipients of some social security assistance.

Duvvury and George (1997) note that the policies of social security for unorganized workers in Kerala were influenced by experiments undertaken by the State's working-class movement before 1957. Citing from Isaac (1984) and Isaac, Franke and Raghavan (1997), they point out that historically, 'the working class movement in Kerala had experimented with integrating the struggle against capitalists and the colonial state with their initiatives for welfare and mutual benefit activities' (Duvvury and George 1997: 14). These experiments included institutional arrangements such as labour associations and cooperatives. The lessons learnt from these arrangements influenced the demands of the labour movement for social security as well as the formulation of labour welfare policies by the state after 1956–57. The establishment of Welfare Funds was an important policy intervention in this period.

Welfare Funds were instituted by the state for the distribution of social security assistance among rural unorganized workers. The benefits from Welfare Funds to workers can be divided into three types (ibid.). First, some Welfare Funds provide provident fund benefits to members upon superannuation, a monthly pension and a gratuity payment. Secondly, some Funds provide social insurance benefits to members, such as payment for medical treatment or physical disability. Thirdly, some Funds provide welfare assistance to members, such as assistance for children's education, for the marriage expenses of daughters and for construction of houses.[12] About nineteen Welfare Funds for different sections of unorganized workers were established in Kerala after 1956–57 (Duvvury and George 1997). In 1995, Welfare Funds covered at least 50 per cent of all unorganized workers in the State, accounting for about 2.6 million workers. In general, the funds for these institutions were generated through contributions from workers, employers and the government over a period of time.

The allowances provided through the major schemes of which members of my surveyed households in Morazha were beneficiaries in 2001 were as follows.

- Agricultural worker pension of Rs 110 per month (Rs 1,320 per year)
- Allowance for physically handicapped persons of Rs 110 per month (Rs 1,320 per year)
- Pension for widows of Rs 100 per month (Rs 1,200 per year)
- Pension for elderly persons of Rs 100 per month (Rs 1,200 per year)
- Pension for traditional artists of Rs 400 per month (Rs 4,800 per year)
- Pension for construction workers of Rs 150 per month (Rs 1,800 per year).

In Morazha, the share of households that received social security benefits was highest for Dalits among all caste groups. About 28 per cent of all Dalit manual labour households involved in agricultural wage work received social security benefits in 2001, while for all manual labour households involved in agricultural wage work the share was 22 per cent. The average income from social security schemes was also the highest for Dalit households among all households – Rs 1,018 per year (Table 9). For Dalit households, the income from social security schemes constituted 6 per cent of the poverty line, while for all castes together, the share was 5.3 per cent.

[12] In this context, see also Kannan (2002).

TABLE 9 *Average income from direct social security schemes, caste-wise, manual labour households involved in agricultural work, Morazha, 2001*

Caste group	Share of households receiving benefit (per cent)	Average income from social security schemes (Rs per household per year)	Average income as share of poverty line (per cent)
Other Castes	25.0	787.1	4.2
Other Backward Classes	18.9	976.7	4.5
Scheduled Castes	28.2	1017.6	6.0
All	22.2	952.3	5.3

Note: I have considered only payments actually received from the government as on the date of survey.
Source: Survey data, 2001.

It is notable that in Morazha, social security benefits have not been captured by elites as in many other Indian States. The difference is primarily because of the shift in the balance of power in the countryside after land reforms.

The estimation of social security income as a share of total income, however, does not fully capture the benefits actually received. A scheme to pay retired agricultural workers a monthly pension is not a programme of poverty alleviation, but a protective social security cover aimed at reducing economic vulnerability and deprivation among the poor. In Morazha, for beneficiaries who were aged and economically dependent on their children due to poor health, the government pension was a matter of great joy and pride; it gave them the feeling that they were also earners, and raised their levels of economic security and self-esteem.

The Public Distribution System

The Public Distribution System (PDS) in Kerala has its origins in the struggle by the peasant movement in 1942 to establish Producers and Consumers Cooperatives (PCCs). The PCCs aimed to provide foodgrain during World War II, when food shortages were acute in the State. Until 1997, the PDS in Kerala was universal. However, under the neo-liberal regime at the Centre, universal PDS was scrapped in 1997 and a Targeted Public Distribution System (TPDS) was introduced. Under the TPDS, the population was classified into above poverty line (APL) and below poverty line (BPL) categories.[13] In 2001, subsidized food was to be made available to only BPL households, and APL households had to pay a price equivalent to the full economic cost of purchasing and handling the foodgrains.

In many Indian villages, Dalits and Adivasis have been systematically excluded from the TPDS as local political regimes have been unsympathetic to their needs. A widespread complaint from other parts of rural India has been

[13] For detailed information on the TPDS, see Swaminathan (2000). Throughout this article, the terms APL and BPL refer to households classified as above poverty line and below poverty line by the government.

that many of the very poor households are not classified as BPL (Swamina-than 2000; Swaminathan and Misra 2002; GoI 2002). NSS data have shown that levels of poverty are higher if we consider a poverty line based directly on calorie intake, rather than a poverty line based on a monetary equivalent adjusted for inflation. In other words, selection of BPL households based on the application of a poverty line not linked directly to calorie intake could lead to large-scale exclusion of nutritionally poor households. As a government committee appointed in 2002 concluded, 'the narrow targeting of the PDS based on absolute income poverty is likely to have excluded a large part of the nutritionally vulnerable population from the PDS' (GoI 2002).

In my survey of Morazha, I tried to match the income status of house-holds with their status regarding access to PDS – whether they were APL or BPL, as per their PDS card. My data show that unlike in other States, there was no systematic exclusion of Dalits from the PDS in Morazha (Table 10). On the other hand, a large number of Dalit households who were not below the poverty line as per their income status, held BPL status on their PDS cards. About 43 per cent of the Dalit households were not income-poor in my survey, yet they had BPL cards. Only 16 per cent of Dalit households in my survey were found to hold APL cards even when they were income-poor. These conclusions from Morazha were quite the opposite of findings from States like Maharashtra, reported by Swaminathan and Misra (2002). In a Maharashtra village, they found that 43 per cent of households were given APL cards when they were actually income-poor.

The low rates of exclusion of income-poor households and high rates of inclusion of non-income-poor households in Morazha were a result of the efforts of the State government and political parties of the Left to bring a larger proportion of households within the ambit of the PDS than that stipulated by the Central government. In 1997, the Central government wanted the State to restrict the supply of subsidized foodgrain to only the income-poor, or 26 per cent of the State's population. As such, the quantity of foodgrain that the Central government provided to the State at subsidized prices was calculated

TABLE 10 *Distribution of number of households by income poverty classification and type of ration card, manual labour households involved in agricultural work, Morazha, 2001*

Type of poverty by income	Type of poverty by colour of ration card	Number of households	
		All	Dalits
Above poverty line	Above poverty line	45	7
Above poverty line	Below poverty line	46	16
Below poverty line	Above poverty line	16	6
Below poverty line	Below poverty line	50	8
All households	All households	157	37

Source: Survey data, 2001.

TABLE 11 *Extent of per capita purchases of commodities from PDS, by caste, manual labour households involved in agricultural work classified as 'below poverty line', Morazha, 2001 in kg/litre per year*

Caste category	Kerosene	Rice	Sugar	Wheat
Other Castes	10.7	66.1	4.5	13.3
Other Backward Class	8.3	64.8	5.1	16.6
Dalit	8.1	65.0	5.2	15.3

Source: Survey data, 2001.

according to the requirements of only 26 per cent of the population. The Left-led government in Kerala argued that the head-count ratio of 26 per cent did not conform to the actual state of poverty in the State, and wanted the benefits of the PDS extended to 42 per cent of the population. Despite the Central government's disagreement, the State government extended the benefits of food subsidy to 42 per cent of Kerala's population. The relatively high coverage of income-poor households under PDS in Morazha was because of this decision of the State's Left-led government to extend food subsidies to an additional section of the population.

In terms of the actual purchase of food from the PDS as well, the difference between Dalit households and non-Dalit households was small in Morazha (see Table 11).

Access to Credit

Field data collected from Morazha in 2001 indicate a revolutionary change in the character of the credit market faced by Dalits since the 1940s. The data show a remarkable expansion in the provision of credit to the poor in the formal sector. Further, credit was provided at terms that were generally favourable to poor households.

In Morazha in 2001, 98 per cent of the principal of loans borrowed by Dalit manual labour households came from the formal sector (Table 12). In other words, landlords, traders and other moneylenders were largely elimi-nated as sources of credit in the village. Within the formal sector, cooperative credit societies accounted for 97 per cent of the credit advanced. About 95 per cent of all loans taken by Dalit households were from the cooperative sector.

One of the most significant outcomes of the ownership of homestead land by Dalit households after land reforms was the improvement in their creditworthiness. These households were able to approach banks and take loans by offering the title-deeds to their homestead plots as collateral. The data in Table 13 show that about 17 per cent of the loans taken by Dalit households offered an immovable property (land) as collateral.

The spread of the cooperative movement in Morazha had a direct link with the political movement for land reform in Malabar led by Left peasant unions. During World War II, at a time when Malabar was experiencing an

TABLE 12 *Distribution of households by different sources of borrowing, manual labour households involved in agricultural work, Morazha, 2001* in per cent

Source of borrowing	Share of number of loans		Share of amount of loan	
	All households	Dalit households	All households	Dalit households
Cooperatives	97.4	95.7	97.3	95.4
Government	1.1	2.1	0.9	3.0
Formal sector	98.4	97.8	98.2	98.4
Moneylenders	0.5	0.0	0.2	0.0
Friends and relatives	0.5	0.0	1.2	0.0
Chit finance	0.5	2.1	0.3	1.6
Informal sector	1.6	0.0	1.8	0.0
Total	100.0	100.0	100.0	100.0

Source: Survey data, 2001.

TABLE 13 *Distribution of borrowings by type of collateral offered, manual labour households involved in agricultural work, by caste, Morazha, 2001* in per cent

Type of collateral	Share of number of loans		Share of amount of loan	
	All households	Dalit households	All households	Dalit households
Third person security	53.4	38.3	43.8	24.7
Immovable property	11.6	17.0	40.8	55.6
Gold	33.3	42.6	13.3	18.1
Others	1.1	0.0	0.8	0.0
No collateral	0.5	2.1	1.2	1.6
All	100.0	100.0	100.0	100.0

Source: Survey data, 2001.

acute food shortage, the peasant movement launched an agitation to prevent the hoarding of foodgrains by landlords and traders. This agitation aimed at forcibly collecting foodgrains from the granaries of landlords and traders, and selling them to the general public through Producers and Consumers Cooperatives or PCCs (Ramachandran 1996). After the War, most of the PCCs were converted into credit societies, called Aikya Nanaya Sanghams (Cooperative Money Societies), that began to advance credit to cultivators at low rates of interest. These Aikya Nanaya Sanghams were later converted into service cooperative banks, the form in which they continue to operate today. Public action thus created a banking institution that helped to eliminate exploitative features of the credit market, and to expand the access of manual labour households to affordable credit.

Concluding Notes

A study of the tortuous and deep road to abolition of their bonded labour, of the winds of modern change which swept over Kerala, the upsurge for

human rights and the success in securing a new deal for the Pulayas, has a
national importance in the perspective of the civil revolution in our country.
(Justice V.R. Krishna Iyer 1981: vii)

In this essay, I have tried to describe and analyse how public action
helped to advance the socio-economic security of Dalit agricultural workers in the Malabar region of Kerala. Specifically, the essay examines social
change in the village of Morazha in Kannur district, with particular reference to changes in land ownership, levels of education, access to credit, and
access to social security schemes and food distribution systems among Dalit
households participating in agricultural wage work. Thomas Shea studied
Morazha village in 1955, before the implementation of land reform in Malabar. His study characterized the conditions of life of agricultural workers in
the village as 'wretched in the extreme'; the worst forms of human insecurity
marked their lives.

In 2001, the conditions of life of Dalits in Morazha were substantially
different from the conditions that Shea wrote about in 1955. Public action was
the driving force behind this transformation, and the break-up of traditional
agrarian power through land reform was the most critical step.

Struggles to transform the conditions of Dalit agricultural workers in
Malabar took place over three distinct phases. In the first phase (from about
1917 to 1934, the year of the Guruvayur struggle), agitations against untouchability were taken up as part of the national movement by members of the
Indian National Congress as well as religious reform movements. The second
phase (roughly 1934 to 1957, the year that the first government of Kerala, led
by the Communist Party, was formed) was a period of elevation of political
consciousness among Dalits; this took place through the integration of Dalit
struggles against untouchability with radical struggles of peasant movements
for land reform. The third phase (1957 and after) witnessed an important
shift in the balance of state power in Kerala. While struggles around land and
different forms of discrimination continued in the third phase, this phase was
distinguished by the implementation of land reforms and the institution of a
number of social security schemes.

Land reforms changed the conditions in which labour power was sold;
it freed the workers to sell their labour power to employers of their choice. *It
hit at the very basis of caste-based atrocities by undermining not only feudal
landlordism, but also the traditional economic base of upper-caste domination.* Land reforms also provided worker households with homestead land
free of cost. The income from homesteads supplemented household incomes
and helped raise food intake and nutrition. Legislation by the State government provided for an innovative pension scheme for unorganized workers.
The public distribution system instituted by the State government served
effectively to improve levels of nutrition. The political movement for land

reform played an important role in eliminating older forms of usury-based exploitation, and in establishing cooperative credit institutions.

My estimates of net income from homesteads, the first for Kerala to my knowledge, show that homestead plots brought in more than marginal monetary benefits to Dalit households. Michael Tharakan has noted that there are 'many scholars who failed to understand the significance of the allotment of homestead land to the poor' in Kerala as part of land reform (Tharakan 2002: 358). He also noted the instrumental benefit of homestead land ownership for Dalit households:

> This provision guaranteed a residential plot to landless agricultural labour households who mainly belonged to the scheduled castes [Dalits] and had been systematically denied access to land by the rules of the caste system. With this gain, however, even landless agricultural labourers were able to bargain better for wages, for a better public distribution system, and better school education and health care. As a result of this provision, the lowest in the caste and agrarian hierarchies gained access to rudimentary social progress, just as the middle-level communities had through the social and ritual reform movements. (Ibid.)[14]

The long struggle for land reform in Kerala was an integrated one. It was a struggle in which there was a convergence of resistance against different forms of class-, caste- and gender-based discrimination. This is the main lesson from Kerala's history for the rest of India.

References

Andhur Panchayat (1997), *Panchayat Development Report*, Andhur.

Appu, P.S. (1996), *Land Reforms in India: A Survey of Policy, Legislation and Implementation*, Vikas Publications, New Delhi.

Balaram, N.E. (1973), *Keralathile Communist Prasthanam: Aadyanalukaliloode* (The Communist Movement in Kerala: The Initial Days), Prabhatham Printing and Publishing Company Ltd., Trivandrum.

Buchanan, Francis A. (1870), *A Journey from Madras through the Countries of Mysore, Canara and Malabar*, vols 1, 2 and 3, Higginbothams and Company, Madras.

Centre for Development Studies (CDS) (1975), *Poverty, Unemployment and Development Policy: A Case Study of Selected Issues with Reference to Kerala*, Orient Longman, Chennai.

Centre for Human Rights and Global Justice (2007), *Hidden Apartheid*, NYU School of Law and Human Rights Watch, New Delhi.

---

[14] A comparison of the results from Kerala with observations in a recent national-level report on the status of Indian Dalits is revealing. In the report, titled *Hidden Apartheid*, the continued discrimination against Dalits in India on social and economic grounds is vividly highlighted. The report says: 'The right to own property is systematically denied to Dalits. Landlessness – encompassing a lack of access to land, inability to own land, and forced evictions – constitutes a crucial element in the subordination of Dalits. When Dalits do acquire land, elements of the right to own property – including the right to access and enjoy it – are routinely infringed. Land reform legislation is neither implemented nor properly enforced. Dalits' efforts to secure land have been met with state violence or retaliation by private actors in the form of violence or economic sanctions' (Centre for Human Rights and Global Justice 2007).

Dev, S. Mahendra (2002), 'Growth-mediated and Support-led Social Security in the Unorganized Sector in India', *Indian Journal of Labour Economics*, vol. 45, no. 2, pp. 219–42.

Duvvury, Nata and George, Sabu M. (1997), 'Social Security in the Informal Sector: A Study of Labour Welfare Funds in Kerala', UNDP Project Report, Centre for Development of Imaging Technology, Thiruvananthapuram.

Edona, E.J. (1940), *The Economic Condition of the Protestant Christians in Malabar with Special Reference to the Basel Mission Church*, Empire Press, Calicut.

Ganesh, K.N. (1990), *Keralathinte Innalekal* (The Yesterdays of Kerala), Department of Cultural Relations, Government of Kerala, Thiruvananthapuram.

George, Jose (1992), *Unionization and Politicization of Peasants and Agricultural Labourers in India (With Special Reference to Kerala)*, Commonwealth Publishers, New Delhi.

Government of India (GoI) (2002), 'High Level Committee on Long-Term Grain Policy', Ministry of Food and Public Distribution, Government of India, New Delhi.

Herring, Ronald J. (1980), 'Abolition of Landlordism in Kerala: A Redistribution of Privilege', *Economic and Political Weekly*, vol. 15, no. 26, pp. A59–69.

Herring, Ronald J. (1983), *Land to the Tiller: The Political Economy of Agrarian Reform in South Asia*, Oxford University Press, Calcutta.

Hjejle, Benedict (1967), *Slavery and Agricultural Bondage in South India in the Nineteenth Century*, Joint Reprint Series no. 1, The Scandinavian Institute of Asian Studies, Copenhagen.

Isaac, T.M. Thomas (1984), 'Class Struggle and Industrial Structure: A Study of Coir Weaving Industry in Kerala, 1859–1980', unpublished Ph.D. thesis submitted to Centre for Development Studies, Thiruvananthapuram.

Isaac, T.M. Thomas, Franke, Richard W. and Raghavan, Pyarelal (1998), *Democracy at Work in an Indian Industrial Cooperative: The Story of Kerala Dinesh Beedi*, Cornell University Press, Ithaca, New York.

Isaac, T.M. Thomas and Ramakumar, R. (forthcoming), 'Kerala: An Agenda for Sustainable, Equitable and Rapid Growth', in T.M. Thomas Isaac, ed., *Kerala: Towards a Development Agenda*, Sage Publications, New Delhi.

Kumar, Dharma (1965), *Land and Caste in South India: Agricultural Labour in the Madras Presidency during the Nineteenth Century*, Cambridge University Press, Cambridge.

Iyer, V.R. Krishna (1981), 'Foreword', in K. Saradamoni, *Divided Poor: Study of a Kerala Village*, Ajanta Publications, New Delhi.

Kannan, K.P. (1988), *Of Rural Proletarian Struggles: Mobilization and Organization of Rural Workers in Southwest India*, Oxford University Press, New Delhi.

Mayer, Adrian (1952), *Land and Society in Malabar*, Oxford University Press, London.

Mencher, Joan (1980), 'The Lessons and Non-Lessons of Kerala: Agricultural Labourers and Poverty', *Economic and Political Weekly*, vol. 15, nos 41–43, pp. 1781–802.

Menon, Dilip M. (1994), *Caste, Nationalism and Communism in South India: Malabar, 1900–1948*, Cambridge University Press, Cambridge.

Nair, Adoor K.K. Ramachandran (1986), *Slavery in Kerala*, Mittal Publications, Delhi.

Namboodiripad, E.M.S. (1940), 'Dissenting Note', in *Report of the Malabar Tenancy Committee – 1940*, Government of Madras, Madras; reprinted in *Selected Writings*, vol. 2, National Book Agency, Calcuttta.

Namboodiripad, E.M.S. (1948), *Agrarian Question in Kerala*, People's Publishing House, Delhi.

Namboodiripad, E.M.S. (1977), 'Castes, Classes and Parties in Modern Political Development', *Social Scientist*, vol. 6, no. 4, pp. 3–25.

Namboodiripad, E.M.S. (1981), 'Once Again on Castes and Classes', *Social Scientist*, vol. 9, no. 12, pp. 12–25.

Namboodiripad, E.M.S. (1994a), 'Inaugural Address', International Congress on Kerala Studies, Thiruvananthapuram; reprinted in *International Congress on Kerala Studies, Abstracts*, vol. 1, A.K.G. Centre for Research and Studies, Thiruvananthapuram.

Namboodiripad, E.M.S. (1994b), *The Communist Party in Kerala: Six Decades of Struggle and Advance*, National Book Centre, New Delhi.

Nayanar, E.K. (1982), *My Struggles: An Autobiography*, Vikas Publishers, New Delhi.

Panikkar, K.N. (1978), 'Agrarian Legislation and Social Classes: A Case Study of Malabar', *Economic and Political Weekly*, vol. 13, no. 21, p. 880.

Radhakrishnan, P. (1989), *Peasant Struggles, Land Reforms, and Social Change: Malabar 1836–1982*, Sage Publications, New Delhi.

Ramachandran, V.K. (1996), 'On Kerala's Development Achievements', in Jean Dreze and Amartya Sen, eds, *Indian Development: Selected Regional Perspectives*, Oxford University Press, New Delhi, pp. 205–356.

Ramachandran, V.K. (2000), 'Replicating Human Development Achievements', in Govindan Parayil, ed., *Kerala's Development Achievements: Issues of Sustainability and Replicability*, Zed Press, London.

Ramachandran, V.K. and Ramakumar, R. (2001), 'Agrarian Reforms and Rural Development Policies in India: A Note', in *Agrarian Reform and Rural Development*, Department of Agrarian Reform, Government of the Philippines and the Philippines Development Academy, Manila.

Saradamoni, K. (1981), *Divided Poor: Study of a Kerala Village*, Ajanta Publications, New Delhi.

Shea, Thomas W. (1955a), 'Economic Study of a Malabar Village', *Economic Weekly*, vol. 7, no. 34, pp. 997–1003.

Shea, Thomas W. (1955b), 'Economic Study of a Malabar Village', *Economic Weekly*, vol. 7, no. 35, pp. 1030–33.

Shea, Thomas W. (1956), 'Implementing Land Reform in India', *Far Eastern Survey*, vol. 25, no. 1, pp. 1–8.

Shea, Thomas W. (1964), 'Barriers to Economic Development in Traditional Societies: Malabar – A Case Study,' *Journal of Economic History*, vol. 19, pp. 504–22.

Sivaswamy, K.G. (1946), *Food Control and Nutrition Surveys, Malabar and South Kanara*, Servindia Kerala Relief Centre, Madras.

State Planning Board (SPB) (1997), *Report of the Task Force on Agrarian Institutions*, Government of Kerala, Thiruvananthapuram.

Swaminathan, Madhura (2000), *Weakening Welfare: The Public Distribution of Food in India*, LeftWord Books, New Delhi.

Swaminathan, Madhura and Misra, Neeta (2002), 'Errors in Targeting: Public Food Distribution in a Maharashtra Village, 1995–2000', *Economic and Political Weekly*, 30 June, pp. 2447–50.

Tharakan, P.K. Michael (1982), 'The Kerala Land Reforms (Amendment) Bill, 1979: A Note', Thiruvananthapuram.

Tharakan, P.K. Michael (2002), 'Land Relations in Kerala', in V.K. Ramachandran and Madhura Swaminathan, eds (2003), *Agrarian Studies: Essays on Agrarian Relations in Less-Developed Countries*, Tulika Books, New Delhi.

Vishnubharateeyan (1980), *Adimakalengane Udamakalaayi* (How Did the Slaves Become Owners), Chinta Publishers, Trivandrum.

Glossary

Aikya Nanaya Sangham	Cooperative Money Society
amsam	a unit of revenue administration in Malabar consisting of two or three *desams*.
cent	a measure of area of land; 100 cents = 1 acre and 247 cents = 1 hectare
Dalit	caste group classified as Scheduled Caste in the Indian Constitution
desam	a sub-division of a revenue village; was the territorial unit of military organization in Malabar
devaswam	temple administration; property belonging to a temple
janmam land	land held traditionally as birthright
janmi	a person in whom the proprietary right over *janmam* land is vested, and includes in the case of a *devaswam* owning *janmam* land, the managing trustee or trustees of the *devaswam*

jati	caste
moplah/mappila	Muslims of Malabar
mundu	a loose garment worn around the waist; *dhoti*
naduvazhi	a chieftain, usually belonging to the Nair caste
Nair	a caste group of Kerala who were historically soldiers and administrators; technically Sudras and lowermost in the caste Hindu scale, but given the status of Kshatriyas by Brahmans; were chieftains and members of the landed community; practised matriliny
Namboodiri	Malayalam-speaking Brahman caste of Kerala
Pulaya/Paraya/Cherumar	Dalit caste groups who were the oppressed castes or the traditional slave castes
tehsildar	a revenue administrative officer in charge of collecting taxes from a *tehsil*
thampuran (thambran)	lord, usually belonging to an upper caste
Tiyya/Ezhava	caste group 'below' the Nairs but 'above' the traditional slave castes in terms of ritual status
yajaman	lord, usually belonging to an upper caste

The Peasant Movement and Dalit Rights in East Thanjavur, Tamil Nadu

G. Ramakrishnan

This essay presents a comparison of the conditions in which the Dalit people of East Thanjavur lived in the 1940s and the living conditions of the Dalits after agrarian struggles were launched, up to 1991. Some of the challenges that remain to be overcome are also outlined here.

Although the Dalit people of East Thanjavur in Tamil Nadu remain income-poor, and victims of different forms of social and economic deprivation, it is nevertheless important to recognize that as a result of decades of struggle, there have been important changes in their economic and social status – especially in the forms of caste oppression against them and in the criminal practice of untouchability. The struggles of the Dalits of East Thanjavur from the 1940s were led by the Kisan Sabha, the Agricultural Workers' Association and the Communist Party of India – and, after 1964, by the Communist Party of India (Marxist). The struggles of the rural masses since 1940 in East Thanjavur are unparalleled in the history of the peasant movement in Tamil Nadu.

At the outset, I shall clarify two methodological features of this essay. First, the area that I call 'East Thanjavur' refers to the eastern part of the old district of Thanjavur (or Tanjore), and, more specifically, to the present-day districts of Thiruvarur and Nagapattinam in Tamil Nadu. Secondly, this essay is not an attempt at a scholarly history of the movement of agricultural workers, in particular Dalit agricultural workers, of the East Thanjavur region, or of agrarian relations in the area. There is much valuable scholarly work on the area that I have not reviewed or summarized.[1] This essay's specific feature is that it draws extensively on two published Tamil works, by B. Srinivasa Rao (1947) and G. Veerayyan (1998), which are invaluable sources of information and analysis, and have not hitherto been available to a non-Tamil-reading public. I have supplemented these secondary sources with primary material from interviews that I have conducted with agricultural workers and tenant cultivators in the region.

[1] See, for example, Menon, Saraswathi (1979a, 1979b, 1983); Gough (1981, 1989); Bouton (1985); Sivaraman (1970); Menon, Parvathi (1986); Surjit (2008); and the extensive Thanjavur-centred bibliographies in each of them.

Agrarian Relations in East Thanjavur before Independence
Concentration of Land

Historically, Thanjavur district in Tamil Nadu, called the 'granary' (*nel-kalanjiyam*) of Tamil Nadu, has been an area of surplus rice production. Its fertile lands are irrigated by waters from the Cauvery river, released from the Grand Anicut, an advanced engineering feat of the Chola period. Agriculture was the main occupation of the people and two crops were raised every year.

In the early twentieth century, land relations in Thanjavur district, especially in its eastern part, were characterized by a huge concentration of land in the hands of a few landlords, zamindars and temple authorities. *Ryotwari* landlords – or *mirasdars*, as they were then called – owned thousands of acres of land. The holdings of an individual landlord could span many villages. Srinivasa Rao (1947: 6) wrote:

> The whole of Thanjavur district was under the domination of three categories of land holdings. In the northern part of the district the land was owned by Dharmapuram Adheenam, Thiruvaaduthurai Adheenam, Thirupanandal Matam, Sankara Matam and Akobila Matam. These *matam*s [*matham*s] were controlled and managed by the mutt chiefs. In the central part of the district, the land was owned by landlords like Vadapathimangalam, Nedumbalam, Kottur, Vallivalam, Kunniyur Iyer, Poondi Vandayar, Ukkadai Thevar and Kapisthalam Moopanar. In the southern part of the district, land was owned by zamindars, as in the Madhukkoor Zamin, Pappanadu Zamin, Sikkavalem Zamin and some other zamins. These three groups owned almost all the agricultural land in the undivided Thanjavur district.

Srinivasa Rao goes on to give an account of the landholdings of the major landlords of Thanjavur district:

1. Vadapathimangalam Thiagaraja Mudaliar family: 15,000 acres
2. Kunniyur Sambasiva Iyer: 600 acres agricultural land and 500 acres of coconut grove
3. Rao Bahadur Samiyappa: 2,500 acres
4. K.G. Estate: 400 acres
5. K.M.K. Estate: 300 acres
6. Mannargudi Gopalakrishna Iyer: 2,000 acres

The nature of landholdings in East Thanjavur differed from the nature of landholdings in the rest of Tamil Nadu. In other districts, Dalit labourers were allotted a separate area of habitation, often called the 'colony'. In East Thanjavur, on the other hand, Dalits were not permitted to own even a small piece of land on which to raise a hut, especially since the roads and all other common spaces in the village were privately controlled, either by landlords or temple authorities. There is an old saying in the region that other than landlords and caste Hindus among tenants, no person could own even 'a needlepoint of space'.

A substantial section of the East Thanjavur population worked as tenants of the landlords and the temples, paying different forms of rent. The majority of agricultural workers – mainly Dalits, but also caste Hindus – worked on land owned by landlords. The Dalit workers were both economically and socially dependent on the landlords on whose farms and land they worked. Those among them who were not wage workers but long-term bonded labourers were called *pannaiyal*s, or farm servants.

Thanjavur was annexed by the British in 1799. The colonial administration seized the opportunity to generate large revenues from the rural areas of the district. They imposed very high fixed rents, collecting the rents in cash from landlords and cultivators irrespective of the quality or quantity of the harvest. High rates of rent, forcible collection of revenue and cheap procurement prices constituted the main features of the British land revenue policy. The colonial administration also protected the backward aspects of agrarian relations in order to extract higher revenues from the landlords. The landlords, in turn, squeezed the agricultural labourers and tenant cultivators in order to generate more surplus. This led to a sharpening of contradictions, and the agricultural workers had to fight for their rights against both the landlords and the colonial rulers.

Conditions of Tenant Cultivators and Agricultural Labourers

The living conditions of the tenant cultivators and farm servants in the 1940s, more so of the Dalit farm servants, were miserable, as opposed to that of the landlords, who lived in luxury and in palatial homes. Landlords exercised control over not just the land, but also the water bodies, even appropriating the fish from the village tanks. Many of them were moneylenders, charging high rates of interest. They controlled the village and district-level decision-making committees, and cooperative credit societies, and the colonial administration did everything possible to further their interests.

The worst forms of caste oppression in Tamil Nadu existed in the district of Thanjavur. In the 1940s, a majority of the Dalits there were farm servants, while most of the cultivating tenants and a few landless labourers were caste Hindus. All the landlords, *matham* chiefs and zamindars were caste Hindus, with most of them belonging to the ritually 'upper' castes. Though the landlords had different political affiliations – some directly supported British rule, others were part of the national movement led by the Congress, and yet others were supporters of the Dravidian movement – they were united in suppressing the movements of farm servants and tenant cultivators.

Forms of Landlord Oppression: Two Interviews
V. Ramu, Tenant Cultivator, Thenparai Village, East Thanjavur
In a detailed interview I conducted with V. Ramu (who was about 80 years old at the time of the interview, in 2006), a Dalit and a former tenant cultivator of Thenparai village, he described to me the conditions that

prevailed in his village in the 1940s. Thenparai is a place of great significance in the history of the peasant movement in Tamil Nadu for the movement of the Kisan Sabha began here.

Ramu told me that there were about 600 households in Thenparai, of which about 50 were Dalit. The rest belonged to eighteen Other Castes, with the Muthuraja caste (now classified as a 'Most Backward Caste') claiming the largest numbers. Almost all the households in the village worked on land as tenants or farm servants. Most of the Dalits and many of the Muthuraja caste were farm servants.

All the land in Thenparai village, approximately 362 *veli* (1 *veli* = 6.5 acres), was initially owned by the Rettai Rayar landlord family, who leased out land to tenants for cultivation. Later, the ownership of all the land was transferred to a Hyderabad-based mutt called Uthirapathi Matham, but the collection of rent and other forms of traditional payments continued as before. 'The tenant paid rent either as *vaaram* (sharecropping) or *kuthagai* (fixed rent). *Vaaram* was more common at the beginning of the nineteenth century. Under this system, the tenant paid a fixed share of the yield to the landlord. The tenant's share varied markedly in different parts of the district' (Menon 1979a: 26–27).

While tenants had to pay the equivalent of three-fourths to four-fifths of the crop yield to the landlords in the form either of fixed rent (*kuthagai*) or share rent (*vaaram*), they could not be certain of getting the same land for cultivation the next year. In addition to the share of the yield they received as rent, the landlords managed to extract still more surplus in one form of payment or the other, and sometimes appropriated almost all of the output.

Tenants had to pay 8 *kalam* and 4 *marakkal* of paddy per *maa* (0.33 acre) as principal rent to landlords.[2] The yield per *maa* in the 1940s was 10 *kalam* of paddy, which meant that there was little left for the tenants to take home. In addition, there were ten dues (*pathu pathu*) they had to pay:

1. *Kidakattuthal/Mattukidai Kattuthal*. In those days the manure used in the fields was dung, the droppings of cattle tethered on the land for the purpose. Out of every ten times that the cattle were brought to the field the tenant had to pay for five, at the rate of one *kalam* of paddy each time.

2. *Vandisatham*. The manure required for 1 acre of land was ten cartloads. The tenant had to pay 50 per cent of the rent for these carts.

3. *Neeranikkam* (irrigation work). The tenant had to pay 6 *marakkal* of paddy per year to the water supplier or irrigation worker.

4. *Koilpathu*. The tenant had to pay 6 *marakkal* of paddy per year towards the expenses of holding the annual village temple festival.

5. *Vakkalada*. For every bundle of hay he took home, the tenant had to pay one measure (a quarter of a *marakkal*) of paddy. One *maa* of land yielded ten bundles of hay.

---

[2] Both *kalam* and *marakkal* are local volumetric measures.

6. *Verapathu* (seed rent). Six *marakkal* of paddy seeds were required to cultivate one *maa*. The landlords provided the seeds, and the tenants had to pay.

7. *Kaatchappadu.* For every 12 *marakkal* of paddy, the tenant had to pay one measure as *kaatchappadu* or compensation for loss of weight in the paddy.

8. *Marakkalthundu.* For every bag of paddy taken by the landlord as his share, the tenant had to pay 2 *marakkal* as *marakkalthundu.* This was paid on the assumption that for every bag of paddy there would be a shortfall of 2 *marakkal.*

9. *Koothadipathu.* During the festival in the village temple, each tenant family had to pay 3 *marakkal* of paddy to the folk art troupe engaged for entertainment.

10. *Tharisukooli.* If the landlord paid cash wages for transplantation, the sum had to be paid back in the form of paddy, at the rate of 6 *marakkal* per *maa.*

Punishment for non-payment of rent, in whole or in part, took several forms. If there was a shortfall in the rent paid by the tenant, the landlord made a note of it as *vasakkattu* (rent due). If the owed amount was not paid by the next year, the landlord would seize the tenant's cattle. If the tenant did not own any cattle, he would be tied up and beaten severely, and the pulley (*vittam*) would be confiscated from the drinking-water well of his household.

Tenant cultivators were exploited in various other forms as well. They were forced to first work on lands cultivated directly by the landlord before they could work on land they leased in. For working in the landlord's fields, they were paid wages of 3 to 4 *marakkal* of paddy. If a tenant refused to work on the landlord's fields, his house would be locked up, and he and his family prevented from entering their home. The locks could be opened only on the intervention of the headman or *nattamai* (there was one *nattamai* for every twelve households in the village). Landlords have been known even to poison the water in wells that belonged to tenants if they refused to work on *mirasdar*-owned lands.

Tenants also had to volunteer as free labour at the 17 kilometre-long canal near Thenparai village. If they refused to do this work, they were evicted from their leased land. While tenant cultivators might receive a share of the fish caught from the village tank, *pannaiyals* were not entitled to any share.

T. Ponnan, Former Farm Servant, Umamaheswarapuram Village, East Thanjavur

Another interview I conducted was with T. Ponnan, a former farm servant of Umamaheswarapuram revenue village, Thiruvarur taluk. All the land in the village was owned by the landlord Vadapathimangalam Thiyagaraja Mudaliyar. He owned land in seventeen other villages as well. While he lived in Vadapathi village, his land in the other villages was looked after by his agents, and by village *munsiffs* and *karnams*. Other functionaries under the landlord's command who administered the farms were *neeranikam* (irrigation worker), *vettumai*, *visarippu*, *thalaiyari* and *maniyam*. These served as the landlord's henchmen and implemented his orders.

Although the village was a multi-caste village, only Dalits worked as farm servants there. Landless agricultural workers of Other Castes worked in the fields, drove carts and tended cattle for the landlord. Both the Dalit farm servants and the Other Caste Hindu agricultural workers were allotted small pieces of land by the landlords on which to raise huts.

The farm servants in the village, as in the entire district, worked under extremely oppressive conditions. The landlord's agent would wake them up at 4 in the morning; the workers went to the fields and returned from work only after sunset. They were paid a pittance, three-fourths of a *marakkal* of paddy, for a whole day's work. They were given two meals during the day at the work-site: cold rice (*palaiya sadam*) left over from the previous day in the morning, and hot rice gruel at noon – both served in mud pots. Their wages were paid once a week ($5^1/_4$ *marakkal*). If a farm servant did not turn up for work he was whipped and made to drink liquid cowdung, which meant that he was forced to work even in ill health. On rare occasions, such as a marriage in the family, farm servants would be given Rs 30 and 5 *kalams* of paddy by the landlord.

There were times when farm servants sought to escape these oppressive conditions by fleeing to Singapore, Burma and Malaya, travelling by ship from the sea-port of Nagapattinam. However, there would be agents of the landlord waiting at Nagapattinam, who forcibly brought back those they recognized to the village.

The families of farm servants – parents, wives and children – also had to work for the landlord. While the men worked in the fields, their wives were employed in tending cattle, and at transplantation and weeding. Women workers' wages were two measures of paddy a day. When a child was born to a farm servant, the village *munsiff* and, more important, the landlord had to be informed immediately. If he failed to do so, he was punished. Children too were not spared from work. Boys aged 6 had to work as cowherds; at the age of 10 they had to clear cowdung from the cattle-sheds; at the age of 15 they worked as cart drivers; and by the age of 18 they became bonded labourers like their fathers. Girls were put to work to gather fodder for the cattle.

The hut of a farm servant's family typically measured 12 x 18 feet with a 3-foot-high mud wall. There were no locks and keys to these huts; in any case their occupants possessed nothing of value to protect. Even the vegetables the farm servants raised belonged to the landlord. Only pots and pans made of mud were permitted in the hut for use as cooking and eating utensils. Every aspect of family life including childbirth was confined to this small space.

A farm servant had to seek permission from the landlord when his son or daughter was to marry, often having to plead his case on the grounds that the marriage would bring another hand to work at the farm. To conduct a marriage ceremony, the farm servant was dependent on the landlord for paddy, money and the *thali* (*mangalsutra*) for the bride. The newly-wed couple had to seek the blessings of the master soon after the marriage.

The farm servant was expected to pay obeisance to the landlord as if he were god. Whenever he appeared before the landlord he had to kneel down with folded hands. The customary piece of cloth draped on his shoulder would have to be removed and tied at the waist as a sign of 'respect'. Tending the landlord's cattle was his responsibility, and it was often said that the cattle led better lives than the farm servant.

Dalit farm servants were subjected to far greater indignities. They were not permitted to enter the street on which caste Hindus lived. If they had something to say to the landlord, they had to go round to the back of his house and speak from a distance. They could wear only dirty clothes in the landlord's presence; if seen in clean clothes, the landlord's henchmen would tear the clothes off their bodies. A strip of loin-cloth made of cotton was the only clothing they were allowed to wear. The landlord invariably addressed the farm servants in foul language and abused them, irrespective of their seniority or age.

Dalits lacked graveyards in which to bury the dead. Even where a graveyard was available, access to it through the fields of the master was prohibited. Burials thus had often to wait for permission from the landlord. Dalit farm servants could not enter temples, were not permitted footwear, and could not touch even the clothes of caste Hindus. During feasts or on special occasions, Dalits were given food in the metal *marakkal* (volumetric measure); they were forbidden from eating food served on banana leaves as was customary. Separate glasses were set aside for them to drink from in toddy-shops and tea-shops. Dalits were not permitted to draw drinking water from common wells, or to ask for water even in rest houses run by charity organizations.

There was an undeclared law that Dalit farm servants' children could not go to school since they were 'born to serve the landlord'. The biographer of P.S. Dhanushkodi (who later became President of the Tamil Nadu Agricultural Workers' Union and a Member of the Legislative Assembly) writes that when Dhanushkodi was sent to a Burma-returned Dalit youth to learn the Tamil alphabet, his farm servant father was summoned by the landlord, tied to a tree and whipped. The outraged landlord asked his farm servant who would look after the cattle if his son went to school (N. Ramakrishnan 1995). It took years of bitter struggle before Dalits in rural Thanjavur gained the right to attend school. 'Historically, Dalits in Palakurichi [a village in East Thanjavur] have been discriminated in terms of access to educational facilities. . . . Paraya and Palla children were not admitted to schools till 1937' (Surjit 2008).

Struggles against Caste and Class Oppression: The Beginnings

In East Thanjavur all sections of the peasantry – farm servants, tenant cultivators, small and middle peasants, and even rich peasants – were exploited and oppressed by the landlords and the colonial administration, to different degrees.

> The root causes of the misery of the peasantry, which involved a complex jungle of tenancy rules, land rights, forms of work of labour, rack rents and indebtedness, was sustained by the colonial exploitation of India. In this vital aspect, the peasant movement was an integral part of the freedom movement in India. (Menon 1979b: 53)

In the early years of the twentieth century, they began to fight against the worsening living conditions and oppression through spontaneous acts of protest.

> An interesting example of such struggle surfaced in the estate of the Brahmin landlord, Ganapathy Subramania Iyer of Kaliyakudi village in Nannilam Taluk, who owned 100 *veli* (1 *veli* = 6.61 acres) of land. He had *pannaiyals* working for him and paid them lower than customary wages. In March 1938, in a militant protest against inhuman treatment, they refused to work and petitioned the Government. The *mirasdar* was forced to raise their wages, but, not unexpectedly, still kept the wages below the demanded level. In retaliation, the landlord organized a group of rowdies from nearby villages and in league with other influential landlords in the neighbourhood, attacked the men and molested the women labourers who had defied the traditional hierarchy on 28th April 1938. (Ibid.: 53–54)

Efforts to channelize and organize these protests of the farm servants and tenant cultivators began in the late 1930s, especially after a unit of the Kisan Sabha, the first in Tamil Nadu, was set up in Thenparai. Although the All India Kisan Sabha (AIKS) was established at the national level in 1936, it took a further five to eight years for it to take root in Tamil Nadu.

In 1938–39, Manalur Maniammai, a Brahmin widow, in defiance of orthodoxy, dedicated herself to organizing Dalits in Thanjavur. She learnt martial arts in order to face attacks by toughs employed by the landlords. She held a meeting of Dalit farm servants in her village and exhorted them to revolt against the landlords and against the British colonial power, and to support the slogan of *swaraj* or self-rule. She urged them to join the Kisan committees to fight for their rights. Manalur Maniammai later became a member of the Communist Party of India (CPI) and the AIKS, and went on to become one of its leaders. She is widely believed to have been murdered while at the house of a landlord, where she had gone for negotiations on behalf of the peasants. The landlord claimed that she had been gored to death by a stag.

Struggle of Tenant Cultivators in Thenparai

The struggle of tenant cultivators began in Thenparai village, where all the lands previously owned by the Rettai Rayar family were sold to the Uthirapathi Matham in 1939. The tyrannical modes of exploitation practised by the Retti Rayars were continued by the Matham. It asked the tenants to execute bonds (*sasanam*) and to cut tattoos on their hands. When the tenants started putting up a resistance to these and other forms of oppression, the Matham brought in *goonda*s from other villages to assault them.

At the first all-India conference of the AIKS, held in Lucknow on 11 April 1936, a decision had been taken to mobilize peasants and agricultural labourers all over the country. Upon hearing of the conflict between the landlord and tenant cultivators in Thenparai, a meeting held in Madras of the State Committee of the CPI resolved to send B. Srinivasa Rao, from the Kisan Sabha, to Thanjavur. (At that time Srinivasa Rao, born in the South Canara district of the then Madras Presidency, could speak, but not read or write Tamil.) He was accompanied by Amirthalingam, Venkatesa Solagar and Ramanujam, local peasant leaders from Thanjavur, and Ramachandra Nedungadi from the Kisan Sabha's all-India centre. In 1943, Srinivasa Rao formed the first unit of the Kisan Sabha in Tamil Nadu, in Thenparai village of East Thanjavur. Thus began the organized movement of peasants and agricultural labourers in the district, a movement of which agricultural workers were the backbone.

On his way to Thenparai, Srinivasa Rao was given a rousing reception at Kalappal, a village in Mannargudi taluk, Thiruvarur district. Addressing the farm servants of the village, he said:

> What is the difference between you and the landlords? Are you not also human beings, born of your mother's wombs and with two arms and legs?
>
> If you are hit, hit back. It is illegal to whip *pannaiyals* and to force cow-dung into their mouths. If the landlords try to impose such punishment on you, retaliate, chase them down and fight back. If goondas come to attack you, tie them to a tree. If a single one of you is attacked, the entire village should unite against the attack and in defence of the victim.
>
> Establishing unity and strengthening the Kisan Sabha are of the utmost importance. Hoist the red flag in every village. If you establish a Kisan Sabha everywhere, and if you begin to hit back, you can indeed instil fear in the landlords. The police too will have to reconsider their position, and they will be unable to cause the same fear that they did. Do not hold back: face this challenge boldly and move forward.

One of the first demands put forward by the Kisan Sabha unit in Thenparai on behalf of the tenant cultivators was that 33 per cent or one-third of the product be given as share rent; in other words, that tenants receive 67 per cent in place of the 18 per cent they had hitherto received as their share from Uthirapathi Matham. The retaliation was swift: Veerasamy, who had been elected Secretary of the Thenparai Kisan Sabha unit and who was himself a tenant cultivating 3 acres, was evicted from his leased-in land. With the help of leaders like Srinivasa Rao, Manali Kandasamy and others, the peasants of Thenparai began an agitation. Despite the near-famine conditions in the countryside in 1943, Uthirapathi Matham, through their local agent Seetharamachari, issued orders preventing the tenants from harvesting the paddy they had cultivated. The Matham told the peasants that they would let the crop wither rather than allow the Kisan Sabha to grow in the village.

A meeting was held in which the district leaders of the Kisan Sabha participated. The peasants and workers of the village decided, for the first time ever, to defy the authority of the Matham. They harvested and threshed the paddy, leaving the landlords' share at the threshing floor for them to collect. They had gained in confidence, and the news of their struggle spread rapidly across the district. In one village after another, peasants came to the Kisan Sabha asking for units to be established in their own villages. The landlords were furious that they were unable to stop the tenants from threshing the paddy; and their plans to burn the paddy at the threshing floor proved futile. At the instigation of the landlords, Veerasamy was attacked and his house burned down. The police filed false criminal charges against both peasants and leaders of the Kisan Sabha, following which Venkatesan and six others were sentenced to several months of imprisonment. The peasants of Thenparai, however, were undeterred.

To break the stalemate, Madhavan, Deputy Superintendent of Police, held a tripartite meeting in Kalappal village in 1944, and negotiated an agreement that provided for a wage increase for the farm servants, and gave the tenant cultivators the right to thresh the harvested paddy at their own threshing floors rather than at the threshing floors of the landlords. Amirthalingam, Kalappal Kuppusamy and Rajagopal represented the Kisan Sabha at this meeting, and V.S. Thiagaraja Mudaliar (Vadapathimangalam) and the head of the Thirukkalar Matham represented the landlords. In December that year, the District Collector, Ismail, held a second meeting and drafted a new agreement, by which it was further decided that:

(i) the share of paddy due to the tenant would be given at the threshing floor and the landlords would sign receipts on receiving their share;

(ii) standard volumetric measures approved by the government would be used to measure the shares of paddy.

However, the peasants had to struggle to implement the terms of the agreement. The government and the landlords joined hands against them. Acting on a demand made by the landlords, the district administration issued an externment order to Amirthalingam and Manali Kandasamy, instructing them to leave Thanjavur district for Tiruchirapalli. The impact of the externment was felt as far away as the British Parliament, where Communist members raised their voice against it until the order was withdrawn.

Revolt of Farm Servants in Thenparai

The victory achieved by tenant cultivators in reducing the back-breaking rents in Thenparai not only enthused the tenants of the district, but also inspired farm servants working under the Kalappal and Nedumbalam landlords, and under Vadapathimangalam Mudaliyar, Valivalam Desikar and Kunniyur Sambasiva Iyer. Determined to fight against the caste and class oppression to which they were subjected, Dalit farm servants joined the Kisan Sabha in large numbers, not only in and around Thenparai village but throughout East Thanjavur. About 15,000 farm servants and tenants attended the first conference of the State Kisan Sabha, held in Mannargudi in 1944. The Kisan Sabha flag soon came to be known as the flag of the Dalits, and it was hoisted wherever they lived.

The Kisan Sabha lent leadership to and fought on behalf of farm servants and Dalits on a wide range of issues, including wages, land, rents and discriminatory practices such as untouchability. On all issues that affected their livelihood and dignity, including attacks by landlords, the Dalits were asked to resist and retaliate. The Kisan Sabha called upon the farm servants to start wearing full *dhoti*s instead of the loin-cloth, to speak out whenever necessary, and to physically resist if the landlords' *goonda*s tried to flog them or force them to drink cowdung-water. Dalit women were asked to wear blouses, a right they had been denied. The Kisan Sabha fought for the right of Dalits to sit together with caste Hindus in teashops and to drink tea in common glasses. The Kisan Sabha demanded that Dalit children go to school rather than to work in cattlesheds. Farm servants were told to go to work after 6 am instead of at 4 am, and to return from work before sunset. Higher wages for farm servants were also demanded.

The landlords tried their best to stem the tide but in vain. The methods of repression attempted by them included attacks by hired *goonda*s, foisting of false criminal cases and threats to the *pannaiyal*s that they would be driven away from their native villages. But the Dalit upsurge could not be stopped. The government came under pressure to intervene and bring about a settlement between farm servants and landlords.

At the tripartite meeting of 1944 (mentioned above) that was held at the instance of the Deputy Superintendent of Police, representatives of farm servants sat for the first time with landlords at a negotiating table where the two sides were treated alike. This was a victory in itself for the Dalit farm servants. The terms of the agreement that went in their favour were as follows:

(i) to stop the whipping of farm servants and forcing them to drink cowdung;

(ii) to pay farm servants 2 small measures of paddy a day as wages;

(iii) at harvest time, to pay farm servants 3 small measures of paddy per *kalam* and 4 small measures of paddy per day.

Further gains were achieved in the agreement negotiated in December that year, at the intervention of the District Collector. These included:

(i) an increase in the daily wages of agricultural labourers from 2 small measures of paddy to 3 small measures (from half a *marakkal* to three-fourths of a *marakkal*);

(ii) in addition, one-seventh of the total yield of paddy, i.e. 2 measures, were to be given to farm servants as *kalavadi*.

Caste Hindu tenants, sharecroppers and small peasants were initially suspicious of the Kisan Sabha and took some time to come under its influence in the fight for peasants' rights. The landlords were quick to realize that if caste Hindu peasants joined hands with Dalit workers, they would be faced with a formidable opposition, and their citadel of feudal and caste oppression would come under threat. Following in the footsteps of their British colonial masters, the landlords too attempted a strategy of divide and rule. The response of the Kisan Sabha and the Communist Party was to continue in their attempts to unify all sections of the peasantry, and the attempts of the landlords to split the movement along caste lines did not succeed. They were forced finally to come to an understanding with the Kisan Sabha and to participate in the tripartite meeting organized by the Thanjavur District Collector to discuss the problems faced by the peasantry. Manali Kandasamy represented the Kisan Sabha at this meeting.

The landlords, who agreed to the terms of the settlement at the official meeting albeit reluctantly, later went back on their word and refused to implement it. But by then the Kisan Sabha movement had spread all across the district, and militant peasants rallied behind the organization. General body meetings, rallies and public meetings were held, and peasants struck work all over East Thanjavur. Once they understood the full impact of the terms of the tripartite settlement, caste Hindu tenants began to set aside their anti-Dalit prejudice and to gravitate towards the Kisan Sabha.

The district administration and the landlords were alarmed at the rapid rise of peasant militancy. The government took immediate measures to suppress the movement. Section 144, the provision in the Indian Penal Code relating to unlawful assembly, was promulgated across the entire district, and Manali Kandasamy and Amirthalingam, leaders of the Kisan Sabha, were externed. The landlords launched a rival peasant organization with the help of N.G. Ranga and one G. Narayanasamy Naidu.

Arbitration and Intervention by the Government

The 1946 Assembly election saw the Congress Party coming to power in Madras province. Immediately after the election a delegation of landlords from Thanjavur district, led by Vadapathimangalam Thiagaraja Mudaliar, met the Congress ministers to brief them about the Communists who, in their view, were instigating riots and spreading terror in Thanjavur. They demanded that the government intervene against the Communist-led peasant movement.

The government appointed the Thanjavur District Sessions Judge as arbitrator to look into the problems between the Kisan Sabha and the landlords in the Mannargudi revenue division, which comprised four taluks: Mannargudi, Thiruthuraipoondi, Needamangalam and Vedaranyam. The arbitrator, after holding a three-day-long meeting with Kisan Sabha leaders and landlords, gave the following verdict: that farm servants' wages should be increased from 3 measures of paddy to $3^{1}/_{2}$ measures, and that landlords will not evict tenants from their leased-in fields or farm servants from their huts (Veerayyan 1998).

Both sides accepted the verdict, and Kunniyur Sambasiva Iyer and the other landlords as well as the Kisan Sabha leaders signed the arbitration award announced by the judge. However, some of the landlords, who had not expected the verdict to go in favour of the peasants, refused to implement it. Bashyam Iyengar, then Revenue Minister, heeding the complaint of these dissident landlords, went personally to East Thanjavur and convened another tripartite conference at Needamangalam.

Bashyam Iyengar said that it had been foolishness on the part of the government to appoint an arbitrator and that the government did not have the powers to implement the arbitration award. He further declared that landlords could evict any tenant from their lands and any person from huts put up on their lands, as their right to do so was absolute. The conference convened by the Revenue Minister ended without an agreement being reached between the Kisan Sabha and the landlords. Since the Minister went a step further and publicly announced that landlords could elicit help from the police, what followed was a reign of terror against the peasants. The police also fabricated false cases against members and leaders of the Kisan Sabha.

> On January 3, 1943, while addressing a meeting in Kumbakonam, the State Revenue Minister openly declared that he would not tolerate the Communists and the Kisan Sabha. He said that the Kisan Sabha was enacting a 'mini Noakhali' in Mannargudi and Thiruthuraipoondi. The Kisan Sabha was responsible for arson and murder. In the name of opposing capitalism, they are destroying everything in the district, he said. He said that, in order to protect law and order, he would take stringent action against the Communists. After this, Section 144 was promulgated to ban AIKS meetings. Most taluks in East Thanjavur were brought under this section of the Indian Penal Code. Reserve Police from Tiruchi were brought into the district. (Ibid.: 15)

The declarations made by the Revenue Minister emboldened the landlords. They issued press statements demanding that the Kisan Sabha be banned in the district, which received wide publicity in all the newspapers. All this contributed to large-scale repression of the peasant movement.

Repressive Tactics of the Government after 1947
This was the situation in East Thanjavur when India gained independence in 1947. The peasants of East Thanjavur had hoped that the government of an independent nation would come to their rescue and solve their

problems. Contrary to their expectations, however, the landlords – who had by then switched their loyalties from the British colonial administration to the Congress Party – used the government to once again suppress the peasant movement. The Kisan Sabha was banned, as was the Communist Party.

In many parts of Tamil Nadu, especially Thanjavur, Section 144 was enforced for four years, from 1948 through 1951. The peasant and labour movement in Thanjavur was sought to be crushed: hoisting the red flag was banned, and peasants were forbidden to wear red towels and were threatened with dire consequences if they became members of the Kisan Sabha. (Veerayyan 1998).

Kalappaal Kuppu, a farm servant who became a leader of the movement in Mannargudi, became the first peasant martyr in independent India. He was one of the Kisan Sabha leaders who had signed the settlement that abolished whipping of farm servants and forcible drinking of cowdung-water. Kuppu was arrested on false charges on 18 April 1948, at the age of 35, and interned in the central jail in Tiruchirapalli – where he was killed by poisoning.

Apart from Kuppu, several hundreds of cadres of the agrarian movement were arrested by the police on trumped-up charges of conspiracy, put behind bars without any investigation, and beaten and tortured in prison. The Nanalur conspiracy case, Nedumbalam conspiracy case, Thiruppoonthuruthy conspiracy case and Ambalapattu conspiracy case were some of the cases that were falsely brought against the leaders and cadres of the movement. In 1950, all these were merged and redesignated the Thanjavur Conspiracy Case. The accused were tried in court at Mayiladuthurai and sentenced to three years of rigorous imprisonment.

In a bid to split the Kisan Sabha, a settlement was sought to be reached in Mayiladuthurai between the rival peasant organization leader G. Narayanasamy Naidu and the landlords, called the Mayiladuthurai settlement. But the peasant movement ignored the settlement and the protests continued. Section 144 was once again promulgated in Thanjavur district and the Malabar Special Police was called in to tackle the situation. The district soon resembled a vast police camp. The huts of Dalit farm servants were destroyed in many villages, either by the police or by landlords' *goondas*.

Peasant leaders Sivaraman from Jambavan Odai, Iraniyan from Vattakudi, Arumugam from Ambalappattu, Raju from Kottur and Natesan from Nanalur were shot dead in the police firing. The police smashed the house of Manali Kandasamy in rage against their inability to apprehend him. The newspapers in the State colluded with the landlords' campaign, publishing mainly what was handed out to them by the landlords and the State administration. All this did not succeed, however, in preventing the spread of the Kisan Sabha, which continued to fight for the dignity of Dalits and the livelihood of peasants in the decade 1940–50 (Ramakrishnan 2002). Dalits and other sections of the peasantry bravely faced all kinds of opposition: bullets, *goondas*, foisted conspiracy cases and false campaigns by the press. The

Kisan Sabha grew in influence in East Thanjavur, as well as in the adjacent Pattukkottai and Aranthangi taluks of West Thanjavur.

The 1952 Assembly Elections

In the first Assembly elections held in Madras province after independence, in 1952, the Congress lost its majority and Chief Minister Kumarasamy Raja was defeated. Out of nineteen Assembly constituencies in Thanjavur district, the Congress lost in ten, the Communist Party of India won in six, and independent candidates supported by the CPI won in another four constituencies. Manali Kandasamy, who had been forced to remain underground throughout the election campaign, won the Mannargudi Assembly seat by a huge margin. Landlord candidates Kunniyur Iyer, Nedumbalam Mudaliar and Poondi Vandayar were defeated.

The victorious CPI candidates were Manali Kandasamy and A.K. Subbiah in Mannargudi, N. Sivaraj and S. Vadivel in Nagapattinam, P. Venkatesa Solagar in Needamangalam, and S. Ramalingam in Thanjavur. E.V. Ramasami supported CPI candidates in the Thanjavur region. The CPI won fourteen Assembly seats in the State, of which six were from Thanjavur district. The victory in the Assembly elections proved to be a shot in the arm for the activities of the Kisan Sabha in East Thanjavur.

The Congress did not get a majority but they formed the government nevertheless, with the help of the Commonweal Party and Toilers' Party which had stood against the Congress in the run-up to the election. C. Rajagopalachari became Chief Minister of Madras State.

New Phase of the Peasant Movement
The Pannaiyal Protection Act of 1952

On 20 August 1952, the Kisan Sabha held a conference at Thiruthuraipoondi, attended by about 60,000 tenant cultivators and farm servants, to protest the eviction of tenants from their lands. On 22 August, a day after the conference concluded, the newly elected State government passed the Pannaiyal Protection and Cultivation Ordinance, applicable only to Thanjavur district. Addressing a meeting in Thanjavur after promulgation of the ordinance, Chief Minister Rajagopalachari said: 'The spectre of Communism is haunting the peasants and agricultural labourers of Thanjavur district. I have brought out the Act only to liberate them. Landlords should accept this Act' (Veerayyan 1998). The ordinance ruled that:

1. Tenants who cultivate the lands of those who own more than 6.5 acres were not to be evicted.
2. Tenants were to keep a share of 40 per cent of the output of paddy; 60 per cent was to go to the landlords and they were to give receipts for their share.
3. The wage increase mentioned in the 1948 Mayiladuthurai settlement for farm servants was to be implemented.

4. If a landlord wanted to evict a farm servant from his farm, he would have to pay the farm servant Rs 150 or six months' wages, whichever was higher, as compensation. In 1952, Rs 150 was equivalent to the price of 12.5 bags of paddy (the price of one bag was Rs 12).

The ordinance had a great impact in Thanjavur district, especially in East Thanjavur. It was seen as a victory achieved through pressures exerted on the government by struggles of the peasants and their organizations. The Fifth State Conference of the Kisan Sabha was held in Mannargudi in 1953. More than one lakh people participated in the rally on its closing day.

Over the next four years, the Thanjavur Pannaiyal Protection Act (the ordinance was passed as an Act later) brought about a qualitative change in agrarian relations in the district, and in master–slave relations that hitherto existed between farm servants and landlords. It struck a blow at the conditions of bondage in which farm servants and their families had worked for landlords, whereby a landlord could proclaim the farm servant as 'mine' and the farm servant and his family had to address the landlord as master (*ejamaan*).

The Act legislated that landlords had to pay farm servants the prescribed wages if they wanted to keep them on their farms. If they did not want the farm servants to work for them, they had the option of paying the prescribed compensation and relieving them. Some landlords chose to pay Rs 150 and retain the farm servants as wage labourers, after accepting an undertaking from them that they were no longer farm servants. A landlord could now employ anybody as an agricultural worker on his farm. An erstwhile farm servant also could choose to work wherever he received better wages. The agricultural worker was becoming free in a double sense: free from ownership of the means of production, and free to sell his labour power. Thus the Pannaiyal Protection Act of 1952 paved the way for transforming the relationship between landlords and farm servants into one between landlords and agricultural workers, although other agrarian and social conditions, such as land concentration and untouchability, continued to exist as before. 'The system of *pannaiyal* has practically gone out of vogue except in the case of about 5 per cent of the landlords. Neither landlords nor labourers desire resuscitation of the odious system' (Government of Tamil Nadu 1969: 6).

New Demands and New Struggles

Once the farm servants became daily wage labourers, new demands – such as assured work, higher wages and right to homesteads – came to the fore. Earlier, workers had been allowed to raise huts on the farms of the landlords for whom they worked. Now that they had the freedom to work for different landlords, they began to be evicted from their huts. Thus, in addition to wage increase and assured work, the demand had to be raised for title deeds to their homesteads.

The new situation also gave birth to a conflict of interests between tenant cultivators and small landowners, and farm servants-turned-agricultural labourers. During the years 1943–53, tenants and sharecroppers, small land-owners, and farm workers of Thanjavur had come together under a single peasant organization (the Kisan Sabha), which addressed their common griev-ances and organized common struggles against the landlords and the state. Now, difficulties arose in continuing this form of united struggle. While joint struggles could continue for basic demands such as 'land to the tiller' and abolition of untouchability, issues such as wage increase and regular employ-ment in agricultural operations strained the unity of tenants and agricultural labourers. The Pannaiyal Protection Act introduced a divide between land-owning peasants (including poor peasants) and landless agricultural workers. The need was felt, therefore, to have separate organizations to represent the interests of both these classes. An agricultural workers' conference was held in Thiruvarur in 1956, at which it was decided to establish the Tamil Nadu Agricultural Workers Association.

The years between 1956 and 1960 witnessed several militant wage struggles being launched across East Thanjavur. After the Pannaiyal Protection Act came into force, landlords began to deny jobs to local workers by bring-ing in agricultural labourers from other villages. The agricultural workers of East Thanjavur, under the leadership of the Communist Party of India, fought against these new tactics of the landlords by pressing three main demands: jobs for local workers, uniform wages throughout the district, and higher wages. The strike actions of agricultural labourers in some villages went on for days together – up to forty-five days in some instances.

From 1966 to 1968 the struggles entered a new phase, marking a milestone in the history of the Left movement and agricultural workers' move-ment in the district. In 1966 the landlords, to counter the growing militancy of agricultural workers, formed the Paddy Growers Association, functioning from Nagapattinam taluk, whose membership and leadership consisted mainly of landlords. It formed a network of *goonda*s and held public meetings to incite violence against agricultural labourers; to pit caste Hindus against Dalits; and to campaign against the Left by saying that paddy growers should not engage workers belonging to the Left for agricultural operations. The police and the revenue administration supported the Paddy Growers Association, as did the Congress Party. This new direction taken by the landlords led to a tense situation in the district, one of open confrontation. The District Committee of the Communist Party of India (Marxist) (CPI[M]) and the Agricultural Workers Association put forward the demand that a tripartite conference be held to resolve the wage dispute, in support of which a one-day strike was organized throughout the district.

The DMK Government Years: Renewed Militancy

In the 1967 Assembly elections, the Dravida Munnetra Kazhagam (DMK) came to power in the State of Tamil Nadu. As part of their elec-tion campaign the DMK leaders had exposed the anti-people policies of the

Congress government, especially focusing on police firings against agricultural labourers. But after coming to power, they showed no signs of intervening to settle the wage dispute and other demands of the workers. In October 1967, at the time of the *kharif* harvest, CPI(M) leaders A. Balasubramaniam and N. Sankaraiah met the DMK Chief Minister C. Annadurai, and urged that the State government settle the wage dispute in East Thanjavur through negotiation at the earliest opportunity. But the government did not intervene. The Agricultural Workers Association resolved that workers would undertake harvesting work only for landlords who were prepared to pay 6 litres of paddy a day as wages. One landlord in Mannargudi taluk was willing to pay the stipulated wages and agricultural labourers went to work for him, while the Paddy Growers Association attacked him for compromising the stand taken by landlords.

Workers' struggles continued in most parts of the district, as did the repressive measures against them. In Poonthalangudi village (Mannargudi taluk), when *goonda*s of the landlord tried to remove the red flag from a flagpost, agricultural workers resisted them and protected it. The police came to the assistance of the *goonda*s and opened fired on the workers, killing one of them on the spot. A district-wide protest movement was organized against the police action. After this incident the State government finally convened a tripartite conference to resolve the conflict, which resulted in an agreement on the following lines.

1. Half a litre of paddy would be added to the existing daily wage.
2. In places where 6 litres of paddy had been paid as wages during the previous year, the wage rate would continue as it was.
3. Preference would be given to employment of local workers in agricultural operations; workers from outside would be brought in only if there were not enough local workers to meet the demand.
4. The State government would appoint a wage commission to decide the wage rates.
5. The agreement would apply for a period of one year.
6. The agreement would be applicable only to East Thanjavur.
7. Revenue authorities would take the initiative to implement the agreement.

As usual, government officials and landlords were reluctant to implement the agreement, and agricultural workers had to struggle for its implementation. At this juncture there was a change in the leadership of the Paddy Growers Association. Gopalakrishna Naidu (from Irinjur village, adjacent to Kilvenmani), a notorious anti-communist, became its president.

During the harvesting season of 1968–69, the Agricultural Workers Association put forward the demand that the State government should once again convene a conference to discuss revision of wages, to which the government had agreed in June 1968. Even as the campaign for wage increase was under way in the entire district, the Paddy Growers Association kidnapped

Chinnapillai, branch president of the Irinjur Agricultural Workers Union, and murdered him. The landlords' message was clear: since the period of validity of the agreement of the previous year had expired, they would revert to paying the old wages, which were less than the existing wages. Once again a situation of conflict arose between the agricultural workers and the Paddy Growers Association.

The State government, instead of trying to settle the issue through negotiation, formed a special police force called the Kisan Police to suppress the struggles of the agricultural workers and the Left movement. During the freedom struggle the Malabar Special Police had been brought in to crush the peasants' movement; now it was the DMK government's turn to form a special police cell to suppress the militant struggles of workers in East Thanjavur. The police openly sided with the landlords to break the agricultural workers' strike for wage increase. The targets of attacks by the Paddy Growers Association and the police, aided by the *goonda* force of the landlords, were not only the workers who were engaged in wage struggles, but also the Left movement as a whole, which had been fighting against untouchability, caste and other forms of oppression since the 1940s.

The landlords were adamant that since the validity of the earlier agreement had expired, they would go back to giving wages at the old rates. In opposition to this, agricultural workers began renewed struggles. *Goonda*s attacked Left cadres and workers in many villages. A landlord by the name of Ramachandran, of Kekkarai village, was also murdered by the *goonda*s as he was seen as a supporter of the Communist movement.

There were widespread workers' struggles in Nagapattinam, Thiruvarur, Thiruththuraipoondi, Mannargudi and Nannilam in East Thanjavur. In places where the landlords accepted the 6-litre wage formula, harvesting was completed; where it was not accepted and workers were brought in from outside, there was conflict. The repression unleashed to counter this was brutal. False cases were framed and thousands arrested – premises of the courts were filled with agricultural workers. The police and *goonda*s, who were guests of the landlords' hospitality, targeted and attacked agricultural labourers in their homes, and destroyed their property. Despite the repression, however, the agricultural workers did not succumb and continued their struggle.

> 'Several heads would have rolled on the field, blood would have flowed like the Kaveri in flood, if only we had not been restrained by the higher-ups. But for that instruction from our leaders, we would have put real fear in their hearts. We would have shown them who we really are.'
>
> Adilingam, a thin man with bright, piercing eyes, seemed to be reliving that tense September day in 1968 as he continued:
>
> 'There were twelve police vans carrying hundreds of Madras Special Police forces. We gheraoed the vans, they couldn't move an inch without killing

several of us. We carried every bit of equipment we could get hold of, sticks, spears, sickles, kitchen knives. Twelve of their men were wounded, not a single one on our side. The Superintendent of Police planted several white flags on the ground and asked for peace. We said, "We will release one van if you go and bring our women, whom you arrested last night, like cowards under cover of darkness. Go, get them!" And our women were brought back in an hour's time from Kivalur station. For the first time in the history of our village, the police took orders from the labourers. It was a great day.'

This was how a confrontation between agricultural labourers and land-lords, backed by the police, was described to me by a leading participant. (Sivaraman 1970: 246)

This was in the village of Puducheri in Nagapattinam sub-division of East Thanjavur. The incident was part of a familiar pattern of struggles in the late 1960s.

'There is no security for our cadres. We have to organize our own volunteer force to protect ourselves' – P. Ramamurti issued this statement after a visit to East Thanjavur. Chief Minister Annadurai denied that such a situation existed in the district.

A protest meeting was held at Nagapattinam on 15 November 1968 to condemn the attacks by the police and the *goonda*s. Pakkiri, a movement activist, was slain on the road while returning from the meeting, at Sikkal village. The Left and the peasants' movement organized further protests against this dreadful combined attack by the Kisan Police, the local police, officials of the administration, the Paddy Growers Association and the landlords' *goonda* force.

The Kizhvenmani Massacre

The agricultural workers were intransigent in their resolve to not suc-cumb to either the false assurances or the intimidatory tactics of the Paddy Growers Association and the police. The landlords tried to wean peasants and agricultural workers from the influence of the Communist Party by mak-ing promises to them of assured work and higher wages, but on condition that they bring down the red flag. Organized sections of agricultural workers declared, however, that they would not uproot the symbol of the movement that had given them dignity of life and work.

The landlords chose the village of Kizhvenmani in Nagapattinam taluk, whose agricultural workers were firmly committed to continue the struggle, as their next target of attack. On 25 December 1968, at about 8 pm, more than a hundred *goonda*s led by Gopalakrishna Naidu (president of the Paddy Growers Association), and armed with guns, choppers, petrol cans and other lethal weapons, drove into the village in a blue van. Naidu ordered the *goonda*s to burn down the entire village. Forty-four people of the village who sought shelter in a nearby hut were all burnt alive.

The Venmani massacre was condemned at protest meetings organized not only in Thanjavur but in the entire State of Tamil Nadu, and also in other States where the Left movement was strong. The hut in which the forty-four victims were burnt alive, which belonged to an agricultural worker named Ramayya, is today the site of the Venmani Memorial. Every year, 25 December is observed as a day to commemorate the martyrs of 1968, and as a day of pledges to eradicate untouchability and end feudal exploitation.

The Venmani massacre was not just retaliation against the workers' wage struggles, but an attack by landlords against Dalits who were fighting against caste and feudal oppression. This fact came out clearly in an interview that Mythili Sivaraman conducted with a landlord in East Thanjavur.

> Not only did the labourers deny that the wage issue was basic to the troubles, but even the landlords shrugged it off as secondary. An emaciated old man, owner of about 15 acres, lectured me on what he considered to be the source of the present problems. 'Things used to be very peaceful here some years ago. The labourers were very hardworking and respectful. But now . . . the fellow who used to stand in the backyard of my house to talk to me comes straight to the font door wearing slippers and all. . . . And at 5.30 sharp he says, "Our leader is speaking today at a public meeting. I have to leave." His leader holds a meeting right next door to me and parades the streets with the red flag. These fellows have become arrogant and lazy, thanks to the Communists. They have no fear in them any more.'
>
> The root of the problem was easy to locate. It was the emergence of the new fearless, politically aware [Dalit] labourer and his militant union. (Sivaraman 1970: 248)

After the Venmani massacre, the government appointed a one-man commission under a retired judge, Ganapathia Pillai, to go into the question of wages for agricultural labourers and to make recommendations. Pending the release of the final recommendations of the commission, the District Collector, in a tripartite meeting held at Thanjavur on 16 January 1969, announced that wages were to be increased, and that outside labourers were to be employed only after local labourers had been given work and only if there was a real need for such employment.

Ganapathia Pillai Commission Report

The salient features of the Ganapathia Pillai Commission's report and its recommendations were as follows.

1. The judge pointed out that a special feature of the working population of the East Thanjavur area was that 90 per cent belonged to the Scheduled Castes. In the western part of Thanjavur district, not more than half of the working population belonged to the Scheduled Castes. According to the 1961 Census, of the total population of the East Thanjavur taluks of Srikali, Mayavaram, Nannilam, Nagapattinam, Mannargudi and Thiruthuraipoondi,

nearly 28 per cent belonged to the Scheduled Castes. In the western part of Thanjavur district this proportion was 18 per cent.

2. Ganapathia Pillai believed that fixing different wage rates for different taluks would create unnecessary discontent and encourage unnecessary migration of labour from one place to another, and decided to recommend uniform rates for wages for all six taluks (the whole of East Thanjavur).

3. The judge further stated that the state had the 'legal power to restrict the freedom of contract of landholders to refuse work to local labour totally and to import outside labour by enacting appropriate labour legislation'.

4. While the minimum wages of agricultural workers could be determined under the provisions of Central Act 11 of 1948, Ganapathia Pillai was of the opinion that the State government should bring out a special legislation designed to settle the labour problems in Thanjavur.

5. Wages once fixed were to be reviewed by a committee once in three years.

6. He recommended 6 local measures out of 54 measures as the harvest wage (6 local measures plus 420 ml or 360 grams in weight, that is, 6 litres).

7. The judge also pointed out that while the problem of shortage of house sites was not very acute at the time, a long-term policy for solution of this problem had to be worked out. He suggested, in this regard, that all available methods of acquiring lands for house sites be utilized.

On the basis of these recommendations, the State government of Tamil Nadu legislated an Act on Fair Wages. The law was applicable only to East Thanjavur to begin with, and was to be implemented throughout the State from 1998 onwards.

Struggles for Titles to House Sites and Farm Land

In addition to struggles to end the scourge of untouchability, to liberate agricultural labourers from serfdom and to ensure minimum wages, the Left and the Agricultural Workers Union in Thanjavur began a movement centred on another important aspect of the right to life of agricultural workers: title-deeds for house-sites.

Once the relations of bondage between landlords and farm labour were broken, landlords began to evict agricultural workers from homes built on their employers' land. In order to protect their homes, the workers began a movement demanding title-deeds to homesteads. Given also the recommendation of the Ganapathia Pillai Commission in this regard, the State government announced legislation to grant agricultural workers title-deeds to house sites on private land owned by landlords. In Thanjavur district, the office from where these title-deeds were issued was located at Mannargudi, and title-deeds were given to 180,000 agricultural workers in the district.

The next movement launched by peasants throughout the State and in Thanjavur related to the Land Ceiling Act that had been enacted by the Congress government in 1961. The Act legislated a ceiling of 30 standard acres of land, but it had many loopholes that were used by the landlords to escape the ceiling – for instance, by assigning land to trusts, *máthams* and so on. The peasants demanded that the Act be amended along the lines of a law enacted in the neighbouring State of Kerala by the CPI(M)-led State government with E.M.S. Namboodiripad as Chef Minister. Pickets were organized throughout Tamil Nadu to press the demand. Srinivasa Rao, a leader of the peasants' and agricultural workers' movement, travelled across the State to help organise the pickets. The strain of this campaign took a severe toll on his health, and he fell ill and died on 30 September 1961.

The struggle for land distribution gathered momentum in the 1970s and continued for twenty years thereafter in East Thanjavur. In 1971, the DMK government amended the Land Ceiling Act and fixed the ceiling at 15 standard acres. The peasants' struggle then pressed the state to take over surplus land and to distribute it under the provisions of the amended Act. Details of land that was finally distributed as a result of this struggle are given below, district-wise.

Thiruvarur District

Thiagaraja Mudaliar of Vadapathimangalam owned 6,000 acres of sugarcane land, all under tenant cultivation. All the land was distributed among 6,500 agricultural labourers – 1,500 acres in 1971 and 4,500 acres in 1991.

Kottur Mudaliar owned 4,000 acres of land, all of which has been distributed.

Sambasiva Iyer of Kunniyur owned 900 acres of land. Of this, 700 acres were distributed to agricultural labourers between 1970 and 1990. The remaining 200 acres of land, of which 130 acres are dry land, remain with the family of the landlord.

Samiappa Mudaliar of Nedumbalam owned nearly 2,000 acres of land, of which 1,800 acres were distributed and 200 acres remain with the landlord's family.

In Keevalur, Valivalam Desikar owned nearly 2,000 acres of land; 1800 acres were distributed and 200 acres are with the landlord's family.

In Tirukkottaram village, Nannilam taluk, all 150 acres of land owned by Gurusamy Pillai were distributed.

In Kodavasal block, all 1,500 acres owned by Solingapuram Iyer were distributed.

Three Brahmin families owned 500 acres of land between them in Sirukalathur village, Kodavasal taluk. They left the village and all their land, barring 10 acres, was distributed. In Adipuliyur village, all the land owned by two Brahmin families was distributed.

Of nearly 370 acres owned by four Brahmin family farms in Sithadi village, Kudavasal taluk, all but 6 acres were distributed.

Swaminatha Iyer of Melapaliyur village, Kudavasal taluk, owned

300 acres of land. At present, his family owns only 6.5 acres; the rest has been distributed.

Nearly 2,000 acres of land in Vikkirapandiapuram, Viswapuram and Mudikondan villages in Kodavasal taluk, and Anathandapuram in Mayavaram taluk, were distributed.

In Narthankudi, Narikkudi, Vedambur, Vadamangalam, Araiyur, Saranatham, Pulavarnatham and Manickamangalam villages in Valangaiman block, 1,500 acres were distributed to agricultural workers.

Nagapattinam District

Thannilappadi Naidu owned nearly 300 acres of land in Keelaiyur block, all of which were distributed. All temple lands in the block were brought under tenant cultivation.

In Meenambanallur, about 1,000 acres belonging to a landlord were distributed to landless labourers.

In the villages of Keelaiyur, Ottathattai and Periyathambur, about 150 acres of land were distributed.

A Brahmin family at Konerirajapuram village, Kuttalam block, owned 600 acres of land; all of it has been distributed.

Brahmin landlords owned nearly 800 acres of land in Kodimangalam, Nallavur, Paruthikkudi and Kanchivoy villages in Kuttalam block; all of it has been distributed.

In Pangal, Kolappadu and Panangudi villages of Thalaignayiru block, 2000 acres were distributed.

Trust, Temple and Matham Land

Trusts are exempted from the provisions of the Land Ceiling Act. There are fourteen trusts in East Thanjavur. Nearly 1,500 acres owned by these trusts are cultivated by tenants.

The following is a list of the extent of land owned by temples and cultivated by tenants in East Thanjavur:

  (i) 400 acres in Thevur, Keevalur block;
 (ii) 400 acres in Sikkal village, Nagapattinam block;
(iii) 200 acres owned by Sembianmadevi Temple in Nagapattinam block;
 (iv) 500 acres owned by Dharmapuram Matham at Thirukuvalai, Keelai-yur block;
  (v) 600 acres in Nattirupu village, Keelaiyur block;
 (vi) 200 acres owned by Ettikkudi Temple in Keelaiyur block;
(vii) 12,000 acres owned by Vedaranyam Temple in Vedaranyam block;
(viii) 2,000 acres owned by Mannargudi Temple in Mannargudi block;
 (ix) 300 acres owned by Nachiarkoil Temple in Kodavasal block;
  (x) 250 acres owned by Tirukkalar Temple in Kodavasal block;
 (xi) 400 acres in Tiruppugalur, Nannilam block; and
(xii) all the land owned by temples in Tirukkannamangai, Tiruvanchiyam,

Tirukkannapuram, Tiruchankattankudi, Tirumarugal and Tirukalam-
bur villages in Nannilam block.

A total of 39,152 acres of wet land and 28,815 acres of dry land are
owned by 241 temples in Sirkali and Tarangambadi in Nagapattinam district,
and Tiruvidaimarudur and Kumbakonam in Thanjavur district. The wet land
is entirely under tenant cultivation; 20,000 acres of the dry land are covered
by coconut and banana groves, and house sites.

There are about 600,000 acres of cultivable wet land in East Thanjavur, of which trusts and temples own 300,000 acres. Between 1970 and 1991,
of these 600,000 acres of wet land, 200,000 acres were distributed to landless
agricultural labourers as a result of sustained struggle by the Agricultural
Workers Union and Kisan Sabha. If the exemptions given to temples and
trusts are withdrawn, there is a possibility of distributing a further 300,000
acres to tenants.

Conclusion

A distinctive feature of the pre-independence movement in East
Thanjavur is that it brought together the anti-colonial, anti-landlord and social
liberation demands of the working people into a single movement. From 1940
to 1991, the Left movement in East Thanjavur (comprising the present districts of Nagapattinam and Thiruvarur) struggled hard for the eradication of
untouchability and the liberation of Dalits; for the liberation of farm servants
from the worst forms of pre-capitalist extra-economic oppression; to ensure
tenancy rights; and to secure wage increases for agricultural workers. In the
years after 1970, the movement was instrumental in ensuring that large parts
of the vast estates of local landlords were redistributed to erstwhile tenants.

This essay stops at 1991, when the Tamil Nadu State government,
following the lead of the central government, began to implement neoliberal
economic policies. A separate study needs to be undertaken to analyse the
impact of these neoliberal policies on the agrarian situation in East Thanjavur,
especially on the status and rights of Dalits and the peasantry.

References

Bouton, M.M. (1985), *Agrarian Radicalism in South India*, Princeton University Press, Princeton.
Gough, Kathleen (1981), *Rural Society in Southeast India*, Cambridge University Press,
    Cambridge.
Gough, Kathleen (1989), *Rural Change in Southeast India, 1950s to 1980s*, Oxford University
    Press, New Delhi.
Pillai, Ganapathia (1969), *Report of the Commission of Enquiry on the Agrarian Labour
    Problems of East Thanjavur District*, Government of Tamil Nadu, Madras.
Menon, Parvathi (1986), 'The Agrarian Economy of the Carnatic in the 17th and 18th Centuries',
    unpublished Ph.D. thesis submitted to Aligarh Muslim University, Aligarh.
Menon, Saraswathi (1979a), 'Responses to Class and Caste Oppression in Thanjavur District,
    1940–1952, Part I', *Social Scientist*, vol. 7, no. 6, January, pp. 14–31.
Menon, Saraswathi (1979b), 'Responses to Class and Caste Oppression in Thanjavur District,
    1940–1952, Part III', *Social Scientist*, vol. 7, no. 10, pp. 52–64.
Menon, Saraswathi (1983), 'Social Characteristics of Land Control in Thanjavur District during

the Nineteenth Century: A Sociological Study', unpublished Ph.D. thesis submitted to Jawaharlal Nehru University, New Delhi.

Ramakrishnan, N. (1990), *Pannai Adimaithanathai Ethirtha Porattathil PSD* (PSD [P.S. Dhanushkodi] in the Struggle against Agrarian Slavery), South Vision Publications, Chennai.

Ramakrishnan, N. (2002), *History of the Communist Movement in Tamil Nadu, 1917–1964*, Vaigai Publishers, Chennai.

Rao, B. Srinivasa (1947), *Thanjaiyil Nadappathu Enna?* (What is Happening in Thanjavur?) Communist Party of India, Thanjavur District Committee, Thanjavur.

Sivaraman, Mythili (1970), 'Thanjavur: Rumblings of Class Struggle in Tamil Nadu,' in Kathleen Gough and Hari P. Sharma (eds), *Imperialism and Revolution in South Asia*, Monthly Review Press, New York and London.

Surjit, V. (2008), *Farm Business Incomes in India: A Study of Two Rice Growing Villages of Thanjavur Region, Tamil Nadu*, unpublished Ph.D. thesis submitted to University of Calcutta, Kolkata.

Vaimainathan (1998), *Thyagi Kalappal Kuppu* (Kalappal Kuppu, Martyr), New Century Book House, Chennai.

Veerayyan, G. (1998), *Tamizhnadu Vivasayigal Iyakka Varalaru* (A History of the Peasant Movement in Tamil Nadu), South Vision Publications, Chennai.

Land Reform and Access to Land among Dalit Households in West Bengal

Aparajita Bakshi

This essay deals with an important form of discrimination in the Indian countryside, the lack of access of Dalit (Scheduled Caste / SC) and Adivasi (Scheduled Tribe / ST) households to ownership and operational holdings of land in rural India. It includes a case study of the impact of land reforms in one State of India, West Bengal, on landholdings among Dalit and Adivasi households.

Access to land in an agriculture-based rural economy is important because land is the primary means and instrument of agricultural production. The social distribution of land in a village economy determines the economic position and power relations between different social groups in the village. Chakrabarty and Ghosh (2000), using National Sample Survey (NSS) data on ownership holdings of land, showed that in most States of India, the proportion of land owned by Dalit households was much lower than their share in the population. However, in rural India, the proportion of land owned by Dalit households increased in the period between 1982 and 1992 (ibid.). Thorat (2002) noted that in 1993–94, only 19 per cent of Dalit households were self-employed in agriculture, while the comparable statistic for non-Dalit, non-Adivasi households was 42 per cent. According to Thorat: 'The limited access to agricultural land and capital assets is both due to the historical legacy associated with restrictions imposed by the caste system and the ongoing discrimination in the land market, capital market and other related economic spheres' (ibid.).

It is important in a village economy to distinguish land that is used for productive purposes from land that is not directly used for agricultural production. Land used for income-bearing activities, for example, crop land, plantations and orchards, constitute productive agricultural land, while house-site land, fallow and barren lands are categories of land that are not generally used directly for regular crop production. Our aim in this essay is to determine Dalit households' access to land for agricultural production, and to compare this access with that of other social groups.

Secondary Data Sources on Landholdings in India

There are three major sources of secondary data on landholdings in India: the National Sample Survey Organization's (NSSO's) Land and Livestock Holdings (L&LH) surveys, the NSSO's Employment and Unemployment (E&U) surveys and the World Agricultural Census.

The L&LH surveys of the NSSO were initiated in 1954–55 as part of the World Agricultural Census, and since 1970–71 these surveys have been carried out decennially. The NSSO conducted its most recent L&LH survey in 2002–03 (59th round). In these surveys, the NSSO deals with two kinds of landholding: household ownership holdings and household operational holdings.

Household *ownership* holdings include all land owned or held in owner-like possession by households. The published reports of the NSSO provide data on households disaggregated by social groups. The household *operational* holding is the extent of land managed – whether it be owned, leased or otherwise possessed – as a techno-economic unit of production, in which some agricultural production was carried out in the reference period. Operational holdings are thus a better measure of access to land for production than ownership holdings. The NSSO reports do not, however, publish data on operational holdings of land disaggregated by social group.

The NSSO's E&U surveys provide data on land possessed and land cultivated by rural households. The published reports present the data disaggregated by social group. 'Land possessed' by households includes all land owned and occupied by households. It also includes all types of land: agricultural, homestead and non-agricultural. As in the case of ownership holdings in the L&LH surveys, this kind of classification of land tends to underestimate the incidence of landlessness with respect to productive land.

'Land cultivated' includes all crop land, plantations and orchards cultivated by households. It excludes homestead land and non-agricultural land. This category includes land owned and self-cultivated, land occupied and land leased in, but excludes land leased out by households. It is equivalent to an operational holding of agricultural land.

The Agricultural Census of India was initiated in 1950 as part of the World Agricultural Census programme organized by the Food and Agriculture Organization (FAO). Until 1960, the Agricultural Census of India was carried out by the NSSO. From 1970, the Agricultural Census has been carried out every five years by the Department of Agriculture. The Agricultural Census is a census of landholdings, and provides data on the distribution of operational holdings of land. The available published data are disaggregated by social group. In States where plot-wise land records are revised annually (typically in the erstwhile non-zamindari areas), the Agricultural Census is simply a re-tabulation of the existing land records. In States that do not have plot-wise land records, the Agricultural Census is a sample survey of households that operate land. In any case, being a survey of *holdings* rather than *households*, the Agricultural Census does not provide us estimates of landlessness among households (see Ramachandran 1980).

This essay is concerned with access to land for production purposes. Household operational holding is a better indicator of access to productive land than household ownership holding. The definition of household owner-ship holding includes all kinds of land owned by households, including home-stead land and non-agricultural land. As the preceding definition indicates, households that have no land for production are nevertheless not counted as 'landless' if they own homesteads or other types of land. According to the NSSO's L&LH report for 2003, only 6.6 per cent of rural households in India did not own any land in that year (NSSO 2006a). Further, the incidence of landlessness declined between 1992 and 2003. According to the same survey, 31 per cent of rural households in India did not operate any land in 2002–03, and landlessness with respect to operational holdings increased sharply, from 20 per cent in 1991–92 to 31 per cent in 2002–03 (NSSO 2006b). The con-tradiction arises because of the inclusion of homestead land in the definition of ownership holding.

Access to Land: Results from Secondary Data

I have used two indicators to assess access to land. Absolute depriva-tion of access to productive land is measured by incidence of landlessness. Inequality in access to land is measured by an index of access to land for cultivation.

First, I present the data on households that were landless with respect to operational holdings from the L&LH 59th round of 2003. Secondly, I use data on operational holdings of land from the L&LH 59th round of 2003 to construct an index of access of rural households, belonging to different social groups, to productive agricultural land.

Landlessness in NSSO's Land and Livestock Holdings Survey, 2003

By the NSSO's 2003 data, 31.2 per cent of rural households in rural India did not operate any land (Table 1). Incidence of landlessness was higher among Dalit households than among Adivasi households and non-Dalit/Adi-vasi households. While 41 per cent of Dalit households did not operate land, 23.6 per cent of Adivasi households and 29.3 per cent of non-Dalit/Adivasi households did not operate land. The data substantiate the impression that while Dalit households are generally landless, Adivasi households have small plots of land of low productivity.

The proportion of Dalit households that do not operate land was highest in Andhra Pradesh, Tamil Nadu, Kerala and Maharashtra.[1] The States with lowest incidence of landlessness were Jammu & Kashmir, Uttaranchal

---

[1] Some of the North Eastern States, such as Mizoram, Meghalaya and Arunachal Pradesh, also record high incidence of landlessness among Dalit households. The number and proportion of Dalit households in these States, however, are small.

TABLE 1 *Households that do not operate land as a proportion of all households, by social group, rural India, 2002–03 (kharif season)* in per cent

State	Adivasi	Dalits	Other Castes	All
Mizoram	6.3	100.0	1.7	6.3
Tamil Nadu	47.1	69.2	54.7	58.4
Andhra Pradesh	45.7	64.1	47.4	51.3
Kerala	48.0	59.6	35.9	38.7
Meghalaya	15.5	56.5	55.0	19.6
Maharashtra	46.7	54.9	31.3	37.4
Arunachal Pradesh	3.0	53.6	52.1	13.8
Gujarat	28.8	48.7	34.0	34.7
Karnataka	28.0	46.5	30.6	33.2
Bihar	19.8	46.4	24.3	29.3
Punjab	30.0	45.4	23.8	32.2
Haryana	0.0	42.9	27.8	32.1
Manipur	4.3	41.6	20.3	13.5
Orissa	19.5	36.2	27.0	26.7
Tripura	20.4	33.5	35.3	30.7
West Bengal	23.4	32.9	31.0	31.0
Rajasthan	7.3	28.1	12.5	14.7
Sikkim	25.7	26.7	30.9	29.1
Madhya Pradesh	18.1	25.0	23.8	22.8
Jharkhand	14.7	23.5	18.4	17.6
Uttar Pradesh	37.7	22.9	16.5	18.4
Chhattisgarh	11.6	20.8	20.4	17.1
Assam	12.9	20.5	18.7	18.2
Himachal Pradesh	12.8	19.2	22.2	20.8
Uttaranchal	2.3	18.5	17.9	17.8
Jammu & Kashmir	0.0	15.4	6.5	7.7
Nagaland	7.5		39.8	9.7
Goa	100.0		60.8	62.1
India	23.6	41.0	29.3	31.2

Source: Computed from unit-level data, NSSO (2003a) and NSSO (2003b).

and Himachal Pradesh. In West Bengal, 31 per cent of households did not operate land. This is close to the national average. However, the proportion of *landless* Dalit households in West Bengal is below the national average in respect of operational holdings and of ownership holdings.

Index of Access

To measure the inequality in access to productive land across different social groups I have used a simple index of access.[2] The access index is defined as the ratio of the share of total land owned by group *j* to the share

---

[2] See, for example, K. Nagaraj, cited in Ramachandran (1990).

of this group in total number of households. Thus, the index of access to land for Dalits, denoted as A_D, can be represented as:

A_D = Percentage of total land owned by Dalit households / Percentage of Dalit households in total households

The value of the access index ranges between 0 and ∞. If A_D takes the value 1, it represents a situation where the access of Dalit households to land is in proportion to the share of Dalit households in the population. Where the access index is less than 1, it represents a situation in which the proportion of Dalit households in the population is greater than the share of total land Dalit households own.

TABLE 2 *Index of access to operational holding, by social group, 2002–03 (kharif season)*

State	Adivasi	Dalit	Other Castes
Nagaland	1.07	0.00	0.01
Mizoram	1.01	0.00	0.50
Goa	0.00	0.00	1.03
Meghalaya	1.06	0.01	0.54
Punjab	0.10	0.05	1.60
Haryana	0.01	0.13	1.37
Arunachal Pradesh	1.12	0.19	0.60
Kerala	0.81	0.29	1.10
Bihar	0.95	0.30	1.22
Andhra Pradesh	1.83	0.33	1.14
Tamil Nadu	1.28	0.35	1.23
Maharashtra	0.74	0.38	1.20
Manipur	1.23	0.39	0.83
Jharkhand	1.30	0.40	0.93
Karnataka	0.93	0.43	1.14
Madhya Pradesh	0.80	0.49	1.25
Uttar Pradesh	0.48	0.52	1.19
Gujarat	0.56	0.53	1.23
Rajasthan	0.54	0.56	1.27
Sikkim	1.22	0.56	0.94
Orissa	1.11	0.64	1.07
Tripura	1.35	0.65	0.95
Himachal Pradesh	1.01	0.66	1.11
Chhattisgarh	1.14	0.70	0.98
Assam	1.39	0.87	0.97
Uttaranchal	2.52	0.88	1.01
West Bengal	0.98	0.90	1.05
Jammu & Kashmir	0.74	1.11	0.98
India	**1.14**	**0.44**	**1.16**

Source: Computed from unit-level data, NSSO (2003a) and NSSO (2003b).

I have calculated the access indices from unit-level data on household operational holdings from the 59th round L&LH survey (Table 2).

The index of access to operational holding is 1.16 for non-Dalit/ Adivasi households, and only 0.44 for Dalit households (Table 2) – numbers that illustrate the inequality between the two social groups very clearly. The data indicate that the access index for land for cultivation in West Bengal is 0.9, which is double the all-India average. Comparing the values of this index across different States, we find that West Bengal is second only to Jammu & Kashmir. For Adivasi households, however, the index value in West Bengal is 0.98, which is lower than the national average of 1.14.

Access to Land: Results from Primary Data for West Bengal

The preceding analysis shows that West Bengal stands out from other high agricultural growth States in India with respect to the *social* distribution of land. The agricultural growth experience in West Bengal was quite distinct from the all-India experience. Agriculture in West Bengal stagnated for three decades, from the 1950s to the early years of the 1980s (Boyce 1987). Agrarian conditions in the State were characterized by backwardness in relations of production, high levels of socio-economic inequality and stagnation of forces of production (Mishra and Rawal 2002). From the early 1980s onwards, Bengal came out of the 'agricultural impasse' (the term is from Boyce 1987) with agricultural output showing marked growth (Swaminathan and Saha 1994; Sen and Sengupta 1995; Swaminathan and Rawal 1998; Sanyal, Biswas and Bardhan 1998). Growth of agricultural production in the State decelerated, however, in the 1990s (Ramachandran, Swaminathan and Bakshi 2009; Bhattacharyya and Bhattacharyya 2007; Chattopadhyay 2005; Swaminathan and Rawal 1998; Ramachandran, Rawal and Swaminathan 2002).

The distribution of ownership and operational holdings of land in West Bengal is more equal than in other States of India. Most of the agricultural land in the State is owned and operated by small and marginal farmers. According to NSSO estimates for 2002–03, of the total households with ownership holdings in West Bengal, 98 per cent were marginal and small farmers, and the holdings they owned was 84 per cent of total ownership holdings. The NSS data record no large landowners in West Bengal (NSSO 2006a).[3] NSSO estimates of the Gini coefficients of distribution of operational holdings of land in fifteen States of India for 2002–03 show West Bengal as having the lowest concentration of operational holdings (NSSO 2006b).

Institutional transformation in the countryside was a major feature of rural change in West Bengal. While rural policy concentrated on agricultural growth in most parts of India, development planning in West Bengal since 1977 emphasized, for an extended period, land reform and the decentraliza-

---

[3] By the NSSO's definition, marginal farmers own up to 1 hectare of land, small farmers 1–4 hectares, medium farmers 4–10 hectares, and large farmers, above 10 hectares.

tion of power and resources to institutions of local government, as well as production growth. West Bengal is a State where policy efforts have been directed to distribute land to the landless and the poor, and specifically to Dalits, Adivasis and other deprived social groups, and also to issue joint title-deeds to men and women. Some of the social-distributive effects of the land reform programme show up in recent village-based research and analyses of secondary data. These show that West Bengal is ahead of other States with respect to distribution of agricultural and homestead land to Dalit and Adivasi households, and also with respect to purchase of agricultural land by the rural poor, including Dalit households (Mishra and Rawal 2002; Rawal 2001).

The non-farm sector plays an important role in the rural economy of West Bengal. The proportion of non-agricultural workers in rural West Bengal increased from 29.3 per cent of all workers in 1991 to 41.6 per cent in 2001 (Census 2001). NSS Employment and Unemployment Survey estimates after 1980 indicate that West Bengal has a higher proportion of rural non-agricultural workers than all other States in India, with the exception of Kerala (Chandrasekhar 1993; Bhaumik 2002).

Village-Level Data

In this section I examine specific features of the ownership of agricultural land by Dalit, Adivasi and Other households from village-level data collected from different parts of West Bengal. The village-level data come mainly from a series of surveys conducted in May–June 2005 in seven villages in different agro-climatic zones in West Bengal: Dalkati in West Medinipur district, Bidyanidhi and Kalinagar in Barddhaman, Kalmandasguri in Koch Bihar, Amarsinghi in Malda, Thuthipakar in Uttar Dinajpur, and Tentultala in North 24 Parganas.[4]

Dalkati, located in the red laterite zone of West Medinipur district, has a population that is predominantly Adivasi. Levels of agricultural productivity in the village are low, and since it is situated on the fringes of a forest, collection of forest produce forms an important source of livelihood. Bidyanidhi and Kalinagar are in Barddhaman district, where paddy yields have traditionally been high. Kalmandasguri in Koch Bihar district and Amarsinghi in Malda district are villages where paddy and jute cultivation predominates, and where mechanization (other than energization of well irrigation) is low. Thuthipakar is a village in Uttar Dinajpur where the cropping pattern recently shifted from paddy to tea and pineapple. Tentultala, in the estuarine region of North 24 Parganas, also witnessed major changes in cropping pattern in recent years. Cultivation in the village has shifted from paddy to prawn cultivation.

While Dalkati village in West Medinipur district did not have a Dalit population (Table 3), in the other villages Dalits constituted over 30 per cent of all households. Tentultala and Kalmandasguri each had a significant

---

[4] The survey was directed by V.K. Ramachandran and Vikas Rawal.

TABLE 3　*Social composition of the study villages, West Bengal, May–June 2005*

Village	District	As percentage of total households			
		Dalit	Adivasi	Muslim	Others
Dalkati	West Medinipur	–	69.3	–	30.7
Bidyanidhi	Barddhaman	47.9	–	18.3	33.8
Kalinagar	Barddhaman	32.8	38.8	–	28.4
Kalmandasguri	Koch Bihar	46.1	5.5	39.8	8.6
Amarsinghi	Malda	43.0	0.9	–	56.1
Thuthipakar	Uttar Dinajpur	36.2	55.9	–	7.9
Tentultala	North 24 Parganas	39.0	0.4	59.4	1.2

Source:　Survey data.

TABLE 4　*Index of access to agricultural land (ownership holdings), by social group*

Village		Access index – ownership holdings			
		Dalit	Adivasi	Muslim	Others
Tentultala	North 24 Parganas	1.5	5.8	0.6	2.3
Kalmandasguri	Koch Bihar	1.4	1.2	0.5	1.1
Thuthipakar	Uttar Dinajpur	1.3	0.8		1.4
Amarsinghi	Malda	0.5	0.0		1.4
Kalinagar	Barddhaman	0.3	0.3		2.8
Bidyanidhi	Barddhaman	0.2		0.4	2.4
Dalkati	West Medinipur		0.6		1.8

Source:　Survey data.

TABLE 5　*Index of access to agricultural land (operational holdings), by social group[5]*

Village	District	Access index – operational holdings			
		Dalit	Adivasi	Muslim	Others
Tentultala	N 24 Parganas	1.6	2.2	0.6	0.0
Kalmandasguri	Koch Bihar	1.5	1.3	0.5	0.7
Thuthipakar	Uttar Dinajpur	1.4	0.8		1.1
Amarsinghi	Malda	0.7	0.0		1.3
Kalinagar	Barddhaman	0.5	0.4		2.4
Bidyanidhi	Barddhaman	0.3		0.4	2.4
Dalkati	West Medinipur		0.6		1.9

Source:　Survey data.

[5] Muslim households are treated as a separate social group because there are considerable differences between them and Other non-Dalit non-Adivasi households in terms of economic conditions and access to land.

Muslim population, and Thuthipakar and Kalinagar each had a significant Adivasi population.

In three of the seven villages, the index of access to agricultural land of Dalit households was greater than 1 (Table 4). The index value was 1.49, 1.28 and 1.41 in Tentultala, Thuthipakar and Kalmandasguri repectively. In other words, in these villages the share of Dalits in land ownership was greater than their share in the population. In the two villages of Barddhaman district, the index values for Dalits were as low as 0.2 and 0.3. In Tentultala, Kalmandasguri and Bidyanidhi, Muslim households constituted a substantial part of the population, but the index value for Muslims was low.

The access index for operational holdings of land is shown in Table 5. In each of the seven villages, the index value of operational holdings for Dalit households was marginally higher than the corresponding index for ownership holdings. This indicates that tenancy has helped Dalit households gain access to operational holdings of land. The case of Tentultala is interesting. Here, the extension of prawn cultivation has had a striking effect on the pattern of land distribution. Operational holdings in Tentultala are highly concentrated in the hands of a few prawn-tank owners who lease in most of the village land for prawn cultivation. The tank owners in the village belong to Dalit and Muslim households, and that is reflected in the new position of these two social groups with respect to land.

To sum up, in three of the six villages with a Dalit population, the value of the access index for Dalits was greater than 1.

Participation of Dalits and Adivasis in Agrarian Struggles in West Bengal

Results from secondary and primary data show that Dalit households in West Bengal have better access to agricultural land than their counterparts in other parts of India. This is a direct outcome of land reform measures in the State, of which Dalits and Adivasis were the major beneficiaries. The programmes of land reform and decentralization of administrative and political power in rural Bengal that were implemented in the 1970s were a culmination of peasant struggles and organized peasant movements in the region since the 1930s. This section briefly revisits the major agrarian struggles in Bengal, and assesses the participation of Dalits and Adivasis in these movements.

The history of pre-independence peasant movements in Bengal cannot be dissociated from the history of the Kisan Sabha, which took a leading role in organizing the peasantry and voicing their demands in the larger political sphere. The Kisan Sabha was established in the mid-1930s.[6] In its initial years, it was a multi-party organization drawing members from among the Socialists, Communists and the Congress (Sen 1972). However, the Kisan Sabha gradually lost its political base among other parties and in 1945, after

---

[6] The Congress Socialist Party (CSP) took a leading role in the formation of the Kisan Sabha. The All India Kisan Committee (later renamed the Kisan Sabha) was formed at the All India Kisan Congress held at Meerut on 11 April 1936 (Sen 1972).

the exit of Swami Sahajananda as its president, Communists predominated in the leadership (ibid.).

At one of the first meetings of the All India Kisan Congress (later renamed Kisan Sabha) held in Meerut in 1936, the fundamental demand raised was abolition of zamindari and recognition of ownership rights to land of the actual tillers of the land. Other demands included moratorium on debts, abolition of land revenue and rent on uneconomic holdings, reduction of land revenue and rents, licensing moneylenders, and minimum wages for agricultural workers (ibid.). The demands raised by the Bengal Provincial Kisan Sabha sought to reconcile the common interests of all sections of the peasantry and agricultural workers, and to 'unite Hindus and Scheduled Castes, Muslims, Rajbansis and tribals in a common organization to realize common demands' (ibid.). This feature of the Kisan Sabha is perhaps crucial in explaining why the mobilization of peasants and agricultural workers on demands associated with the status and rights of specific oppressed castes did not take place in West Bengal in the same way as in other States of India.

Organized peasant movements in West Bengal since the mid-1930s can be divided into three phases: movements before Tebhaga, the Tebhaga movement, and movements for implementation of land reforms after independence.

Peasant Movements before Tebhaga

Immediately after the establishment of the All India Kisan Sabha, provincial Kisan Sabhas were set up in the districts of Bengal. The provincial Kisan Sabhas were particularly active in Dinajpur, Jalpaiguri, Rangpur (now part of Bangladesh) in the northern part of Bengal, Barddhaman, Birbhum, 24 Parganas, Hooghly and Medinipur. The provincial Kisan Sabhas led active movements in different parts of Bengal, organizing the peasantry against landlords and moneylenders, against government policies, and raising region-specific demands. Some of the well-known interventions by the provincial Kisan Sabhas in Bengal were the mobilization of small peasants against 'haat tola', a market tax imposed by landlords on produce sold by farmers at markets in Dinajpur, Jalpaiguri and Rangpur; for lowering the interest rates of 'karja' or paddy loans taken by sharecroppers from landlords at the beginning of the agricultural season and repaid after harvest; and against the increase in canal tax in the Damodar Canal area in Barddhaman district in 1938–39 (Sen 1972; interview with Benoy Konar, 4 November 2010). In 1939 the Kisan Sabha also submitted a memorandum to the Floud Commission stating the problems of agriculture and the land system in Bengal, and advocating abolition of the zamindari system (Sen 1972).[7]

Between 1942 and 1943, Bengal was plagued by natural disasters

---

[7] The Floud Commission was set up by the Fazlul Haque ministry in 1938 to enquire into the problems of land revenue administration in Bengal. The Commission submitted its report in 1940, recommending abolition of the Permanent Settlement and all rent-receiving interests in Bengal.

and famines. During these years the Kisan Sabha worked extensively for disaster and famine relief. Community kitchens were set up in villages, and '*dharma-gola*' or common granaries were organized for storage of paddy. During this period of scarcity, for the first time, landlords began hoarding paddy for capitalist gains, and stopped advancing paddy loans or *karja* to share-croppers. The Kisan Sabha campaigned against the hoarding of paddy and embarked on a 'grow more food' campaign (Sen 1972; interview with Benoy Konar, 4 November 2010).

All the demands raised by the Kisan Sabha were for the peasantry as a whole. There were no specific demands for Dalit or Adivasi peasants and agricultural labourers. However, because Dalit and Adivasi peasants and workers formed the bulk of the rural population in large parts of Bengal, the Kisan Sabha drew its strength from these Dalit and Adivasi masses – and rural Muslim masses – in the province. The Kisan Sabha was particularly strong in Dinajpur district, where the Rajbanshi and Adivasi populations were in the majority (Singha Roy 1999). In March 1946, Rupnarayan Ray, a poor Rajbanshi peasant, was elected to the Legislative Assembly from Dinajpur.[8]

The Tebhaga Movement

The Tebhaga movement was the first State-wide movement organized by the Kisan Sabha in Bengal. One of the recommendations of the Floud Commission, whose report was submitted in 1940, was a reduction in the landlord's share of the produce in sharecropped areas to one-third, leaving a two-thirds share for the *bargadar* or sharecropper. In September 1946, the Bengal Provincial Kisan Sabha organized the first State-wide struggle for *tebhaga* or two-thirds share for the sharecropper, as recommended by the Floud Commission (Sen 1972). The demand for *tebhaga* received support from both peasants and sharecroppers, and the movement quickly spread from the districts of North Bengal to East Bengal, and Medinipur, Birbhum, Hooghly, Howrah and 24 Parganas in southern Bengal (Sen 1972; interviews with Benoy Konar and Shibdas Bhattacharya, 4 November 2010). Sharecroppers started taking the harvested paddy to their own threshing floors for division of the produce. According to Sen (1972), 'by the middle of December the agrarian struggle had spread to eleven districts and lakhs of *bargadar*s had carried the crop to their *khamar*'. As the movement gained momentum, it faced stiff resistance from landlords and the police (ibid.; Singha Roy 1999).

The Rajbanshi and Namashudra peasantry were the fighting force of the Tebhaga movement (interview with Benoy Konar, 4 November 2010). The Dalit and Adivasi peasants of Dinajpur and adjoining districts had a very strong presence within the Kisan Sabha, and they not only participated but also gave leadership to the Tebhaga movement in the region. The movement

---

[8] Three Communists were elected to the Legislative Assembly that year; the other two were Jyoti Basu and Ratanlal Brahman (Sen 1972).

spontaneously spread to the Dooars region in North Bengal, where Santhal and Oraon sharecroppers cultivated reclaimed forest land owned by Muslim *jotedars*. The peasants of the Dooars received support from tea-garden workers, who were also Adivasis (Sen 1972: 52–57). In Medinipur, the sharecroppers were mostly Dalits and Adivasis. The Tebhaga movement gained their support and it spread to different pockets of the district (ibid.: 43–44). In 24 Parganas, where reclaimed coastal land was auctioned off in 'lots' to *lotdars*, and was cultivated by Dalit and Adivasi sharecroppers, these groups also participated in the movement (interview with Shibdas Bhattacharya, 4 November 2010). Many of the peasants who lost their lives to landlord and police atrocities during the Tebhaga struggle were Dalit and Adivasi members of the movement.

As the Tebhaga movement intensified, the Muslim League government promised to introduce a Bargadar Bill to legislate a two-thirds share of the produce of sharecropped land for the tenant. However, no such Bill materialized, and the agrarian struggle was crushed with severe police repression, mass arrests of peasants and Kisan Sabha activists, and eviction of sharecroppers by landlords (Sen 1972).

In April 1947, the government introduced the State Acquisition and Tenancy Bill for abolition of zamindari in Bengal. It sought to impose a ceiling on landholdings of zamindars of up to 100 *bigha*s per family or 10 *bigha*s per head. The remaining land was to be purchased by the state at a fair price. Ceiling-surplus land was also to be redistributed to landless peasants to the extent that the size of the holdings remained economic. The Bill did not deal with the rights of sharecroppers. The Congress Party effectively opposed the Bill by walking out of the Legislative Assembly and not participating in the debate (ibid.: 74–76).

Implementation of Land Reforms in West Bengal after Independence

After independence, although land reform Acts were passed in all the States of India, implementation of these Acts was limited. In West Bengal, despite the West Bengal Estates Acquisition Act being passed in 1953 and the West Bengal Land Reforms Act in 1954, they were not implemented till the United Front government came to power in 1967 (Mukherjee 1973).[9] In the one-and-a-half years that the United Front was in power, 153,178 acres of land were vested with the government. However, its efforts to redistribute the land met with resistance from landowners, who obtained injunctions from the court. It was then that Harekrishna Konar, Minister for Land and Land Revenue, called for active help from the peasantry for implementing the land

---

[9] The major constituents of the United Front government of 1967 were the Bangla Congress, the Communist Party of India (Marxist) (CPI[M]), the Communist Party of India (CPI) and the Forward Bloc, with Ajoy Mukherjee of the Bangla Congress as Chief Minister and Jyoti Basu of the CPI(M) as Deputy Chief Minister.

reform programme in the State. With the support of the government, peasants started to cultivate the ceiling-surplus land and harvest the produce (ibid.).

The United Front government was dissolved in March 1969. The Left Front government came to power eight years later, in 1977. The land reforms programme was a major development effort taken up by the Left Front government in West Bengal. Land reforms in West Bengal had three components: tenancy reforms, redistribution of ceiling-surplus land to the landless and the poor, and distribution of homestead land.

The programme was implemented within the framework of existing laws. The only changes made to the West Bengal Land Reforms Act (1954) were adjustment of ceiling limits according to family size of the cultivator, and inclusion of water bodies and orchards within the ceiling limits.[10] However, the unique feature of implementation of the land reform programme in West Bengal was active participation of the peasantry in identifying ceiling-surplus and *benami* land, and identifying beneficiaries for land distribution (see Bandyopadhyay 2000; Mukherjee 1973). The struggles of peasants in Bengal since the mid-1930s thus came to fruition.

The land reform programme of the Left Front government in West Bengal brought land to new sections of the peasantry (Mishra and Rawal 2002). As on February 2008, about 1,122,116 acres of land had been redistributed to 2,971,875 million landless and marginal-cultivator households. This constituted 22.6 per cent of the total land distributed in all of India (Ramachandran 2008). After 1994–95, joint title-deeds were issued to cultivators who acquired land through redistribution. In many cases, title-deeds were issued singly in favour of women. The total number of recorded *bargadar*s under 'Operation Barga' in 2008 was 1.51 million (ibid.). By 2003, according to State government estimates, 86 per cent of *bargadar*s in West Bengal had been registered (Government of West Bengal 2004: 31–32).

Though beneficiaries of land reforms were not identified on the basis of caste, Dalit and Adivasi households were the major beneficiaries as they formed a significant section of landless and small peasants in the State. In a State where 23 per cent of the population is Dalit and 5.5 per cent Adivasi (Census of India 2001), of the new title-deed holders, 37 per cent were Dalits and 19 per cent were Adivasis (Government of West Bengal 2006). The social-distributive effects of the land reform programme are well acknowledged. The *West Bengal Human Development Report 2004* states that 'the disproportionate granting of *patta* rights to Scheduled Castes and Tribes is likely to have led not just to some degree of economic empowerment, but also a greater sense of social dignity as well' (Government of West Bengal 2004: 39).

---

[10] See Sections 14L, 14M, and Section 2 Clause 7 of the West Bengal Land Reforms Act, 1954. These sections were amended by the West Bengal Land Reforms (Amendment) Act, 1972, and West Bengal Land Reforms (Amendment) Act, 1981, respectively. See also Ghosh and Nagaraj (1978).

Class and Caste in Peasant Movements in Bengal

Class was the basis of peasant mobilization in the organized peasant movements of West Bengal. The two major demands raised by these agrarian struggles were the abolition of zamindari and an increase in the sharecropper's share of output. Describing the positions taken by different classes in Bengal towards agrarian struggles, Sen (1972) writes that although the peasants were not an undifferentiated category, with respect to abolition of zamindari the class interests of all sections of the peasantry were the same. The Tebhaga movement, on the other hand, was for the rights of the sharecropper, and therefore sharecroppers played the leading role in the movement. Agricultural workers also participated in large numbers, since this class 'shared with the *bargadar* a common hatred against the *jotedar* who had grabbed his land'. Middle peasants also supported the movement (ibid.: 81–83).

Dalits and Adivasis, who formed a dominant section of poor peasants, sharecroppers and agricultural workers in West Bengal, participated in the agrarian struggles in a big way. According to Benoy Konar, the social empowerment of Dalits and Adivasis in West Bengal was achieved through the historical role played by them in anti-feudal agrarian struggles and for the economic empowerment of the rural working masses. Land reforms and the participation of Dalits and Adivasis in local decision-making through panchayats also played a role in weakening traditional caste relations in Bengal (interview with Benoy Konar, 4 November 2010; see also Bandopadhyaya 2002).

On the Contribution of Land Reforms: Results from Primary Data

The analysis of village-level data from seven selected villages in West Bengal in this section deals with the distribution of ceiling-surplus land and homestead land. First, let us consider the redistribution of crop land to the landless and rural poor. Table 6 shows that the implementation of land reforms varied across the seven villages. In Dalkati almost 60 per cent of households received agricultural land, while in Thuthipakar only 7 per cent of households benefited from redistribution of agricultural land. This included households that obtained *patta*s directly and households that inherited assigned land. In terms of the land area redistributed, the highest was in Dalkati, where 32 per cent of the total area of household ownership holdings was acquired in the course of land reforms. The area of redistributed land was lowest in Bidyanidhi, where only 1.9 per cent of total agricultural land owned was redistributed land.[11] It is interesting to note that not one of the study villages was untouched by land reforms.

---

[11] Though the area redistributed in Bidyanidhi was only 2 per cent of total area of ownership holdings, nearly 20 per cent of the households acquired land. This reflects a situation where, even when there is a demand for land and a political will to redistribute land, the availability of ceiling-surplus land that can be acquired and redistributed poses a problem.

TABLE 6 *Redistribution of agricultural land in the study villages till May–June 2005*

Village	District	Number of assignees	Share of assignees in total households	Area of agricultural land redistributed (in acres)	Share of redistributed land in total ownership holdings
Dalkati	West Medinipur	107	59.8	47.3	32.0
Kalinagar	Barddhaman	27	40.3	4.5	13.6
Amarsinghi	Malda	33	30.8	11.6	15.0
Kalmandasguri	Koch Bihar	36	28.1	16.9	18.2
Bidyanidhi	Barddhaman	28	19.7	2.8	1.9
Tentultala	North 24 Parganas	19	7.6	5.5	3.6
Thuthipakar	Upper Dinajpur	9	7.1	9.7	8.8

Source: Survey data.

TABLE 7 *Shares of different social groups in agricultural land distributed in the study villages till May–June 2005*

Village	District	Percentage of total agricultural land redistributed				Total land distributed (in acres)
		Dalit	Adivasi	Muslim	Others	
Dalkati	West Medinipur		73.2		26.8	47.26
Kalmandasguri	Koch Bihar	18.9	24.7	39.5	16.8	19.01
Amarsinghi	Malda	25.9	0.0		74.1	11.64
Thuthipakar	Upper Dinajpur	8.4	45.4		46.3	9.72
Tentultala	North 24 Parganas	70.8	0.0	29.2	0.0	6.50
Kalinagar	Barddhaman	39.2	50.2		10.6	4.52
Bidyanidhi	Barddhaman	82.1		17.9	0.0	2.80

Source: Survey data.

The major beneficiaries of the distribution of agricultural land in the study villages have been Dalit and Adivasi households, and, in Kalmandasguri, Muslim households (Table 7). In Dalkati, Tentultala, Kalinagar and Bidyanidhi, more than 70 per cent of the agricultural land redistributed was assigned to Dalit and Adivasi households. In Kalmandasguri, 40 per cent of the redistributed agricultural land was assigned to Muslim households, and another 43 per cent to Dalit and Adivasi households. In two of the villages, Thuthipakar and Amarsinghi, where the major beneficiaries were non-Dalits, most of the non-Dalit households who were assigned land belonged to Other Backward Classes (OBCs).[12]

Secondly, let us consider the distribution of house-site or homestead land, which is an important component of land reforms in West Bengal. Access

---

[12] The OBC households in Amarsinghi primarily belonged to the Tantubai Tanti caste. These are income-poor migrant households from Bangladesh who were resettled in this village.

to homestead land is also an important aspect of land ownership in India as a whole. Ownership of homestead land means not only a place to live and a changed position in society, but also access to a source of potential nutrition and livelihood support as a result of kitchen-garden cultivation (see, for instance, Government of Tripura 2007). Absence of ownership of a house-site is often a key factor in the unfreedom of peasant and agricultural worker households in India (see the discussion of this dimension in Ramachandran 1990).

In all seven study villages, Muslim, Dalit and Adivasi households were the major beneficiaries of homestead land distribution (Table 8). Out of 210 households that gained homestead land, 23 per cent were Dalit, 46 per cent were Adivasi, 24 per cent were Muslim, and 8 per cent belonged to Other Caste groups. Of the last group, a majority were OBCs. An important feature of the distribution of homestead land in Kalmandasguri, Thuthipakar and Dalkati was that the size of homesteads was larger in these villages than in the others. The average size of homesteads distributed per household in these villages was 0.13 acre, 0.15 acre and 0.17 acre, respectively. Larger homesteads allow for kitchen-garden cultivation and rearing backyard poultry, both common in these villages. Such activities enhance household incomes and nutritional standards.

Thirdly, let us consider the impact of Operation Barga in the seven villages. Incidence of tenancies was low in the villages, except in Tentultala (Table 9). Of the 80 tenant households in Tentultala, 61 households (76 per cent) recorded *barga* land. Most of the tenancies in the other villages were unregistered seasonal contracts.

Tentultala, a prawn-cultivating village, was exceptional in terms of its land relations. In this village, large tracts of agricultural land were leased in by a few prawn farmers and converted to fisheries (see Rawal 2006). Of the total land owned by households in the village, 87 per cent was leased out to prawn farmers. Even registered *barga* lands were sub-leased for prawn-farming, and the rent received was shared equally between landowner and sharecropper. Of the 33 acres of *barga* land in the village, 31.8 acres were leased out to prawn farmers (ibid.).

Table 10 shows the distribution of recorded *bargadar*s in the study villages, by social group. It is important to note that of the 71 recorded *bargadar*s in the seven villages, all but one were either Dalit (42 per cent), Muslim (53 per cent) or Adivasi (3 per cent). Only one household belonging to Other Backward Classes in Amarsinghi had *barga* rights.

In fact, among all the tenant households in the study villages, 45 per cent were Dalit, 40 per cent Muslim and 5 per cent Adivasi. Only 10 per cent were non-Dalit/non-Adivasi households. Dalit and Muslim households had gained access to land through tenancy contracts in the study villages. This is apparent from the higher value of the access index of operational holdings than of ownership holdings for these social groups in our earlier analysis.

TABLE 8 *Share of different social groups in homestead land distributed in the study villages till May–June 2005*

Village	District	Percentage of total assignees				Number of total assignees
		Dalit	Adivasi	Muslim	Others	
Dalkati	West Medinipur		90.5		9.5	74
Bidyanidhi	Barddhaman	50.0		0	50.0	4
Kalinagar	Barddhaman	41.7	58.3		0.0	24
Amarsinghi	Malda	80.0	5.0		15.0	20
Tentulata	North 24 Parganas	13.6	0.0	86.4	0.0	22
Kalmandasguri	Koch Bihar	24.5	9.4	58.5	7.5	53
Thuthipakar	Upper Dinajpur	30.8	69.2		0.0	13
All villages		22.9	45.7	23.8	7.6	210

Source: Survey data.

TABLE 9 *Number of registered tenant households and extent under registered tenancies in the study villages, May–June 2005*

Village	No. of registered tenant households	Total no. of tenant households	Extent under registered tenancy (in acres)	Total extent under tenancy (in acres)
Dalkati	0	5	0.00	1.40
Kalinagar	0	8		3.20
Bidyanidhi	2	16	1.50	6.79
Thuthipakar	1	12	2.60	8.50
Kalmandasguri	3	24	6.08	14.51
Amarsinghi	4	14	2.16	27.17
Tentultala	61	80	33.17	222.96

Source: Survey data.

TABLE 10 *Distribution of recorded tenants by social group, study villages, May–June 2005*

Village	Dalit	Adivasi	Muslim	Others	All
Dalkati	–	0	–	0	0
Kalinagar	0	0	–	0	0
Thuthipakar	0	1	0	0	1
Bidyanidhi	1	–	1	0	2
Kalmandasguri	2	1	0	0	3
Amarsinghi	3	–	0	1	4
Tentultala	24	0	37	0	61
All	30	2	38	1	71

Source: Survey data.

Conclusion

The exclusion faced by Dalits in terms of access to basic economic resources remains a reality in contemporary India. In particular, the right of the Dalit masses to productive resources such as land has generally been left unattended if not grossly violated, since access to land demands deep and radical changes in the social structure. West Bengal is one State in India where efforts have been made to grant land rights to landless households, especially Dalit and Adivasi households. The impact of land reforms in West Bengal is reflected in national-level statistics on landholdings.

Secondary data show that Dalit households in West Bengal have better access to land than in other States. This is indicated by the fact that the proportion of landless Dalit households in terms of operational holdings is lower in West Bengal than the national average, and that their index of access to agricultural land is higher than the national average.

Village-level data show that Dalit, Adivasi and Muslim households have been significant beneficiaries of land reforms in West Bengal. These social groups have gained access to agricultural and homestead land through the process of land reforms. Though cases of tenancy were few in the study villages except for one village, the majority of sharecroppers in the villages were Dalits and Muslims. Dalit and Muslim households also gained access to land through seasonal tenancies. The policy of land reform implemented by the West Bengal government has thus contributed, though in a limited way, to lowering inequalities across social groups in the State.

The land reform programme implemented in West Bengal was a result of agrarian struggles in the State since the mid-1930s. The Dalit and Adivasi populations in West Bengal were historically involved in these agrarian struggles. The participation of Dalits and Adivasis in the economic struggles against pre-capitalist relations of production played no small role in the social empowerment of these groups.

This essay draws upon Bakshi (2008). I am grateful to V.K. Ramachandran and Madhura Swaminathan for their comments and advice on this essay. I am thankful to Vikas Rawal for his suggestions regarding National Sample Survey data, and to V.K. Ramachandran and Vikas Rawal for the West Bengal survey data used here. I interviewed Benoy Konar and Shibdas Bhattacharya on 4 November 2010. This essay draws heavily on these interviews, and I am grateful to them for their time and patience. I am also grateful to Madan Ghosh for his help.

References

Athreya, Venkatesh (2003), 'Redistributive Land Reforms in India: Some Reflections in the Current Context', paper presented at the All India Conference on Agriculture and Rural Society in Contemporary India, Barddhaman, West Bengal, 17–20 December.

Bagchi, Amiya Kumar (2003), 'Agrarian Transformation and Human Development: Instrumental and Constitutive Links', in V.K. Ramachandran and Madhura Swaminathan, eds, *Agrarian Studies: Essays on Agrarian Relations in Less-Developed Countries*, Tulika Books, New Delhi.

Bakshi, Aparajita (2008), 'Social Inequality in Land Ownership in India: A Study with Particular Reference to West Bengal', *Social Scientist*, vol. 35, nos. 9–10, pp. 95–116.

Bandopadhyaya, Jayantanuja (2002), 'Class Struggle and Caste Oppression: Integral Strategy of the Left', *The Marxist*, vol. 18, nos. 3–4, July–December.

Bandyopadhyay, D. (2000), 'Land Reform in West Bengal: Remembering Hare Krishna Konar and Benoy Chaudhury', *Economic and Political Weekly*, vol. 35, nos. 21–22, pp. 1795–97.

Bhattacharyya, Maumita and Bhattacharyya, Sudipta (2007), 'Agrarian Impasse in West Bengal in the Liberalization Era', *Economic and Political Weekly*, vol. 42, no. 52, pp. 65–71.

Bhaumik, Shankar Kumar (2002), 'Employment Diversification in Rural India: A State Level Analysis', *The Indian Journal of Labour Economics*, vol. 45, no. 4.

Boyce, James K. (1987), *Agrarian Impasse in Bengal*, Oxford University Press, New Delhi.

Chakrabarty, G. and Ghosh, P.K. (2000), *Human Development Profile of SCs and STs in Rural India*, National Council of Applied Economic Research, New Delhi.

Chandrasekhar, C.P. (1993), 'Agrarian Change and Occupational Diversification in Non-Agricultural Employment and Rural Development in West Bengal', *Journal of Peasant Studies*, vol. 20, no. 2, 5 February, pp. 205–70.

Chattopadhyay, Apurba Kumar (2005), 'Distributive Impact of Agricultural Growth in Rural West Bengal', *Economic and Political Weekly*, vol. 40, no. 53, pp. 5601–10.

Dreze, Jean and Sen, Amartya, eds (1996), *Indian Development: Selected Regional Perspectives*, Oxford University Press, New Delhi.

El-Ghonemy, M. Riad (2003), 'The Land Market Approach to Rural Development,' in V.K. Ramachandran and Madhura Swaminathan, eds, *Agrarian Studies: Essays on Agrarian Relations in Less-Developed Countries*, Tulika Books, New Delhi.

Ghosh, Jayati and Chandrasekhar, C.P. (2003), 'Why is Agricultural Employment Generation Falling?' *Macroscan*, available at http://www.macroscan.org/fet/apr03/print/prn-t220403Agricultural_Employment.htm, viewed on 10 September 2013.

Ghosh, Ratan and Nagaraj, K. (1978), 'Land Reforms in West Bengal', *Social Scientist*, vol. 6, nos. 6–7, pp. 50–67.

Government of Tripura (2007), *Tripura Human Development Report, 2007*, Government of Tripura, Agartala.

Government of West Bengal (2004), *West Bengal Human Development Report 2004*, Development and Planning Department, Government of West Bengal, Kolkata and United Nations Development Programme (UNDP).

Government of West Bengal (2006), *West Bengal Economic Review 2005–06*, Bureau of Applied Economics and Statistics, Government of West Bengal, Kolkata.

Jodhka, Surinder S. and Newman, Katherine (2007), 'In the Name of Globalization: Meritocracy, Productivity and the Hidden Language of Caste', *Economic and Political Weekly*, vol. 42, no. 41, 13 October, pp. 4125–32.

Mishra, Surjya Kanta and Rawal, Vikas (2002), 'Agrarian Relations in Contemporary West Bengal and Tasks for the Left', in V.K. Ramachandran and Madhura Swaminathan, eds, *Agrarian Studies: Essays on Agrarian Relations in Less-Developed Countries*, Tulika Books, New Delhi.

National Sample Survey Organization (NSSO) (2003a), *Household Ownership Holdings in India, 2003*, National Sample Survey 59th Round (January–December, 2003), Government of India, New Delhi.

National Sample Survey Organization (NSSO) (2003b), *Some Aspects of Operational Land Holdings in India, 2002–03*, National Sample Survey 59th Round (January–December 2003), NSS Report no. 492 (59/18.1/3), Government of India, New Delhi.

Ramachandran, V.K. (1980), *A Note on the Sources of Official Data on Land Holdings in Tamil Nadu*, Data Series No. 1, Madras Institute of Development Studies, Chennai.

Ramachandran, V.K. (1990), *Wage Labour and Unfreedom in Agriculture: An Indian Case Study*, Clarendon Press, Oxford.

Ramachandran, V.K. (1996), 'On Kerala's Development Achievements', in Jean Dreze and Amartya Sen (eds), *Indian Development: Selected Regional Perspectives*, Oxford University Press, New Delhi.

Ramachandran, V.K. (2008), 'Land Reform Continues in West Bengal', *The Hindu*, 22 August, available at http://www.thehindu.com/2008/08/22/stories/2008082255051100.htm, viewed on 11 September 2013.

Ramachandran, V.K. and Swaminathan, Madhura (2002), 'Introduction', in V.K. Ramachandran and Madhura Swaminathan, eds, *Agrarian Studies: Essays on Agrarian Relations in Less-Developed Countries*, Tulika Books, New Delhi.

Ramachandran, V.K., Swaminathan, Madhura and Bakshi, Aparajita (2010), 'Food Security and Crop Diversification: Can West Bengal Achieve Both?' in Banasri Basu, Bikas K. Chakrabarti, Satya R. Chakravarty and Kaushik Gangopadhyay, eds, *Econophysics and Economics of Games, Social Choices and Quantitative Technique*, Springer Verlag Italia, Milan.

Ramakumar, R. (2005), 'Socio-economic Characteristics of Agricultural Workers: A Case Study of a Village in the Malabar Region of Kerala', unpublished Ph.D. thesis submitted to Indian Statistical Institute, Kolkata.

Rawal, Vikas (2001), 'Agrarian Reform and Land Markets: A Study of Land Transactions in Two Villages in West Bengal, 1977–1995', *Economic Development and Cultural Change*, vol. 49, no. 3, April, pp. 611–29.

Rawal, Vikas, Swaminathan, Madhura and Ramachandran, V.K. (2002), 'Agriculture in West Bengal: Current Trends and Directions for Future Growth', background paper submitted for West Bengal State Development Report and Perspective, Kolkata.

Rawal, Vikas (2006), *Landlessness in Rural West Bengal*, report submitted to the Development and Planning Department, Government of West Bengal, Kolkata.

Rawal, Vikas (2008), 'Ownership Holdings of Land in Rural India: Putting the Record Straight', *Economic and Political Weekly*, vol. 43, no. 10, 8 March, pp. 43–48.

Roy, Singha and Debal, K. (1996), 'Land Reforms, Peasant Movements and Scheduled Castes: Issues of Social Justice and Empowerment', in Sanjeeb K. Behera, ed., *Dalits and Land Reforms in India*, Proceedings of the National Seminar on Land Reforms and Schedule Castes, organized by Indian Social Institute, New Delhi, 16–18 December, Indian Social Institute, New Delhi.

Sen, Abhijit and Sengupta, Ranja (1995), 'The Recent Growth in Agricultural Output in Eastern India, with Special Reference to the Case of West Bengal', paper presented at Workshop on Agricultural Growth and Agrarian Structure in Contemporary West Bengal and Bangladesh, Kolkata, January.

Swaminathan, Madhura and Rawal, Vikas (1998), 'Changing Trajectories: Agricultural Growth in West Bengal, 1950 to 1996', *Economic and Political Weekly*, vol. 33, no. 40, pp. 2595–2602.

Swaminathan, Madhura and Saha, Anamitra (1994), 'Agricultural Growth in West Bengal in the 1980s: A Disaggregation by Districts and Crops', *Economic and Political Weekly*, vol. 29, no. 13, 26 March, pp. A2–11.

Sen, Sunil (1972), *Agrarian Struggle in Bengal 1946–47*, People's Publishing House, New Delhi, Ahmedabad and Bombay.

Thorat, Sukhadeo (2002), 'Oppression and Denial: Dalit Discrimination in the 1990s', *Economic and Political Weekly*, vol. 37, no. 6, 9 February, pp. 572–78.

Thorat, Sukhadeo (2004), 'On Reservation Policy for Private Sector', *Economic and Political Weekly*, vol. 39, no. 25, 19 June, pp. 2560–63.

Thorat, Sukhadeo and Newman, Katherine (2007), 'Caste and Economic Discrimination: Causes, Consequences and Remedies', *Economic and Political Weekly*, vol. 42, no. 41, 13 October, pp. 4121–24.

Thorat, Sukhadeo and Attewell, Paul (2007), 'The Legacy of Social Exclusion: A Correspondence Study of Job Discrimination in India', *Economic and Political Weekly*, vol. 42, no. 41, 13 October, pp. 4141–45.

Thorat, Sukhadeo and Sabharwal, Nidhi Sadana (2005), 'Rural Non-farm Employment and Scheduled Castes: Activities, Education and Poverty Inter-linkages', in Rohini Nayyar and Alakh N. Sharma, eds, *Rural Transformation in India: The Role of Non-farm Sector*, Institute for Human Development, New Delhi.

Thorat, Sukhadeo, Mahamallik, M. and Sadana, Nidhi (2010), 'Caste System and Pattern of Discrimination in Rural Markets', in Sukhadeo Thorat and Katherine S. Newman, eds, *Blocked by Caste: Economic Discrimination in Modern India*, Oxford University Press, New Delhi.

Economic Issues in
Contemporary Village India

Dalit Households in Industrializing Villages in Coimbatore and Tiruppur, Tamil Nadu

A Comparison across Three Decades

Judith Heyer

This essay examines the conditions of life of Dalit households with respect to selected socio-economic variables over three decades in selected villages in Coimbatore (now Tiruppur) district in western Tamil Nadu.

Coimbatore district was an early industrializer, the industrialization process going back to the 1920s and 1930s. Its industrialization was linked with agriculture from the start: its textile industry depended on cotton, and its engineering enterprises produced textile machinery as well as pumps for agriculture. The industrial entrepreneurs came from the dominant agricultural castes, and the dominant agricultural castes provided much of the industrial labour force as well (Baker 1984; Chari 2004; and Damodaran 2008).

Capitalist agriculture in the area depended on lift irrigation, which relied on bullocks and leather buckets. The leather work was done by members of the Arunthathiyar (Chakkiliyar) community, one of the main Dalit communities in the region. With the mechanization of irrigation becoming widespread in the 1950s, Arunthathiyar workers shifted to agricultural field operations. As the demand for labour rose with the intensification of agriculture, Arunthathiyar households became the main source of agricultural labour power.

This essay deals with the socio-economic situation of Dalit households in the study villages with respect to four major variables: (1) landholdings, (2) occupations, (3) education, including literacy and schooling, and (4) the criminal practice of untouchability. The data cover the period 1981–82 to 2008–09.

The Database

This essay uses village-level data from Tiruppur district. Tiruppur was created as a separate district of Tamil Nadu in October 2008. Six taluks of Coimbatore district together with one or two taluks from Erode were included in the new district.

The data come from nine separate settlements in two revenue villages in Avinashi taluk, Coimbatore (now Tiruppur) district. All the hamlets in the first revenue village (there were four) were surveyed. The village had a population of 3,417 according to the 1981 Census, and comprised 75 per cent of the 1981–82 survey population. Five adjacent hamlets of the second revenue village, the total population of which was 3,348 in 1981, provided the remainder of the population covered by the study.

In the rest of the essay, I refer to the hamlets as 'villages'. The villages are 40 to 60 km north of Coimbatore, and 20 to 30 km north-east of Tiruppur. The villages are also 4 to 6 km from roads on which there were bus services in 1981, and 10 to 15 km from block and taluk offices in Avinashi town.

Systematic surveys were conducted in 1981–82, 1996 and 2008–09. These were supplemented by in-depth interviews in the survey years, and in 2003, 2004, 2010 and 2011.

The 1981–82 Dataset

A 20 per cent random sample of households drawn from the Census of India 1981 population returns was selected for the 1981–82 survey. For Dalit households in two of the hamlets the Census record was too inaccurate to use, so the settlements in which Dalits lived were mapped and Dalit households were selected on the basis of the maps.[1] There were a total of 230 households in the 1981–82 sample. I interviewed members of 119 of these households, using a check list rather than a questionnaire, and working with a research assistant (V. Mohanasundaram) trained to translate and not interpret what was being said. He then went on to do the remaining interviews on the basis of a questionnaire.

The sample interviews covered demographic information, and information on marriages and dowries. They covered land ownership and operation, and crops grown; wells and investment in wells; investment in houses and buildings, equipment, and machinery; and livestock. The interviews also covered the financing of all assets and the financing of consumption including health care. The focus throughout the sample interviews was on investment and capital accumulation. There were also retrospective questions on land inheritance, and on purchases and sales of land by household heads, their fathers and their grandfathers. There was one set of questions about employment for employers and another for employees. There were questions about employment and self-employment outside agriculture (although there were gaps in the data on female occupations). Finally, there were open-ended questions about the aspirations parents had for their children and the problems they themselves were facing at the time.

In addition to interviewing members of households in the sample, I interviewed all the large landholders, a group that was not numerous enough to be adequately represented in the sample. I also conducted selected interviews aimed at getting more information on specific issues not covered elsewhere.

---

[1] It subsequently became clear that the selection procedure used in conjunction with the maps led to under-representation of Arunthathiyar (Chakkiliyar) caste households in the sample.

Gounders were the most numerous of the landholders in the study villages in 1981–82 (Tables 1 and 2). Naidus were much less numerous but also had significant landholdings. Chettiars were the other major landholding group.[2] Chettiars were strongly represented in trade as well. The Other Caste groups represented in large numbers were the two Dalit groups among workers, Arunthathiyars (Chakkiliyar) and Pannadis.[3] A variety of Other Caste groups were represented in smaller numbers.

In 1981–82, the villages were predominantly agricultural. Caste was used as a means to exploit labour, particularly by Gounder, Chettiar and Naidu employers. The bulk of the village labour force was engaged in agriculture. Virtually all of the remainder was engaged in trade and services derivative of agriculture. Small numbers of sons in Naidu, Gounder and Chettiar households, and one or two from 'Other' castes were also working in mills, factories and workshops outside the villages in 1981–82. There were a small number of sons working in white-collar jobs outside the villages as well.

In 1981–82, land was still irrigated exclusively by deep open wells representing sizeable levels of investment. Bores had been sunk in some of these wells, the deepest of which were about 200 feet. Cotton, sugarcane and turmeric were the major irrigated crops, supplemented by groundnut, banana, tobacco, coconut, tapioca, chilli, mulberry, paddy, sorghum (*cholam*), finger millet (*ragi*), pearl millet (*cumbu*) and a variety of other cereals, vegetables and fruit. Sorghum, groundnut, sesame and a variety of pulses were grown on dry land. There was also a substantial livestock economy. There was relatively little mechanization of field operations. There were only two tractors in the villages in 1981–82.

The 1996 Dataset

In 1996, I returned with two research assistants (M. Srinivas and Paul Pandian) and V. Mohanasundaram to interview members of the 1981–82 sample households and those of their descendants who remained in the villages. We traced all but two of the 1981–82 sample households. Thirty-five had migrated in their entirety. Two had died out. This left 191 (85 per cent) of the households in the original sample still represented in the villages. The two research assistants stayed in the villages to conduct questionnaire-based interviews of the descendants. The questionnaire covered very similar ground to that covered in 1981–82. In focusing on descendants, however, not enough attention was paid to new household formation. This left considerable ambiguity about the membership of individual households. I did some additional interviews in 1996 as well.

By 1996 the villages had become much more fully integrated into

---

[2] These were 501 Chettiars, not to be confused with Devanga Chettiars, a weaver caste, represented only in small numbers in the villages in 1981–82. The Chettiars are Tamil-speaking; Devanga Chettiars speak Telugu.

[3] Pannadis were Pallars, Devendras.

the industrial economy. Large numbers of individuals resident in the villages were commuting to industrial employment in nearby towns and urban centres. Transport and communications had improved. Industrial units were also being set up in the villages and surrounding rural areas. Agriculturalists were doing much less well than they had been in 1981–82. One of the main reasons for this was a decline in the water table.[4] Another reason was the rise in labour costs, as alternative employment opportunities became available.[5] Policy changes associated with the economic reforms introduced in the early 1990s also meant that there was less support from the state. There was evidence of some aspects of the 'agrarian crisis' experienced in other parts of India too.[6] The position of agricultural labourers had improved. The economy had become more open, the old agrarian interests were less powerful, and the state had been intervening to strengthen the position of the poor on a much larger scale than before.

Agriculture was now relying on borewells as much as on open wells, the deepest bores going down to 600 feet in 1996. The number of tractors had risen, but bullocks were still used for most transport and field operations. There was more irrigated cotton, despite the shortage of labour. There was also more banana cultivation. The area under sugarcane had not changed much. There was less rain-fed cultivation than there had been in 1981–82. Fodder shortages limited the role of dairy production, though dairying continued to play a role in 1996.

The 2003–04 Data

I returned briefly in 2003 and in 2004, to do interviews that focused on Dalit housing, panchayati raj institutions (PRIs), self-help groups (SHGs), schools and *balwadi*s, non-agricultural employment, and non-agricultural enterprises. I worked with another research assistant, Selva Murugan. He also conducted a number of interviews on Arunthathiyar housing.

PRIs and SHGs were new features in the villages in 2003 and 2004, striking particularly in that the panchayat presidency in one of the revenue villages was reserved for a Dalit woman, as was the union councillorship that covered both villages. This, and the advent of self-help groups, had given Dalits a new profile in the villages.

Another major event was the establishment of an electricity substation in one of the villages at the end of the 1990s. This had not brought the upsurge in non-agricultural enterprises that had been hoped for, but it had improved the supply of electricity to agriculture. There were more non-

---

[4] Sivanappan and Aiyasamy (1978) noted that the water table had been declining for some time. The decline came to a head in the study villages in the drought of 1983–84.

[5] Chari (2004) and Singh and Sapra (2007) show how sharp the rise in employment in the Tiruppur garment sector was between the mid-1980s and 1996.

[6] As outlined in Government of India (2007), for example.

agricultural enterprises in and around the villages than there had been in 1996, but not many more.

The 2008–09 Dataset

In 2008–09 I returned with two more research assistants (Arul Maran and Gowri Shankar), who interviewed members of households in a new 20 per cent sample in the same hamlets and villages. The sample was drawn from a series of maps that we developed in the case of the revenue village that was included in its entirety in the survey, and from School Census data in the revenue village that was partially covered by the survey. (It only became evident as we were doing the survey that the School Censuses were a good basis for sampling; had we realized this earlier, we would have drawn the whole sample from them.) The two research assistants interviewed members of sample households using a questionnaire that covered ground similar to that covered in the earlier two surveys. I did some additional interviews again.

In 2008–09 industrial and other non-agricultural employment had increased further, with most workers commuting to and from such jobs. There was only a small increase in industrial units in and around the villages. There had been more outmigration and some immigration as well.[7] There had been substantial real estate development. There had also been a proliferation of financial services.

A number of small knitwear manufacturing and associated units had been established in the study villages in 2007 and 2008. A radical break with the past, however, came with the establishment of two steel mills: one with three furnaces that started up in 2009, and the other with more than three furnaces that started up in 2010. The owners were from Kerala and Coimbatore. These were industrial units on an altogether larger scale than the manufacturing units hitherto located in the villages. They occupied large buildings on large plots of land, standing out dramatically in the local landscape. As far as the village economy was concerned, there were more negative than positive linkages associated with the mills. The bulk of the work force came from north India and was accommodated within the mill compounds. The mills competed with agriculturalists and others in the villages for power. They created congestion and degraded the roads. They were major sources of air and water pollution. They made it unlikely that there would be any further development of textile manufacturing in and around the villages. They created problems for agriculture too. On the positive side, it is unclear how much business for local trade and services they will create. They represented additional resources for the panchayat, however, and Dalits in particular hoped to benefit from this.

There had been a marked decline in agriculture in the villages. Much

---

[7] The Census data show that the population of the main village remained more or less unchanged between 1991 and 2001. The School Census data show that this remained the case in 2008 too.

less land was being cultivated than in 1996. Agriculture was suffering from increasing costs of labour and from water shortages in addition to a marked decline in state support, particularly in the form of research and extension on which agriculturalists had hitherto relied a great deal. Water was now being tapped from as deep as 1200 feet. Tractors were being used both for transport and for field operations, particularly land preparation and ploughing. Other vehicles were also being used for transport. It was not uncommon to see bulldozers being hired from outside on occasion. There had been further changes in cropping pattern. There was very little cotton left, and much less sugarcane. There was more banana and turmeric. Among the minor crops that were being grown was maize, linked with poultry units that had emerged on a number of larger farms.

Agricultural labourers from the study villages were now working over a wider geographical area than before. The villages were becoming known for specializing in agricultural labour. There had been significant further expansion of state welfare programmes, including the beginnings of the National Rural Employment Guarantee Scheme (NREGS), which were having noticeable effects both on standards of living and on labour supply.

The 2010–11 Data

I returned in 2010 and 2011 to do more interviews on the NREGS, and to get more details on agricultural labour and on technical change in agriculture. The NREGS was much more widespread than it had been in 2008–09. The impact of the steel mills was becoming clearer too. Technical change in agriculture was also gaining some momentum.

There had been major changes in irrigation technology. Drip irrigation was being introduced, first for tree crops and then for shorter-term crops. Private-sector companies were the main source of advice on this. Farmers were also constructing tanks lined with cement to replace the earth-lined tanks that they had been using earlier, considerably reducing seepage in the process. The combination of drip irrigation and cement-lined tanks helped save water (and labour). Further, in 2011, the first experiments with mechanized harvesting of sugarcane were taking place.

Problems with the Data
1. The 1981–82 and 2008–09 samples are not strictly comparable with the 1996 sample.
2. Arunthathiyars were under-represented in the 1981–82 sample.
3. The 1996 definition of households was unsatisfactory. This was a particular problem in looking at the size distribution of landholdings. It was less of a problem in other contexts.
4. The data on ages are not very reliable, more so for older than for younger people.
5. There are no systematic data on female occupations in 1981–82.

6. The failure to distinguish contract labour, which is piece-rated, from agricultural labour, paid on a daily basis, is a limitation referred to below.

Landholding
Agricultural Land

Average holdings of agricultural land fell, from 3.55 acres per household in 1981–82 to 3.01 acres per household in 1996, and 2.16 acres per household in 2008–09 (Table 1). This included land outside as well as land inside the villages. By 2008–09, considerable inroads had been made by people outside the villages buying agricultural land for real estate and indus-

TABLE 1 *Household ownership holdings of land, by caste, study villages, 1981–82, 1996 and 2008–09* in acres

	1981– 82 HH (no.)	1981– 82 Land (acres)	1981– 82 Land/ HH (acres/HH)	1996 HH (no.)	1996 Land (acres)	1996 Land/ HH (acres/HH)	2008– 09 HH (no.)	2008– 09 Land (acres)	2008– 09 Land/ HH (acres/HH)
Chakkiliyar	43	3.0	0.07	47	3.0	0.06	63	2	0.03
Pannadi	27	5.5	0.20	50	10.7	0.21	38	7	0.18
Dalit	**70**	**8.5**	**0.12**	**97**	**13.7**	**0.14**	**101**	**9**	**0.09**
Naidu	14	108.3	7.74	12	104.7	8.73	11	109	9.91
Gounder	80	468.7	5.86	94	511.3	5.44	77	336	4.36
Chettiar	35	171.6	4.90	42	185.8	4.42	42	87	2.07
Other	30	56.8	1.89	37	34.8	0.94	26	13	0.50
Non-Dalit	**159**	**805.4**	**5.07**	**185**	**836.3**	**4.52**	**156**	**545**	**3.49**
All	229	813.9	3.55	282	850.1	3.01	257	554	2.16

Note: HH = households.
Source: Village surveys, 1981–82, 1996 and 2008–09.

TABLE 2 *Households by caste as a proportion of all households and land owned by each caste group as a proportion of all land owned, study villages, 1981–82, 1996 and 2008–09* in per cent

	1981–82 Households	1981–82 Land	1996 Households	1996 Land	2008–09 Households	2008–09 Land
Chakkiliyar	19	0.4	17	0.4	25	0.4
Pannadi	12	0.7	18	1.3	15	1.3
Dalit	**31**	**1.0**	**34**	**1.6**	**39**	**1.6**
Naidu	6	13.0	4	12.0	4	20.0
Gounder	35	58.0	33	60.0	30	61.0
Chettiar	15	21.0	15	22.0	16	16.0
Other	13	7.0	13	4.0	10	2.0
Non-Dalit	**69**	**99.0**	**66**	**98.0**	**61**	**98.0**
All	100	100.0	100	100.0	100	100.0

Source: Village surveys, 1981–82, 1996 and 2008–09.

trial use. People who had left the villages were holding on to agricultural land in the villages too.

The average agricultural landholding per household of Dalits had increased from 0.12 acre in 1981–82 to 0.14 acre in 1996, and then fallen to 0.09 acre again in 2008–09 (Table 1). Both the numbers of households and the extents involved were small. The increase from 1981–82 to 1996 consisted of a few individual households, mainly Pannadi, acquiring small areas of land. The improvement between 1981–82 and 1996 was not sustained in the more competitive conditions between 1996 and 2008–09.

In 1981–82 Dalits made up 31 per cent of the households and owned 1 per cent of the land; in 1996 they made up 34 per cent of the households and owned 1.6 per cent of the land; and in 2008–09 they made up 39 per cent of the households and still owned only 1.6 per cent of the land (Table 2). They had improved their relative position (very marginally) by 1996. Their relative (and absolute) position had worsened again by 2008–09.

The size distribution of landholdings is shown in Tables 3a, 3b, 4a,

TABLE 3a *Ownership holdings of land, by size-class of holdings and caste group, study villages, 1981–82* in numbers

Size-class of holding (acres)	Number of households								
	Chakkiliyar	Pannadi	**Dalit**	Naidu	Gounder	Chettiar	Other	**Non-Dalit**	All
0	42	16	58	3	12	7	11	33	91
Less than 1		10	10		2		5	7	17
1 to 2.4		1	1		9	10	8	27	28
2.5 to 4.9	1		1	1	16	7	1	25	26
5 to 9.9				7	25	7	4	43	43
10 and above				3	16	4	1	24	24
All	43	27	70	14	80	35	30	159	229

Source: Village surveys, 1981–82.

TABLE 3b *Proportion of land owned, by size-class of ownership holdings and caste group, study villages, 1981–82* in per cent

Size-class of holding (acres)	Proportion of households								
	Chakkiliyar	Pannadi	**Dalit**	Naidu	Gounder	Chettiar	Other	**Non-Dalit**	All
0	98	59	83	21	15	20	37	21	40
Less than 1		37	14		3		17	4	7
1 to 2.4		4	1		11	29	27	17	12
2.5 to 4.9	2		1	7	20	20	3	16	11
5 to 9.9				50	31	20	13	27	19
10 and above				21	20	11	3	15	10
All	100	100	100	100	100	100	100	100	100

Source: Village surveys, 1981–82.

4b, 5a and 5b for 1981–82, 1996 and 2008–09. Forty per cent of the households resident in the villages were landless in 1981–82. This had risen to 45 per cent by 1996 and 51 per cent by 2008–09. Among Dalits the proportions were much higher, having risen from 83 per cent in 1981–82 and 82 per cent in 1996 to 92 per cent in 2008–09. Twenty-nine per cent of the households in the villages had holdings of 5 acres or more in 1981–82. This had fallen to 20 per cent in 1996 and 14 per cent in 2008–09. The proportion of Dalit households with less than 1 acre was 97 per cent throughout.

Thus the agricultural landholdings of non-Dalit households in the villages were smaller in 1996, and smaller again in 2008–09, than in 1981–82. There were more non-Dalit households in the villages who were landless in 1996, and in 2008–09 too. Dalits living in the villages were in a marginally better position in some respects as far as agricultural land was concerned in 1996, but they were in a worse position again in 2008–09 as compared to 1981–82.

TABLE 4a *Ownership holdings of land, by size-class of holdings and caste group, study villages, 1996* in numbers

Size class of holding (acres)	Number of households								
	Chakkiliyar	Pannadi	**Dalit**	Naidu	Gounder	Chettiar	Other	**Non-Dalit**	All
0	47	35	82	1	14	9	22	**46**	128
Less than 1		12	12		1		6	**7**	19
1 to 2.4		2	2		16	12	6	**34**	36
2.5 to 4.9		1	1	1	26	11	1	**39**	40
5 to 9.9				7	22	8	1	**38**	38
10 and above				3	15	2	1	**21**	21
All	47	50	97	12	94	42	37	**185**	282

Source: Village surveys, 1996.

TABLE 4b *Proportion of land owned, by size-class of ownership holdings and caste group, study villages, 1996* in per cent

Size-class of holding (acres)	Proportion of households								
	Chakkiliyar	Pannadi	**Dalit**	Naidu	Gounder	Chettiar	Other	**Non-Dalit**	All
0	0	4	2	0	17	29	16	**18**	13
Less than 1		2	1		28		3	**21**	14
1 to 2.4		0	0		23	19	3	**21**	13
2.5 to 4.9			0	25	16	5	3	**11**	7
5 to 9.9				100	100	100	100	**100**	100
10 and above				0	0	0	0	**0**	0
All	100	100	100	0	0	0	0	**0**	0

Source: Village surveys, 1996.

TABLE 5a *Ownership holdings of land, by size-class of holding and caste group, study villages, 2008–09* in numbers

Size-class of holding (acres)	Number of households								
	Chakkiliyar	Pannadi	**Dalit**	Naidu	Gounder	Chettiar	Other	**Non-Dalit**	All
0	61	31	92		10	11	18	39	131
Less than 1	1	4	5			2	1	3	8
1 to 2.4	1	2	3		20	16	4	40	43
2.5 to 4.9		1	1	3	23	10	2	38	39
5 to 9.9				3	17	1	1	22	22
10 and above				5	7	2		14	14
All	63	38	101	11	77	42	26	156	257

Source: Village surveys, 2008–09.

TABLE 5b *Proportion of land owned, by size-class of ownership holdings and caste group, study villages, 2008–09* in per cent

Size-class of holding (acres)	Proportion of households								
	Chakkiliyar	Pannadi	**Dalit**	Naidu	Gounder	Chettiar	Other	**Non-Dalit**	All
0	97	82	91		13	26	69	25	51
Less than 1	2	11	5			5	4	2	3
1 to 2.4	2	5	3		26	38	15	26	17
2.5 to 4.9		3	1	27	30	24	8	24	15
5 to 9.9				27	22	2	4	14	9
10 and above				45	9	5		9	5
All	100	100	100	100	100	100	100	100	100

Source: Village surveys, 2008–09.

House-Sites

There was a substantial amount of Dalit housing development in the State as a whole from the 1980s through the 2000s. This was clearly visible in Coimbatore and Tiruppur districts, where Dalit settlements are now part of the landscape in a way they were not before.

Dalits owned their own house-sites in settlements in the four villages where there were Dalit populations in 1981–82. Three of these settlements were Arunthathiyar and one was Pannadi. The settlements were all very overcrowded. New settlements were in the process of being established in two of the four villages in 1981–82.

In 1996, the new Arunthathiyar settlements being established in 1981–82 were up and running, doubling the number of house-sites in each case. The house-sites in the new settlements were 2.1 cents each, which was an improvement on the 1.5 cents in the old Dalit settlements. The streets were also wider and there was some other public space as well. New settlements were being planned for Dalits in the two villages where no new settlements had been established earlier, although they were still some way off in 1996.

In 2008–09, the new settlements in the remaining two villages being planned in 1996 were up and running. One was Arunthathiyar, the other Pannadi. The new Pannadi settlement had plots of 3 cents each with 20-feet streets in between the rows, making both plots and streets larger than those in the new Arunthathiyar settlements. Pannadis had also got an extension of their old settlement by grouping together to buy 1.5 acres, and dividing that into twenty-eight plots of varying sizes. In addition, Pannadis had bought houses in the main village. This was something that would have been unthinkable for Arunthathiyars. Pannadi leaders estimated that they still needed another 55 house-sites to satisfy the demand in 2008–09. There were fifteen thatched huts on public land where Pannadis were squatting, hoping eventually to establish legal rights there.

In one of the villages in which Arunthathiyars had got a new settlement in 1981–82, another small settlement had been added by 2008–09. Efforts were being made to get a further thirty house-sites on another piece of land as well. There seemed to be an insatiable demand for house-sites in all the study villages with Dalit populations in 2008–09. Some of this was a demand for house-sites for children in future, though much was simply to get away from multiple occupancy, still quite widespread in 2008–09.

Occupations
Changes in Occupational Structure
The proportion of households getting the major part of their income from agriculture fell from 77 per cent in 1981–82 to 64 per cent in 1996 (Table 6). The proportion of men and boys engaged in farm activities fell even more, from 75 per cent to 54 per cent over the same period (Table 7).[8] This was a period over which there was significant integration of the local economy into the wider regional economy. Between 1996 and 2008–09, there was a further decrease in the proportion of households getting the major part of their income from agriculture, from 64 per cent to 54 per cent. There was, however, a small increase in the proportion of men and boys engaged in farm activities over this latter period.

The proportion of Dalit households getting the major part of their income from agriculture fell from 97 per cent in 1981–82 to 80 per cent in 1996 (Table 6). The proportion of Dalit men and boys engaged in farm activities fell from 98 per cent to 72 per cent over the same period (Table 7). The decrease was larger among Pannadis than among Arunthathiyars. While the proportion of Dalit households among households in the farm sector rose from 39 per cent in 1981–82 to 43 per cent in 1996, their proportion in the non-farm sector rose from 4 per cent to 19 per cent. Between 1996 and 2008–09, the proportion of Dalit households getting the majority of their income from agriculture fell further, from 81 per cent to 77 per cent. The proportion of Dalit males engaged in farm activities barely changed between

---

[8] See Heyer (2011) for data on the occupations of women and girls. This essay focuses on the occupations of men and boys.

TABLE 6 *Farm and non-farm households, by caste group, study villages, 1981–82, 1996 and 2008–09*

	Number of households					Column %					Row %				
	Chakki-liyar	Pannadi	Dalit	Non-Dalit	All	Chakki-liyar	Pannadi	Dalit	Non-Dalit	All	Chakki-liyar	Pannadi	Dalit	Non-Dalit	All
1981–82															
Non-farm households	1	1	2	51	53	2	4	3	32	23	2	2	4	96	100
Farm households	42	26	68	106	174	98	96	97	68	77	24	15	39	61	100
All households	43	27	70	157	227	100	100	100	100	100	19	12	31	69	100
1996															
Non-farm households	5	13	18	76	94	11	30	20	44	36	5	14	19	81	100
Farm households	42	30	72	97	169	89	70	80	56	64	25	18	43	57	100
All households	47	43	90	173	263	100	100	100	100	100	18	16	34	66	100
2008–09															
Non-farm households	12	13	25	86	111	20	34	26	59	46	11	12	23	77	100
Farm households	47	25	72	59	131	80	66	74	41	54	36	19	55	45	100
All households	59	38	97	145	242	100	100	100	100	100	24	16	40	60	100

Note: Households entirely dependent on pensions or remittances are excluded.
Source: Village surveys, 1981–82, 1996 and 2008–09.

TABLE 7 *Male farm and non-farm workers, by caste group, study villages, 1981–82, 1996 and 2008–09*

	Number of workers					Column %					Row %				
	Chakki-liyar	Pannadi	Dalit	Non-Dalit	All	Chakki-liyar	Pannadi	Dalit	Non-Dalit	All	Chakki-liyar	Pannadi	Dalit	Non-Dalit	All
1981–82															
Farm	84	63	147	192	339	98	98	98	64	75	25	19	43	57	100
Non-Farm	2	1	3	109	112	2	2	2	36	25	2	1	3	97	100
All male workers	86	64	150	301	451	100	100	100	100	100	19	14	33	67	100
1996															
Farm	64	38	102	114	216	81	61	72	44	54	30	18	47	53	100
Non-Farm	15	24	39	146	185	19	39	28	56	46	8	13	21	79	100
All male workers	79	62	141	260	401	100	100	100	100	100	20	15	35	65	100
2008–09															
Farm	72	26	98	107	205	76	60	71	49	58	35	13	48	52	100
Non-Farm	23	17	40	111	151	24	40	29	51	42	15	11	26	74	100
All male workers	95	43	138	218	356	100	100	100	100	100	27	12	39	61	100

Source: Village surveys, 1981–82, 1996 and 2008–09.

1996 and 2008–09, though the proportion of Arunthathiyars fell a bit further over that period. Dalits represented a slightly larger proportion (23 per cent) of households in the non-farm sector than in 1996.

Changes in Farm-based Occupational Structure
Landlords, Peasants, Workers

Table 8 shows the numbers of agriculturalist and agricultural labourer households in the farm sector. In 1981–82, a distinction was made between '*thottam* farmers', with enough land irrigated by wells to justify the employ-ment of permanent labourers, and 'small farmers'. There were no very large landowners, and no 'landlords' not working on their land. The last of these had left in the 1970s. According to the definition adopted in 1981–82, 14 per cent of the households getting the bulk of their income from agriculture were '*thottam* farmers', and 30 per cent were small farmers. It was not pos-sible to disaggregate the 1996 or 2008–09 data in a similar way. Permanent labourers no longer had the same significance in the work force that they had in 1981–82.

While the numbers of agriculturalist households getting the bulk of their income from agriculture barely changed between 1981–82 and 1996, these numbers fell sharply between 1996 and 2008–09. The number of households getting the bulk of their income from agricultural labour was unchanged between 1981–82 and 1996, and then fell only slightly between 1996 and 2008–09. The proportion of agricultural labourer households among farm households (column per cent) rose from 56 per cent in 1981–82 to 57 per cent in 1996, and 67 per cent in 2008–09. While there was a decline in agriculture within the villages, people from the study villages were working further afield as agricultural labourers. They had acquired a reputation as agricultural labourers who were available for work in areas where there were shortages of agricultural labourers in 1996, and even more acute shortages in 2008–09.

The proportion of Dalits among agricultural labourer households increased from 70 per cent to 73 per cent between 1981–82 and 1996, and from 73 per cent to 81 per cent between 1996 and 2008–09.

Distinctions within the Agricultural Labour Force

The main distinctions within the agricultural labour force were between (i) farm servants (*pannaiyal*), who were permanent labourers with an advance that tied them to a particular employer for a year; (ii) daily wage labour; (iii) piece-rated contract labour other than for sugarcane-crushing; and (iv) migrant sugarcane-crushing labour working on contracts (Table 9). Contract labour other than for sugarcane-crushing was an arrangement in which a group of workers was paid an agreed sum for a particular agricultural task. This form of labour first appeared in 1996. It was the dominant form of agricultural labour in 2008–09. The data do not distinguish between daily

TABLE 8 *Farm households: agricultural labourer and agriculturalist, by caste group, 1981–82, 1996 and 2008–09*

	Number of households					Column%					Row %				
	Chakki-liyar	Pannadi	Dalit	Non-Dalit	All	Chakki-liyar	Pannadi	Dalit	Non-Dalit	All	Chakki-liyar	Pannadi	Dalit	Non-Dalit	All
1981–82															
Agricultural labour	42	26	68	29	97	100	100	100	27	56	43	27	70	30	100
Agriculturalist (small farmer)				53	53				50	30				100	100
Agriculturalist (*thottam* farmer)				24	24				23	14				100	100
All farm households	42	26	68	106	174	100	100	100	100	100	24	15	39	61	100
1996															
Agricultural labour	41	30	71	26	97	98	100	99	27	57	42	31	73	27	100
Agriculturalist	1		1	71	72				73	43	1		1	99	100
All farm households	42	30	72	97	169	100	100	100	100	100	25	18	43	57	100
2008–09															
Agricultural labour	47	24	71	17	88	100	96	99	29	67	53	27	81	19	100
Agriculturalist		1	1	42	43				71	33		2	2	98	100
All farm households	47	25	72	59	131	100	100	100	100	100	36	19	55	45	100

Note: *Thottam* farmers = farmers who cultivate well-irrigated land and employ permanent labourers.
Source: Village surveys, 1981–82, 1996 and 2008–09.

TABLE 9 *Male agricultural labourers, by caste group, study villages, 1981–82, 1996 and 2008–09*

	Number of male agricultural labourers					Column %					Row %				
	Chakki-liyar	Pannadi	Dalit	Non-Dalit	All	Chakki-liyar	Pannadi	Dalit	Non-Dalit	All	Chakki-liyar	Pannadi	Dalit	Non-Dalit	All
1981–82															
Casual*	47	43	90	41	131	59	70	64	79	68	36	33	69	31	100
Pannayal#	30	3	33	2	35	38	5	23	4	18	86	9	94	6	100
SCC**	3	15	18	9	27	4	25	13	17	14	11	56	67	33	100
All male agricultural labourers	80	61	141	52	193	100	100	100	100	100	41	32	73	27	100
1996															
Casual*	39	11	50	23	73	64	30	51	96	60	53	15	68	32	100
Pannayal#	20	2	22	1	22	33	5	22	4	18	91	9	100		100
SCC**	2	24	26	1	27	3	65	27	4	22	7	89	96	4	100
All male agricultural labourers	61	37	98	24	122	100	100	100	100	100	50	30	80	20	100
2008–09															
Casual*	71	23	94	18	112	99	100	99	100	99	63	21	84	16	100
Pannayal#	1		1		1	1		1		1	100		100		100
SCC**															
All male agricultural labourers	72	23	95	18	113	100	100	100	100	100	64	20	84	16	100

Notes:　* Daily and contract labour.
　　　　** Sugarcane crushers.
　　　　# Permanent tied workers.

Source:　Village surveys, 1981–82, 1996 and 2008–09.

and contract workers other than for sugarcane-crushing however, many of whom do some of both.

1. Eighteen per cent of male agricultural labourers were farm servants in 1981–82, the majority Arunthathiyars, as Table 9 shows. Although a similar proportion of a smaller and older male agricultural labour force were farm servants in 1996, the absolute numbers had fallen considerably. By 2008–09, there were very few farm servants left.

2. Fourteen per cent of the male agricultural labour force were sugarcane crushers in 1981–82, the majority Pannadis. In 1996 the figure had risen to 22 per cent. Significant numbers of women not included in this figure were participating too, unlike in 1981–82. By 2008–09, however, sugarcane-crushing had completely disappeared. All sugarcane was being processed in mills.

3. The proportion of daily and contract labour other than for sugarcane-crushing fell from 68 per cent to 60 per cent between 1981–82 and 1996 as sugarcane-crushing assumed a more important role. By 2008–09, the proportion of daily and contract labour had risen to 99 per cent as there was no more sugarcane-crushing and farm servant employment was very rare.

Changes in Relations of Agricultural Production

1. Relations between farm servants and their employers were extremely oppressive and exploitative in 1981–82.[9] They were inseparable from untouchability practices (see below). In 1981–82, farm servants were beck-and-call labourers working long hours on a continuous basis on most days of the year. They were required to stay on the farm at night to look after livestock, equipment and stores if their employer did not live on the farm. They also did a considerable amount of night irrigation work. Their annual earnings were higher than those of casual labourers. There were discretionary benefits, which included time off, loans, and 'help' with expenditure on health care, life-cycle ceremonies and so on. These were key instruments of control that farm servants resisted by changing employers, buying produce in the local markets instead of from their employers, and getting loans from elsewhere. Employers complained bitterly about these strategies in 1981–82.

In 1996, farm servants were no longer beck-and-call labourers. They had fixed hours of work, similar to those of casual labourers; and they had leave that was negotiated at the beginning of the year. It was no longer easy for employers to get farm servants to stay overnight on their farms. Employers complained that state provision of televisions meant that farm servants would no longer work long hours. Employers also complained that farm

---

[9] Cederlof's (1997) account of relationships between Gounders and Arunthathiyars in the 1930s and 1940s had points of similarity with the situation in the villages in 1981–82. See Breman (1974) for a similar situation in Gujarat. See Heyer (2000 and 2010) for more detailed accounts of these relationships in the study villages.

servants taken on at the beginning of the year often left without completing their contracts, and that it was no longer possible to get other Arunthathiyars to bring them back. There had been a general improvement with respect to language and body language, as noted in the discussion of untouchability practices below.

There were few farm servants left by 2008–09. Those that were left were treated better, on par with the improvement in the treatment of agricultural labourers.

2. Relations between employers and daily wage labour improved over time as 'labour shortages' meant that employers felt they had to treat labour with more respect. In 2008–09, employers talked about having to treat their labourers with more respect, use different language and make them feel appreciated (see also De Neve and Carswell 2010). In a discussion with an agricultural employer in 2011 about the advantages of daily wage labour and the difficulty of getting it any more, the employer said that he had to treat his daily labourers extremely carefully, giving as an example that if he stood over them and supervised their work, as he used to do, the workers would not come for work any more.

There were differences in the treatment of Dalit and non-Dalit labourers throughout. This was apparent in language, body language and conventions relating to physical space, particularly space around the house.

3. There were important changes in the relations between employers and contract labour, implied by the move from daily work to contract labour paid at piece-rates. Contract labour was preferred by most labourers because, although it meant working hard, they could earn more in a shorter time that way. Contracts were negotiated informally by individuals who would bring a group to do the work. There was minimal supervision by employers where contract labour was concerned. It involved much less interaction, much less contact, between employers and individual labourers. The whole relationship was more distant, but it became more respectful over time as well.

Other Changes in the Farm Sector
While there had been some adaptation to increased water and labour shortages, and some response to new market opportunities, the reduction in state expenditure on research and extension services made agriculture more difficult than before. In 1981–82, the Tamil Nadu Agricultural University (TNAU), together with the Department of Agriculture, Government of Tamil Nadu, was a major source of technical advice and support. Agricultural officers had a high profile in the villages. By 1996 they were much less in evidence. By 2008–09 they were providing still less technical advice and support. In 2008–09, private sector companies were beginning to provide technical advice, but only selectively. In the case of irrigation equipment, the private sector appeared to be playing a positive if belated role. The introduction of mechanized harvesting by sugar mills was another important development.

The expansion of welfare programmes had a significant impact on the farm sector, as did the introduction of the NREGS (see also Heyer 2012). In 1981–82 welfare programmes were not very significant, and what there was barely reached Dalits at all. By 1996 they had expanded greatly, and Dalits were benefiting as much as anyone else. These schemes were already having an impact on the supply of agricultural labour at the time. By 2008–09 they had expanded again, and workers spoke of not having to do as many days of work as before in order to feed their families because of the public distribution system. The NREGS was having an impact on the supply of female labour to agriculture as well, more so in 2010 and 2011 than in 2008–09.

Non-Farm Employment
Industry and Services

There was a relatively small non-farm sector in the villages in 1981–82 and what did exist was virtually all services (the exceptions were a few weavers, potters and others) (Tables 10 and 11). In 1996, the proportion of households whose primary source of income was services, 22 per cent, was the same as in 1981–82. The proportion of individual men and boys whose main occupation was services had increased slightly, from 20 per cent to 23 per cent. There had been much larger changes where industry and manufacturing were concerned. Thirteen percent of the households in the villages were now getting most of their income from manufacturing, compared with only 1 per cent in 1981–82; and 22 per cent of the main occupations of individual men and boys were in manufacturing, compared with only 4 per cent in 1981–82. By 2008–09 there had been a further increase in the proportion of households getting the bulk of their income from manufacturing, and a decrease in the proportion getting the bulk of their income from services. Thirty per cent of the households in the villages were now getting most of their income from employment in the manufacturing sector, and 28 per cent of the main occupations of individual men and boys were employment in manufacturing. In 2008–09, the proportion of individual men and boys whose main occupation was in the manufacturing sector was much nearer the proportion of households getting the bulk of their income from employment in manufacturing than in 1996. The proportion of households getting the bulk of their income from employment in services had fallen to 16 per cent, and the proportion of men and boys whose main income was from employment in services to 15 per cent.

There were very few Dalit households in the non-farm sector in 1981–82 (Tables 10 and 11). In 1996 there was a larger number, more Pannadis than Arunthathiyars, and they were divided roughly equally between industry (8 per cent of the total) and services (11 per cent of the total). The corresponding proportions of men and boys whose main occupations were in industry and services were 15 per cent and 11 per cent. By 2008–09, the proportion of Dalit households getting the bulk of their income from non-farm activities had increased. Twenty-one per cent were getting the bulk of

TABLE 10 *Non-farm households: industry, traditional manufacturing and services, by caste group, study villages, 1981–82, 1996 and 2008–09*

	Number of households					Column %					Row %				
	Chakki-liyar	Pannadi	Dalit	Non-Dalit	All	Chakki-liyar	Pannadi	Dalit	Non-Dalit	All	Chakki-liyar	Pannadi	Dalit	Non-Dalit	All
1981–82															
Industry															
Traditional manufacturing				3	3				2	1				100	100
Services	1	1	2	48	50	2	4	3	31	22	2	2	4	96	100
All non-farm households	1	1	2	51	53	2	4	3	32	23	2	2	4	96	100
All households	43	27	70	157	227	100	100	100	100	100	19	12	31	69	100
1996															
Industry	1	6	7	28	35	2	14	8	16	13	3	17	20	80	100
Traditional manufacturing	1		1		1	2		1			100		100		100
Services	3	7	10	48	58	6	16	11	28	22	5	12	17	83	100
All non-farm households	5	13	18	76	94	11	30	20	44	36	5	14	19	81	100
All households	47	43	90	173	263	100	100	100	100	100	18	16	34	66	100
2008–09															
Industry	11	9	20	52	72	19	24	21	36	30	15	13	28	72	100
Traditional manufacturing	1	4	5	34	39	2	11	5	23	16	3	10	13	87	100
Services	12	13	25	86	111	20	34	26	59	46	11	12	23	77	100
All non-farm households	24	26	50	117	167	41	69	52	81	69	14	16	30	70	100
All households	59	38	97	145	242	100	100	100	100	100	24	16	40	60	100

Source: Village surveys, 1981–82, 1996 and 2008–09.

TABLE 11 *Male non-farm workers: industrial, traditional manufacturing and services, by caste group, study villages, 1981–82, 1996, 2008–09*

	Number of male workers					Column %					Row %				
	Chakki-liyar	Pannadi	Dalit	Non-Dalit	All	Chakki-liyar	Pannadi	Dalit	Non-Dalit	All	Chakki-liyar	Pannadi	Dalit	Non-Dalit	All
1981–82															
Industrial				20	20				7	4				100	100
Traditional manufacturing				1	1				0	0				100	100
Services	2	1	3	88	91	2	2	2	29	20	2	1	3	97	100
All male non-farm workers	2	1	3	109	112	2	2	2	36	25	2	1	3	97	100
All male workers	86	64	150	301	451	100	100	100	100	100	19	14	33	67	100
1996															
Industry	9	12	21	69	90	11	19	15	27	22	10	13	23	77	100
Traditional manufacturing	3		3		3	4	2	2	0	1	100		100		100
Services	3	12	15	77	92	4	19	11	30	23	3	13	16	84	100
All male non-farm workers	15	24	39	146	185	19	39	28	56	46	8	13	21	79	100
All male workers	79	62	141	260	401	100	100	100	100	100	20	15	35	65	100
2008–09															
Industry	21	12	33	66	99	22	28	24	30	28	21	12	33	67	100
Traditional manufacturing															
Services	2	5	7	45	52	2	12	5	21	15	4	10	13	87	100
All male non-farm workers	23	17	40	111	151	24	40	29	51	42	15	11	26	74	100
All male workers	95	43	138	218	356	100	100	100	100	100	27	12	39	61	100

Source: Village surveys, 1981–82, 1996 and 2008–09.

their income from employment in industry. This included almost as many Arunthathiyars as Pannadis. Only 5 per cent of Dalit households, and 5 per cent of Dalit men and boys, were getting the bulk of their income from services in 2008–09.

In 2008–09 Dalits, who made up 40 per cent of the total number of households in the villages, represented 28 per cent of the total number of households getting their main income from employment in industry, and 13 per cent of the total number of households getting their main income from employment in services. They were under-represented in both, and in services more than in industry.

The fact that the share of employment in services declined from 1996 to 2008–09 was partly due to fewer households turning to residual low-income services because they did not have other opportunities, and partly due to better transport and more mobility.

Self-Employed: Capitalist Entrepreneurs and Small Vendors

Table 12 shows the number of households in the sample getting the bulk of their income from self-employment, disaggregated into small, medium and large. Table 13 shows the numbers of individual men and boys with self-employment as their main occupation. The numbers are quite small. Information on non-sample households is included in the discussion below.

In 1981–82, 19 per cent of the total number of households in the sample relied primarily on income from self-employment (Table 12), and 13 per cent of the men and boys were self-employed. Self-employment included small-scale washermen, barbers, potters, weavers, and petty traders and shopkeepers with very low incomes, and medium-scale carpenters, blacksmiths, shopkeepers and produce traders who earned somewhat more. The only significant large-scale entrepreneurs in the villages at that time were people engaged in cotton trade and business, one or two of whom either owned or rented ginneries as well as engaging in cotton trade; an agricultural inputs dealer whose business was substantial; and an astrologer whose business was very large.

In 1996 a smaller proportion of households, 12 per cent, relied primarily on income from self-employment (Table 12), and a slightly larger proportion of men and boys, 15 per cent, was self-employed (Table 13). In addition to the self-employment registered for 1981–82, small-scale self-employed included people plaiting coconut leaves, making charcoal and repairing footwear. The medium-scale self-employed now included tailors, powerloom operators, fertilizer salesmen, electrical fitters, a rice trader, a household owning an oil-pressing business and the owner of a small metal workshop (which did not survive for very long). There were fewer blacksmiths, carpenters and produce traders in the villages than before. The only large-scale entrepreneurs were those involved in cotton trade and business, including one who had taken up cotton seed business, and one person who had started stitching men's

TABLE 12 Self-employed non-farm households, by size of enterprise and by caste group, study villages, 1981–82, 1996 and 2008–09

	Number of households					Column %					Row %				
	Chakki-liyar	Pannadi	Dalit	Non-Dalit	All	Chakki-liyar	Pannadi	Dalit	Non-Dalit	All	Chakki-liyar	Pannadi	Dalit	Non-Dalit	All
1981–82															
Small				18	18				11	8				100	100
Medium				21	21				13	9				100	100
Large				5	5				3	2				100	100
All self-employed non-farm households				44	44				28	19				100	100
All households	43	27	70	157	227				100	100	19	12	31	69	100
1996															
Small	1	1	2	9	11	2	2	2	5	4	9	9	18	82	100
Medium		2	2	14	16		5	2	8	6		13	13	88	100
Large				4	4				2	2				100	100
All self-employed non-farm households	1	3	4	27	31	2	7	4	16	12	3	10	13	87	100
All households	47	43	90	173	263	100	100	100	100	100	18	16	34	66	100
2008–09															
Small		1	1	5	6		3	1	3	2		17	17	83	100
Medium		1	1	7	8		3	1	5	3		13	13	88	100
Large				6	6				4	2				100	100
All self-employed non-farm households		2	2	18	20		5	2	12	8		10	10	90	100
All households	59	38	97	145	242	100	100	100	100	100	24	16	40	60	100

Notes: Small: dhobi, barber, potter, weaver, coconut-leaf plaiting, charcoal, chappal plaiting, low-income petty trader and shopkeeper, electrical fitter, elastic unit. Medium: bullock-cart hire, carpenter, blacksmith, shopkeeper, produce trader, tailor, fertilizer sales representative. Large: cotton trade and business, astrologer, agriculture inputs dealer, cotton seed trade, rice trade, oil pressing, banana trade, transport business, powerloom operator, garments, road contractor, builder, spinning mill, LIC agent.
Electrical fitter, bullock cart hire and cycle shop were medium in 1996, and small in 2008–09.

Source: Village surveys, 1981–82, 1996 and 2008–09.

TABLE 13   *Self-employed non-farm male workers, by size of enterprise and caste group, study villages, 1981–82, 1996 and 2008–09*

	Number of workers					Column %					Row %				
	Chakki-liyar	Pannadi	Dalit	Non-Dalit	All	Chakki-liyar	Pannadi	Dalit	Non-Dalit	All	Chakki-liyar	Pannadi	Dalit	Non-Dalit	All
1981–82															
Small				43	43				14	10				100	100
Medium				9	9				3	2				100	100
Large				7	7				2	2				100	100
All self-employed non-farm workers				59	59				20	13				100	100
All households	86	64	150	301	451	100	100	100	100	100	19	14	33	67	100
1996															
Small	3	5	8	21	29	4	8	6	8	7	10	17	28	72	100
Medium				21	21				8	5				100	100
Large				10	10				4	2				100	100
All self-employed non-farm workers	3	5	8	52	60	4	8	6	20	15	5	8	13	87	100
All households	79	62	141	260	401	100	100	100	100	100	20	15	35	65	100
2008–09															
Small	1	2	3	8	11	1	4	2	4	3	9	18	27	73	100
Medium		1	1	8	9		2	1	4	3		11	11	89	100
Large				9	9				4	3				100	100
All self-employed non-farm workers	1	3	4	25	29	1	7	3	11	8	3	10	14	86	100
All households	95	43	138	218	356	100	100	100	100	100	27	12	39	61	100

Notes: As in Table 12.
Source: Village surveys, 1981–82, 1996 and 2008–09.

underwear for the low end of the domestic market. Households involved in large-scale non-farm business, including the agricultural inputs dealer, had left the villages and settled in nearby towns.

In 2008–09, the proportion of households relying primarily on income from self-employment had fallen further, to 8 per cent (Table 12). The proportion of individual men and boys who were self-employed had also fallen, to 8 per cent (Table 13). There were a number of vendors who travelled by bicycle, selling a range of cheap consumer goods. The numbers relying on traditional services and produce trade had decreased further. Several small units making elastic for the garment industry had started up, linked to two larger entrepreneurs who were subcontracting the production of elastic as well as producing and selling their own. There were large entrepreneurs resident in the villages involved in a wider range of activities than before: a banana trader, an owner of a transport business, a road contractor, a builder, garment factory owners, a spinning mill owner and a Life Insurance Corporation agent who was doing very well. Many of the large entrepreneurs, however, operated from outside the villages.This was even more true in 2008–09 than in 1996.

There were very few Dalit households relying primarily on incomes from self-employment and relatively few self-employed Dalits throughout the period under consideration. This reflects the fact that it has always been difficult for Dalits to flourish in self-employment in villages like these (cf. Harriss-White and Vidyarthee 2010; and Prakash 2010).

Employees: Manual Labour, Semi-Skilled Labour,
Non-Manual Labour

Employees have been classified as manual (or 'unskilled'), semi-skilled (or blue collar, i.e. working in mills, factories and workshops in which some conventionally recognized skill is required) and non-manual, which includes village assistants as well as white-collar workers.

There were very few households (4 per cent) relying primarily on non-farm employment in the villages in 1981–82 (Table 14), and relatively few men and boys (12 per cent) whose main occupation was non-farm employment (Table 15). Those relying primarily on non-farm employment relied on government employment classified as non-manual, on industrial employment and on construction. Most would have had to migrate to take up non-farm employment. There was not very much available in the villages at the time.

The number of households relying primarily on non-farm employment was much higher in 1996, by which time commuting had become a possibility. Twenty-four per cent of households now relied on non-farm employment for the bulk of their income, and 31 per cent of the men and boys recorded non-farm employment as their main occupation. Relatively large numbers were now relying on semi-skilled employment in factories, mills and workshops. There were more people relying on construction work. Cutting firewood had become a significant source of manual employment income too. The percent-

TABLE 14 *Non-farm employee households: manual, semi-skilled, non-manual, by caste group, study villages, 1981–82, 1996 and 2008-09*

	Number of households					Column %					Row %				
	Chakki-liyar	Pannadi	Dalit	Non-Dalit	All	Chakki-liyar	Pannadi	Dalit	Non-Dalit	All	Chakki-liyar	Pannadi	Dalit	Non-Dalit	All
1981–82															
Manual				2	2				1	1				100	100
Semi-skilled				2	2				1	1				100	100
Non-manual	1	1	2	3	5	2	4	3	2	2	20	20	40	60	100
All non-farm employee households	1	1	2	7	9	2	4	3	4	4	11	11	22	78	100
All households	43	27	70	157	227	100	100	100	100	100	19	12	31	69	100
1996															
Manual	1	4	5	8	13	2	9	6	5	5	8	31	38	62	100
Semi-skilled	1	6	7	30	37	2	14	8	17	14	3	16	19	81	100
Non-manual	2		2	11	13	4		2	6	5	15		15	85	100
All non-farm employee households	4	10	14	49	63	9	23	16	28	24	6	16	22	78	100
All households	47	43	90	173	263	100	100	100	100	100	18	16	34	66	100
2008–09															
Manual	1	2	3	3	6	2	5	3	2	2	17	33	50	50	100
Semi-skilled	11	9	20	51	71	19	24	21	35	29	15	13	28	72	100
Non-manual				14	14				10	6				100	100
All non-farm employee households	12	11	23	68	91	20	29	24	47	38	13	12	25	75	100
All households	59	38	97	145	242	100	100	100	100	100	24	16	40	60	100

Source: Village surveys, 1981–82, 1996 and 2008–09.

TABLE 15 *Male non-farm employees: manual, semi-skilled, non-manual, by caste group, study villages, 1981–82, 1996 and 2008–09*

	Number of male non-farm employees					Column %					Row %				
	Chakki-liyar	Pannadi	Dalit	Non-Dalit	All	Chakki-liyar	Pannadi	Dalit	Non-Dalit	All	Chakki-liyar	Pannadi	Dalit	Non-Dalit	All
1981–82															
Manual				2	2				1	0				100	100
Semi-skilled				27	27				9	6				100	100
Non-manual	2	1	3	21	24	2	2	2	7	5	8	4	13	88	100
All male non-farm employees	2	1	3	50	53	2	2	2	17	12	4	2	6	94	100
All male workers	86	64	150	301	451	100	100	100	100	100	19	14	33	67	100
1996															
Manual	1	5	6	11	17	1	8	4	4	4	6	29	35	65	100
Semi-skilled	9	14	23	70	93	11	23	16	27	23	10	15	25	75	100
Non-manual	2		2	13	15	3		1	5	4	13		13	87	100
All male non-farm employees	12	19	31	94	125	15	31	22	36	31	10	15	25	75	100
All male workers	79	62	141	260	401	100	100	100	100	100	20	15	35	65	100
2008–09															
Manual		2	2	10	12		5	1	5	3		17	17	83	100
Semi-skilled	21	12	33	63	96	22	28	24	29	27	22	13	34	66	100
Non-manual	1		1	13	14	1		1	6	4	7		7	93	100
All male non-farm employees	22	14	36	86	122	23	33	26	39	34	18	11	30	70	100
All male workers	95	43	138	218	356	100	100	100	100	100	27	12	39	61	100

Source: Village surveys, 1981–82, 1996 and 2008–09.

age involved in non-manual employment was still small, though the range of non-manual employment provided by the state had increased. There was no private sector non-manual employment accessible to those residing in the villages in 1996.

By 2008–09, the proportion of households relying on non-farm employment for the bulk of their income had risen to 38 per cent, and the proportion of individual men and boys whose main occupation was non-farm employment had risen to 34 per cent. The proportion relying primarily on semi-skilled employment had more than doubled since 1996. The proportion of households relying primarily on non-farm manual employment had barely changed, but there were now private-sector non-manual employees living in the villages, commuting to work in banks and in information technology.

There were very few Dalit households relying primarily on non-farm employment in 1981–82. By 1996, the proportion had risen to 16 per cent (higher among Pannadis and lower among Arunthathiyars). The proportion of individual Dalit men and boys with non-farm employment as their main occupation had risen from 2 per cent to 22 per cent. By 2008–09, the proportion of Dalit households relying primarily on non-farm employment had risen further, to 24 per cent, and the proportion of individual Dalit men and boys with non-farm employment as their main occupation had risen to 26 per cent. Arunthathiyars were catching up with Pannadis too. Nearly all Dalit men and boys involved in non-farm employment relied on work in mills, factories and workshops. One or two relied on construction.

Other Changes in the Non-Farm Sector

There was a distinct change in the character of the non-farm sector between 1981–82 and 2008–09, in which the increase in state employment played a relatively minor role. Agricultural trade and processing, which had been prominent in 1981–82, played a less important role in 1996 and less still in 2008–09. Many of the minor activities that helped make a living in 1981–82 and in 1996 had disappeared by 2008–09. Construction and mechanized transport had become quite prominent in 2008–09. The first small textile units had been set up in the villages by 1996, and there were more by 2008–09. There were small spinning mills in neighbouring villages, the owners of which lived in the study villages. The arrival of steel mills in 2008 and 2009 was a major development, the full impact of which will only become clear over time. A lot of non-farm activities in which people from the villages were involved were located outside the villages. Many of these involved outmigration from the villages.

Child Labour

Table 16 shows the number of boys in the age-group 5–14 years who were working in 1981–82 and in 1996. In 1981–82, 65 per cent of Arunthathiyar boys aged 5–14 years were working. This included all boys

TABLE 16 *Male child labour, by caste group, study villages, 1981–22 and 1996*

Boys: 5–14 years	Caste group				
	Chakkiliyar	Pannadi	*Dalit*	Non-Dalit	All
1981–82					
Boys working	17	9	**26**	6	32
All boys	26	27	**53**	68	121
Working boys as proportion of all boys	65	33	**49**	9	26
1996					
Boys working	7		**7**	1	8
All boys	24	13	**37**	53	90
Working boys as proportion of all boys	29	0	**19**	2	9

Note: Some numbers in the above table changed – not tracked.
Source: Village surveys, 1981–82, 1996 and 2008–09.

in the age-group 10–14 years, and one or two boys less than 10 years old. The figure was lower for Pannadis. Some of the Pannadi boys were neither in school nor in the work force in 1981–82. There were not insignificant numbers of boys in the age-group 5–14 years, belonging to Chettiar households and 'Other' non-Dalit households, working in 1981–82 as well.

By 1996, the number of boys in the age-group 5–14 years who were in the work force had fallen substantially. Just under 30 per cent of Arunthathiyar boys aged 5–14 years were working in 1996, and there were no Pannadis in the sample who were doing so. There were still Chettiar boys in the age-group 5–14 years and boys in Other non-Dalit households who were working, but fewer than in 1981–82. There were young girls working in elastic factories in 1996, however, and others doing cotton-seed work.

By 2008–09, there were virtually no boys or girls aged 5–14 in the work force, and none in the sample. Almost all were in school.

Education, Literacy and Schooling
School Enrolment among School Age Population

Tables 17 and 19 show the numbers of 5–14-year-old boys and girls in the 1981–82, 1996 and 2008–09 samples, and the proportions in school, by caste group. In 1981–82, only 48 per cent of boys aged 5–14 were in school, and only 39 per cent of girls in the same age-group. There were striking differences between caste groups. Whereas a relatively large proportion of non-Dalit boys were in school, the proportion of Dalit boys in school was very low. In all caste groups except Other, the proportion of 5–14-year-old girls in school was much lower than that of boys.

By 1996 there had been considerable improvement, even more for girls than for boys. This was part of a more general improvement in the State as a whole. Mid-day meals, free uniforms and books were introduced in the schools of Tamil Nadu in the mid-1980s, after which there was an upsurge in the level of participation in education at the State level (Kajisa and Palanichamy 2010). In 1996, 76 per cent of boys aged 5–14 in the sample were in school, and 75 per cent of girls. In all caste groups other than Arunthathiyar, 80 per cent or more of boys were in school, and 70 per cent or more of girls. Only 42 per cent of Arunthathiyar boys and 52 per cent of Arunthathiyar girls in the sample were in school.

By 2008–09, nearly all children aged 5–14 were in school, even Arunthathiyar. The small numbers still not in school included some 5-year-olds who had not yet started school, and a very small number of 13 and 14-year-olds who had dropped out before they were 15 years old. It was state policy that all students should complete Standard VIII, and teachers were trying to ensure that this was so.

Tables 18 and 20 show the numbers in the samples studying beyond Standard X. It was only in 2008–09 that significant numbers were doing this, though even then the numbers were quite small. These numbers included both young men and young women who were Dalits, and more young women than young men who were Dalits.

There had been a striking change in attitudes to education, particularly

TABLE 17 *Boys' school attendance, by caste group, study villages, 1981–82, 1996 and 2008–09*

Boys: 5–14 years	Number of boys				
	Chakkiliyar	Pannadi	Dalit	Non-Dalit	All
1981–82					
All boys	26	27	53	68	121
Boys in school	4	3	7	51	58
Proportion in school (%)	15	11	13	75	48
1996					
All boys	24	13	37	53	90
Boys in school	10	11	21	47	68
Proportion in school (%)	42	85	57	89	76
2008–09					
All boys	29	10	39	47	86
Boys in school	27	9	26	46	82
Proportion in school (%)	93	90	67	98	95

Source: Village surveys, 1981–82, 1996 and 2008–09.

TABLE 18 **Men and boys studying beyond SSLC, by caste group, study villages, 1981–82, 1996 and 2008–09**

Years of survey	Number of men and boys				
	Chakkiliyar	Pannadi	Dalit	Non-Dalit	All
1981–82				1	1
1996				5	5
2008–09	3	2	5	20	25

Source: Village surveys, 1981–2, 1996, and 2008–9.

TABLE 19 *Girls' school attendance, by caste group, study villages, 1981–82, 1996 and 2008–09*

Girls: 5–14 years	Number of girls				
	Chakkiliyar	Pannadi	**Dalit**	Non-Dalit	All
1981–82					
All girls	16	17	**33**	67	100
Girls in school	1		**1**	38	39
Proportion in school (%)	6	0	**3**	57	39
1996					
All girls	21	17	**38**	57	95
Girls in school	11	12	**23**	48	71
Proportion in school (%)	52	71	**61**	84	75
2008–09					
All girls	23	9	**32**	33	65
Girls in school	22	9	**31**	33	64
Proportion in school (%)	96	100	**97**	100	98

Source: Village surveys, 1981–82, 1996 and 2008–09.

TABLE 20 **Women and girls studying beyond SSLC, by caste group, study villages, 1981–82, 1996 and 2008–09**

Years of survey	Number of women and girls				
	Chakkiliyar	Pannadi	Dalit	Non-Dalit	All
1981–82					
1996					3
2008–09	4	4			24

Source: Village surveys, 1981–82, 1996 and 2008–09.

among Dalits, both between 1981–82 and 1996, and again between 1996 and 2008–09. In 1996, Dalits were keen to send their children to school not because they thought this would increase their employment opportunities, but because they thought it would enable them to 'hold their heads up high' in interactions with officials and others. In 2008–09, they saw education as doing more than this. Children had become the centre of attention, their hope for the future and the focus of investment.

Educational Attainment in the Population as a Whole

The historical legacy of low participation in education is clear from Tables 21 and 22, which show the educational attainment of males in the sample aged 7 and above who were not in school. In 1981–82, 56 per cent had never been to school at all. Only 24 per cent had gone further than primary school. By 1996, the proportion who had never been to school had fallen to 41 per cent, and the proportion who had gone further than primary school had risen to 36 per cent. By 2008–09, the proportion who had never been to school was still 31 per cent, while the proportion who had gone further than primary school was 44 per cent. Fifty six per cent had not had more than primary schooling. The adult male population was relatively poorly educated even in 2008–09.

Among Dalits, the situation was much worse. In 1981–82, 87 per cent of Dalit males aged 7 and above had never been to school, and only 5 per cent had gone further than primary school (Table 21). In 1996 the figures were 72 per cent and 15 per cent respectively, and in 2008–09, 54 per cent and 25 per cent. Among Dalits, the proportion that had not had more than primary schooling was 75 per cent. The remaining 25 per cent had had some secondary schooling, but very few had reached Standard X even in 2008–09.

For females the situation was much worse. In 1981–82, 86 per cent of the sample women and girls aged 7 and above who were not in school had never been to school at all, and only 5 per cent had gone further than primary school (Table 22). By 1996, the proportion who had never been to school had fallen to 66 per cent, and the proportion who had gone further than primary school had risen to 18 per cent. By 2008–09, the proportion who had never been to school was still 58 per cent, and the proportion who

TABLE 21 *Educational level of non-school-attending men and boys aged 7 years and above, by caste group, study villages, 1981–82, 1996 and 2008–09*

Educational level	Number of men and boys					Column %				
	Chakki-liyar	Pan-nadi	**Dalit**	Non-Dalit	All	Chakki-liyar	Pan-nadi	**Dalit**	Non-Dalit	All
1981–82										
0	86	67	**153**	125	278	91	83	**87**	39	56
Grades 1 to 5	5	9	**14**	84	98	5	11	**8**	26	20
Grade 6 to SSLC	3	5	**8**	98	106	3	6	**5**	31	21
Above SSLC				13	13				4	3
All men and boys	94	81	**175**	320	495	100	100	**100**	100	100
1996										
0	62	49	**111**	73	184	73	69	**71**	25	41
Grades 1 to 5	12	9	**21**	76	97	14	13	**13**	26	22
Grade 6 to SSLC	11	13	**24**	120	144	13	18	**15**	42	32
Above SSLC				19	19				7	4
All men and boys	85	71	**156**	288	444	100	100	**100**	100	100
2008–09										
0	54	25	**79**	40	119	53	56	**54**	17	31
Grades 1 to 5	25	6	**31**	64	95	25	13	**21**	27	25
Grade 6 to SSLC	18	13	**31**	86	117	18	29	**21**	37	31
Above SSLC	5	1	**6**	45	51	5	2	**4**	19	13
All men and boys	102	45	**147**	235	382	100	100	**100**	100	100

Notes: The individuals for whom data on educational achievements were missing are not included in the tables.
SSLC = Secondary School Leaving Certificate.
Source: Village surveys, 1981–82, 1996 and 2008–09.

TABLE 22 *Educational level of non-school-attending women and girls aged 7 years and above, by caste group, study villages, 1981–82, 1996 and 2008–09*

Educational level	Number of females					Column %				
	Chakki-liyars	Pann-adis	**Dalit**	Non-Dalit	All	Chakki-liyars	Pann-adis	**Dalit**	Non-Dalit	All
1981–82										
0	77	64	**141**	208	349	97	98	**98**	79	86
Grades 1 to 5	2	1	**3**	37	40	3	2	**2**	14	10
Grade 6 to SSLC				19	19				7	5
Above SSLC										
All women and girls	79	65	**144**	264	408	100	100	**100**	100	100
1996										
0	59	59	**118**	146	264	92	89	**91**	55	66
Grades 1 to 5	5	5	**10**	51	61	8	8	**8**	19	15
Grade 6 to SSLC		2	**2**	63	65		3	**2**	24	16
Above SSLC				7	7				3	2
All women and girls	64	66	**130**	267	397	100	100	**100**	100	100
2008–09										
0	68	36	**104**	110	214	72	72	**72**	48	58
Grades 1 to 5	10	4	**14**	48	62	11	8	**10**	21	17
Grade 6 to SSLC	11	7	**18**	53	71	12	14	**13**	23	19
Above SSLC	5	3	**8**	16	24	5	6	**6**	7	6
All women and girls	94	50	**144**	227	371	100	100	**100**	100	100

Notes: The individuals for whom data on educational achievements were missing are not included in the tables. There were more females than males for whom this was the case.
SSLC = Secondary School Leaving Certificate
Source: Village surveys, 1981–82, 1996 and 2008–09.

had gone further than primary school was 25 per cent. Although as many girls as boys were going to school in 2008–09, the legacy of past deprivation meant that the educational levels in the adult female population were still considerably lower than in the case of men. Seventy five per cent had not had more than primary schooling in 2008–09.

Among Dalit females the situation was worse. In 1981–82, 98 per cent of Dalit women and girls aged 7 and above who were not in school had never been to school, and none had gone further than primary school (Table 22). In 1996 the figures were 92 per cent and 0 per cent respectively, and in 2008–09 they were 72 per cent and 17 per cent. There had been considerable improvement by 2008–09, although 82 per cent had not had more than primary schooling.

Untouchability Practices

Untouchability is still a serious issue in Tamil Nadu (see the Introduction to this volume) as in other parts of rural India (Shah *et al.* 2006). In the study villages, untouchability practices were more severe for Arunthathiyars than for Pannadis.

In 1981–82, Arunthathiyars faced restrictions on such things as how they got water,[10] where they lived, where they were served and in what tumblers they were served at the tea-shop, where their children sat and in what vessels they drank water at school. There were also language and body language conventions that were demeaning and strict. These were all rigidly enforced too.[11]

The restrictions on Arunthathiyars had decreased considerably by 1996. They could move about more freely and interact with others more easily in public spaces in the villages. More significantly, they had begun to organize independently of members of the dominant castes, through the Ambedkar People's Movement (APM). The activities of an APM cell established in one of the hamlets in 1994 illustrate how significantly relations with dominant caste members had changed. When the establishment of the cell was announced, members of the dominant castes objected, and threatened 'to stop Arunthathiyars from riding bicycles in the village', 'not to give employment to initiators in the village' and 'to file police cases against them'. They also approached Members of the Legislative Assembly in a bid to prevent the APM branch from being set up. The first issue taken up by the APM was the construction of a temple in one of the new Arunthathiyar settlements. When Arunthathiyars began construction work, Other Caste Hindus came with axes, knives and spades to destroy the building. The matter went to the police and the *tahsildar,* who came to the village and got a 'no objection' letter from village leaders, after which there was no further trouble over the construction of the temple. The next move of the APM was to petition the Collector for separate water taps and for the right of Arunthathiyars to fill their pots themselves from the taps in the centre of the village if their own taps ran dry. Both of these demands were met. An APM cell set up in one of the other Arunthathiyar settlements in the early 1990s took up similar issues, but with somewhat less success. That settlement was in a village with some big temples and temple entry was one of the issues there.

There were further moves in the late 1990s, the most notable of which was the abolition of separate seating and separate drinking vessels for

---

[10] They got water from the main village borehole where non-Dalits filled their pots first, and then filled the pots of Arunthathiyars who were not allowed to fill their pots themselves. It looked as though this was designed to humiliate, or at least to keep Arunthathiyars "in their place." It served as one of the more obvious daily reminders of their subordinate status.

[11] When I started fieldwork in 1981–82, I had to negotiate an arrangement to make it possible for me to interview Arunthathiyars as well as caste Hindus. It was finally agreed that if I left the village after interviewing Arunthathiyars and did not return until the next day, others would talk to me, because they could assume that I had had a bath and as a result they would no longer regard me as polluting. This was no longer an issue in 1996 or 2008–09.

Arunthathiyars and Pannadis in schools. The APM was not, however, success-ful in abolishing the practice of using separate glasses for Dalits in tea-shops. In one case the tea-shop was fined for continuing the practice, but after a brief period the practice began again. A tea-shop next to one of the Dalit settlements did stop using the two-glass system permanently, however, at the instigation of the All India Anna Dravida Munnetra Kazhagam (AIADMK), the owner of the shop being an AIADMK supporter. In the late 1990s, the APM cells in both Dalit settlements in which cells had been established were disbanded. In one case this was said to be due to intimidation by members of the dominant castes who broke the APM flagpole outside the settlement. In the other case, lack of support from fellow Arunthathiyars was said to be the reason for the leader switching to the Democratic Youth Federation of India (DYFI).

Thus, as elsewhere in Tamil Nadu, despite dynamic changes in the local economy, untouchability practices remain a serious issue in the study villages. Pannadis have been able to move into the main village in which they live but Arunthathiyars still have to live separately. Arunthathiyars are nowhere near being able to function on an equal footing with others in the villages. A recent illustration of this is the comment of a young man who went on a bus to work in Tiruppur. Once they left the village, the fact that those on the bus came from the same village meant that they formed something of a common bond. When they returned to the village, however, they got off the bus separately. There was no question of going to each other's houses, or even hanging out together on the road once they were back. This does not mean that untouchability is not an issue in Tiruppur and other urban areas. There are plenty of examples of untouchability practices there too.[12]

Conclusions

This essay has shown (i) that Dalits in these villages of Tamil Nadu had very little agricultural land and the situation had changed very little over the period under review; (ii) that they had got considerably more land for house-sites; (iii) that they were only slowly reducing their dependence on agriculture, much more slowly than Other Caste groups; (iv) that within agriculture they were still very predominantly labourers; (v) that to the extent they were entering the non-agricultural economy, they were doing so as employees rather than as self-employed persons; and (vi) that they lagged behind other groups of employees in that they were manual and/or semi-skilled workers rather than non-manual workers. Further, (vii) Dalits were not getting anywhere in self-employment, either in trade or other forms of business; (viii) their educational record was very poor until recently; and (ix) they were still suffering severely from untouchability practices, though less severely than was the case in 1981–82.

---

[12] See Carswell and De Neve (forthcoming), for a contrary view.

Dalits were lagging behind other groups in every respect. This was all within a context in which emigration had been greater among other groups than among Dalit groups. The differences would appear even more marked if emigrants had been included in the analysis above.

The research on which this essay is based has been funded by the U.K. Department of International Development (DFID, formerly ODA), Oxford University Webb Medley Fund, Leverhulme Trust and the Queen Elizabeth House Oppenheimer Fund at different stages, and in 2008–09 by a grant from DFID and ESRC. It has benefited greatly from the participation of Dr V. Mohanasundaram who has been my interpreter and co-researcher for most of the fieldwork since 1981–82, and from the contributions of M.V. Srinivasan, Paul Pandian, Selva Murugan, Arul Maran and Gowri Shankar who did some of the fieldwork interviews. It has also benefited from discussions at seminars in Oxford and elsewhere, and with a large number of individuals, particularly Barbara Harriss-White, J. Jeyaranjan, C. Lakshmanan, Raman Mahadevan, K. Nagaraj and M. Vijayabaskar. I owe a particular debt of thanks to V.K. Ramachandran, Madhura Swaminathan and others at the Foundation for Agrarian Studies in Kolkata for comments and discussions.

References

Baker, Christopher John (1984), *An Indian Rural Economy, 1880–1955: The Tamilnad Countryside*, Clarendon Press, Oxford.

Breman, Jan (1974), *Patronage and Exploitation: Changing Agrarian Relations in South Gujarat, India*, University of California Los Angeles Press, Berkeley.

Carswell, Grace and De Neve, Geert, 'T-Shirts and Tumblers: Caste, Politics and Industrial Work in Tiruppur's Textile Belt, South India', *Contributions to Indian Sociology* (forthcoming).

Cederlof, Gunnel (1997), *Bonds Lost: Subordination, Conflict and Mobilization in Rural South India, c. 1900–70*, Manohar, New Delhi.

Census of India (1971), *Population Census 1971*, Government of India, New Delhi.

Census of India (1981), *Population Census 1981*, Government of India, New Delhi.

Census of India (1991), *Population Census 1991*, Government of India, New Delhi.

Census of India (2001), *Population Census 2001*, Government of India, New Delhi.

Chari, Sharad (2004), *Fraternal Capital: Peasant Workers, Self-Made Men and Globalization in Provincial India*, Permanent Black, New Delhi.

Damodaran, Harish (2008), *India's New Capitalists: Caste, Business and Industry in a Modern Nation*, Permanent Black, New Delhi.

De Neve, Geert and Carswell, Grace (2010), 'From Field to Factory: Tracing Bonded Labour in the Coimbatore Powerloom Industry', unpublished draft manuscript.

Harriss-White, Barbara and Vidyarthee, Kaushal (2010), 'Stigma and Regions of Accumulation: Mapping Dalit and Adivasi Capital in the 1990s', in Barbara Harriss-White and Judith Heyer, eds, *Comparative Political Economy of Development: Africa and Asia*, Routledge, London.

Heyer, Judith (2000), 'The Changing Position of Agricultural Labourers in Villages in Rural Coimbatore, Tamil Nadu, between 1981–02 and 1996', Working Paper no. 27, Queen Elizabeth House, Oxford.

Heyer, Judith (2010), 'The Marginalization of Dalits in a Modernizing Economy', in Barbara Harriss-White and Judith Heyer, eds, *Comparative Political Economy of Development: Africa and Asia*, Routledge, London.

Heyer, Judith (2011), 'Dalit Women Becoming "Housewives": Lessons from the Tiruppur Region, 1981–2 to 2008–9', revised version of paper presented at the Conference on 'Mobility or Marginalization: Dalits in Neo-Liberal India', Oxford University, 1–2 September.

Heyer, Judith (2012), 'Social Policy and Labour Standards: A South Indian Case Study', *Global Labour Journal*, vol. 3, no. 1, pp. 91–117.

Kajisa, Kei and Palanichamy, Venkatesa N. (2010), 'Schooling Investments over Three Decades in Rural Tamil Nadu, India: Changing Effects of Income, Gender and Adult Family Members' Education', *World Development*, vol. 38, no. 3, pp. 298–314.

Ministry of Finance (2007), *Report of the Expert Group on Agricultural Indebtedness*, Government of India, New Delhi.

Prakash, Aseem (2010), 'Dalit Entrepreneurs in Middle India', in Barbara Harriss-White and Judith Heyer, eds, *Comparative Political Economy of Development: Africa and Asia*, Routledge, London.

Shah, Ghanshyam, Mander, Harsh, Thorat, Sukhadeo, Deshpande, Satish and Baviskar, Amita (2006), *Untouchability in Rural India*, Sage Publications, New Delhi.

Singh, Navsharan and Sapra, Mrinalini Kaur (2007), 'Liberalization in Trade and Finance, India's Garment Sector', in Barbara Harriss-White and Anushree Sinha, eds, *Trade Liberalization and India's Informal Economy*, Oxford University Press, New Delhi.

Sivanappan, R.K. and Aiyasamy, P.K. (1978), *Land and Water Resources of Coimbatore District*, Tamil Nadu Agricultural University, Coimbatore.

Vijayabaskar, M. (2011), 'Global Crises, Welfare Provision and Coping Strategies of Labour in Tiruppur', *Economic and Political Weekly*, vol. 46, no. 22, pp. 38–45.

Tenancy and Distress in Thanjavur Region, Tamil Nadu

A Case Study of Palakurichi Village

V. Surjit

Historically, Dalits in the Thanjavur region of Tamil Nadu have been subjected to the worst forms of caste oppression by the dominant oppressor castes. Dalits here have faced discrimination in the form of untouchability, differential access to various public goods and inequality in the ownership of various forms of assets. This discrimination, as well as political organization and mobilization among the oppressed castes in Thanjavur, have been well documented in several scholarly studies (van Schendel 1991; Guhan 1983; Gough 1981; Menon 1979a, 1979b, 1979c and 1983; Sivaraman 1973).

This essay is a case study of landless Dalit households who are now tenant cultivators of land in Palakurichi village, Thanjavur region, Tamil Nadu. Its main objective is to examine the levels of income from cultivation among Dalit cultivators and the factors that determine agricultural incomes in the village. The study attempts to show how Dalit cultivators, because of their lack of ownership of means of production, incur higher costs and earn lower incomes than non-Dalit cultivators. The Thanjavur region has in recent years been experiencing constraints in the availability of irrigation water, which has affected agriculture and cultivator's incomes. In this situation of distress, Dalit cultivators have been worse off than non-Dalit cultivators.

The Thanjavur region (comprising the present districts of Thanjavur, Tiruvarur and Nagapattinam) is historically known as the 'rice bowl' of South India for its rice production systems. The importance of this region in terms of its contribution to rice production in the country has been widely noted in the literature (Gough 1981; van Schendel 1991; Swenson 1973; Menon 1983). The delta of the river Cauvery covers the region. The irrigation system of the Cauvery delta is one of the oldest water control facilities in India, dating back to second century AD in the early Chola period (Bouton 1985).[1] The alluvial soils of the delta are very good for wet cultivation of rice.

From the 1940s and through the early decades of independence, Thanjavur benefited from many government programmes aimed at augmenting rice production. These include the Grow More Food Campaign (1942),

---

[1] See Surjit (2008) for a review of the literature on development of irrigation facilities and changes in agrarian relations in the Thanjavur region over different periods.

the Intensive Agricultural Area Programme (IAAP) (1960–61), and the High Yielding Variety Programme (HYVP) (1966–67) (see Rukmani 1993). Thanjavur was one among seven districts selected for implementation of the Intensive Agricultural District Programme (IADP) in 1962.

Dalit households constitute a substantial share of the population in the region. They are mainly landless agricultural workers.[2] The region also has a long history of oppressive landlordism, under which landless Dalits were the most oppressed section of society. However, Dalits in Thanjavur at present have gained some access to land as a result of years of struggle under the leadership of political forces led by the Left.

The study village, Palakurichi, belongs to Kilvelur taluk of the Old Delta Cauvery zone, and scholars have studied it in detail at different points of time (Figure 1).[3] Gilbert Slater surveyed Palakurichi in 1917; P.J. Thomas and K. C. Ramakrishnan resurveyed the village in 1936; Margaret Haswell studied it in 1961; and S. Guhan resurveyed the village in 1983. These studies provide information about the village and changes that have taken place over almost a century.

The soil of the Old Delta Cauvery zone, to which Palakurichi belongs, is sandy and has often suffered from problems of salinity.[4] The only source of irrigation has been the network of canals branching out of the Cauvery. The region has been affected by low levels of water availability, poor drainage facilities, floods and uncertainty in availability of water through canals.

The region had a bipolar agro-economic structure with the agricultural work force sharply divided between large landowning cultivators belonging (mainly) to non-Brahmin castes and a large body of Dalit agricultural labourers.[5] There was an 'isomorphism of caste and class relations' in the region, and the bond was much stronger than in any other region (Bouton 1985). This peculiar agro-economic structure resulted in a higher degree of agrarian radicalism in this area than in any other part of Thanjavur (Bouton 1985; Gough 1981, 1989; Beteille 1974).

The entire Cauvery delta is irrigated by a network of rivers and canals

[2] According to Census 2001, the share of Dalits in the total population of Thanjavur region (25 per cent) is higher than for the State of Tamil Nadu as a whole (19 per cent).

[3] Palakurichi was a part of Nagapattinam taluk during the 1991 Census.

[4] Marshall M. Bouton classified the Cauvery delta into various agro-ecological zones based on two major criteria: the nature of irrigation facilities, and the nature and composition of the agricultural work force. In order to characterize the nature of irrigation facilities, Bouton examined (i) whether there was irrigation or not, (ii) the 'pervasiveness' of canal irrigation facilities, and (iii) the quality and dependability of water delivered through the irrigation system. For characterizing differences in the composition of the agricultural work force, Bouton looked at the share of agricultural labourers and cultivators in the agricultural work force and in total population, as well as the agrarian density, defined as the number of agricultural workers per unit area of land.

[5] In this zone, the agricultural labourers were organized and mobilized against the large landowners.

Source: Bouton (1985).

that branch out from the river at the Grand Anicut. Irrigation water from the Grand Anicut is carried to the delta through its main branches and canals (the Cauvery, Vennar and Grand Anicut canals), which further branch out into small rivulets and canals. The outflow from the Grand Anicut through this network of small rivers and canals determines the levels of availability of irrigation water for cultivation in different parts of the region.

Although several factors influence the delivery of irrigation water at the field level, the volume of outflow from the Grand Anicut is a broad indicator of the availability of irrigation water. Data on the quantum of water released from the Grand Anicut for the period 1950–51 to 2006–07 are plotted in Figure 2. Over the last 56 years, the highest amount of irrigation water flow (359 thousand million cubic feet) was recorded during 1954–55.

FIGURE 2 *Total flow of irrigation water from Grand Anicut, 1950–51 to 2006–07* in tmc ft

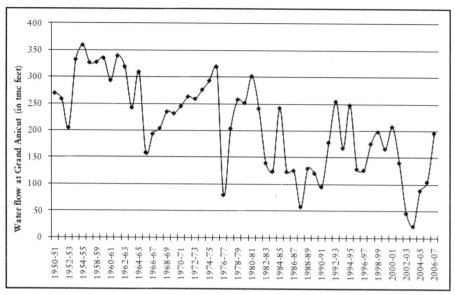

Outflow of water from the Grand Anicut has never reached even 300 thousand million cubic feet (tmc ft) after 1980–81.[6] In 2003–04, the reference year for this village study, the outflow from the Grand Anicut was only 23 tmc ft, the lowest ever in the last five decades. The average outflow during the last five decades (1950–51 to 2006–07) was 210 tmc ft, and the median outflow was 208 tmc ft. Non-availability of irrigation water imposed severe constraints on agricultural production in the region. In Palakurichi, the standing crop of rice when nearing the harvesting stage was severely damaged due to lack of irrigation water, and rice cultivators suffered huge losses due to crop damages.

It must be emphasized that 2003–04, the year of this study, was a year of severe drought in Palakurichi. Availability of irrigation water was extremely low. This exceptional situation in respect of availability of irrigation water had exceptional implications in terms of not only of agricultural yields and profitability, but also for cultivation practices and the labour process.

Method of Data Collection

A detailed house-listing exercise was undertaken in the village in April 2004, which was completed in a week. As part of the house-listing, detailed data were collected on both operational and ownership holdings of land, nature of tenure of land, and type of irrigation. Data were also collected on

---

[6] Data for the period 1950–51 to 1979–80 were collected from the Records of the Superintending Engineer, Public Works Department, Thanjavur Circle, cited in TNAU (1985). Data for the period 1980–81 to 2006–07 were collected from the Records of the Office of Executive Engineer, Public Works Department, Cauvery Division. The total outflow recorded is the amount of water released into Cauvery, Vennar and Grand Anicut Canal alone. Water released into Coleroon and the scouring sluice was not taken into account. Data for 1955–56 and 1956–57 were not available.

demographic and socio-economic characteristics of household members, particularly by caste, age, sex, primary and secondary occupation, literacy levels, and educational status. There were a total of 427 households in Palakurichi village, distributed over three wards.

From the house-listing, households that had cultivated some land during the previous agricultural year (i.e. 2003–04) were identified. Out of the 427 households, 134 households reported operational holdings during the previous agricultural year. These households were then classified into six different size-classes: (1) marginal (0.01 hectare to 1 hectare); (2) small (1.01 hectares to 2 hectares); (3) semi-medium (2.01 hectares to 4 hectares); (4) medium (4.01 hectares to 10 hectares); (5) large (10.01 hectares to 20 hectares); and (6) more than 20 hectares. Households within each size-class of cultivators were further stratified into Dalit and non-Dalit households.

For the detailed survey on farm business incomes in Palakurichi, a sample of 40 per cent of all cultivator households was selected. Out of 134 households with operational holdings, 55 households were selected by simple random sampling without replacement, in proportion to the number of households in each size-class and caste group to which they belonged (Table 1).

In 2004, Palakurichi had a population of 1,647 persons in 427 households.[7] The majority of households (58 per cent) were Dalit households. Of the 247 Dalit households in the village, 135 belonged to the Parayar caste and 112 belonged to the Pallar caste (Appendix Table A1). Among caste Hindus, Padayatchis were the largest caste group, constituting about 16 per cent of total households. This was followed by Pillai, Naidu, Konar, Thevar and Vellala castes, each constituting less than 5 per cent of total households. Naidu households, which accounted for only 4.2 per cent of total households, were historically the largest landowners in the village. Though Dalits constituted a substantial share of the population in Palakurichi, historically they faced various kinds of overt and covert discrimination. At the time of the study

TABLE 1 *Details of sample households, by caste, by size-class of operational holdings, Palakurichi village, 2004* in numbers

Size-class (in hectares)	Dalits	Non-Dalits	All
0.01 to 1	13	20	33
1.01 to 2	2	8	10
2.01 to 4	1	2	3
4.01 to 10	1	4	5
10.01 to 20	0	2	2
> 20	0	2	2
All	17	38	55

Source: Survey data, 2004.

[7] The total number of households according to the 2001 Census was 424, with a population of 1,649 (PCA Census 2001).

there were seven distinct habitations in Palakurichi; caste Hindus occupied the main habitation, and the Dalit settlements were located far away from it.[8] The picture was not very different from a century ago, when it was observed that 'the Dalit settlements are built at a furlong distance from the caste village connected only by the small narrow earth banks' (Rajalu 1918: 79).

Although the physical separation between the habitations of Dalits and Other Castes remained unchanged over the years, there was a marked decline in overt forms of discrimination against Dalits in Palakurichi. This came about mainly on account of their organization under the leadership of the Communist Party of India (Marxist) since the late 1960s (Guhan 1983).[9]

Conditions of Agricultural Production in Palakurichi

Agriculture was the single most important source of livelihood in Palakurichi. In 2004, the primary occupations of about 78 per cent of workers in the village were agriculture-based. The agricultural economy of Palakurichi has been a rice-based one for the last nine decades. The most important factors that have determined the course of agricultural transformations over this period are, first, the construction of the Mettur dam in 1934 and the consequent availability of irrigation water; secondly, the thrust for agricultural modernization as part of the 'green revolution' from the early 1960s; and thirdly, the decline in availability of irrigation water from the Cauvery irrigation system from the late 1980s.

At present, the entire village is primarily dependent on a single crop of direct-sown, long-duration rice (the *samba* crop). In 2003–04, out of the gross cropped area of 961 acres, 957 acres were under rice cultivation. In Palakurichi, the *samba* crop of rice is sown in August, and harvested in January and February the following year. The timing of various operations in rice cultivation depends largely on the availability of canal water from the Cauvery river. In a normal year, water is released from the Mettur dam at the beginning of June, and it reaches the tail end of the delta, where Palakurichi is situated, only by the second week of July. Cultivators start their field preparation and ploughing depending on the arrival of water from the Cauvery. During the last two decades, there have been unprecedented delays in releasing adequate supplies of water from the dam. On several occasions, water was not available for a sufficiently long period of time to raise the crop.

---

[8] In 2004, the farthest Dalit settlement in Palakurichi village was situated at a distance of more than a kilometre from the main caste Hindu settlement.

[9] With respect to this Guhan notes: 'In the perception of Harijans, a very significant contribution of the Party [Communist Party of India (Marxist)] has been to free them from traditional repression by landlords. Older pannayals recalled how 20 to 25 years ago, it was normal for landlords to flog their pannayals, physically tie them to ploughs, and make them drink cow dung soaked in water as a punishment. . . . If today these practices were things of the past, the credit went largely to the party. "We have no fear as long as the red flag flies" was a statement that was frequently repeated' (Guhan 1983: 103).

Under these circumstances, cultivation practices had to be modified to make optimum use of the limited amount of irrigation water available for a short period of time. Although rice cultivation in Palakurichi uses modern inputs, it lacks proper adoption of new technology and farming practices as recommended for similar production environments by research institutions. This is mainly reflected in the quality of field operations and the use of higher seed rates than the recommended levels.

Agrarian Structure in Palakurichi

As mentioned earlier, 78 per cent of the work force in Palakurichi depended on agriculture for their livelihood. Among them, agricultural labourers constituted 64 per cent and 14 per cent were cultivators. There was strict caste-based division within the work force dependent on agriculture. In 2004, the majority of agricultural labourers (83 per cent) were Dalits, and the majority of cultivators (68 per cent) were Other Caste Hindus.

In an agrarian economy, access to land plays a key role in determining livelihoods, as well as the position of households in the social and economic structure of the village. The pattern of land ownership in Palakurichi in 2004 reflected exceptionally high levels of inequality. The most striking feature of this unequal distribution of land was that 80 per cent of the households were landless (Table 2). At the other end of the distribution, about 3.2 per cent of landowning households owned over 67 per cent (115.9 hectares) of total land.

Inequality in operational holdings was also of similar magnitude. About 69 per cent of all households did not operate any land. On the other hand, about 4.9 per cent of households operated over 70 per cent of total land. In 2004, the Gini coefficient of distribution of ownership holdings in Palakurichi was 0.92, and the Gini coefficient of distribution of operational holdings was 0.89 (Table 3).

Historically, inequality in the distribution of ownership holdings has been high in Palakurichi. In his study of 1917, Rajalu (1918: 81) observed:

TABLE 2 *Distribution of number of households and extent of ownership holdings, by size-class of ownership holdings, Palakurichi village, 2004*

Size-class (in hectares)	Number of households	Share (in per cent)	Extent of land (in hectares)	Share (in per cent)
0	341	79.9	0.0	0.0
0.01 to 1	54	12.6	27.2	15.9
1.01 to 2	13	3.0	16.4	9.6
2.01 to 4	5	1.2	12.2	7.1
4.01 to 10	12	2.8	77.4	45.1
10.01 to 20	1	0.2	14.2	8.3
>20	1	0.2	24.3	14.2
Total	427	100.0	171.7	100.0

Source: Survey data, 2004.

'evidence from tradition shows that the whole village was for generations in the hands of large landlords'. The resurvey in 1983 by Guhan showed that inequality in ownership of landholdings had increased over time. According to Guhan (1983), inequality in ownership of land holdings (excluding landless households), estimated in terms of the Gini coefficient, increased from 0.69 in 1896 to 0.71 in 1980 (Table 4). Data collected in 2003–04 show that the inequality in distribution of ownership holdings of land among landed households declined marginally between 1983 and 2004. However, this decline was accompanied by an increase in the proportion of landless households. The proportion of landless households increased from 72.5 per cent in 1983 to 80 per cent in 2004.

The disparity in ownership and operational holdings between households belonging to different caste groups is very striking. About 93 per cent of Dalit households (constituting 58 per cent of all households in the village) and 62 of non-Dalit households did not own any land in 2004 (Table 5). Pallars and Parayars were the Dalit castes in Palakurichi, and among them, 54 per cent of Parayar households and 46 per cent of Pallar households were landless. Further, 83 per cent of Dalit households and 49 per cent of non-Dalit

TABLE 3   *Gini coefficient for distribution of landholdings among households, Palakurichi village, 2004*

Type of household landholding	Including landless households	Excluding landless households
Ownership	0.92	0.61
Operational	0.89	0.66

Source: Survey data, 2004.

TABLE 4   *Gini Coefficient for distribution of ownership holdings, Palakurichi Village, 1896 to 2004*

Year	Gini coefficient
1896	0.69
1980	0.71
2004	0.61

Sources: Guhan (1983); survey data, 2004.

TABLE 5   *Share of landless households and average size of ownership holding, by caste, Palakurichi village, 2004*

Village	Percentage of households with no ownership holdings			Average size of ownership holding per landowning household (in hectares)		
	Dalits	Non-Dalits	All	Dalits	Non-Dalits	All
Palakurichi	93.1	61.7	80.0	0.71	2.31	2.00

Source: Survey data, 2004.

households did not possess any operational holdings of land. The per capita extent of ownership holding among Dalit households that owned land was 0.71 hectare, and the corresponding figure for non-Dalit households was 2.31 hectares (Table 6). A similar gap existed between Dailt and non-Dalit households in respect of operational holdings (0.84 hectare and 2.91 hectares).

The wide disparity in relative access to land between Dalit and non-Dalit households in Palakurichi in 2004 is reflected in the index of access to land (Table 7). The access index for a social group j, denoted as A_j, can be represented as follows:

$$A_j = \frac{\text{Percentage of total extent of landholding owned or operated by group } j}{\text{Percentage of households in group } j \text{ among total households}}$$

A higher value of access index indicates better access to land (Nagaraj 2007). In terms of ownership holdings of land in Palakurichi, the access index for Dalits was 12.2 while the same for non-Dalits was 220.5.

The access index of operational holding of land for Dalits was better than that with respect to ownership holding of land. This is also reflected in the better relative access index with respect to operational holdings than ownership holdings of land. This is mainly due to the fact that in recent years Dalits have gained some access to land through tenancy because of their struggles under the leadership of the Communist Party of India (Marxist) (CPI[M]) (see Bouton 1985; Gough 1989; Guhan 1983).[10]

TABLE 6 *Share of landless households and average size of operational holding, by caste, Palakurichi village, 2004*

Village	Percentage of households with no operational holdings			Average size of operational holding per land-operating household (in hectares)		
	Dalits	non-Dalits	All	Dalits	non-Dalits	All
Palakurichi	83.0	48.9	68.6	0.84	2.91	2.26

Source: Survey data, 2004.

TABLE 7 *Access to land, by caste, Palakurichi village, 2004* in per cent

Village	Access to ownership of land			Access to operational holding of land		
	Access index for Dalits	Access index for non-Dalits	Relative access index*	Access index for Dalits	Access index for non-Dalits	Relative access index
Palakurichi	12.2	220.5	18.1	20.1	209.6	10.4

Note: *Relative access index is the ratio of access index for non-Dalits to that for Dalits.
Source: Survey data, 2004.

[10] A detailed account of the agrarian struggles in Thanjavur region is given in Rama-krishnan (2014).

Tenancy in Palakurichi

Reviewing the early studies on Palakurichi, Guhan (1983: 74) observed that 'historically, tenancy has not been prominent in Palakurichi'. In 1917, Rajalu reported that there were 132 households who owned land in the village, and all but five of them cultivated some part of their own land (Rajalu 1918: 78). More than 75 per cent of the land was cultivated by the owners themselves. He also mentioned that there were nineteen cultivating tenants who did not own any land, and that ten owned small holdings but leased in some more land for cultivation (ibid.). The situation was almost the same twenty years later, in 1937, when Tirumalai observed that of the total land under cultivation (1049.6 acres), 105.9 acres were leased out and cultivated by tenants (Tirumalai 1940: 122–23). This accounted for 10 per cent of the total cultivated land. In 1983 Guhan reported that 45 acres of land (which mainly belonged to temples) were being cultivated by 34 tenants who did not own any land themselves (Guhan 1983: 74). This accounted for less than 5 per cent of the net cropped area of 1006 acres.[11] In my survey of 2004, the degree of tenancy (defined as the ratio of total land leased in for cultivation to the total extent of operational holdings of land) was very high, at 43 per cent.

A special feature of landholdings in Palakurichi village in 2004 was that temples and religious institutions owned the land that was leased out for cultivation. Two temples, Varadarajaperumal Kovil and Parvatheeswaran Kovil, owned wet land (*nanjai*) that was leased out to individual cultivators. In 2004, these two temples leased out 8.5 hectares of land to fourteen individuals. A notable feature of temple-land tenancies is that the tenants are predominantly from caste Hindu families. Of the fourteen temple tenants in 2004, only one was a Dalit cultivator. However, thirteen of the fourteen tenants sub-leased some of the temple land to other cultivators. Historically, only Other Castes were tenants of temple lands. From 1978 onwards, in response to the movement led by the CPI(M), Dalits gained some access to temple lands. However, as my survey of 2004 shows, the majority of temple-land tenants continue to be caste Hindus, and Dalits have access to temple lands mainly as sub-tenants of the official tenants.[12]

As noted above, a significant change in the agrarian structure after the 1980s was the rise in incidence of tenancy in Palakurichi. In contrast with previous studies, in 2003–04 it was found that out of the total operational holdings of 303.33 hectares in the village, nearly 130 hectares of land (43 per cent of the total extent) were leased in for cultivation (Table 8). There are two major reasons for the increase in incidence of tenancy between 1983

[11] The net cropped area reported by Guhan was the average net cropped area for the period 1974–78, taken from the Village Statistical Register (Guhan 1983: 41, Table 19). We assume that there would not have been a major increase or decrease in the net cropped area of the village in a short period.

[12] Thus, in the Record of Tenancy Rights (RTR), it is the name of the caste Hindu cultivator that is recorded and not that of the actual Dalit cultivator.

TABLE 8   *Details of lease and mortgage transactions of land, Palakurichi village, 2004*

Degree of tenancy	Percentage of tenant households among cultivators	Lease transactions		Mortgage transactions		Total operated land as percentage of total owned land
		Amount of land leased in (in hectares)	Amount of land leased out (in hectares)	Amount of land mortgaged in (in hectares)	Amount of land mortgaged out (in hectares)	
42.8	18.5	129.9	2.6	1.0	5.3	176.7

Source: Survey data, 2004.

TABLE 9   *Details of lease transactions of land, by caste, Palakurichi village, 2004*

	Dalits	Non-Dalits
Degree of tenancy	68.40	39.50
Percentage of tenant households among cultivators	11.70	27.80
Total amount of land leased in (in hectares)	24.13 (18.60)*	105.75 (81.40)*
Total amount of land leased out (in hectares)	1.34	1.21
Percentage of lessor households	1.20	1.70

Note: * Indicates share of total land leased in for cultivation.
Source: Survey data, 2004.

and 2004. First, in a number of Naidu households that were traditional land-owners, young adult members moved out of the village and settled in cities. These households then began to lease out their land for cultivation. Secondly, some large cultivators who depended on wage labour for cultivation shifted to tenancy arrangements when rice cultivation came under stress from the uncertainty and inadequacy of irrigation water.

The major share of land under tenancy was held by non-Dalit households. Of the total land leased in by cultivator households in Palakurichi, about 81 per cent was leased in by non-Dalit households (Table 9). At the same time, it was through tenancy that Dalit households gained some access to land for cultivation. Of the total operational holdings cultivated by Dalit households, about 68 per cent was leased-in land. In comparison, about 40 per cent of land operated by non-Dalit households was leased-in land.

Historically, as elsewhere in Thanjavur, two major forms of tenancy existed in Palakurichi: share tenancy (*varam*) and fixed-rent tenancy (*kuthagai*). During the early part of the twentieth century, sharecropping was the prevalent form of tenancy in the region. Later, sharecropping gave way to fixed-rent tenancy, though the pace of change was different in different parts of the Cauvery delta. Tirumalai (1940) noted that land in Palakurichi was mostly leased out on fixed rent, and in cases where there was a failure of rain or the land was less fertile leading to an uncertainty in yields, the sharecropping system was practised. About the fixed-rent system of tenancy, Tirumalai observed, though the system of Kuttagai is meant to give the tenants an opportunity to improve the land and profit by the increased yield, actually the reverse is the case, because the tenants generally have no capital to meet the initial costs of cultivation. The short period of the lease offers no incentive either. (Ibid.: 125)

In 2004, all leased land was under fixed-rent tenancy.

In 2003–04, the system of tenancy was *kuthagai* or fixed-rent tenancy and none of the lease arrangements were registered. Among the 55 sample cultivators, twenty-three cultivators had leased in land for cultivation from twenty-seven lessors. Out of these twenty-seven lessors, ten were temples. In all cases, the lessor was an Other Caste cultivator (twelve out of seventeen individual lessors belonged to the Naidu caste and of the remaining five, none were Dalits). As already mentioned, temple land is usually leased out to caste Hindu cultivators with large landholdings. Other cultivators sub-lease temple land from these lessees. In my sample, only one Dalit cultivator sub-leased land from a Naidu landowner who in turn had leased it from a temple. Guhan (1983: 74) had also noted that 'in most of these cases, there was a main lessee who was usually a resident Naidu landowner connected with the temple as a trustee. He sublet the land to a number of his farm servants or other workers.'

Rent was usually paid in kind by the tenant. However, because of low agricultural production in the recent past, some tenants paid the rent in cash to the owner of the land. In 2003–04, out of the twenty-three sample cultivators who had leased in land, sixteen cultivators paid the rent in kind and the remaining six paid in cash. One Dalit cultivator was sowing government land owned by the Public Works Department and he did not pay any rent. Though some cultivators paid the rent in cash, the owner of the land did not share the costs of any of the inputs used for cultivation.

Over the years, as the fortunes of rice cultivation changed, the amount of rent to be paid to the landowner also changed (Table 10). In 1918, the rent paid in kind, as reported by Rajalu (1918), was 834 kg per hectare, constituting 74 per cent of the total produce. Yield levels rose in 1940 and the rent paid in kind was 1,704 kg per hectare (74 per cent of the produce)

TABLE 10 *Amount of rent paid in kind and its share in total produce for leased-in land, Palakurichi village, 1918–2004* in kg per hectare

Year	Rent paid in kind (in kg)	Yield	Share of produce paid as rent (in per cent)
1918	834	1130	74
1940	1704	2320	73
1983	1112–1667	3160	35–53
2004	672–1254	1240	54–101
2004*	889–1112	1240	72–90

Note: *This was the information about rental rates which I got from discussions with cultivators in the village.

Sources: Rajalu (1918); Tirumalai (1940); Guhan (1983); Survey data 2004.

(Tirumalai 1940). By the 1980s, yield levels had increased considerably and the rent paid in kind varied from 1,112 kg to 1,667 kg per hectare, constituting 35 to 53 per cent of the total produce. Though the rent paid increased, the share of produce paid as rent declined due to the rise in yield from 2,320 kg per hectare in 1940 to 3,160 kg per hectare in 1983. Analysing the terms and conditions of tenancy, Guhan (1983) observed: 'Tenancy is worthwhile only if two crops could be grown as otherwise the rent was about a third to one half of gross output and over three-fourths of the net return on a single crop.'

In 2003–04, the average rent paid by tenants was 988 kg per hectare. This was lower than the absolute level of rent in 1983. However, given the yields that year, it constituted about 79 per cent of the average yield. Thus, the share of produce paid as rent in 2004 was higher than the corresponding share paid in 1983. The average hides large variations. The rent paid ranged from 672 kg per hectare to 1,254 kg per hectare. In general, temple lands were leased at a higher rent than land leased out by individual lessors. Among the sample cultivators, the average rent per hectare paid in kind for temple lands was 1,014 kg per hectare, whereas the average rent for land leased from individual cultivators was 968 kg per hectare. This differential was because some individual lessors reduced the rents in 2003–04 in view of the low level of yields. There was no such reduction in rents to be paid to the temples. The Executive Officer in charge of the temple land reported that rents on temple land were waived only if the State government announced such waiver as policy and issued orders to that effect.[13]

Six tenants in the sample paid the rent for leased-in land in cash. This was done mostly in cases of land leased in from individual cultivators (other than one cultivator who paid the rent in cash for temple land taken on sublease from a large cultivator). The remaining sixteen cultivators paid rent in kind.

Among twenty-three tenant cultivators in the sample, only two had not paid the rent for the last two years. In some cases, the landowner had allowed the tenant to defer payment of rent. But in no case had the rent been written off because of crop failure. In 2003–04, because of losses in rice production, the State government announced a relief amount of Rs 1,000 per acre for those who had lost their crops. Since all lease arrangements in the village were unregistered, none of the tenants got any such monetary relief. The relief was taken by the lessors who had the legal rights over the land leased out. In a few cases the lessor reduced the rent payments of the actual cultivator.

Farm Business Incomes in Palakurichi

Farm business income is defined here as the difference between the gross value of output realized by a cultivator and Cost A2 incurred for cultivation of crop. Cost A2 is the value of all paid-out costs, including rents.

---

[13] Personal communication from the Executive Officer, Varadarajaperumal Kovil, Nagapattinam.

A detailed definition of the components of farm business income is given in Appendix A7. The striking result from my data on farm business incomes in Palakurichi is that, in 2003–04, 51 cultivators (93 per cent) out of a sample of 55 cultivators suffered losses.[14] On average, the gross value of output per hectare was Rs 7,423. In comparison, the average level of cost of cultivation (Cost A2) per hectare was Rs 17,487. In other words, on average, a cultivator in Palakurichi incurred a loss of Rs 10,064 on every hectare of land cultivated with rice in 2003–04 (Table 11).

Negative farm business incomes in Palakurichi in 2003–04 were essentially on account of low rice yields. Given that the average Cost A2 was Rs 17,487 and the average price of rough rice received by cultivators was Rs 5.42 per kg, a yield of 3.23 tonnes per hectare would have been required for an average cultivator to break even. In fact, the average yield in Palakurichi in 2003–04 was only 1.24 tonnes per hectare. It may be noted that the average yield of rice in Nagapattinam district was below 3.23 tonnes per hectare for half the years between 1992–93 and 2005–06. The yield level was consistently below 3.23 tonnes per hectare in the four years from 2002–03 to 2005–06 (see Appendix Table A2).

It is also important to point out that in 2003–04, total household incomes (that is, income from all sources) of most households in Palakurichi were very low. About 40 per cent of the households were unable to cover losses incurred in crop production with income from other sources. In other words, in the case of 40 per cent of households, the total net income from all sources – including income from labouring out in agriculture and non-agricultural activities, dairying, hiring out machinery like diesel pump-sets and tractors, businesses, services, traditional caste occupations, salaried jobs, government pensions, and remittances – was negative. Such households had to cover their losses by using their past savings, by borrowing or by selling assets accumulated in the past. The official poverty line for rural Tamil Nadu

TABLE 11 *Farm business incomes, Cost A2 and gross value of output per hectare, by size-class of operational holdings, Palakurichi village, 2003–04* in Rs per hectare at current prices

Size-class (in hectares)	Gross value of output	Cost A2	Farm business income
0.1 to 1	7159	18347	−11188
1.01 to 2	9256	18234	−8978
2.01 to 4	3833	14614	−10781
4.01 to 10	6928	15418	−8490
10.01 to 20	10080	13412	−3333
> 20	6589	13116	−6527
All	7423	17487	−10064

Source: Survey data, 2004.

[14] The four cultivators who made profits from rice cultivation had their land in other villages.

estimated from the 61st round of the NSS survey on consumer expenditure for the year 2004–05 was Rs 4,239 per capita per annum. In Palakurichi, in 2003–04, only 25 per cent of cultivator households had per capita household incomes above the official poverty line.

While almost all cultivators in Palakurichi produced low yields of rice in 2003–04, the magnitude of loss they incurred varied significantly by caste. The data show that on average, non-Dalit cultivators had higher levels of gross value of output and lower levels of Cost A2 than Dalit cultivators. On balance, non-Dalit households made a smaller net loss (Rs 8,886 per hectare) than Dalit households (Rs 12,696 per hectare) (Table 12). A *t* test was carried out to verify the equality of means of farm business incomes and Cost A2 between Dalit and non-Dalit cultivators. It was found that Dalit cultivators had significantly (10 per cent level of significance) higher levels of Cost A2 and significantly (5 per cent level of significance) lower levels of farm business incomes (higher levels of loss) than non-Dalit cultivators (see Appendix Tables A3, A4). Most Dalit cultivators had very small operational holdings; only two Dalit households in the village cultivated more than 2 hectares of land. In the lower size-categories of operational holdings, in which a substantial number of the Dalit households were situated, Dalit cultivators incurred

TABLE 12 *Farm business incomes, Cost A2 and gross value of output per hectare, by caste, by size-class of operational holdings, Palakurichi village, 2003–04* in Rs per hectare at current prices

Size-class	Gross value of output		Cost A2		Farm business income	
(in hectares)	Dalits	Non-Dalits	Dalits	Non-Dalits	Dalits	Non-Dalits
0.1 to 1	5841	8016	18777	18068	–12935	–10053
1.01 to 2	4198	10520	22757	17104	–18559	–6583
2.01 to 4	7834	1832	18121	12861	–10287	–11028
4.01 to 10	11205	5859	11486	16401	–280	–10542
10.01 to 20	NA	10080	NA	13412	NA	–3333
> 20.0	NA	6589	NA	13116	NA	–6527
All	6081	8024	18777	16910	–12696	–8886

Note: NA = not applicable.
Source: Survey data, 2004.

TABLE 13 *Average farm business incomes and total household incomes, by caste, Palakurichi village, 2003–04* in Rs per annum per household

Size-class (in hectares)	Total farm business incomes	Total other incomes	Total household incomes	Household income per capita
Dalits	–9845	13914	4069	1115
Non-Dalits	–21709	40981	19272	5339
All	–18042	32615	14573	4033

Source: Survey data, 2004.

TABLE 14   *Levels of Cost A2, gross value of output and farm business income from all crops among cultivators in Palakurichi village during 2003–04, by terms of possession of operational holding* in Rs per hectare

Terms of possession of land	Gross value of output	Cost A2	Farm business income
Owner cultivator	5988	16520	–10532
Owner-cum-tenant cultivator	10265	19075	–8810
Pure tenant cultivator	6739	23781	–17043

Source: Survey data, 2004.

considerably higher levels of losses than non-Dalit cultivators (Table 13).[15]

Between Dalit and non-Dalit cultivators, total losses from crop production were higher for non-Dalit cultivators. But incomes from other sources and, on balance, total household incomes were more than four times higher for non-Dalit households than Dalit households (Table 13). It is important to note this ability of non-Dalit households to earn incomes from other sources to compensate for losses from crop cultivation.

As discussed in the earlier section, the distribution of ownership holdings of land was very unequal, and Dalits gained some access to land through tenancy. I have classified cultivators into three categories, based on the terms of possession of land cultivated: (i) owner cultivators, (ii) owner-cum-tenant cultivators, and (iii) pure tenant cultivators. The levels of farm business incomes and costs varied significantly across the three categories. Pure tenants had significantly higher levels of costs and lower levels of farm business incomes than other cultivators (Table 14).[16] Owner cultivators, who were mainly rich peasants and landlords, had lower levels of gross value of output than pure tenants and owner-cum-tenant cultivators. This is because the rich peasants and landlords, realizing that the yields were going to be abysmally low, did not harvest the crop from plots that were severely damaged and thus saved on the costs of harvesting the crop.

Pattern of Input Use in Rice Cultivation

Table 15 presents the structure of cost of cultivation of rice in Palakurichi. The largest item of cost in rice cultivation was human labour. It

---

[15] There was only one Dalit household in the size-category 4–10 hectares of operational holding. This household had higher gross value of output and slightly lower Cost A2 than non-Dalit cultivators in this category. This Dalit cultivator possessed a private pond near his field and could save his crop in the reference year by utilizing water from the pond for irrigation.

[16] The ANOVA for differences in levels of farm business incomes and Cost A2 of cultivators showed that they varied significantly (5 per cent level of significance) across owner cultivators, owner-cum-tenant cultivators and pure tenant cultivators (Appendix Tables A5 and A6). I performed *t* tests for significant differences in mean values of farm business incomes and Cost A2 between owner cultivators, owner-cum-tenant cultivators and pure tenant cultivators. The tests showed that owner cultivators and owner-cum-tenant cultivators had significantly higher levels of farm business incomes and lower levels of Cost A2 than pure tenant cultivators.

constituted, on average, 34 per cent of the total cost. This was followed by expenditure on machine labour and fertilizers, each of which constituted, on average, nearly 17 per cent of Cost A2. The fourth major item of cost the rental value of leased-in land, which constituted, on average, 10 per cent of Cost A2. These four items together constituted nearly 75 per cent of the total paid-out cost of rice cultivation. Other items of cost were irrigation and seeds, each of which constituted, on average, 7 per cent of Cost A2. Expenditure on interest on working capital accounted for 4 per cent of Cost A2.

TABLE 15 *Average cost of cultivation of rice, by item of cost, Palakurichi village, 2003–04*

Item	Cost per hectare	Share in Cost A2 (in per cent)
Hired human labour	5992	34
Machine labour	2952	17
Seed	1229	7
Plant protection chemicals	240	1
Farmyard manure	335	2
Fertilizer	2810	16
Irrigation	1193	7
Interest on working capital	744	4
Rental value of leased-in land	1715	10
Depreciation and maintenance	177	1
Land revenue	35	0.2
Miscellaneous	64	0
Cost A2	17487	100

Source: Survey data, 2004.

TABLE 16 *Item-wise cost of cultivation of rice, by caste, Palakurichi village, 2003–04* in Rs per hectare

Item	Dalits		Non-Dalits	
	Amount	Share (in per cent)	Amount	Share (in per cent)
Hired human labour	5921	32	6024	36
Machine labour	3405	18	2750	16
Seed	1380	7	1162	7
Plant protection chemicals	238	1	241	1
Farmyard manure	257	1	370	2
Fertilizer	2721	14	2849	17
Irrigation	1386	7	1107	7
Interest on working capital	660	4	782	5
Rental value of leased-in land	2635	14	1303	8
Depreciation and maintenance	36	0	240	1
Land revenue	57	0	25	0
Miscellaneous	81	0	56	0
Cost A2	18777	100	16910	100

Source: Survey data, 2004.

TABLE 17 *Expenditure on input use among cultivators in Palakurichi village during 2003–04, by terms of possession* in Rs per hectare

Item	Owner cultivator	Owner-cum-tenant cultivator	Pure tenant cultivator
Hired human labour	5440	6476	6425
Machine labour	2775	2934	3926
Seed	1255	1128	1298
Plant protection chemical	271	232	194
Farmyard manure	299	234	516
Fertilizer	2662	2377	3569
Depreciation and maintenance charges	2338	686	1484
Irrigation	637	1197	2183
Land revenue	136	59	11
Rental value of leased-in land	0	2969	3160
Interest on working capital	686	690	909
Miscellaneous	21	94	105
Cost A2	16520	19075	23781

Source: Survey data, 2004.

Table 16 shows the item-wise costs for cultivators disaggregated by caste groups. Dalit cultivators in Palakurichi incurred a higher level of Cost A2 than non-Dalit cultivators. The item-wise costs of cultivation of rice for Dalit and non-Dalit cultivators show that Dalit cultivators spent more than non-Dalit cultivators on machine labour, seed, irrigation and rental value of leased-in land.

Similarly, if we analyse the expenditure on various inputs with respect to the degree of tenancy among cultivators, we can see that pure tenants, who are mainly Dalit, spent much more than others on the rental value of leased-in land, machine labour, irrigation and interest on working capital (Table 17). This difference in levels of expenditure was mainly due to lack of ownership of land and of machinery used for cultivation, particularly tractors and diesel pumps. Pure tenants paid more to hire these means of production.

Differences in levels of expenditure on these inputs between Dalit and non-Dalit cultivators are discussed below.

Expenditure on Rental Value of Land

There was a significant difference in expenditure on rental value of land incurred by different caste groups. Dalit cultivators spent Rs 2,635 per hectare as rent (14 per cent of Cost A2), whereas non-Dalit cultivators spent less than half that amount (Rs 1,303, or 8 per cent of Cost A2). We know that about 93 per cent of Dalit households in Palakurichi did not own any agricultural land. Dalit households primarily cultivated and obtained land through tenancy. As a result, an average Dalit household incurred a substantially higher cost on account of rental payments than an average non-Dalit household (Table 16). In 2003–04, the year of my survey, the rent paid by tenant cultivators constituted a substantial component of Cost A2. The average value of rental payments for tenant households was Rs 3,144 per hectare. This constituted about 16 per cent of their average Cost A2. When averaged over all cultivators, about 10 per cent of Cost A2, constituting Rs 1,715 per hectare, was spent on rent. Rental payments constituted a substantial share of Cost A2 for small peasants and Dalit cultivators. In Palakurichi, since all tenancy contracts were fixed-rent contracts, the losses due to lower yields had to be absorbed by the tenant alone.

Expenditure on Machine Labour and Irrigation

Machine labour was the second biggest item of cost in rice cultivation in Palakurichi. The machines used in the village were tractors, diesel pumps and sprayers.[17] Machines were used for ploughing, irrigation, spraying plant protection chemicals and threshing the harvested crop. All tillage operations in Palakurichi were done with the help of tractors. It needs to be noted that in a village entirely dependent on public canal irrigation, cultivators had to incur substantial costs for the delivery of irrigation water to the field. On account of being situated at the tail end of the canal system, irrigation water was available in Palakurichi only for a short duration. Also, in 2003–04, the flow rate of water in the canal was low. Some fields in Palakurichi were at a higher elevation than the irrigation channel, and water did not flow to these fields by force of gravity. Given these constraints, most cultivators in Palakurichi had to incur substantial expenditure to pump water from the irrigation channel to their fields.

Differences across cultivators in the cost of machine labour and irrigation were related, most importantly, to a highly unequal pattern of ownership of machines. The Gini coefficient for distribution of the value of means of production, excluding land, was 0.95. Table 18 gives the pattern of ownership of machines among Dalit and non-Dalit cultivators. It shows that there were large inequalities in ownership of machines as between cultivators belonging to different caste groups.

In 2003–04, there were sixteen tractors in the village. Among the

TABLE 18 *Number of tractors, diesel pumps and sprayers owned by households, by caste, Palakurichi village, 2003–04*

Caste	Tractor	Diesel pump	Sprayer	Average value of means of production (in Rs)	Total number of households
Dalits	0	1	1	41535	17
Non-Dalits	2	15	4	220187	38
All	2	16	5	164968	55

Source: Survey data, 2004.

[17] Apart from these machines, cultivators also possessed implements like sickles, axes, crowbars and pickaxes.

sample cultivator households, one landlord household and one household deriving its main income from non-farm businesses owned tractors. No Dalit household in the village owned a tractor.

The distribution of ownership of diesel pumps was also highly unequal: households with relatively large operational holdings owned disproportionately higher numbers of pump-sets. There was only one Dalit household that owned a diesel pump, whereas non-Dalit households owned fifteen pumps.

Similarly, sprayers were owned by rich peasants, landlords and households deriving most of their income from non-farm businesses. Of seventeen Dalit households in the sample, only one household owned a sprayer.

Owning a tractor helped non-Dalit cultivators time their ploughing operations in such a manner that land preparation and sowing of seeds was finished just before the irrigation water arrived in the village. This helped in efficient utilization of the limited quantity of water available for proper germination and crop establishment. Cultivators who did not own tractors, on the other hand, had to hire them for ploughing and threshing. These cultivators not only spent more on machines than those who owned tractors, but also faced problems in timely availability of machine labour. The rate for hiring tractors for three rounds of ploughing was Rs 1,500 per hectare. In some cases, cultivators had to resort to wet ploughing. Under such circumstances, when ploughing was not timed according to the availability of irrigation water, tilling the soil took more time and resulted in a further increase in the expenditure on ploughing.

Water for irrigation was a scarce commodity in Palakurichi. There were two main constraints faced by cultivators in Palakurichi with respect to irrigation water. The first constraint was that too little canal water was supplied to the village and even that arrived very late in the season. The second constraint was that on account of being located in the coastal area, the groundwater was saline and could not be used for irrigation.

Apart from that, some fields were at higher elevation than the irrigation channels, thus blocking the free flow of irrigation water. Therefore, to make use of the limited quantity of water that was available for a short time, cultivators in Palakurichi used diesel pumps to lift water from irrigation channel to field. The distribution of ownership of diesel pumps was, as mentioned, highly unequal. Since non-Dalit cultivators in the village owned diesel pumpsets, they managed to irrigate the crop when there was water in the irrigation channels at lower costs than Dalit cultivators. Dalit cultivators had to hire diesel pumps from owners of pump-sets. Non-Dalit cultivators who owned diesel pumps rented them out only after meeting their own requirements of water. At times, Dalits had to hire diesel pumps from neighbouring villages at still higher rents. This further raised the cost of irrigation for them.

To sum up, ownership of agricultural machinery was concentrated in the hands of non-Dalit cultivators who operated relatively large operational holdings. Because they owned means of production, these households were able to obtain machine labour and irrigation at much lower costs than Dalit households that cultivated relatively small plots of land. On average, Dalit households spent Rs 3,405 per hectare on machine labour and Rs 1,386 per hectare on irrigation. By comparison, non-Dalit households spent Rs 2,750 per hectare on machine labour and Rs 1,107 per hectare on irrigation (Table 16).

Expenditure on Seeds

In 2003–04, about 7 per cent (Rs 1,229) of Cost A2 was spent on seeds. Dalit households incurred higher costs on seed material than non-Dalit households. The seed rates adopted by Dalit cultivators (153 kg per hectare) were much higher than the recommended rates for directly sown rice (75 kg per hectare).[18] Dalit households in Palakurichi used higher seed rates in anticipation of higher mortality of seedlings due to the water scarcity.

The use of high seed rates by small cultivators in Thanjavur region has been noted in earlier studies as well. The Farm Management Studies conducted in Thanjavur district from 1967–68 to 1969–70 observed that: (i) the average seed rates adopted by cultivators in the study villages were very high; (ii) smaller farms had higher seed rates per hectare than large farms; and (iii) the proportion of purchased seed in the total seed used was higher among small farms than large farms (GoI 1973: 34). Swenson, in a study of the costs and returns from rice cultivation among cultivators operating various sizes of farms in two villages in Thanjavur district, observed that small farms used higher seed rates per acre than large farmers (Swenson 1973: 276).

Further, the share of home-produced seeds in total seed used was smaller for small and medium cultivators (who were Dalits) than for large cultivators (who were non-Dalits) (Table 19). From the little that they produced, particularly during successive years of low production, small cultivators were unable to preserve seeds for the next crop, and had to buy them either from the market or from other cultivators. Finally, it must be pointed out that although, for the sake of consistency with the CCPC methodology, both

TABLE 19 *Share of home-produced seed in total seed used for rice cultivation, by size-class of operational holding, Palakurichi village, 2003–04* in per cent

Size-class of operational holding (in hectares)	Share
0.01 to 2	23
2.01 to 10	29
> 10	46
All	25

Source: Survey data, 2004.

[18] The seed rate recommended by the State Agricultural University and Department of Agriculture for semi-dry rice (dry seeded irrigated un-puddled lowland rice with supplemental irrigation) was 75 kg per hectare (GoT and TNAU 2005: 25–26).

home-grown and purchased seeds are valued at market prices prevailing at the time of sowing when calculating Cost A2, in reality, marginal and small cultivators procured seeds at higher prices prevailing at the time of sowing, while large cultivators kept a part of the previous year's harvest for use as seeds.

Inequalities in the distribution of means of production (including land) made for relatively high levels of costs of cultivation among Dalit cultivators, who were mainly tenant cultivators. This resulted in lower farm business incomes from rice cultivation for Dalit cultivators.

Conclusions

This essay has attempted to study the levels of income and returns to Dalit cultivators from rice cultivation in the Thanjavur region, a region historically known as the 'rice bowl' of South India. The study brings out the extreme inequality in ownership of landholdings in the region. In terms of land ownership, Dalit households were worse off than non-Dalit households. However, Dalits had some access to land for cultivation through tenancy. Information on tenancy shows that over the years there was an increase in the incidence of tenancy in Palakurichi village.

In 2003–04, cultivators in the village suffered losses and faced a distress situation due to low availability of irrigation water. Though the majority of cultivators suffered losses, the extent of loss varied between Dalit and non-Dalit cultivators. Dalit cultivators, because of the higher cost levels, gained lower incomes from cultivation than non-Dalit cultivators. A detailed, item-wise listing of costs of cultivation shows that Dalit cultivators had higher levels of expenditure for machine labour, irrigation, seed and rents on leased-in land. These differences in costs were mainly due to lack of ownership of means of production, particularly machinery and land, among Dalit cultivators. The majority of Dalit cultivators being tenants, they had to incur large expenditures on rent. Though their incomes from cultivation were low, non-Dalit households had higher levels of household incomes than Dalit cultivators on account of incomes from sources other than cultivation. In the situation of distress, it was the rich caste Hindu households, who owned an unequally high share of the means of production, who broke even.

I am grateful to Madhura Swaminathan and V.K. Ramachandran for comments on earlier drafts. I also thank participants in the workshop on Dalit Households in Village Economies at the Indian Statistical Institute, Kolkata, for their useful suggestions.

References

Beteille, A. (1974), *Studies in Agrarian Social Structure*, Oxford University Press, Delhi.

Bouton, Marshall M. (1985), *Agrarian Radicalism in South India*, Princeton University Press, Princeton.

Gough, Kathleen (1981), *Rural Society in Southeast India*, Cambridge University Press, Cambridge.

Gough, Kathleen (1989), *Rural Change in Southeast India, 1950s to 1980s*, Oxford University Press, New Delhi.

Government of India (GoI) (1973), *Economics of Farm Management in Thanjavur District,*

Tamil Nadu: Combined Report 1967–68 to 1969–70, Directorate of Economics and Statistics, Ministry of Agriculture.

Government of Tamil Nadu (GoT) and Tamil Nadu Agricultural University (TNAU) (2005), *Crop Production Guide 2005*.

Guhan, Sanjivi (1983), 'Palakurichi: A Resurvey', Working Paper No. 42, Madras Institute of Development Studies, Madras.

Menon, Saraswati (1979a), 'Responses to Class and Caste Oppression in Thanjavur District: 1940–52', Part I, *Social Scientist*, vol. 7, no. 6, January, pp. 14–30.

Menon, Saraswati (1979b), 'Responses to Class and Caste Oppression in Thanjavur District: 1940–52', Part II, *Social Scientist*, vol. 7, no. 7, February, pp. 57–68.

Menon, Saraswati (1979c), 'Responses to Class and Caste Oppression in Thanjavur District: 1940–52,', Part III, *Social Scientist*, vol. 7, no. 10, May, pp. 52–64.

Menon, Saraswati (1983), 'Social Characteristics of Land Control in Thanjavur District during the Nineteenth Century: A Sociological Study', unpublished Ph.D. thesis submitted to Jawaharlal Nehru University, New Delhi.

Rajalu, K.S. (1918), 'Tanjore District: Palakurichi Village', in G. Slater, ed., *Some South Indian Villages*, Volume 1, Economic Studies, University of Madras and Oxford University Press, Madras.

Ramakrishnan, G. (2014), 'The Peasant Movement and Dalit Rights in East Thanjavur, Tamil Nadu', in V.K. Ramachandran and Madhura Swaminathan, eds, *Dalit Households in Village Economies*, Tulika Books, New Delhi (this volume).

Rukmani, R. (1993), 'The Process of Urbanization and Socioeconomic Change in Tamil Nadu 1901–1981', Ph.D. thesis submitted to University of Madras, Madras.

Sivaraman, M. (1973), 'Thanjavur: Rumblings of Class Struggle in Tamil Nadu', in Kathleen Gough and H.P. Sharma, eds, *Imperialism and Revolution in South Asia*, Monthly Review Press, New York.

Swenson, Geoffrey Clyde (1973), 'The Effect of Increases in Rice Production on Employment and Income Distribution in Thanjavur District, South India', unpublished Ph.D. thesis submitted to Michigan State University, Michigan.

Tamil Nadu Agricultural University (TNAU) (1985), *Techno-Economic Survey of Thanjavur District*, Centre for Agricultural and Rural Development Studies, TNAU.

Tirumalai, S. (1940), 'Palakurichi', in P.J. Thomas and K.C. Ramakrishnan, eds, *Some South Indian Villages: A Resurvey with Analysis and Observations*, University of Madras, Madras.

van Schendel, Willem (1991), *Three Deltas: Accumulation and Poverty in Rural Burma, Bengal and South India,* Indo-Dutch Studies on Development Alternatives 8, Sage Publications, New Delhi.

TABLE A1 *Number and share of households, by caste, Palakurichi village, 2004*

Caste	Number of households	Share (in per cent)
Parayar	135	31.6
Pallar	112	26.2
Padayatchi	67	15.7
Pillai	20	4.7
Naidu	18	4.2
Konar	15	3.5
Thevar	13	3.0
Vellalar	11	2.6
Kammalar	7	1.6
Chettiyar	5	1.2
Vanniyar	5	1.2
Asari	4	0.9
Vadukar	3	0.7
Yadava	3	0.7
Brahman	2	0.5
Agamudayan	2	0.5
Pandaram	2	0.5
Kallar	1	0.2
Kownder	1	0.2
Muthaliyar	1	0.2
Total	427	100.0

Source: Survey data, 2004.

TABLE A2 *Average yield of rice in Nagapattinam district during 1992–93 to 2005–06* in tonnes per hectare

1992–93	5.0
1993–94	3.0
1994–95	5.5
1995–96	3.5
1996–97	2.5
1997–98	2.6
1998–99	4.3
1999–2000	5.0
2000–01	4.9
2001–02	3.8
2002–03	1.7
2003–04	2.9
2004–05	1.4
2005–06	2.3

Source: Season and Crop Report for Tamil Nadu, various years.

TABLE A3 *'t' test for differences in means of farm business incomes among Dalit and non-Dalit cultivators in Palakurichi village, 2003–04*

Two-sample 't' test with unequal variances

Group*	Obs	Mean	Std. Err.	Std. Dev.	[95% Conf. Interval]	
NSC	23	−7611.153	1639.687	7863.662	−11011.66	−4210.65
SC	15	−11985.94	1799.36	6968.892	−15845.18	−8126.696
Combined	38	−9338.043	1254.889	7735.657	−11880.69	−6795.395
Diff		4374.787	2434.393		−580.3337	9329.909

Satterthwaite's degrees of freedom: 32.5998

Ho: mean (NSC) − mean (SC) = diff = 0

Ha: diff < 0	Ha: diff ~= 0	Ha: diff > 0
t = 1.7971	t = 1.7971	t = 1.7971
P < t = 0.9592	P > |t| = 0.0816	P > t = 0.0408

Note: NSC = non-Dalit cultivators; SC = Dalit cultivators.

TABLE A4 *'t' test for differences in means of Cost A2 among Dalit and non-Dalit cultivators in Palakurichi village, 2003–04*

Two-sample 't' test with unequal variances

Group*	Obs	Mean	Std. Err.	Std. Dev.	[95% Conf. Interval]	
NSC	23	15872.87	1238.2	5938.199	13305	18440.74
SC	15	18877.53	1500.812	5812.62	15658.61	22096.45
Combined	38	17058.92	972.87	5997.174	15087.7	19030.14
Diff		−3004.667	1945.656		−6975.279	965.9459

Satterthwaite's degrees of freedom: 30.5405

Ho: mean (NSC) − mean (SC) = diff = 0

Ha: diff < 0	Ha: diff ~= 0	Ha: diff > 0
t = -1.5443	t = -1.5443	t = -1.5443
P < t = 0.0664	P > |t| = 0.1328	P > t = 0.9336

Note: NSC = non-Dalit cultivators; SC = Dalit cultivators.

TABLE A5 *ANOVA for differences in means of Cost A2 among cultivators categorized by terms of possession of land, Palakurichi village, 2003–04*

Summary of Cost A2

Category	Mean	Std. Dev.	Freq.		
Owner cultivator	16519.82	8414.192	25		
Owner-cum-tenant cultivator	19074.76	4790.313	16		
Pure tenant cultivator	23781.45	8417.813	14		
Total	19111.49	7978.915	55		

Analysis of Variance

Source	SS	Df	MS	F	Prob > F
Between groups	4.73E+08	2	236629358	4.15	0.0213
Within groups	2.96E+09	52	57010542		
Total	3.44E+09	54	63663090.4		

Bartlett's test for equal variances: $\chi^2 (2) = 5.4737$ Prob $> \chi^2 = 0.065$

TABLE A6 *ANOVA for differences in means of farm business incomes among cultivators categorized by terms of possession of land, Palakurichi village, 2003–04*

Summary of farm business income

Category	Mean	Std. Dev.	Freq.		
Owner cultivator	−10531.5	8613.816	25		
Owner cum tenant cultivator	−8809.67	8706.374	16		
Pure tenant cultivator	−17042.7	7149.265	14		
Total	−11688	8766.133	55		

Analysis of Variance

Source	SS	Df	MS	F	Prob>F
Between groups	5.67E+08	2	283708187	4.12	0.0219
Within groups	3.58E+09	52	68888807.2		
Total		54			

Bartlett's test for equal variances: $chi^2 (2) = 0.6462$ Prob $> chi^2 = 0.724$

Farm business income = gross value of output – Cost A2

Cost A2 includes all the variable costs.

The components of Cost A2 are:
1. Value of hired human labour
2. Value of hired and owned bullock labour
3. Value of owned machine labour
4. Value of hired machine labour
5. Value of seed (both farm-produced and purchased)
6. Value of insecticides and pesticides
7. Value of manures (owned and purchased)
8. Value of fertilizers
9. Irrigation charges
10. Depreciation of implements and farm buildings
11. Land revenue, cesses and other taxes
12. Interest on working capital
13. Rent paid for leased in land.
14. Other miscellaneous expenses

Land Conflicts and Attacks on Dalits

A Case Study from a Village in Marathwada

R. Ramakumar and Tushar Kamble

The right to own property is systematically denied to Dalits. Landlessness – encompassing a lack of access to land, inability to own land, and forced evictions – constitutes a crucial element in the subordination of Dalits. When Dalits do acquire land, elements of the right to own property – including the right to access and enjoy it – are routinely infringed. (Centre for Human Rights and Global Justice 2007)

In 1996, a nongovernmental organization undertook a door-to-door survey of 250 villages in the state of Gujarat and found that, in almost all villages, those who had title to land had no possession, and those who had possession had not had their land measured or faced illegal encroachments from upper castes. (Human Rights Watch 1999)

. . . the distinction and discrimination based on caste still prevails in Maharashtra. A slight provocation like a dispute at the water pump leads to polarization as Dalits and non-Dalits; non-Dalits attack Dalit *bastis*, destroy their houses and even kill them. . . . The Dalits are not supposed to assert their rights and equality before the law. If they do, they have to pay a price. (PUCL 2003)

Landlessness is a pervasive feature of Dalit households in rural India. Landlessness is foundational to the existence of Dalits as a distinct social group in rural areas; it forms the material basis for the domination and exploitation of Dalits in non-economic spheres as well. The caste system thus contains elements of both social oppression and class exploitation.

Caste discrimination has also acquired the status of an ideology. The conception and practice of caste as an ideology implies that a person is primarily perceived by another not on the basis of his or her capabilities, but on the basis of the caste that he or she is born into. In this context, it is no surprise that the efforts of upper-caste groups to sustain 'cultural differentiations' transgress into non-cultural spheres, including the economic sphere.[1] Thus,

---

[1] As Guru (2012) notes on the caste system in India, 'cultural difference may subsume within itself elements of both material and social hierarchy'. In the Marxist literature,

even Dalits who own land are subjected to discrimination and harassment by upper-caste groups.

This essay attempts to verify the hypothesis formulated in the preceding paragraph through a case study of a Dalit household from one village in rural Maharashtra. It is based on repeated visits to the village by the authors in May and July 2012.

Takwiki is a village in Osmanabad taluk of Osmanabad district in Maharashtra (see Figures 1 and 2). The district belongs to the larger Marathwada region, which is a drought-prone region and relatively backward in social and economic indicators. According to the 2001 Census, Takwiki had a total population of 2,396 persons, residing in 486 households. About 14 per cent of its population belonged to the Scheduled Castes (SCs). The overall

FIGURE 1 *Map of the State of Maharashtra with Osmanabad district*

Source: Adapted from www.mapsofindia.com.

there is appreciation of what Hobsbawm (2011) calls the 'relative autonomy of . . . super-structural elements' in the evolution of society. In his famous letter to Mehring in 1893, Frederick Engels criticized the argument that 'ideological spheres' do not have 'independent historical development' or 'any effect upon history'. Engels wrote that 'the basis of this is the common *undialectical conception of cause and effect as rigidly opposite poles*, the total *disregarding of interaction*; these gentlemen often almost deliberately forget that once an historic element has been brought into the world by other elements, ultimately by economic facts, *it also reacts in its turn* and may react on its environment and even on its own causes' (Engels 1893, emphasis added).

FIGURE 2 *Map of Osmanabad district in Maharashtra State, with Takwiki village*

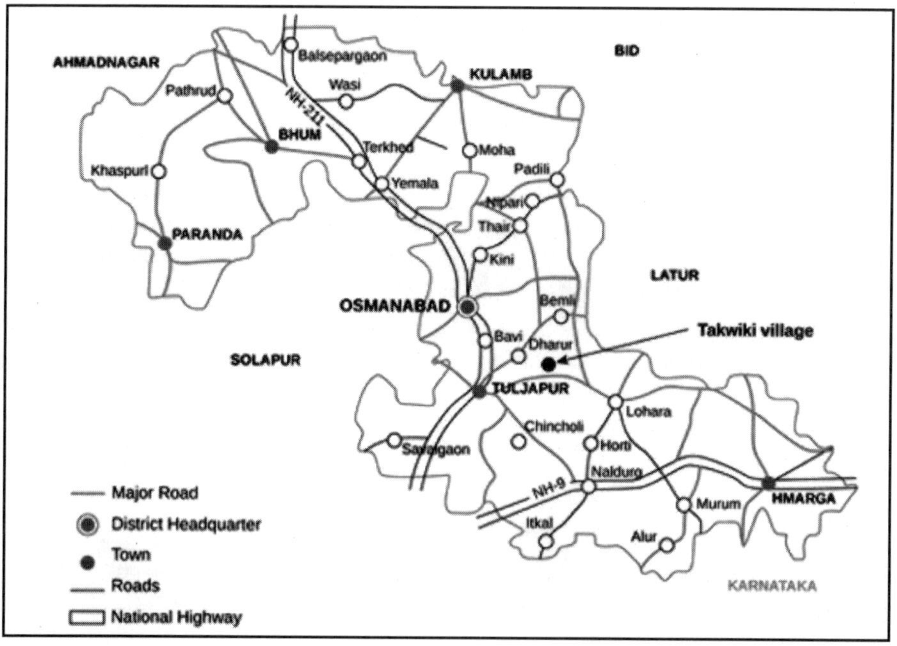

Source: Adapted from www.mapsofindia.com.

literacy rate in the village was 54.5 per cent. Of all main workers in the village, 47 per cent were cultivators and 36 per cent were agricultural labourers.

This is a case study of a household headed by Dhondiba Raut. The authors learned of the predicament of this household when a household member approached one of them (R. Ramakumar) for help.

The Raut household, belonging to the Chambhar caste, has been living in Takwiki village for more than a century. Until recently, Takwiki and the surrounding villages were dominated by Muslim landlords. The Marathwada drought of 1971–72 and the acute squeeze on incomes that it inflicted on peasants at large forced some of the Muslim landlords in the region to sell a part of their land. In consequence, Tulsiram Raut (Dhondiba's father) purchased 7.5 acres of land in 1972 from Taher Khan Lal Khan Pathan, who owned a large area of land in Takwiki (interview with Dhondiba Raut, May 2012). Tulsiram was a cobbler; he used his savings and a loan to purchase the plot at a relatively low cost of Rs 250–500 per acre. While the transfer of land had taken place in 1972 itself, the official transfer of land in the village land records (*fer far nondani*) took place only in 1979. The 7.5 acres of land were part of Block Number (*gut kramank*) 133 in the land records. In Block Number 133 in the village map, Tulsiram's plot formed three pieces of about 4 acres each (see the larger area with black borders in Figure 3).

Tulsiram had three sons when he purchased the land: Kondiba Tulsiram Raut, Dhondiba Tulsiram Raut and Vithoba Tulsiram Raut. The land

FIGURE 3 *Aerial photograph of the plots under dispute, Takwiki village, Maharashtra, 2012*

Source: Google earth.

he purchased was equally divided among the three sons, with one rectangular piece of land going to each. In 2012, all these plots were irrigated by a well dug at the western side of Block Number 133. The Rauts grew sugarcane in these plots.

In 1988, Dhondiba and his brother Vithoba pooled savings and purchased some more land in Takwiki (interview with Dhondiba Raut, May 2012). The plots of land newly purchased were geographically fragmented, and a 1-acre plot was located just across the eastern bund (marked white in Figure 3) of Block Number 133. At the time of purchase, this 1-acre plot, belonging to Block Number 132, was registered in the name of Vithoba. In 2007, Vithoba transferred the ownership of this 1-acre plot to Dhondiba, in exchange (no extra cash was paid) for another 1-acre plot owned by Dhondiba located elsewhere. Thus, Dhondiba came to own the 1-acre plot in Block Number 132 from 2007. This plot was valued at between Rs 6 and 8 lakhs in 2012, and was registered in the name of Dhondiba's wife, Hirabai Raut.

Much of the land in Block Number 132 belonged to the Kedar household, a large landowning, upper-caste (Maratha) household from Patoda, the village adjacent to Takwiki. According to the residents of Takwiki, the Kedar household owned more than 120 acres of land in 2012. They also leased in large areas of land from others on a long-term basis, about which no estimate was available. Before the 1970s, according to the people we interviewed in the village, the Kedar household owned only about 10–15 acres of land. In those days, the household mainly ran a tempo-transport business. Being the only tempo-owning household in the region allowed the Kedars to accumulate substantial savings, which were channelled into purchasing land after the 1972 drought. According to some accounts, since the Kedar household members were also the local moneylenders in the 1970s, widespread default on loans during and after the 1972 drought enabled them to attach additional areas of land. However, it was not possible to independently verify these accounts.

In 2011–12, the Kedar household enjoyed considerable economic clout. They were the largest landowners in Takwiki and Patoda. They owned two tractors, which were partly rented out, a dairy farm, a jaggery-making unit, a timber agency, and an electrical rewinding shop in the two villages. They continued to own tempo vans which plied on rent, and were involved in moneylending. Many Takwiki villagers assert that with all this clout, the Kedar household effectively had the right of first refusal in any land transaction that took place in the region. They cited a number of cases where the Kedar household bid up the land price to such high levels that no one else stood a chance of buying the land going on sale.

Politically, the Kedar household was attached to the Nationalist Congress Party (NCP) in the region and generally enjoyed a close relationship with the party's district leadership. Members of the Kedar household were also regularly chosen as members of the gram panchayat as well as of boards of local credit societies in Patoda (interview with Bharat Raut, July 2012; and interview with Imran Pathan, July 2012).

The 1-acre plot that Dhondiba had swapped with Vithoba in 2007 was located within a series of plots owned by the Kedar household beyond the eastern bund of Block Number 133 (these plots belong, according to the village land records, to Block Numbers 126, 130, 131, 134, 135, 147, 149, 150, 151, 155, 156, 157, 167 and so on). If the Kedar household were to annex the 1-acre plot owned by Dhondiba, the advantages to them would be many. First, they would get to own a large piece of contiguous land totally under their possession on the eastern side of the bund. In fact the Kedar household had made an offer to Dhondiba in 2011 to buy out all his land including the 1-acre plot, but Dhondiba had refused; the convenience of owning all his land at one place was paramount for him too. Secondly, the newly established dairy farm and the jaggery-making unit of the Kedar household were situated close to Dhondiba's plot. If the Kedars possessed this plot, they could build a direct approach road to these units; in its absence, they were obliged to reach these units over a longer route from Patoda village.

While the economic advantages of taking Dhondiba's land were substantial for the Kedars, there was another dimension that was too evident to be missed. Dhondiba was a Chambhar who owned an irrigated plot cultivated with sugarcane right under the nose of the powerful Maratha household. Apparently, the Kedars believed that their social prestige was lowered by a Dalit owning a plot in the midst of their lands. Getting rid of the Dalit from the plot would raise the prestige of the Kedar household.

FIGURE 4 *Aerial photograph of the plots under dispute showing the nature of encroachment, Takwiki village, Maharashtra, 2012*

Source: Google earth.

When efforts to persuade Dhondiba to sell the plot failed, encroachment began (interview with Bharat Raut, July 2012). From the beginning of 2011, the Kedars began to drive tractors and tempos through Dhondiba's plot to travel to their dairy farm and jaggery-making unit. In Figure 4, this encroachment is depicted pictorially: it was in the form of driving from point A to point B, and then proceeding to point C. The objective, according to the Raut household, was to harass them to the point of forcing them to sell the land to the Kedars and moving them out.

After tolerating the encroachment for a few days, Dhondiba's son Bharat Raut confronted some of the Kedars and asked them to stop driving through their plot. However, Bharat was greeted with a flurry of abuse, including the use of caste names (interview with Bharat Raut, July 2012). The caste dimension of the encroachment now came out into the open. According to Bharat, some of the abusive language went like this:

> हे चाम्भारड्या, तुम्हाला शेताची काय गरज आहे? खेतर शिवून खाणारी जात तुमची
> (You Chambhar, what business do you have in farming? Your caste is to work with animal skin.)

> हे चाम्भारड्या, मस्ती चढली आहे का तुला? तुम्ही चांभार हे शेत कसे कसता आम्ही पाहून घेऊ
> (You Chambhars appear to be enjoying [cultivation]. We will see how you Chambhars cultivate this land.)

Bharat says he was afraid to approach the police at this stage. The encroachment continued on a regular basis after this incident. A few days later, while driving through the plot, the Kedars ran their tractor over the irrigation pipeline on the eastern side of Kondiba Raut's plot (interview with Bharat Raut, July 2012). The pipeline was destroyed. Kondiba confronted the Kedars over this action. The reaction from members of the dominant household, according to the police complaint filed by Kondiba, was to hurl abuse at him with caste names and severely assault him with wooden sticks.

Deciding that enough was enough, Kondiba and Bharat approached the Bembili police station to file a complaint under The Scheduled Castes and The Scheduled Tribes (Prevention of Atrocities) Act, 1989 (henceforth Atrocities Act). In the beginning, the Head Constable at the police station (the exact date is not available) refused even to accept the complaint from Kondiba and Bharat (interview with Bharat Raut, July 2012). However, forced by Bharat's insistence, the police finally accepted their complaint on a piece of paper. Kondiba's statement was recorded and he was asked to leave. Bharat wanted to file the case under the Atrocities Act. But the Head Constable refused and told him: 'All that cannot be done. You do not know what the Atrocities Act is. This incident does not fall under its purview' (interview with Bharat Raut, July 2012).

The next day, Bharat went to the police station and demanded to be shown the statements recorded the previous day. He was refused at first, but eventually he was given a copy of the FIR. To his surprise, Bharat found that the recording of Kondiba's statement was incomplete: only the instance of physical attack was recorded and there was no mention of the verbal abuse using caste names (interview with Dhondiba Raut, May 2012). Evidently, the statement was recorded in such a way that no complaint could be filed under the Atrocities Act. Kondiba's complaint was being considered as a non-cognizable offence.

For more than two weeks after the attack no action was taken on the complaint filed by Bharat. No arrests were made and there was no questioning of the Kedars. On 29 January 2011, Dhondiba's younger son, Karan Raut, approached the police station to press for lodging the complaint under the Atrocities Act. He was also told that no case under the Atrocities Act could be registered against the Kedars for several reasons (interview with Karan Raut, July 2012). First, he was told, land encroachment issues did not fall under the purview of the Atrocities Act: 'This is a civil case, we cannot register the case as a criminal offence.' Secondly, special permission was required from the Superintendent of Police (SP) of the district to file such a case. Thirdly, a person from the caste of the accused persons (that is, a person from the Maratha caste) had to present himself as a witness for such a case to be filed under the Atrocities Act.

Each of these reasons cited for not registering a case under the Atrocities Act was wrong (interview with Uddhav Kamble, formerly Special Inspector General of Police (Protection of Civil Rights), Maharashtra, July 2012). First, Chapter II of the Atrocities Act clearly states that the list of offences under the Act includes 'whoever, not being a member of a Scheduled Caste or a Scheduled Tribe . . . wrongfully dispossesses a member of a Scheduled Caste or a Scheduled Tribe from his land or premises or interferes with the enjoyment of his rights over any land, premises or water'. The Act also states that offences are to be treated as criminal, under the Code of Criminal Procedure, 1973. Secondly, no permission from the SP is required to register a case under the Atrocities Act. According to the guidelines, a case can be independently registered at the local police station; after registering the case, the investigation has to be handed over to an officer not below the level of a Deputy Superintendent of Police (DySP). Thirdly, the caste of the witness is nowhere a consideration under the Atrocities Act.

The absence of police action encouraged the Kedar household to continue with aggressive encroachment. On 18 January 2011, according to a complaint filed by Bharat Raut at the Bembili police station, four brothers of the Kedar household reached Dhondiba's plot with a bulldozer. Coming in from the northern end of Dhondiba's plot (point A in Figure 4), they first levelled the bund on the eastern side of Block Number 133. After this, they encroached about 10 feet into Dhondiba's plot and cleared the land for a road on its western side (from point A to point B, north to south) and then, bending eastward, on the southern side (from point B to point C, west to east). The levelling ended once the encroached pathway reached the Kedars' jaggery-making unit (point D). During the encroachment, the Kedars broke Dhondiba's irrigation pipeline and threw it away to one side. A tree that stood on the bund was also felled.

Photographs of the encroachment were taken by Dhondiba's family the same day; one of these, given to us by Bharat, is presented here as Figure 5. These photographs show that the newly built road was wide enough to allow a truck or tempo-van or tractor to pass through.

That very night, Bharat went to the Kedars to question their latest act of violent and lawless encroachment (interview with Bharat Raut, July 2012). However, he was again abused with caste names and threatened with dire consequences if he resisted further. Faced with encroachment and threats to life, Dhondiba and Bharat approached the court of the Taluk Judicial Magistrate (First Class) for justice. The court, on 10 March 2011, stayed the encroachment and restrained the Kedar household from using the newly built pathway. Dhondiba Raut was to collect the official stay order after two days (interview with Bharat Raut, July 2012).

Confident now of their right over the plot, Hirabai and Bharat went to work on the land on the morning of 11 March 2011 (interview with Bharat Raut, July 2012). What greeted them was a shower of abuse and a violent physical attack. Angry over Dhondiba's victory in the court, members of the Kedar household came armed with wooden poles and began to hit Hirabai

FIGURE 5 *Photograph showing the encroachment into Dhondiba Raut's plot, taken in 2001 from near point B in Figure 3, facing point C* (photograph courtesy Bharat Raut)

and Bharat. Hirabai was hit on the back of her head, leaving her bleeding. Bharat was beaten by more than one person for over 10 minutes, and suffered a fracture of his left arm and bruises all over his body.

Throughout the physical attack, the Kedars also abused Hirabai and Bharat severely, using caste names (interview with Bharat Raut, July 2012). For instance, Bharat was told: 'हे चाम्भारड्या, असले स्टे मी बांधून हिंडतो' ('You Chambhar, we wear such stay orders like a garland and roam around').

Bleeding profusely, Hirabai and Bharat rushed to the Bembili police station to file a complaint. However, the Assistant Police Inspector refused to accept a formal complaint against the Kedar household (interview with Bharat Raut, July 2012). Instead, the police asked Hirabai and Bharat to go to the hospital for treatment. Bharat had no choice but to agree, as his mother was bleeding. They went to the Primary Health Centre at Bembili village, from where they were referred to the Civil Hospital at Osmanabad. They were admitted there the same day.

The next day Bharat got himself discharged, went to the court of the Taluk Judicial Magistrate (First Class) and obtained an official copy of the order staying the encroachment. Armed with the court order, he approached the Bembili police station once again. Once again, the police refused to consider Bharat's complaint under the Atrocities Act. Just as Kondiba was told in January 2011, Bharat was informed that the attack on him did not come under the purview of the Atrocities Act. His complaint too would be treated as a normal case of alleged assault (interview with Bharat Raut, July 2012).

The attack on Hirabai and Bharat was not without witnesses. Razak

Pathan, a middle peasant who owned a plot of land close to Dhondiba's, was a witness to the attack on them on 11 March. Razak Pathan's name was specifically cited in Bharat's police complaint as a witness, and he personally appeared at the police station to give a statement against the Kedars. Razak Pathan's son, Imran Pathan, was the police *patil* of Takwiki village. Yet the Pathan family faced a severe backlash from the Kedar household. According to Imran, his father was first asked by the Kedars to withdraw the statement given to the police: 'Why are you interfering in favour of the Chambhars?' he was asked (interview with Imran Pathan, July 2012). Imran told us in an interview that his family decided to stick to their statement because, 'If it is the Rauts today, tomorrow it may be us. So we have to unitedly move against this big landlord. Otherwise, he will eat us all one day' (interview with Imran Pathan, July 2012).

When Razak Pathan refused to withdraw his statement, it was his family's turn to face harassment (interview with Imran Pathan, July 2012). First, the Kedars arranged to send a complaint to the District Collector demanding Imran's removal as the police *patil*. When Imran came to know of the complaint, he approached every village person whose signature was on the complaint. All of them denied having signed such a complaint; it turned out that the signatures were forged. But that was not all. The approach to Razak Pathan's plot of land passed through the bund of a few plots owned by the Kedar household. Razak Pathan used to take his tractor and other implements to his field through this rather wide bund. Soon after the incident, the Kedars closed down this path by fencing it off (a photograph of the fence is given as Figure 6). The Pathans were forced to travel to their field by taking another road, which meant a detour of about 1 km. 'What to do?' Imran said dejectedly when we spoke to him (interview with Imran Pathan, July 2012).

With the matter reaching a dead end, Karan Raut decided to take external help. He brought the matter to the notice of a few leaders of the All India Kisan Sabha in Solapur and a leading journalist based in Mumbai. The journalist spoke personally to the District Collector, who promised swift action in the case. Karan sent a direct complaint to the Collector by email. Based on the email, the Collector, a Dalit himself, instructed the Superintendent of Police of the district to file a case under the Atrocities Act. On the SP's orders, a case was finally filed under the Atrocities Act at the Bembili police station. A DySP visited the village and the encroached land, as per the requirements, and recorded the statements of all concerned. Further, two officials from the State Social Welfare department visited Dhondiba's house and recorded their statements (interview with Bharat Raut, July 2012).

Just as it appeared that some positive action was forthcoming, the Assistant Police Inspector and the Head Constable of the local police station began to intervene again in favour of the Kedars. According to a written complaint from Karan to the District Collector, the day after the visit of the DySP to the village,

FIGURE 6 *Photograph of the fence (circled) that blocked entry into Razak Pathan's plot, 2012* (photograph by R. Ramakumar)

... my brother and mother were called to the Police Station. At the Police Station, a constable, in the absence of an officer, tried to record a statement of my mother that suggested that we would appeal in the court, though in the meantime would allow the Kedar family to use the road illegally constructed across our field. We refused to sign the statement. (Email sent to Pravin Gedam, District Collector, Osmanabad, dated 9 April 2011)

Even after the visits of the DySP and government officials to the village, no arrests were made. Dhondiba Raut's family sent another complaint to the Collector, and managed to get the supporting journalist to speak to the Collector once again. Finally, following repeated orders from the Collector and the SP, an arrest warrant was issued in the names of four members of the Kedar household. Now facing heat, the four accused members of the Kedar household absconded. After spending about twenty days in hiding, they appeared in the court of the Taluk Judicial Magistrate (First Class) to surrender, but the police recorded their arrest before they could surrender. They remained in custody for about eighteen days, after which the court granted them bail. At the time of writing this, the arrested members of the Kedar family were back in Takwiki village. No further action had been taken by the police and it appeared that the case would drag on. There has been no further hearing in the case.

But if anyone thought that the arrests would restrain the Kedars from harassing the Raut family any further, they were mistaken. According to Bharat, there has been no end to the harassment even after the arrests. In fact the acts of oppression extended from farm to home, and were continuing at the time of writing this.

First, there were continuing efforts to harass Bharat on his farm by trying to divert surplus water into his field (interview with Bharat Raut, July 2012). Topographically, the fields of the Kedar household are at an elevation from where excess water drained downwards through a canal by the side of Dhondiba's fields. After the arrests, the Kedars reduced the height of the bund that separated their plots from that of the Rauts. As a result, the excess water, instead of flowing into the canal by the side, spilled over the bund and flowed into the fields owned by the Rauts. According to Bharat, this presented a constant threat to their standing crop of sugarcane.

Secondly, going by informally laid out village rules, all plots of land lying within the boundaries of one village should be reachable by a pathway that originates from the same village. In Takwiki, these pathways were roughly 7 feet wide. While laying such pathways, an equal extent of land (i.e. 3.5 feet each) was to be given away by every landowner whose land lay in the way. The village road from Takwiki (marked as a horizontal black line in Figure 3) was constructed by acquiring 3.5 feet each from the plots of the Rauts (on the northern side) and the Kedars (on the southern side). However, after the conflict, the Kedar household recaptured their share of 3.5 feet of the road and began to insist with the panchayat that if a road had to be built, all 7 feet had to be acquired from the plot of the Rauts. According to Bharat, there was constant tension in the fields after this act by the Kedars (interview with Bharat Raut, July 2012).

The Rauts were also subjected to new forms of harassment within the village residential area. Bharat alleged that a tough with criminal antecedents had been contracted to harass his family in the village (interview with Bharat Raut, May 2012). Widely known and feared for his thuggish acts, including his alleged recent involvement in a case of burning the house of a Pardhi household, this man, who had no *locus standi* in the matter, had begun to threaten Dhondiba and Bharat, asking them to vacate the concerned plot to the Kedars.

Threats aside, according to Bharat, the tough was harassing the Raut family in other, less direct ways (interview with Bharat Raut, July 2012). First, there was a common village plot that the Raut family had been using for many years as dumping ground for garbage. The tough had recently fenced off that land for himself and prevented the Rauts from dropping garbage there. Secondly, there was a well in a vacant and commonly held plot that the Rauts used to draw water. More recently, the tough had fenced off that plot of land too, claiming that he had leased it in from the government.

The nature and pattern of these acts led the Raut household to conclude that the tough had been unleashed on them by members of the Kedar household. According to Bharat, one of the Kedars had told him, in a recent threatening conversation, that '10 एक्कर जमीन गेली तरी हरकत नाही, पण तुला जीवंथ सोडणार नाही' ('Even if we lose 10 acres of land, it does not matter; we will not leave you till you die').[2] Bharat and other villagers have reasonably interpreted this threat as implying an instruction to the tough not to worry about the consequences of physically harming Dhondiba or Bharat, and that the Kedars were ready to spend an equivalent of the value of 10 acres of land (about Rs 30–40 lakhs) on the cases that might follow.

The oppression of the Raut household shares elements of one of the most gruesome cases of caste-related violence in recent times: the Khairlanji massacre on 29 September 2006, in Bhandara district of Maharashtra. On that day, four members of the family of Bhaiyalal Bhotmange (belonging to the Dalit community) were brutally murdered by an upper-caste Hindu mob in Khairlanji village (for reports on the massacre, see Dhawale 2006 and Teltumbde 2007). There too, it was encroachment into land owned by the Bhotmange family that culminated in the killings. Dhawale (2006) notes that the 'the immediate cause of the massacre' was that 'whatever little land they had was also sought to be taken away from them'. According to Teltumbde (2007), 'the dispute over the passage through Bhotmange land provided a backdrop to the incident'. He further notes:

> The land, which was used as a common passage by the villagers as long as it was uncultivated, became unavailable to villagers [after the Bhotmange household purchased it for cultivation]. The matter had gone to revenue court, but eventually Bhaiyalal Bhotmange emerged unscathed. . . . The injury to the caste pride of the caste Hindus simmered and grew with the increasing assertiveness of Bhotmanges, which was perceived to be partly due to their upward economic mobility and cultural progress, the latter in terms of the educational achievements of the Bhotmange children. . . . While the origin of dispute thus appears to be land, the caste prejudice of the caste Hindu villagers played a major role, right from the articulation of dispute through the development and eventual precipitation in to a heinous crime (Teltumbde 2007: 1019).

Basing his argument on different cases of atrocities on Dalits in Maharashtra, including Khairlanji, Teltumbde argues that the most important problem is 'complicity of the state machinery':

> . . . the record of atrocities on Dalits reflects the utter failure of the state in the discharge of its constitutional responsibility. . . . The state's complicity has

---

[2] Interview with Bharat Raut, July 2012. There are similarities between this statement from the Kedars and the statements of upper-caste landlords in other States. In a recent article in *Indian Express*, a land surveyor in Siwan in Bihar quotes an upper-caste landlord illegally holding Bhoodan land thus: 'When we are born, our parents keep a big bundle of currency notes wrapped in a red cloth so that we are able to fight land-related cases' (Singh 2012).

manifested even in its post-atrocity dealings in refusing to register the case, or, if registered, in not conducting proper investigation, and thereby weakening the case in the court of law. . . . The very process of Dalits registering a crime with the police is fraught with hurdles. . . . The case gets counted in the statistics of crimes against SCs only after it gets past these hurdles. More often than not, the local police clearly take sides with the perpetrators of the crime against the Dalit victims and do everything possible to suppress the crime at the first instance. . . . Even if the crime is registered, it is the police who investigate the crime and collect evidence for prosecution. The shoddy investigation by the police in such cases is legion, as evidenced by the extremely paltry rate of conviction. There is a tacit assurance to the upper castes that the official protectors of the law would not come in their way in their dealings with Dalits. This assurance has played a key role in sustaining the growth of atrocities year after year. (Ibid.: 1020).

The case of the Raut household studied here exemplifies each of the hurdles that Teltumbde lists.[3] The harassment of the Rauts is a continuing one, and though it has not yet grown into the extreme form of violence inflicted on the Bhotmange household, the commonalities in the methods of oppression are revealing.

In May 2012, when we interviewed members of the Raut household, they were living a life of fear and growing stress. They had fought oppression bravely, resorting to nothing but the law and claiming what was theirs by right. But even Bharat appeared to be tired of fighting the case. He told us:

> In the field, Kedar harasses us. At home, [the tough] harasses us. We live our lives to be happy and joyous. But there has been no happiness or joy in my life for about two years now. At the same time, I cannot sell all my land and go away. That is exactly what the Kedars want me to do, and I will not let them win this game. However, I will not deny that I often have doubts about what to do. (Interview with Bharat Raut, July 2012)

---

[3] For Maharashtra as a whole, there were 304 cases registered under the Atrocities Act in 2011 (NCRB 2012). According to a news report in 2010, 'Maharashtra's conviction rate in caste atrocity cases is one of the lowest in India'. For the year 2007, the share of convictions in offences against SCs was 2.9 per cent only. This share declined between 2005 and 2007, from 6.3 per cent to 2.9 per cent.

This article first appeared in *Review of Agrarian Studies*, vol. 2, no. 2, 2012.

References

Centre for Human Rights and Global Justice (2007), *Hidden Apartheid*, NYU School of Law and Human Rights Watch, New Delhi.

Dhawale, Ashok (2006), 'The Khairlanji Massacre and after', *People's Democracy*, 10 December.

Engels, Frederick (1893), 'Engels to Franz Mehring', in *Marx and Engels Correspondence*, International Publishers, London, available at http://www.marxists.org/archive/marx/works/1893/letters/93_07_14.htm, viewed on 5 July 2012.

Gaikwad, Rahi (2010), 'Maharashtra's Record in Conviction Rate in Caste Atrocity Cases Dismal', *The Hindu*, 20 June.

Guru, Gopal (2012), 'Conversation on Caste Today', *Seminar*, issue 633, May.

Hobsbawm, Eric (2011), *How to Change the World: Reflections on Marx and Marxism*, Abacus, London.

Human Rights Watch (1999), *Broken People: Caste Violence Against India's Untouchables*, New York, available at http://www.hrw.org/reports/1999/india/index.htm, viewed on 5 July 2012.

National Crime Records Bureau (2012), *Crime in India 2011*, Ministry of Home, New Delhi.

People's Union for Civil Liberties (PUCL) (2003), *The Caste Cauldron of Maharashtra: A Report by the Fact Finding Team*, Mumbai, November.

Singh, Santosh (2012), 'No Half Measures,' *Indian Express*, 8 July.

Teltumbde, Anand (2007), 'Khairlanji and Its Aftermath: Exploding Some Myths', *Economic and Political Weekly*, vol. 35, no. 12, 24 March.

Access of Dalit Borrowers in Rural Areas to Bank Credit

Pallavi Chavan

Financial liberalization has brought about a striking shift in banking policy in India, and led to changes in the regional and sectoral pattern of banking. There has been: (i) large-scale closure of commercial bank branches in rural areas; (ii) a widening of inter-State inequality in credit provision, accompanied by a fall in the proportion of bank credit directed towards rural areas as well as regions where banking has historically been underdeveloped; (iii) a sharp fall in the growth of credit flow to agriculture, followed by a revival in the 2000s but with a changed pattern of distribution of agricultural credit in favour of urban-based borrowers, and corporate and institutional groups; (iv) relative exclusion of the disadvantaged and dispossessed sections of the rural population from the formal financial system; and (e) strengthening of moneylending in the countryside. (See Ramachandran and Swaminathan 2005; Shetty 2004; Chavan 2005; Ramakumar and Chavan 2007; Chavan 2010.)

These changes are associated with a reversal of the policy of social and development banking, a policy that was introduced after bank nationalization in 1969. This policy aimed at expanding the geographical and sectoral reach of the banking system. Further, it aimed at bringing the deprived sections of the population within the ambit of the banking system. After nationalization, targets were fixed for opening bank branches in un-banked or under-banked regions. Targets were also fixed for lending at regulated rates of interest to priority sectors including agriculture and the 'weaker sections', comprising socio-economically backward sections of the population.

By contrast, the approach in the period of financial liberalization has been to allow for a market-determined and market-oriented mode of operation of the banking system. The focus of policy has been on increasing the efficiency – narrowly defined – and profitability of the domestic banking sector, in order to enable it to compete with the rapidly expanding foreign banking network in the country. As a result, interest rates on almost all categories of loans have been deregulated.[1] While the norms applicable to lending to

---

[1] With the application of the base rate system in July 2010, interest rates on all loans, including the small borrowal accounts with a credit limit of Rs 2 lakh, have been deregulated (RBI 2010a).

priority sectors have been left untouched, the definitions of various priority sectors, particularly agriculture, have been widened considerably, leading to a dilution of the very notion of 'priority' attached to these sectors.[2]

It is in the period of financial liberalization that a new term, 'financial inclusion', has been coined. The term may appear similar, in name, to the policy of social and development banking, but it is inherently different with respect to policy essentials. Financial inclusion has been defined as the provision of affordable financial services to those who have been left unattended or under-attended by the formal agencies of the financial system, but *without compromising on commercial and profitability considerations* in order to ensure the 'long-term sustainability' of such services (RBI 2008: 204).

This recent approach of financial inclusion is more individual-specific than previous policy. It incorporates two main instruments: first, a no-frills, basic saving bank deposit account facility (including a small overdraft facility); and secondly, a collateral-free, small borrowal facility under microfinance at market-determined rates of interest (RBI 2006b). Both these instruments have been used rather rigorously by banks in the 2000s, either directly or through intermediaries. Intermediaries of banks mainly include business correspondents (BCs) and microfinance institutions (including non-banking financial companies, trusts and cooperative societies). Further, there has been a growing emphasis on the introduction of advanced technological solutions by banks and their intermediaries. These solutions include hand-held devices and mobile phones, measures intended to bring down the costs of administering the large numbers of small-volume transactions required under financial inclusion (see RBI 2010b). The Reserve Bank of India (RBI) also places emphasis on designing market-based regulatory incentives for banks, for financial inclusion. The RBI set a target of providing, by 2012, banking services through a banking outlet to every village in India with a population of over 2,000 (see RBI 2009 and 2010a).

Database

Dalits constitute an important segment of the rural poor in India. The policy of financial inclusion is expected to improve the access that rural Dalit households have to banking services in the period of financial liberalization. In order to evaluate this claim, I analyse the trends in (i) the debt profile of rural Dalit households, and (ii) the flow of bank credit to Dalits since the early 1990s.

I use secondary data from the All India Debt and Investment Surveys (AIDIS) in order to analyse the debt profile of rural Dalit households. The AIDIS provide data on the debt profile of rural households classified into various socio-economic groups, including Dalits. These data are available from the two most recent rounds of the survey, conducted in 1991–92 and

---

[2] See Ramakumar and Chavan (2007) for a series of changes in the definition of 'agriculture" in this regard since the second half of the 1990s.

2002–03.[3] Further, I use data from six sample surveys of Small Borrowal Accounts (SBAs) conducted by the RBI from 1993 onwards, to examine changes in the supply of commercial bank credit to Dalits. These sample surveys were conducted in 1993, 1997, 2001, 2004, 2006 and 2008.[4]

Debt Profile of Rural Dalit Households

According to the AIDIS, in 2002, more than half of the total debt outstanding of Dalit households in rural India was from informal sources (Table 1). The share of formal sources in the total debt of Dalit households was only 44.8 per cent, much lower than the corresponding share (59 per cent) for non-Dalit households. Among formal sources, the largest share of debt of Dalit households was owed to commercial banks, followed by cooperatives. Among informal sources, professional moneylenders were the single most important source of debt for these households.

An inter-round comparison of the AIDIS data from 1962 onwards shows that with regard to the share of formal sources in the total debt of all rural households, there was a distinct break in the overall trend after 1992. The share of formal sources, of commercial banks in particular, rose steadily between 1962 and 1992, and then fell between 1992 and 2002 (Table 2). The rise in the share of formal sources was particularly striking between 1972 and 1982, the period following the establishment of the policy of social and development banking.[5]

---

[3] Data from the AIDIS need to be treated with some degree of caution on account of the reduced sample size of villages and households across various rounds of this survey. The 1972 round was based on a Central sample (canvassed by the NSSO field staff), a State sample (canvassed by State field staff) and a matching RBI sample. The 1982 round was based on pooled data from the Central and State samples as RBI did not offer a matching sample. However, both the 1992 and 2002 rounds were based on only the Central sample. As a result, the number of villages and households surveyed was much smaller in these two rounds than the earlier rounds. The reduced sample size is expected to have some impact on the quality and reliability of the AIDIS estimates; see the observations made by the Report of the Committee on Informal Financial Sector Statistics at <www.iibf.org.in/uploads/Committee_Report_Informal_Sector. doc>. The Committee submitted its Report to the RBI in 2001, which became a part of the Report of the National Statistical Commission.

[4] Data on small borrowal accounts (SBAs) are also collected every year as part of the Basic Statistical Returns and published under the annual RBI publication of Basic Statistical Returns of Scheduled Commercial Banks in India (BSR). However, the BSR publication does not provide a break-up of SBAs across the socio-economic groups of Dalits and Adivasis.

[5] The results from the 1982 round of the AIDIS have been questioned by many studies on account of a sharp reduction in the village and household sample size by the NSSO during this round compared with the 1972 round (Narayana 1988; Prabhu et al. 1988; Gothoskar 1988; and Bell 1990). Most of these studies have noted the possibility of an underestimation of indebtedness, particularly the incidence of indebtedness, in the 1982 round. However, there is no clear consensus about whether the 1982 round also underestimated the relative share of formal sources; see the findings by Bell (1990) about an underestimation of the share of informal sources and an overestimation of the share of formal sources by the AIDIS. Also see the findings by Gothoskar (1988) about an underestimation of the amount of debt owed to formal sources.

TABLE 1 *Distribution of outstanding debt of rural Dalit and non-Dalit/Adivasi households by source of credit, 1992 and 2002, India* in per cent

Type of source	Dalit households		Non-Dalit households		Non-Dalit and non-Adivasi households		All households	
	1992	2002	1992	2002	1992	2002	1992	2002
All formal sources	**61.1**	**44.8**	**64.6**	**59.0**	**64.6**	**58.5**	**64.0**	**57.1**
Government	9.2	2.9	5.6	2.2	5.5	2.1	6.1	2.3
Cooperatives	15.0	18.3	22.9	28.8	23.3	28.7	21.6	27.3
Commercial banks	34.6	21.6	33.6	25.0	33.3	24.5	33.7	24.5
Insurance companies	0.2	0.1	0.3	0.3	0.3	0.3	0.3	0.3
Provident funds	1.1	0.2	0.7	0.3	0.7	0.2	0.7	0.3
Other formal sources	1.0	1.7	1.7	2.4	1.6	2.5	1.6	2.4
All informal sources	36.6	55.2	31.9	41.0	31.8	41.5	32.7	42.9
Landlords	8.5	2.3	3.1	0.7	3.1	0.8	4.0	1.0
Agriculturist moneylenders	8.0	15.1	6.8	9.2	6.8	9.2	7.1	10.0
Professional moneylenders	10.4	27.6	10.5	18.4	10.5	18.8	10.5	19.6
Traders	2.4	1.4	2.5	2.8	2.5	2.8	2.5	2.6
Relatives and friends	3.7	6.4	5.8	7.2	6.0	7.3	5.5	7.1
Doctors, lawyers and other professionals	0.3	0.3	0.2	0.3	0.2	0.3	0.2	0.3
Other informal sources	**3.3**	**2.1**	**2.9**	**2.4**	**2.6**	**2.4**	**3.0**	**2.3**
Sources not specified	**2.3**	-	**3.5**	-	**3.6**	–	**3.3**	**0.0**
All sources	**100.0**	**100.0**	**100.0**	**100.0**	**100.0**	**100.0**	**100.0**	**100.0**

Source: NSSO (1998 and 2006).

Separate data on Dalit households are not available from the AIDIS rounds before 1992. Nevertheless, the data do indicate that Dalit households in rural areas gained new and often unprecedented access to formal sector credit. The Integrated Rural Development Programme (IRDP), which 'channelled funds on a hitherto unprecedented scale for creating supplementary incomes amongst the relatively poor in rural areas all over India' (Guhan 1986), was the most important means of such access.[6]

Between 1992 and 2002, as was the case with all rural households, the share of formal sources in the total debt of rural Dalit households declined. However, the decline for Dalit households was greater than for non-Dalit households (Table 1). Debt from formal sources as a percentage of the total debt came down by about 16 percentage points between 1992 and 2002

---

[6] For a discussion of the general expansion of bank credit in rural areas in the 1970s and 1980s after the adoption of the model of social and development banking, see Chavan (2005). An assessment of the IRDP in the 1980s showed that of the total families assisted by this scheme across the country, 92 per cent belonged to Dalit and Adivasi groups (Basu 2003). Further, evidence from village surveys conducted across the country in the 1980s made similar observations (see Swaminathan 1990 on West Bengal; Dreze 1990 on Gujarat; and Mahajan 1991 on Punjab – cited in Mishra and Nayak 2004).

TABLE 2   *Distribution of outstanding debt of all rural households by source of credit, 1962–2002, India* in per cent

Type of source	1962	1972	1982	1992	2002
All formal sources	16.9	29.1	55.6	64.0	57.1
Government	2.3	6.7	4.1	6.1	2.3
Cooperatives	13.9	20.1	25.7	21.6	27.3
Commercial banks	0.7	2.2	25.2	33.7	24.5
Insurance companies	–	0.1	–	0.3	0.3
Provident funds	–	0.1	–	0.7	0.3
Other formal sources	–	–	0.6	1.6	2.4
All informal sources	83.1	70.9	44.4	32.7	42.9
Landlords	0.7	8.6	4.8	4.0	1.0
Agriculturist moneylenders	33.9	23.1	23.6*	7.1	10.0
Professional moneylenders	12.7	13.8	–	10.5	19.6
Traders	10.1	8.7	–	2.5	2.6
Relatives and friends	8.8	13.8	10.0	5.5	7.1
Doctors, lawyers and other professionals	–	–	–	0.2	0.3
Other informal sources	17.0	2.8	6.0	3.0	2.3
Sources not specified	–	–	–	3.3	–
All sources	100.0	100.0	100.0	100.0	100.0

Note: *Figure pertains to debt from agriculturist and professional moneylenders and traders together.

Source: RBI (1965, 1975, 1989); NSSO (1998, 2006).

for Dalit households as compared to five percentage points for non-Dalit households.[7] Thus, in the 1990s, Dalits suffered more than Others from the cutbacks in formal credit to rural areas.

The AIDIS data also show that, between 1992 and 2002, the number of Dalit households reporting at least one outstanding loan from formal sources fell by about five percentage points. The corresponding fall for non-Dalit households was only about one percentage point (Table 3).

As outstanding debt is a stock variable, it misses out on loans that are taken during the survey year and settled prior to the date of survey. Hence, it is also important to look at the incidence of fresh loans taken during the survey year. The percentage of Dalit households that reported at least one fresh loan from the formal sector during the survey year was 4.7 per cent in 2002–03 as compared to 7.6 per cent in 1991–92 (Table 4). At the same time, there was a rise between 1991–92 and 2002–03, by about four percentage points, in the number of Dalit households that reported at least one new borrowing from informal sources.

The fall in the share of debt from formal sources among Dalit households between 1992 and 2002 was attributable to a sharp fall in debt

---

[7] Even if the share of debt taken from non-specified sources was entirely added to the debt from formal sources, the fall in the share of formal sources for non-Dalit households was still much smaller than the corresponding figure for Dalit households.

TABLE 3 *Percentage of rural Dalit and non-Dalit/Adivasi households reporting at least one loan outstanding from formal and/or informal sources, India, 1992 and 2002*

Type of source	Dalit		Non-Dalit and Non-Adivasi		All	
	1992	2002	1992	2002	1992	2002
Formal sources	17.1	11.9	15.8	14.3	15.6	13.4
Commercial banks	9.1	5.9	7.3	5.8	7.5	5.7
Informal sources	11.2	17.0	9.9	16.1	9.8	15.5
Professional moneylenders	3.2	7.7	3.3	7.1	3.1	6.9
Any source	25.9	27.1	23.6	27.6	23.4	26.5

Source: NSSO (1998, 2006).

TABLE 4 *Percentage of rural Dalit and non-Dalit and non-Adivasi households reporting at least one cash borrowing from formal and/or informal sources, India, 1991–92 and 2002–03*

Type of source	Dalit households		Non-Dalit and Non-Adivasi households		All households	
	1991–92	2002–03	1991–92	2002–03	1991–92	2002–03
Formal sources	7.6	4.7	9.5	9.5	8.7	7.9
Informal sources	12.6	16.5	11.8	14.3	11.5	14.1
Any source	19.8	20.5	20.9	22.3	19.9	20.8

Source: NSSO (1998, 2006).

outstanding to commercial banks rather than from other formal sources. Of the total reduction of about 16 percentage points in the share of debt from formal sources between 1992 and 2002, about 13 percentage points were on account of commercial banks (Table 1). In 1992, commercial banks were the largest source of debt for Dalit households; in 2002, they were replaced by professional moneylenders. Between 1992 and 2002, the share of rural Dalit households that owed at least one loan to commercial banks fell by about three percentage points (Table 3). During the corresponding period, there was a rise of a little over four percentage points, from 3.2 per cent to 7.7 per cent, in the share of Dalit households that reported at least one loan outstanding from professional moneylenders.

When households were classified by the rates of interest at which they borrowed, it was clear again that informal sources predominated in Dalit debt portfolios (Table 5). Between 1992 and 2002, there was a decline in the share of debt taken at annual interest rates ranging between 6 and 15 per cent and a rise in the share of debt taken at interest rates above 20 per cent. Another disturbing feature was a rise between 1992 and 2002 in the share of total debt taken at compound rates of interest by Dalit households (Table 6). In the same period, the proportion of interest-free debt and debt

TABLE 5　*Outstanding debt of rural Dalit and non-Dalit and non-Adivasi households, by size-class of interest rate, 1992 and 2002, India* in per cent

Size-class of interest rate (in per cent per annum)	Distribution of outstanding debt of							
	Dalit households		Non-Dalit households		Non-Dalit and and non-Adivasi households		All households	
	1992	2002	1992	2002	1992	2002	1992	2002
Nil	9.3	8.2	8.2	8.5	8.4	8.6	8.4	8.4
Less than 6	7.6	2.1	2.3	2.1	2.3	2.2	3.2	2.1
6 to 10	3.8	3.1	3.0	2.4	3.1	2.2	3.1	2.5
10 to 15	35.9	29.0	40.5	33.7	40.2	33.8	39.8	33.1
15 to 20	10.1	11.3	16.9	22.3	17.5	21.9	15.8	20.8
20 and above	27.8	45.5	23.7	30.6	23.4	31.0	24.4	32.6
Not specified	5.5	0.9	5.2	0.4	5.0	0.3	5.3	0.4
Total	100.0	100.0	100.0	100.0	100.0	100.0	100.0	100.0

Source:　NSSO (1998, 2006).

TABLE 6　*Outstanding debt of rural Dalit and non-Dalit and non-Adivasi households, by type of interest rates, 1992 and 2002, India* in per cent

Interest rate type	Dalit households		Non-Dalit households		Non-Dalit and non-Adivasi households		All households	
	1992	2002	1992	2002	1992	2002	1992	2002
Interest-free	9.3	8.2	7.5	8.5	8.4	8.6	8.4	8.4
Simple	65.4	70.7	61.2	68.5	62.2	68.2	62.5	68.8
Compound	15.8	18.5	23.5	21.4	21.9	21.8	21.2	21.0
Concessional	5.9	2.6	4.6	1.7	3.7	1.5	4.2	1.8
Not reported	3.6	–	3.1	–	3.8	–	3.6	–
Total	100.0	100.0	100.0	100.0	100.0	100.0	100.0	100.0

Source:　NSSO (1998, 2006).

taken at concessional rates of interest declined. These findings reflect the rise in the percentage of debt taken from informal sources, especially professional moneylenders.

The AIDIS data show that the fall in the share of formal sources in the total debt of rural Dalit households between 1992 and 2002 occurred in every State of India other than Maharashtra and Himachal Pradesh (Table 7). In Maharashtra, the rise in the share of formal sources of debt was mainly on account of cooperatives and not commercial banks.

The AIDIS data indicate that cooperatives were less important as a source of credit than commercial banks for rural Dalits. In 2002, credit cooperatives had a share of 18.3 per cent in the total debt of rural Dalit households, and commercial banks a share of 21.6 per cent. Nevertheless, there was some increase in the share of cooperatives, from 15 per cent to 18.3 per cent,

TABLE 7   *Share of debt from formal sources in total debt of rural Dalit and non-Dalit and non-Adivasi households, State-wise, 1992 and 2002* in per cent

State	Dalit households		Non-Dalit households		Non-Dalit and non-Adivasi households		All households	
	1992	2002	1992	2002	1992	2002	1992	2002
Andhra Pradesh	36	16	26	29	31	29	31	27
Assam	78	31	61	61	60	60	64	58
Bihar	65	25	74	54	73	53	72	37
Gujarat	96	80	72	66	71	67	74	67
Haryana	55	41	74	52	74	52	72	50
Himachal Pradesh	69	76	56	73	56	73	59	74
Jammu and Kashmir	81	79	75	72	74	72	76	73
Karnataka	73	53	73	68	73	69	73	67
Kerala	84	75	91	82	92	82	91	81
Madhya Pradesh	70	50	71	72	70	69	71	59
Maharashtra	72	90	81	84	81	84	80	85
Manipur	-	-	55	–	57	–	55	–
Meghalaya	–	–	91	–	100	–	91	–
Nagaland	-	-	55	–		–	55	–
Orissa	85	61	72	76	71	73	74	74
Punjab	73	28	81	61	81	61	79	56
Rajasthan	27	24	40	36	40	32	37	34
Tamil Nadu	62	31	56	78	56	78	57	47
Tripura	95	–	88	–	85	–	89	–
Uttar Pradesh	73	47	66	61	65	61	67	56
West Bengal	87	70	80	67	81	67	82	68
India	61	45	65	59	65	59	64	57

Note: – not available.
Source: NSSO (1998, 2006).

between 1991–92 and 2002–03, a period in which the share of commercial banks declined significantly, from 34.6 per cent to 21.6 per cent (Table 1).

Commercial Bank Credit to Dalits

Credit given by commercial banks to Dalits is included in the banks' advances to 'weaker sections'. Domestic commercial banks (public and private sector banks, but not foreign banks) have been required to direct at least 10 per cent of their (adjusted net) bank credit to 'weaker sections' as part of priority sector lending. This sub-target for 'weaker sections' was introduced by the RBI in 1980 as part of its social and development banking policy.[8] Weaker

[8] The sub-target for agriculture and weaker sections was introduced based on the recommendations of the Working Group on the Modalities of Implementation of Priority Sector Lending and the Twenty Point Economic Programme by Banks (Chairman: K.

sections were then defined as small and marginal farmers (with landholdings of less than 5 acres), landless agricultural labourers and tenant farmers, in addition to Dalits and Adivasis.

Over the years, new groups have been included as part of the definition of 'weaker sections', including members of minority communities engaged in specified occupations. More recently, in the 2000s, loans to self-help groups (SHGs) have also been included as part of the credit given to 'weaker sections'. All these new sub-categories have been clubbed together, thus effectively reducing the importance that each sub-category individually deserves as a weaker section.

Despite the fact that the category of weaker sections has been broadened in recent years, banks have consistently failed to meet the prescribed target of lending (Table 8). At the aggregate level, there has been an upward movement in the share of credit given to weaker sections (that is, of adjusted net bank credit) from 2007 onwards for both public and private sector banks. However, the picture at the aggregate level conceals disturbing trends at the

TABLE 8   *Commercial bank credit to 'weaker sections', India, 1991–2010* in Rs 10 million

Year	Public sector banks	% of net bank credit	Private sector banks	% of net bank credit	Total	% of net bank credit
	1	2	3	4	5 = 1+3	6
1991	10260	9.7	246	5.2	10506	9.5
1992	10881	9.7	269	4.5	11150	9.4
1993	11865	8.9	283	4.0	12148	8.7
1994	12779	9.1	300	3.1	13079	8.7
1995	13918	8.2	339	2.5	14257	7.8
1996	15579	8.4	381	2.1	15960	7.8
2001	24899	7.2	959	1.7	25858	6.4
2002	28974	7.3	1142	1.8	30116	6.5
2003	32303	6.7	1223	1.5	33526	5.9
2004	41589	7.4	1495	1.3	43084	6.4
2005	63492	8.8	1913	1.2	65405	7.4
2006	78373	7.7	3909	1.6	82282	6.5
2007	94285	7.2	5229	1.55	99514	6.0
2008	126935	9.3	7228	2.1	134163	7.8
2009	166843	9.9	15844	3.9	182687	8.7
2010	212214	10.2	25691	5.5	237905	9.3

Note: Data are not available for the years between 1997 and 2000.
Source: *Reserve Bank of India Report on Trend and Progress of Banking in India*, various issues.

S. Krishnaswamy) in 1980; see master circular, 'RBI/2010-11/80 RPCD. CO. Plan. BC. 10 /04.09.01/ 2010-11', dated 1 July 2010, for a history of priority sector credit.

disaggregated level. First, at the bank-group level, the performance of private sector banks has been poor when compared with public sector banks. The credit allocation to weaker sections by private sector banks has been far lower than the prescribed target. Secondly, at the bank level, the performance has been even poorer. In every year between 2006 and 2009, about 40–70 per cent of public sector banks failed to meet the target. Further, over 80 per cent of private sector banks failed to meet the target in each of these years. In fact, in 2006–07 and 2007–08, no private sector bank met the target. Even in 2010, when the percentage of credit given to weaker sections at the aggregate level was at its highest level since 1993, fifteen out of twenty-two private sector banks (68 per cent) and eight out of twenty-seven public sector banks (30 per cent) failed individually to meet the target for lending to weaker sections (RBI 2010a).[9]

An analysis of small borrowal accounts (SBAs) shows even more disturbing trends as regards the access of Dalits to bank credit in recent years. SBAs are accounts with an individual credit limit of up to Rs 2 lakhs (the limit was Rs 25,000 till 1998). In 2008, about 56 per cent of total SBAs were held with rural and semi-urban branches of commercial banks, and about 37 per cent of these accounts were for direct finance under agriculture and allied activities (Table 9). Thus, credit flow through SBAs forms an important part of credit flow to rural areas.

The survey of SBAs shows a sharp fall in the percentage share held by Dalits in the total number of SBAs as well as in the total amount of bank credit outstanding between 1993 and 2008. In 2008, both these shares were only about one-sixth of their corresponding shares in 1993 (Table 10).

On an average, there were only sixteen SBAs per 1,000 Dalits in the population in 2008 as compared to 77 in 1993 (Table 11).[10] Further, credit

TABLE 9 *Distribution of number of accounts and amount outstanding under small borrowal accounts held with bank offices, by population group, India, 2008* in per cent

Population group	No. of accounts	Amount outstanding
Rural	33.1	31.5
Semi-urban	22.9	26.5
Urban	11.8	17.1
Metropolitan	32.6	25.3

Source: RBI (2011).

[9] For details about the years between 2006 and 2009, see Report on Trend and Progress of Banking in India, various issues.

[10] Between 1993 and 1997, there was a sharp decline in the total number of SBAs per 1,000 persons. According to Shetty (2004), this speaks of the increasing 'bias' of commercial banks against small-size borrowers in general in the 1990s. However, the surveys after 2001 showed an increasing trend in the total number of SBAs per 1,000 persons. It may be noted that as the cut-off limit for SBAs was changed in 1999, the figures for 1993 and 1997 are not strictly comparable with those from 2001 onwards.

TABLE 10   *Percentage share in the number of small borrowal accounts, amount outstanding, and population of Dalits and non-Dalits, India, 1993–2008*

Caste category	Population		Accounts						Amount					
	1991	2001	1993	1997	2001	2004	2006	2008	1993	1997	2001	2004	2006	2008
Dalit	16.5	16.2	18.0	17.8	12.2	6.7	5.4	3.3	12.4	12.7	7.1	4.6	3.9	2.4
Non-Dalit	83.5	83.8	80.9	81.6	86.8	91.1	94.0	96.7	86.7	86.7	91.6	92.6	96.2	97.6
Non-Dalit and Non-Adivasi	75.4	75.6	71.3	72.7	80.7	87.4	91.0	95.0	81.5	80.1	87.8	90.0	94.1	96.4
Total	100.0	100.0	100.0	100.0	100.0	100.0	100.0	100.0	100.0	100.0	100.0	100.0	100.0	100.0

Note: Small borrowal accounts are accounts with an individual credit limit of up to Rs 2 lakh after 1999, and Rs 25,000 before that.

Sources: RBI (1993, 1997a, 2004, 2006a, 2008); http://www.indiastat.com for the population data.

TABLE 11   *Amount of credit per capita and number of small borrowal accounts per 1000 persons, for Dalit and non-Dalit and non-Adivasi populations, India, 1993 to 2008*

Caste category	Amount of credit per capita (Rs)						Number of small borrowal accounts per 1000 persons					
	1993	1997	2001	2004	2006	2008	1993	1997	2001	2004	2006	2008
Dalit	768	316	439	365	414	295	77	46	37	23	22	16
Non-Dalit	1055	419	1094	1407	1949	2284	68	41	51	60	75	89
Ratio of Non-Dalit to Dalit	1.4	1.3	2.5	3.9	4.7	7.7	–	–	–	–	–	–
Non-Dalit and Non-Adivasi	1098	429	1162	1517	2115	2503	67	41	52	64	80	97
Ratio of Non-Dalit and Non-Adivasi to Dalit	1.4	1.4	2.6	4.2	5.1	8.5	–	–	–	–	–	–
All	1017	402	1001	1240	1701	1967	70	42	49	54	66	78

Notes: Figures of credit per capita have been deflated using GDP deflator at the base of 1999–2000.
The population for each year is worked out applying an exponential rate of growth of population between 1991 and 2001 for each of the categories.

Sources: RBI (1993, 1997a, 2004, 2006a, 2008, 2011); Population Census of India (1991, 2001); RBI, *Handbook of Statistics on Indian Economy* (2006).

TABLE 12 *Average amount of credit received by a Dalit female borrower for every 100 rupees received by a non-Dalit/Adivasi borrower, India, 1997–2008* in rupees

Variable	1997	2001	2004	2006	2008
Average amount of credit to a Dalit female borrower per 100 rupees of credit to a female non-Dalit and non-Adivasi borrower	23	12	8	6.40	4.00
Average amount of credit to a Dalit female borrower per 100 rupees of credit to a male non-Dalit and non-Adivasi borrower	5	1	1	0.98	0.46

Source: RBI (1993, 1997a, 2004, 2006a, 2008, 2011).

per capita (adjusted for price change) for Dalits fluctuated around a declining trend across the survey years, recording a particularly sharp fall between 2006 and 2008.[11] The amount of credit per capita for non-Dalits was nearly seven times the credit received by Dalits through SBAs in 2008. The gap between credit per capita for Dalits and non-Dalits widened substantially between 1993 and 2008.

Caste differences were aggravated by gender differences. In 2008, Dalit women, on average, received only about Rs 4 of bank credit per SBA for every Rs 100 received by non-Dalit and non-Adivasi women (Table 12). In 2008, Dalit women obtained less than Re 1 of credit per SBA for every Rs 100 received by non-Dalit and non-Adivasi men. Further, the average amount of credit per account going to Dalit women vis-à-vis women and men from non-Dalit and non-Adivasi categories was on a rapid decline between 1997 and 2008.

Concluding Observations

According to the AIDIS, commercial banks were the most important source of credit for Dalit households in 1992. There was, however, a sharp fall in the share of debt of commercial banks between 1992 and 2002. The vacuum thus created was filled by professional moneylenders. While professional moneylenders did emerge in 2002 as an important source of credit for other rural households as well, their hold over Dalit households was much stronger. The expansion of informal debt meant an increased and onerous interest burden on rural Dalit households.

Data from the supply side indicate a continued failure by domestic banks to meet the targets set for credit to 'weaker sections' since the early 1990s. In the 1990s and 2000s, the proportion of commercial bank credit to Dalits through small borrowal accounts also recorded a sharp fall.

To conclude, available secondary data show an increasing exclusion

[11] As the cut-off limit for SBAs was changed in 1999, the figures for 1993 and 1997 are not strictly comparable with those from 2001 onwards. Nevertheless, a fall in the number of accounts and amount of credit through SBAs for Dalits is evident from a comparison of the 1993 survey with the 1997 survey, and of the 2001 survey with subsequent surveys.

of rural Dalits from the early 1990s with respect to access to affordable formal sector credit. This also explains the growing grip of informal sources on their debt portfolio in recent years. Hence, similar to the imbalance in credit flow emerging at the sectoral and regional levels, credit allocation across socio-economic groups too has become increasingly unequal in the period of financial liberalization, notwithstanding the emphasis on financial inclusion.

Exclusion of the disadvantaged and dispossessed sections is intrinsic to the functioning of markets.[12] There is, therefore, an inherent conflict between allowing the banking system to be driven by market forces and expecting greater inclusion from the system. The growing exclusion of rural Dalits from formal credit is a sign of this conflict. It underlines the need to revive the policy of social and development banking, with a stronger commitment than before to the objective of social redistribution.

This article first appeared in *Review of Agrarian Studies*, vol. 2, no. 2, 2012. The views expressed here are the personal views of the author and do not represent the views of the organization to which she belongs. The author thanks V.K. Ramachandran, Madhura Swaminathan, S.L. Shetty, Balwant Singh and R. Ramakumar for useful comments and suggestions on an earlier draft of this paper.

References

Basu, Prahlad K. (2003), 'Monitoring, Benchmarking and Evaluation for Poverty Alleviation Programmes: The Indian Experience', United Nations, New York.

Bell, Clive (1990), 'Interactions between Institutional and Informal Credit Agencies in Rural India', *World Bank Economic Review*, vol. 4, no. 3, pp. 297–328.

Chavan, Pallavi (2005), 'Banking Sector Reforms and Growth and Regional Distribution of Rural Banking in India', in V.K. Ramachandran and Madhura Swaminathan, eds, *Financial Liberalization and Rural Credit in India*, Tulika Books, New Delhi.

Chavan, Pallavi (2010), 'How "Rural" is India's Agricultural Credit?' *The Hindu*, 12 August.

Dreze, John (1990), 'Poverty in India and the IRDP Delusion', *Economic and Political Weekly*, vol. 25, no. 39, September.

Gothoskar, S.P. (1988), 'On Some Estimates of Rural Indebtedness', *Reserve Bank of India Occasional Papers*, vol. 9, no. 4, December, pp. 299–325.

Guhan, S. (1986), 'Rural Poverty Alleviation in India: Policy, Performance and Possibilities', paper presented at the Franco-Indian Colloquium on Technological Choices for Rural Development, Montpellier, France, 18–20 March; reproduced in S. Subramanian, ed., *India's Development Experience: Selected Writings of S. Guhan*, Oxford University Press, New Delhi, 2001.

Mahajan, R.K. (1991), *Integrated Rural Development Programme: A Study of Problems and Prospects in Punjab*, Concept Publishing Company, New Delhi.

Mishra, B. and Nayak, Purusottam (2004), 'Limits of Micro Credit for Rural Development: A Cursory Look', in J.K. Gogoi, ed., *Rural Indebtedness in North East India*, Dibrugarh University, Assam.

Narayana, D. (1988), 'A Note on the Reliability and Comparability of the Various Rounds of the AIRDIS and AIDIS', Centre for Development Studies, Thiruvananthapuram, unpublished.

National Sample Survey Organization (NSSO) (1998), 'Household Assets and Indebtedness of Social Groups – January to December 1992', Report No. 432, Parts I and II, New Delhi.

---

[12] The disadvantage and dispossession can be in terms of assets, income, capabilities and values necessary to participate in markets; see Nayyar (2003). Further, see Thorat (2006), who applies the discussion on social exclusion to financial markets.

National Sample Survey Organization (NSSO) (2006), 'Household Asset Holding, Indebtedness, Current Borrowings and Repayments of Social Groups in India as on June 30, 2002', Report No. 503, New Delhi.

Nayyar, Deepak (2003), 'On Exclusion and Inclusion: Democracy, Markets and People', in A.K. Dutt and J. Ros, eds, *Development Economics and Structuralist Macroeconomics: Essay in Honour of Lance Taylor*, Edward Elgar, Cheltenham.

Prabhu, Seeta K., Nadkarni, Avadhoot and Achuthan, C. V. (1988), 'Rural Credit: Mystery of Missing Households', *Economic and Political Weekly*, vol. 23, no. 50, 10 December, pp. 2642–46.

Ramachandran, V.K. and Swaminathan, Madhura, eds (2005), *Financial Liberalization and Rural Credit in India*, Tulika Books, New Delhi.

Ramakumar, R. and Chavan, Pallavi (2007), 'Revival in Agricultural Credit in the 2000s: An Explanation', *Economic and Political Weekly*, vol. 42, no. 52, 29 December to 4 January.

Reserve Bank of India (RBI) (1965), 'All India Rural Debt and Investment Survey, Outstanding Loan Borrowings and Repayments of Rural Households', *Reserve Bank of India Bulletin*, September.

Reserve Bank of India (RBI) (1978), 'All India Debt and Investment Survey – Outstanding Loan Borrowings and Repayment of Households', Department of Statistical Analysis and Computer Services, Mumbai.

Reserve Bank of India (RBI) (1989), 'Statistical Tables Relating to Cash Borrowings and Repayments of Households – July 1981–June 1982', Department of Statistical Analysis and Computer Services, Mumbai.

Reserve Bank of India (RBI) (1991), *Report of the Committee on the Financial System*, Mumbai.

Reserve Bank of India (RBI) (1993), 'Salient Results of the Survey of Small Borrowal Accounts, March – 1993', available at http://rbi.org.in, viewed on 24 September 2012.

Reserve Bank of India (RBI) (1997a), 'Salient Results of the Survey of Small Borrowal Accounts – 1997', available at http://rbi.org.in, viewed on 24 September 2012.

Reserve Bank of India (RBI) (1997b), 'Credit Flow to Agriculture and Other Priority Sector Areas – Salient Financial Indicators', Rural Credit and Planning Department, Mumbai.

Reserve Bank of India (RBI) (2004), 'Survey of Small Borrowal Accounts – 2001', *Reserve Bank of India Bulletin*, May, Mumbai.

Reserve Bank of India (RBI) (2005), 'Taking Banking Services to the Common Man – Financial Inclusion', Address by V. Leeladhar, Deputy Governor, RBI, 2 December, available at http://www.rbi.org.in, viewed on 24 September 2012.

Reserve Bank of India (RBI) (2006a), 'Salient Results of the Survey of Small Borrowal Accounts – 2004', *Reserve Bank of India Bulletin*, July, Mumbai.

Reserve Bank of India (RBI) (2006b), 'Economic Growth, Financial Deepening and Financial Inclusion', Speech by Rakesh Mohan, Deputy Governor, RBI, 20 November, available at http://www.rbi.org.in, viewed on 24 September 2012.

Reserve Bank of India (RBI) (2009), 'Financial Inclusion: Challenges and Opportunities', Speech by D. Subbarao, Governor, RBI, at the Bankers' Club, 9 December, Kolkata.

Reserve Bank of India (RBI) (2010a), *Report on Trend and Progress of Banking in India – 2009–10*, Mumbai.

Reserve Bank of India (RBI) (2010b), 'Putting Financial Inclusion into Mission Mode', Address by K.C. Chakrabarty, Deputy Governor, RBI at the 23rd Skoch Summit, Mumbai, 17 July, available at http://www.rbi.org.in, viewed on 24 September 2012.

Reserve Bank of India (RBI) (2011), 'Survey of Small Borrowal Accounts – 2008', *Reserve Bank of India Bulletin*, May.

Reserve Bank of India (RBI) (various issues), *Report on Trend and Progress of Banking in India*, Mumbai.

Shetty, S.L. (2004), 'Distributional Issues in Bank Credit – Multi Pronged Strategy to Correct Past Neglect', *Economic and Political Weekly*, July.

Swaminathan, Madhura (1990), 'Village Level Implementation of IRDP: A Comparison of West Bengal and Tamil Nadu', *Economic and Political Weekly*, vol. XXV, no. 13, March.

Thorat, Y.S.P. (2006), 'Indian Banking: Shaping an Economic Powerhouse', Speech, available at http://www.ficci.com, viewed on 4 July 2007.

Dalit Households in Village Economies: Essays from the Project on Agrarian Relations in India

Variations in Land and Asset Inequality

Vikas Rawal

This essay presents data on disparities in ownership of land and other assets between Dalit households and households other than Dalits, Adivasis and Muslims (henceforth called households belonging to 'Other Castes'), from fifteen villages surveyed between 2005 and 2010 as part of the Project on Agrarian Relations in India (PARI). A list of the villages is provided in Table 1.

The PARI surveys enumerate and value all physical assets of households in the survey villages, other than ornaments and jewellery. The enumeration is based on a detailed check-list of assets. In addition, as far as possible, the investigators conduct a visual inspection of assets to ensure that all the assets are covered. The respondents are asked to value each asset on the basis of the price it is likely to fetch if it is sold in its present condition.[1] The values

TABLE 1 *List of Villages*

Village	Taluk/Block	District	State	Year of survey
Ananthavaram	Kollur	Guntur	Andhra Pradesh	2006
Bukkacherla	Raptadu	Anantapur	Andhra Pradesh	2006
Kothapalle	Thimmapur	Karimnagar	Andhra Pradesh	2006
Harevli	Najibabad	Bijnor	Uttar Pradesh	2006
Mahatwar	Rasra	Ballia	Uttar Pradesh	2006
Warwat Khanderao	Sangrampur	Buldhana	Maharashtra	2007
Nimshirgaon	Shirol	Kolhapur	Maharashtra	2007
25 F Gulabewala	Karanpur	Sri Ganganagar	Rajasthan	2007
Rewasi	Sikar	Sikar	Rajasthan	2010
Gharsondi	Bhitarwar	Gwalior	Madhya Pradesh	2008
Alabujanahalli	Maddur	Mandya	Karnataka	2009
Siresandra	Kolar	Kolar	Karnataka	2009
Zhapur	Gulbarga	Gulbarga	Karnataka	2009
Panahar	Kotulpur	Bankura	West Bengal	2010
Amarsinghi	Ratua I	Malda	West Bengal	2010

[1] Respondents are requested to provide the price at which their asset could be sold in its present condition, and not the price at which the asset was purchased or at which a new asset of the same type may be available in the market at the time of the survey.

of assets are carefully examined, both in comparison with valuations reported by other households as well as in relation to prevailing market prices collected from selected informants, to identify outliers and correct them. Data on ornaments and jewellery and on financial assets are not collected because the information provided by respondents on these assets is not verifiable, and because, in our experience, respondents tend to greatly under-report holdings of such assets.

The essay analyses disparities in ownership of assets between Dalit households and households belonging to Other Castes. Other Caste households include caste Hindus, Jat Sikhs (in 25 F Gulabewala, Sri Ganganagar district, Rajasthan), Jains (in Nimshirgaon, Kolhapur district, Maharashtra) and Nomadic Tribes (in Maharashtra villages).

PARI surveys of the study villages were conducted between 2005 and 2010. As an approximation, I have used the all-India Consumer Price Index for Agricultural Labourers (CPIAL) to deflate the value of all assets to constant 2005–06 prices. Since most comparisons in the essay are across caste groups and across categories of assets within each village, and not in levels across villages, use of the CPIAL does not create any distortion. Also, a broad ranking of villages in terms of average asset ownership remains unchanged if we were to use alternative deflators such as the Wholesale Price Index (WPI) or a deflator based on the State Domestic Product (SDP).

The essay is organized as follows. The first section discusses disparities in overall wealth. The second section discusses differences in the structure of asset-holdings between Dalit households and Other households. The third section discusses disparities in the ownership of land, and differences in access to land through tenurial arrangements. The last section discusses disparities in ownership of other productive assets.

Disparities in Total Household Asset-holdings

Tables 2–4 present statistics that summarize disparities in the total value of asset-holdings between Dalit and Other Caste households. Table 2 shows the average value of asset-holdings of Dalit households and households belonging to Other Castes. Table 3 shows an index of ownership defined as the ratio of share of wealth owned by households belonging to a caste group to share of households in the village that belong to the same caste group. A value of less than one indicates that the share in ownership of wealth of a caste group is lower than its share in number of households. Conversely, a value higher than one shows that a caste group has more than proportionate share in total wealth. Table 4 shows the proportion of households belonging to a caste group that fall in the bottom four deciles of wealth-ranking and the top one decile of wealth-ranking in the village. Table 5 shows the average value of assets of the top five Dalit and Other Caste households.

These tables bring out the following points. First, in all the villages, the average value of asset-holdings of Dalit households was substantially lower

TABLE 2 *Average value of household asset-holdings, Dalits and Other Caste households* in rupees

Village	Dalit	Other Caste	Ratio (Other Caste / Dalit)
Ananthavaram	64750	863285	13.3
Bukkacherla	65447	362075	5.5
Kothapalle	107588	411632	3.8
Harevli	136615	1682303	12.3
Mahatwar	150339	1248055	8.3
Warwat Khanderao	118368	584205	4.9
Nimshirgaon	473477	1291905	2.7
25 F Gulabewala	44379	5812284	131.0
Rewasi	544777	1099310	2.0
Gharsondi	514968	1802274	3.5
Alabujanahalli	254798	1331933	5.2
Siresandra	482638	1748799	3.6
Zhapur	235265	1060704	4.5
Panahar	54545	681241	12.5
Amarsinghi	157173	344880	2.2

Source: Survey data.

TABLE 3 *Ratio of share in total wealth to share in number of households, Dalits and Other Caste Households*

Village	Dalit	Other Caste
Ananthavaram	0.15	1.93
Bukkacherla	0.22	1.22
Kothapalle	0.36	1.37
Harevli	0.14	1.77
Mahatwar	0.26	2.12
Warwat Khanderao	0.26	1.27
Nimshirgaon	0.49	1.35
25 F Gulabewala	0.02	2.49
Rewasi	0.56	1.13
Gharsondi	0.35	1.23
Alabujanahalli	0.22	1.13
Siresandra	0.38	1.36
Zhapur	0.39	1.75
Panahar	0.14	1.76
Amarsinghi	0.61	1.34

Source: Survey data.

TABLE 4   *Number of Dalit households in bottom four deciles and top decile of household asset-holdings as a proportion of total number of Dalit households, and number of Other Caste households in bottom four deciles and top decile of household asset-holdings as a proportion of total number of Other Caste households*

Village	Dalit households in bottom 40 per cent as a proportion of all Dalit households	Dalit households in top 10 per cent as a proportion of all Dalit households	Other Caste households in bottom 40 per cent as a proportion of all Other Caste households	Other Caste households in top 10 per cent as a proportion of all Other Caste households
Ananthavaram	54.1	0.0	19.3	20.6
Bukkacherla	82.8	0.0	28.0	13.3
Kothapalle	55.9	2.5	29.1	14.3
Harevli	70.7	0.0	12.3	21.1
Mahatwar	57.9	0.0	12.7	25.4
Warwat Khanderao	68.0	0.0	34.5	14.0
Nimshirgaon	66.3	4.0	22.5	14.6
25 F Gulabewala	63.4	0.0	3.7	25.9
Rewasi	61.9	4.8	34.7	11.9
Gharsondi	51.9	3.7	29.3	12.7
Alabujanahalli	82.9	0.0	32.4	11.9
Siresandra	65.5	0.0	24.0	16.0
Zhapur	41.3	0.0	36.0	24.0
Panahar	60.2	0.0	16.3	23.9
Amarsinghi	54.4	5.3	26.1	14.5

Source: Survey data.

than the average value of asset-holdings of Other Caste households (Table 2).

Secondly, there was great variation in the ratio of average asset-holdings of Other Caste households to average asset-holdings of Dalit households across villages (Table 2). In all the villages, the average asset-holding of Other Caste households was at least double the average asset-holding of Dalit households. In Ananthavaram, Harevli and Panahar, all irrigated villages, the total value of assets of Other Caste households was more than twelve times the value of assets owned by a Dalit household on average. The disparity between average holdings was highest in 25 F Gulabewala. Across villages, the average asset-holding of Dalit households was smallest in 25 F Gulabewala, and the average asset-holding of Other Caste households was highest in 25 F Gulabewala. In 25 F Gulabewala, the ratio of average asset-holdings of Other Caste to Dalit households was 131.

The disproportionality in asset ownership by members of a caste group after adjusting for population strength is brought out by the data in Table 3. This table shows, for example, that in relation to their numbers, Dalit households in the Dalit-majority village of Mahatwar had only a quarter (26 per cent) of the assets of all households.

TABLE 5 *Average asset-holdings of top five rich households* in Rs

Village (1)	Dalit (2)	Other Caste (3)	Ratio (3/2)
Ananthavaram	605648	15474116	26
Bukkacherla	160650	4884243	30
Kothapalle	648664	5040132	8
Harevli	715397	8591981	12
Mahatwar	730595	8228001	11
Warwat Khanderao	323904	5949135	18
Nimshirgaon	2188324	17014774	8
25 F Gulabewala	244736	23322083	95
Rewasi	1419017	10187125	7
Gharsondi	1543173	22857439	15
Alabujanahalli	750272	13855711	18
Siresandra	1136583	6210100	5
Zhapur	691083	6244388	9
Panahar	422627	4390291	10
Amarsinghi	771330	1316678	2

Source: Survey data.

Thirdly, in all the villages, Dalit households were concentrated at the lower end of the distribution of asset-holdings. Table 4 shows that in all the villages, Dalit households were concentrated in the bottom four deciles of the distribution of household assets. In Bukkacherla (Anantapur district, Andhra Pradesh) and Alabujanahalli (Mandya district, Karnataka), about 83 per cent of Dalit households were in the bottom four deciles. On the other hand, in ten out of fifteen villages, no Dalit household made it to the top decile. In six villages, more than 20 per cent of households belonging to Other Castes were in the top decile of the distribution of household assets.

Fourthly, the richest among Dalit households had asset-holdings that are a small fraction of the asset-holdings of the richest among households belonging to Other Castes. In all the villages, the average asset-holding of the top five households belonging to Other Castes was several times higher than the average asset-holding of the top five Dalit households (Table 5).

Overall Structure of Asset-Holdings

Table 6 shows the share of different categories of assets in the total value of assets owned by Dalit households in each village. To take an example from the table, among Dalit households in Ananthavaram, agricultural land and trees accounted for 29 per cent of total value of assets, other land and buildings accounted for 53 per cent of total value of assets, animals accounted for 8 per cent of total value of assets, other means of production accounted for 1 per cent of total value of assets, means of transport accounted for 2

TABLE 6   *Share of different categories of assets in total asset-holdings, Dalit households* in per cent

Village	Agricultural land and trees	Other land and buildings	Animals	Other means of production	Means of transport	Other assets
Ananthavaram	29	53	8	1	2	8
Bukkacherla	40	45	4	2	0	9
Kothapalle	36	51	5	1	2	5
Harevli	61	28	6	2	0	4
Mahatwar	42	49	4	1	1	4
Warwat Khanderao	47	49	1	0	1	3
Nimshirgaon	67	28	2	0	1	2
25 F Gulabewala	9	71	9	0	1	9
Rewasi	54	33	3	1	2	6
Gharsondi	69	25	2	0	1	4
Alabujanahalli	28	66	3	1	0	2
Siresandra	50	44	3	1	0	2
Zhapur	54	38	4	1	1	2
Panahar	25	63	5	1	1	6
Amarsinghi	39	53	3	1	0	4

Source: Survey data.

per cent of total value of assets, and other assets accounted for 8 per cent of total value of assets owned. Table 7 shows the corresponding data for Other Caste households for each village.

Table 6 shows that, in a majority of villages, 'other land and buildings' constituted the most important category of assets for Dalit households. The most important constituents within this category were homestead land and houses. In Harevli (Bijnor), Nimshirgaon (Kolhapur), Rewasi (Sikar), Gharsondi (Gwalior), Siresandra (Kolar) and Zhapur (Gulbarga), 'agricultural land and trees' were the most important category of assets for Dalit households.

On the other hand, as shown in Table 7, in almost all the villages, agricultural land (and trees) was the most important category of assets for households belonging to Other Castes. The only exception in this respect was Alabujanahalli (Mandya), where some of the wealthy Vokkaliga households owned valuable land, houses and commercial buildings in a nearby town.

Table 8 shows the share of Dalit households in the total value of assets of different types. For example, the table shows that Dalit households accounted for about 60 per cent of all households in 25 F Gulabewala, but owned only 0.1 per cent of total agricultural land. They owned 6 per cent of the total value of other land and buildings, 9.2 per cent of the total value of animals, 0.1 per cent of the total value of other means of production, 2 per cent of the total value of means of transport, and 5.4 per cent of the total value of all other assets.

TABLE 7   *Share of different categories of assets in total asset-holdings, Other Caste households* in per cent

Village	Agricultural land and trees	Other land and buildings	Animals	Other means of production	Means of transport	Other assets
Ananthavaram	74	20	1	1	1	2
Bukkacherla	56	28	5	6	1	3
Kothapalle	49	42	3	2	1	2
Harevli	51	32	5	9	0	3
Mahatwar	59	34	2	1	1	2
Warwat Khanderao	57	34	2	2	1	4
Nimshirgaon	77	16	1	2	1	2
25 F Gulabewala	81	13	1	3	1	2
Rewasi	57	31	3	3	2	3
Gharsondi	73	14	1	3	3	6
Alabujanahalli	36	59	1	1	1	2
Siresandra	53	41	2	2	1	1
Zhapur	83	13	3	1	0	1
Panahar	48	45	1	2	1	3
Amarsinghi	64	29	2	0	1	4

Source: Survey data.

TABLE 8   *Share of Dalit households in total value of assets owned by all households, by category of asset* in per cent

Village	Share of Dalit households in total value of assets						
	Agricultural land and trees	Other land and buildings	Animals	Other means of production	Means of transport	Other assets	Share in number of households
Ananthavaram	2.5	14.4	27.4	4.0	12.9	16.8	42.5
Bukkacherla	3.2	6.8	3.5	1.5	0.8	11.4	19.9
Kothapalle	8.7	13.5	19.6	4.2	13.8	21.0	31.8
Harevli	31.2	27.8	34.2	5.9	32.0	33.2	51.9
Mahatwar	26.3	42.0	46.2	20.2	32.3	49.2	65.1
Warwat Khanderao	2.1	3.7	1.4	0.2	1.2	2.0	10.0
Nimshirgaon	14.1	24.5	24.5	1.9	10.8	17.3	32.4
25 F Gulabewala	0.1	6.1	9.2	0.1	2.0	5.4	60.3
Rewasi	5.1	5.7	5.5	2.3	4.0	9.8	9.6
Gharsondi	3.4	5.9	4.4	0.2	0.8	2.4	10.2
Alabujanahalli	2.4	3.4	6.9	2.3	1.0	4.2	14.2
Siresandra	13.0	14.9	17.9	7.7	10.5	15.1	36.7
Zhapur	11.3	34.4	20.2	12.7	19.3	29.3	41.1
Panahar	3.6	11.7	25.1	4.1	5.8	14.2	53.6
Amarsinghi	18.5	40.5	33.0	43.7	24.5	31.9	44.9

Source: Survey data.

Table 9 shows similar numbers for households belonging to Other Castes. For example, in Nimshirgaon, households belonging to Other Castes accounted for 61 per cent of all households in the village. These households owned 85 per cent of agricultural land and trees, 74 per cent of land and buildings, 72 per cent of all animals, 88 per cent of all means of transport, and so on.

As can be seen in Table 8, in every village, the share of Dalit households in the ownership of each category of assets was smaller than their share in the total population. This implies that across all villages, Dalits owned a disproportionately small share of the value of assets in each category. A comparison across different categories of assets shows that in most villages, the share of Dalits was lowest with respect to agricultural land and means of production, other than land and animals. Although lower than their share in the total number of households, the share of total value of animals owned by Dalits was higher than the share of agricultural land or any other means of production owned by them.

In contrast, as shown in Table 9, the share in value of assets owned by households belonging to Other Castes was higher than their share in population in all categories across almost all the villages.

TABLE 9 *Share of households belonging to Other Castes in total value of assets owned by all households, by category of asset* in per cent

Village	Share of Other Caste households in value of assets						
	Agricultural land and trees	Other land and buildings	Animals	Other means of production	Means of transport	Other assets	Share in number of households
Ananthavaram	97.5	83.8	70.7	94.4	83.4	80.9	48.2
Bukkacherla	96.2	91.2	96.0	98.0	90.9	85.4	77.3
Kothapalle	90.3	85.5	79.5	95.5	84.7	77.2	63.9
Harevli	45.6	56.0	52.6	63.4	36.1	49.3	31.6
Mahatwar	73.7	58.0	53.8	79.8	67.7	50.8	34.9
Warwat Khanderao	87.4	87.2	83.6	84.3	83.4	84.2	68.7
Nimshirgaon	84.7	74.3	72.3	97.9	88.0	82.0	61.4
25 F Gulabewala	99.9	93.9	90.8	99.9	98.0	94.6	39.7
Rewasi	91.0	90.4	87.8	93.9	90.0	84.2	80.4
Gharsondi	95.5	91.9	94.5	99.6	99.2	97.1	77.4
Alabujanahalli	97.6	96.5	93.1	97.7	99.0	95.8	85.4
Siresandra	87.0	85.1	82.1	92.3	89.5	84.9	63.3
Zhapur	85.1	55.2	69.9	61.1	25.1	58.3	44.6
Panahar	59.5	71.5	66.6	75.4	85.0	72.8	37.1
Amarsinghi	81.5	59.1	65.7	56.3	75.5	68.0	54.3

Source: Survey data.

Ownership of Land and Buildings

Table 10 shows the proportion of households that own agricultural land, homestead land and houses, other land and buildings used for maintaining animals, and land and buildings used for commercial establishments. To take an example, the table shows that in Ananthavaram, 24 per cent of Dalit households owned agricultural land, while 58 per cent households belonging to Other Castes had agricultural land. The proportion of households that owned homestead land and houses was 99 per cent among Dalits and 95 per cent among households belonging to Other Castes. The proportion of households that owned separate land and buildings for the maintenance of animals (that is, outside their homesteads) was 26 per cent among Dalit households and 34 per cent among households belonging to Other Castes. About 2 per cent of Dalit households and 8 per cent of households belonging to Other Castes owned separate buildings that were used as shops and commercial establishments. The table shows that in all the villages, the proportion of Dalit households that owned agricultural land was smaller than the proportion of Other Caste households that owned agricultural land. Access to agricultural land among Dalits was lowest in 25 F Gulabewala in Sri Ganganagar district, where only 3 per cent of Dalit households owned agricultural land. By contrast, in the

TABLE 10 *Proportion of households that own different types of land and buildings, Dalit and Other Caste households*

Village	Agricultural land		Homestead land and houses		Land and buildings for maintenance of animals		Land and buildings used for commercial establishments	
	Dalit	Other Caste	Dalit	Other Caste	Dalit	Other Caste	Dalit	Other Caste
Ananthavaram	24	58	99	95	26	34	2	8
Bukkacherla	88	90	98	91	11	36	0	4
Kothapalle	58	59	98	95	10	11	1	7
Harevli	55	68	98	96	35	56	0	0
Mahatwar	73	92	100	100	33	63	11	10
Warwat Khanderao	58	78	100	99	17	44	0	8
Nimshirgaon	56	85	100	97	22	58	1	1
25 F Gulabewala	3	85	100	97	40	44	0	4
Rewasi	86	98	100	99	14	10	0	5
Gharsondi	74	83	100	99	22	39	11	5
Alabujanahalli	76	85	100	98	24	17	0	6
Siresandra	82	96	100	100	7	30	0	0
Zhapur	51	76	98	100	7	7	2	2
Panahar	32	71	100	99	3	10	2	11
Amarsinghi	51	76	98	100	2	6	2	7

Source: Survey data.

same village, 85 per cent of households belonging to Other Castes owned agricultural land.

It is not surprising that of all categories of land and buildings, incidence of ownership was highest in the case of homestead land and houses. In several villages, the proportion of Dalit households owning homestead land and houses was marginally higher than the proportion of Other Caste households that owned homestead land and houses. This is because a larger share of Other Caste households lived in houses that belonged to their parents or in joint-family establishments. In all the villages, the proportion of households that had separate land or buildings for animals was substantially higher among Other Caste households than among Dalit households.

Table 11 presents data on the average value of assets in each category of land and buildings owned by households. The table shows that in each category of land and building type, the average value of assets owned by a Dalit household was much lower than the average value of assets owned by a household belonging to Other Castes. For example, in the Vidarbha village of Warwat Khanderao, the average value of homestead land owned by a Dalit household was Rs 57,249, while the corresponding figure for an Other Caste household was Rs 1,43,618. In Zhapur, the average value of land owned by

TABLE 11 *Average value of land and buildings of different types, Dalit and Other Caste households* in rupees

Village	Agricultural land		Homestead land and houses		Land and buildings for maintenance of animals		Land and buildings used for commercial establishments	
	Dalit	Other Caste	Dalit	Other Caste	Dalit	Other Caste	Dalit	Other Caste
Ananthavaram	83234	1220425	36028	189731	2890	12256	5800	113286
Bukkacherla	29502	235441	30061	101838	4000	13666	–	30104
Kothapalle	67149	377275	55665	177536	1308	12700	20000	38533
Harevli	162625	341794	33088	80006	3993	3624	–	–
Mahatwar	88135	364869	70535	181624	3090	7762	4030	8280
Warwat Khanderao	96828	477899	57249	143618	17466	21795	–	50625
Nimshirgaon	624172	1202394	133689	195738	14075	21806	12194	27397
25 F Gulabewala	156773	5663971	34827	675533	3122	28624	–	3044
Rewasi	346214	650246	171441	279131	9241	22690	–	649447
Gharsondi	476396	1608282	119621	222424	5147	28120	25381	140017
Alabujanahalli	93377	571933	174283	452619	9803	77846	–	3661838
Siresandra	298043	1084264	164572	382201	8507	36865	–	–
Zhapur	260757	1285212	81958	139064	18046	45115	77340	38670
Panahar	42605	481440	31263	243400	3340	27072	70140	142619
Amarsinghi	135696	306370	75238	89071	10396	4204	66800	56647

Source: Survey data.

a landowning Dalit household was Rs 2.6 lakhs, whereas the corresponding figure for Other Caste households was Rs 12.85 lakhs.

Table 12 presents the average value per acre of agricultural land owned by Dalit and Other Caste households. The data presented in this table must be interpreted with caution. The unit price of land is determined by a number of factors, including availability of irrigation, soil quality, proximity to roads and towns, and demand for land for non-agricultural purposes.

Given this caveat, the table shows that in most villages, the price per acre of agricultural land owned by Dalit households was considerably lower than the average price per acre of agricultural land owned by Other Caste households. For example, in Rewasi (Rajasthan), the average price of land owned by Dalit households was Rs 70,179 per acre, while the average price of land owned by households belonging to Other Castes was valued at Rs 1 lakh per acre. The disparity in the price of land, measured in terms of the percentage gap between the average price of land owned by Dalit households and Other Caste households, was highest in Bukkacherla (Anantapur), 25 F Gulabewala (Sri Ganganagar) and Ananthavaram (Guntur). There were also some exceptions to this overall pattern. In Harevli (Bijnor) and Gharsondi

TABLE 12 *Average price of agricultural land and land planted with trees, Dalit and Other Caste households, by village* in Rs per acre

Village	Dalit	Other Caste	Percentage difference between average price of land owned by Dalit and Other Caste households
(1)	(2)	(3)	(3–2)*100/2
Ananthavaram	155156	356628	130
Bukkacherla	7983	24262	204
Kothapalle	72070	136993	90
Harevli	166989	164138	−2
Mahatwar	214253	248298	16
Warwat Khanderao	45597	73615	61
Nimshirgaon	363435	362914	0
25 F Gulabewala	61128	153404	151
Rewasi	70179	101142	44
Gharsondi	198189	190897	−4
Alabujanahalli	171334	205031	20
Siresandra	124920	179588	44
Zhapur	56658	104645	85
Panahar	150498	257033	71
Amarsinghi	302286	324467	7

Note: Average price is calculated as the total value of all land owned by households belonging to a caste group divided by the total area of land owned by households in that caste group.

Source: Survey data.

(Gwalior), the average price of land owned by Dalit households was marginally higher than the average price of land owned by Other Caste households. In Nimshirgaon (Kolhapur), Amarsinghi (Malda) and Mahatwar (Ballia), the average price of land owned by Dalit households was marginally lower than the average price of land owned by Other Caste households. Although the average unit price in these villages did not vary very much, there were disparities in the quality of land owned by Dalit and Other Caste households. In Harevli, Dalits owned land near the river that did not have access to tubewell irrigation. In Gharsondi, the majority of Dalit and Other Caste households owned land that received very little irrigation because of the diversion of canal water for an urban water supply scheme. The best plots of land in terms of access to irrigation and proximity to roads were owned by the Thakur landlord family. In Nimshirgaon, the price of land was generally high because most of the land was irrigated (or could be brought under irrigation with moderate investment in groundwater irrigation) and because there was a substantial demand for non-agricultural activities in this industrially developed part of Maharashtra. The average price did not capture the fact that the best irrigated lands, on which sugarcane, grape, fruit, vegetables and flowers were cultivated, were owned by Other Caste households, while Dalit households, with limited access to irrigation, used a greater proportion of their land for the cultivation of jowar and pulses.

The data presented in these tables suggest that the disparity in ownership of land and buildings across caste groups is multi-dimensional. The proportion of landless households among Dalits was higher than among households belonging to Other Castes. Dalit households owned a smaller extent of agricultural land, their houses were smaller, their cattle-sheds were smaller, and their shops were run from smaller buildings than the buildings used by Other Caste households. And, in general, households belonging to Other Castes owned better and more valuable land than Dalit households.

Ownership of Animals

In general, the proportion of households that owned cattle was smaller among Dalit households than among households belonging to Other Castes (Table 13). Among households that owned cattle, Dalit households had fewer cattle than households belonging to Other Castes (Table 14). Animals owned by Dalit households were, on average, of lower value than animals owned by households belonging to Other Castes (Table 15).

The disparity in ownership of animals (in particular, of milch cattle) is a reflection not only of disparities in the economic capacity to acquire animals, but also of disparities in the ownership of land. Given that most villages had small or no common grazing areas, access to fodder from owned land was crucial for a household to be able to own cattle.

The pattern of ownership of draught animals was also related to the variations in the extent to which draught animals were used in agriculture

TABLE 13 *Proportion of households owning draught and milch animals, Dalit and Other Caste households*

Village	Draught animals (adult/calf)		Milch animals (adult/calf)	
	Dalit	Other Caste	Dalit	Other Caste
Ananthavaram	10.2	11.8	39.6	39.3
Bukkacherla	12.1	42.5	3.4	37.2
Kothapalle	20.3	24.5	34.7	35.9
Harevli	34.1	84.0	48.8	88.0
Mahatwar	27.4	49.1	62.1	81.1
Warwat Khanderao	12.0	45.3	24.0	50.0
Nimshirgaon	8.1	12.4	58.7	70.7
25 F Gulabewala	8.1	65.4	52.0	90.1
Rewasi	14.3	47.5	66.7	87.0
Gharsondi	25.9	30.1	55.6	81.6
Alabujanahalli	20.0	30.2	42.9	66.5
Siresandra	31.0	56.9	51.7	84.3
Zhapur	36.2	58.8	36.2	54.9
Panahar	23.3	54.3	54.9	71.7
Amarsinghi	35.1	51.4	59.6	72.9

Source: Survey data.

TABLE 14 *Number of cattle of different types owned by households engaged in maintenance of animal resources, by caste group* per 100 households

Village	Dalit				Other Caste			
	Draught animal (adult)	Male calf	Milch animal (adult)	Female calf	Draught animal (adult)	Male calf	Milch animal (adult)	Female calf
Ananthavaram	17	18	114	66	23	23	190	82
Bukkacherla	188	0	12	38	156	16	122	41
Kothapalle	74	36	179	67	101	21	158	67
Harevli	72	32	92	104	121	96	138	79
Mahatwar	16	33	97	39	41	43	139	52
Warwat Khanderao	29	43	57	29	118	51	111	45
Nimshirgaon	13	14	122	72	23	12	155	78
25 F Gulabewala	3	19	94	51	64	42	338	304
Rewasi	0	29	143	129	15	67	211	171
Gharsondi	0	53	140	47	6	51	237	158
Alabujanahalli	63	5	63	58	68	15	139	63
Siresandra	44	28	94	50	114	27	186	86
Zhapur	86	73	73	91	191	150	138	75
Panahar	18	44	78	76	114	69	163	99
Amarsinghi	35	57	68	84	80	54	88	80

Source: Survey data.

TABLE 15 *Average value per cattle head of adult draught and milch animals owned by Dalit and Other Caste households* in Rs'

Village	Draught animals		Milch animals	
	Dalit	Other Caste	Dalit	Other Caste
Ananthavaram	8800	28833	8492	9035
Bukkacherla	8467	9505	3000	7531
Kothapalle	4887	7692	6245	8147
Harevli	5639	5758	6613	9817
Mahatwar	3900	4986	5190	7306
Warwat Khanderao	9132	10640	959	4816
Nimshirgaon	9132	10137	10506	11233
25 F Gulabewala	2055	2483	3908	11120
Rewasi	–	16797	8751	11124
Gharsondi	–	5203	8843	9783
Alabujanahalli	7412	9906	7605	8628
Siresandra	8217	9737	11010	11441
Zhapur	13311	13263	3480	5071
Panahar	3483	5135	2250	2969
Amarsinghi	4008	4534	3754	3790
Kalmandasguri	4923	4004	3782	3592

Notes: Average value is calculated as total value of a particular category of animals owned by households belonging to a caste group divided by total number of animals of that category owned by households in that caste group.

Source: Survey data.

(which, in turn, was related to a number of factors, including the nature of cropping, the size of operational holdings, the extent of mechanization, the nature of rental markets for animals and machines, and the nature of labour markets), in addition to the economic capability of households to acquire bullocks and access to fodder.

Table 13 shows the proportion of households that owned draught and milch animals. Table 14 shows the average number of cattle owned by households that owned some cattle. Table 13 shows that in Bukkacherla (Anantapur), only 3.4 per cent of Dalit households owned milch animals, while 37.2 per cent of households belonging to Other Castes owned milch animals. Table 14 shows that among those who owned animals, Dalit households had only twelve milch cattle per 100 households, while households belonging to Other Castes had 122 milch cattle per 100 households. A similar pattern of disparity in the ownership of milch animals can be seen across most of the study villages.

In Bukkacherla (Anantapur), Dalit households owned small plots of land and needed to use their limited access to fodder, to maintain the draught animals that they could use in agriculture. On the other hand, non-Dalit households, with better access to land, were able to maintain both draught and milch animals.

In Harevli (Bijnor district), Dalit households were able to keep only small female calves, which were sold when they grew up, because, without reliable access to fodder, these households could not maintain adult milch animals.

In Warwat Khanderao (Buldhana), Panahar (Bankura), Siresandra (Kolar) and Zhapur (Gulbarga), there was a steep disparity between Dalit and Other Caste households in the ownership of both draught and milch animals.

In 25 F Gulabewala (Sri Ganganagar), Rewasi (Sikar), Gharsondi (Gwalior), Nimshirgaon (Kolhapur) and Mahatwar (Ballia), the general levels of ownership of draught animals were low because of mechanization of agriculture. In Nimshirgaon (Kolhapur), access to fodder from sugarcane fields allowed Dalit households to keep a substantial stock of milch animals (though smaller than the number of animals kept by households belonging to Other Castes). In the other three villages, the stock of milch animals maintained by Dalit households was very small, and there was a very sharp disparity in the ownership of milch animals between Dalit and Other Caste households.

Table 15 shows the average value of an adult draught animal and an adult milch animal owned by Dalit households and households belonging to Other Castes. With one exception, the average value of an animal was lower among Dalit households than Other Caste households. In Harevli (western Uttar Pradesh), for example, a milch animal owned by a Dalit household was valued at Rs 6,613, whereas one owned by an Other Caste household was valued at Rs 9,817.

TABLE 16 *Proportions of households owning livestock and poultry, Dalit and Other Caste households*

Village	Sheep and goats		Poultry	
	Dalit	Other Caste	Dalit	Other Caste
Ananthavaram	0.4	1.2	21.9	10.6
Bukkacherla	1.7	6.6	5.2	13.3
Kothapalle	0.8	6.3	33.1	12.7
Harevli	14.6	0.0	4.9	0.0
Mahatwar	41.1	7.5	4.2	0.0
Warwat Khanderao	8.0	4.7	8.0	1.2
Nimshirgaon	28.9	8.7	8.8	0.0
25 F Gulabewala	36.6	6.2	4.9	3.7
Rewasi	100.0	92.7	0.0	0.0
Gharsondi	18.5	15.0	7.4	1.0
Alabujanahalli	37.1	50.5	14.3	13.7
Siresandra	13.8	33.3	62.1	45.1
Zhapur	27.7	23.5	12.8	7.8
Panahar	30.1	21.7	49.6	38.0
Amarsinghi	31.6	32.9	38.6	28.6

Source: Survey data.

While many Dalit households were unable to maintain cattle because of poor economic conditions, and in particular because of lack of access to land, in many villages they owned small holdings of sheep, goat or poultry. As shown in Table 16, in nine villages the proportion of households owning sheep or goats was higher among Dalit households than among Other Caste households. In eleven villages, the proportion of households owning some poultry was higher among Dalit households than among Other Caste households.

Ownership of Agricultural Machinery

Data on asset-holdings show that Dalit households have poor access to productive assets in general and agricultural machinery in particular. As shown in Table 8, in thirteen out of fifteen villages, of all categories of assets, the share of Dalits was lowest for 'other means of production'.

Tables 17 and 18 present detailed data on the proportion of Dalit and Other Caste households that owned different types of agricultural machinery. For the purpose of these tables, all machines were classified into machines used for land preparation (tractors, tillers and associated accessories), irrigation equipment, machines used for harvesting and post-harvest operations, and

TABLE 17 *Proportion of households owning different types of agricultural machinery, Dalit and Other Caste households*

Village	Tractors, power tillers and accessories		Irrigation equipment		Machines for harvesting and post-harvest operations		Other machinery used for agriculture and maintenance of animals	
	Dalit	Other Caste	Dalit	Other Caste	Dalit	Other Caste	Dalit	Other Caste
Ananthavaram	0.0	2.5	1.1	15.6	0.0	0.3	6.0	9.7
Bukkacherla	1.7	10.6	1.7	36.3	0.0	6.2	13.8	50.4
Kothapalle	0.0	2.5	5.9	32.1	0.0	5.9	14.4	28.3
Harevli	0.0	8.0	12.2	40.0	0.0	4.0	34.1	76.0
Mahatwar	0.0	1.9	5.3	24.5	3.2	20.8	48.4	69.8
Warwat Khanderao	0.0	2.3	0.0	12.2	0.0	2.9	4.0	41.9
Nimshirgaon	0.0	11.8	16.9	61.2	0.0	4.4	20.9	37.2
25 F Gulabewala	0.0	67.9	0.0	46.9	0.0	30.9	16.3	85.2
Rewasi	0.0	5.6	23.8	65.0	0.0	2.8	28.6	42.9
Gharsondi	0.0	26.7	3.7	31.1	0.0	11.7	29.6	59.2
Alabujanahalli	2.9	9.4	0.0	18.9	0.0	1.9	34.3	63.2
Siresandra	0.0	5.9	27.6	64.7	0.0	0.0	48.3	74.5
Zhapur	2.1	2.0	0.0	17.6	0.0	2.0	27.7	45.1
Panahar	0.0	13.0	3.0	19.6	7.5	47.8	22.6	60.9
Amarsinghi	0.0	0.0	7.0	5.7	0.0	1.4	15.8	40.0

Source: Survey data.

other equipment used for crop production and the maintenance of animal resources (mainly sprayers, ploughs and other equipment used with draught animals, and fodder cutters). The table presents some very interesting findings.

In most of the villages, no Dalit household owned tractors, power tillers and associated accessories, or machines used for harvesting and post-harvest operations. In all the villages taken together, one Dalit household each in Bukkacherla (Anantapur) and Alabujanahalli (Mandya) owned a power tiller, and one Dalit household in Zhapur (Gulbarga) owned a tractor. Only three Dalit households in Mahatwar (Ballia) and ten households in Panahar (Bankura) owned threshing machines.

Among Dalits, the proportion of households that owned irrigation equipment was higher than the proportion that owned other machines. However, there was a sharp disparity between Dalit and Other Caste households in the ownership of irrigation equipment, both in terms of the proportion of households that owned irrigation equipment and in terms of the average value of irrigation equipment. In all the villages, the average value of irrigation equipment owned by Dalit households was lower than the average value of irrigation equipment owned by Other Caste households (Table 18). Even

TABLE 18　*Average value of agricultural machinery owned by a household, by type of machine, Dalit and Other Caste households* in Rs

Village	Tractors, power tillers and accessories		Irrigation equipment		Machines for harvesting and post-harvest operations		Other machinery used for agriculture and maintenance of animals	
	Dalit	Other Caste	Dalit	Other Caste	Dalit	Other Caste	Dalit	Other Caste
Ananthavaram	–	190456	6000	20880	–	13000	5869	7503
Bukkacherla	2000	36529	8000	36200	–	4264	8281	11477
Kothapalle	–	164450	8286	11682	–	639	1434	2745
Harevli	–	281400	10750	23395	–	40000	2378	4989
Mahatwar	–	75000	2630	11385	3000	3509	1200	1310
Warwat Khanderao	–	102740	–	34481	–	16438	4840	4608
Nimshirgaon	–	90614	3509	8634	–	7049	1065	1915
25 F Gulabewala	–	159646	–	44328	–	29768	760	20134
Rewasi	–	231273	21222	22651	–	51570	4844	5740
Gharsondi	–	139662	5245	32406	–	18198	1808	5351
Alabujanahalli	42537	78457	–	12624	–	25619	4605	10615
Siresandra	–	159642	7299	20975	–	–	4086	6974
Zhapur	77340	154679	–	15210	–	65739	1542	4869
Panahar	–	51102	2669	6405	1250	1475	982	2329
Amarsinghi	–	–	8577	10855	–	2004	222	629

Source:　Survey data.

when Dalit households had irrigation equipment, these were typically of lower capacity or older, and thus of lower value than the equipment owned by households belonging to Other Castes. In many cases, Dalit households owned small diesel pumps that had high operating costs, while many households belonging to Other Castes owned electric pumps that had a higher value and lower operating costs.

Summary

This essay uses data from fifteen villages surveyed as part of the Project on Agrarian Relations in India, to analyse disparities in the ownership of assets between Dalit households and households belonging to castes or communities other than Dalits, Adivasis and Muslims. The data show a very systematic pattern of disparities between Dalit and Other Caste households with respect to ownership of various types of assets.

The data from the study villages reveal very sharp disparities in the ownership of assets between Dalit households and households belonging to Other Castes. On average, the asset-holdings of Dalit households were much smaller than the asset-holdings of households belonging to Other Castes. In all the villages, Dalit households were concentrated at the lower end of the distribution of wealth and their representation at the upper end of the distribution was negligible.

Of all the villages, the disparity in ownership of assets between Dalit households and households belonging to Other Castes was highest in 25 F Gulabewala, in Sri Ganganagar district. In this village, 40 per cent households belonging to Other Castes accounted for 99.6 per cent of total wealth. The average wealth of a household belonging to Other Castes was 131 times the average wealth of a Dalit household.

The most striking feature of the structure of asset-holdings was the dominant share of agricultural land in the asset portfolios of households belonging to Other Castes, and that of homestead land and houses in the asset portfolios of Dalits. It is noteworthy that among all categories of assets, the share of agricultural land and other means of production owned by Dalits was invariably the smallest.

Detailed analysis of data on agricultural land shows that the proportion of landless households was higher among Dalit households than among Other Caste households. Among households that owned land, Dalit households owned less land than households belonging to Other Castes, and, in most villages, land owned by Dalit households was less valuable than land owned by households belonging to Other Castes. Data on other types of land and buildings showed a similar pattern: on average, houses, shops and other buildings owned by Dalit households were of lower value than similar establishments owned by households belonging to Other Castes.

The size of cattle-holdings of rural households depended not only on their economic ability to acquire animals, but also their access to land, since, given limited access to common grazing land in most villages, straw from the operational holdings of households was the most important source of fodder for animals. The number of draught animals owned by a household also depended on the use of animal labour, which in turn depended on the size of holdings, farming practices, the nature of labour markets, levels of mechanization, and rental markets for machines and animals. The data on holdings of animals show that, in general, Dalit households had smaller holdings of both milch and draught animals. Disparities in the ownership of milch cattle were smaller in villages like Kothapalle (Karimnagar), where households had access to common grazing areas. In some villages, given their inability to acquire and maintain cattle, Dalit households owned goats, sheep or poultry.

Other than irrigation equipment, in general, Dalit households did not own any machines. Data on the ownership of other means of production showed that in all the villages surveyed, there was only a single Dalit household that owned a tractor and very few households that owned threshing machines. Among households that owned irrigation equipment, Dalit households owned equipment of lower capacity and value than equipment owned by households belonging to Other Castes.

With such limited access to productive assets, for Dalit households, the opportunities for economic mobility within the rural economy are severely limited.

Asset Poverty among Rural Households

An Illustration from Two Villages in Uttar Pradesh

Partha Saha

In contrast to research on income poverty or consumption poverty, empirical studies on poverty arising from a lack of ownership of assets are relatively scarce. The fact is that poverty involves people's deprivation with respect to crucial assets, which in turn has a long-term impact on households. One of the reasons for the scarcity of research on poverty due to lack of ownership of assets is the lack of reliable data on household assets. In India, though decennial debt and investment surveys have been conducted since 1951–52, detailed unit-level data on household assets are available only after 1991–92 (National Sample Survey [NSS], 48th round). Availability of data at the unit level from the All-India Debt and Investment Survey has made it possible to analyse patterns of asset ownership in India, but such efforts have been mostly confined to the study of asset inequality, rather than focusing on poverty.

Poor households are characterized by the lack of or inadequate ownership of assets, in particular productive assets. Scarcity of assets and poverty (lowness of income or expenditure) need to be viewed as closely related phenomena. Assets are the most visible indicators of material well-being and economic status of households, and, as Harriss (1992) noted, 'assets are the longest-run indicator of material economic status available to social scientists'.

There are three ways of assessing the role of asset ownership in the mitigation of poverty:

(i) by considering the intrinsic value of ownership of assets, that is, assets as wealth;
(ii) by considering assets as a source of income generation (in this case, ownership of the means of production is important); and
(iii) by considering assets as a cushion against income fluctuations.

The objective of this essay is to analyse the importance of ownership of assets in mitigating poverty based on the three approaches mentioned above, with a special focus on differences across social groups. It does so with special reference to two villages in Uttar Pradesh, namely Harevli and Mahatwar.

A Brief Introduction to the Study Villages

Harevli

Harevli village is located in Bijnor district, western Uttar Pradesh. It is at a distance of about 4 km from the nearest town, Mandavli, and about 14 km from the *tehsil* headquarters at Najibabad. There were 112 households and 658 persons in Harevli at the time of the survey. Of them, 46 households and 239 persons belonged to the Dalit castes. Among the Dalits, Chamar households were numerically the largest (forty-one households); there were also a few households belonging to the Balmiki caste (five households). Other Backward Classes (OBCs), with 148 persons, constituted 22.5 per cent of the population of the village. The Other Castes population, 203 persons, represented 30.9 per cent of the village population. All the Other Caste households except for one belonged to the Tyagi caste. Muslims, with 68 persons, constituted 10.3 per cent of the total population of the village.

Agriculture was the mainstay of the economy of Harevli. Ownership of agricultural land in the village was highly unequal, with 73 per cent of agricultural land being owned by the top 16 per cent of households and 33 per cent of households not owning any agricultural land. The distribution of operational holdings was also highly unequal. About 26 per cent of households did not operate any land, while another 26 per cent operated about 5 per cent of the total land. In contrast, the top 19 per cent of household operational holdings accounted for about 65 per cent of the total operated area. The average size of operational holdings in the village was 3.7 acres. Of the total operational holdings of households living in Harevli, 29.3 per cent was leased in. Of the total land owned by resident households, about 20 per cent was leased out.

An important feature of agriculture in Harevli was the availability of good irrigation facilities. The village came under the command area of the Eastern Ganga Canal Project and was fully canal-irrigated. In addition, groundwater, extracted by using diesel or electric pumps, was also used extensively for irrigation. The depth of groundwater varied across different areas of the village, with the depth being 25–30 feet on the eastern side and between 40–60 feet on the west.

Sugarcane was the most important crop grown in the village, accounting for about 53 per cent of the gross cropped area. Sugarcane was generally sown in the months of January–February. After harvesting the first planted sugarcane crop, a ratoon sugarcane crop was harvested nine to ten months later (or, in other words, twenty to twenty-one months after sowing). Cultivation of wheat accounted for about 21 per cent of the gross cropped area. The rest of the cropped area was cultivated with rice and fodder crops (sorghum, pearl millet and clover). Mustard was cultivated as an inter-crop with wheat. Paddy was a kharif crop, sown in June and harvested in October–November. Along with paddy, fodder crops (sorghum and pearl millet) were also grown in the kharif season. After harvesting the kharif crop, the land would be prepared for either wheat or sugarcane cultivation. Wheat was primarily grown for household consumption and only a small part (less than one-fifth) of the total village produce was sold to grain merchants. Sugarcane was the principal cash crop, and it was sold to cane crushers and sugar mills situated outside the village.

Mahatwar

Mahatwar is located at a distance of 5 km from the *tehsil* headquarters at Rasra in Ballia district of eastern Uttar Pradesh. A State highway connecting Rasra to Mau passes through Mahatwar. About 2 km on this road towards Rasra is the nearest town, Pakwainer. The three caste groups of the village – Dalits, OBCs (Yadavs and Koiris) and Other Castes – lived in three distinct settlements, separated by fields and the road.

In Mahatwar, Other Castes constituted only 7 per cent of the total population, while Dalits constituted the largest caste group with a population share of 59 per cent. Among Dalits, Chamars were the largest community and accounted for about 50 per cent of the population. OBCs had a significant presence in the village, accounting for 34 per cent of its total population.

Eastern Uttar Pradesh is noted for the small size of its agricultural landholdings.[1] This was also the case in Mahatwar. Mahatwar did not have very large land owners. The largest ownership holding in the village was 10.33 acres, while the average was only 0.9 acre. The average size of operational holding was 1.06 acres. With respect to the distribution of land across social groups, 83 per cent of Dalit households were either landless or owned less than 0.5 acre of agricultural land.

Agriculture in Mahatwar was organized predominantly as owner cultivation, and, on the whole, incidence of tenancy was relatively low. However, tenancy was an institution through which Dalit and OBC households obtained access to land. About 44 per cent of the land operated by Dalit households was leased in. The terms of the tenancy contracts in Mahatwar were based on standard village norms. In the case of fixed-rent contracts, 3 quintals (300 kg) of paddy (or wheat) per acre of land were given as rent. In the case of share tenancy, the crop output was equally shared between landowners and tenants. In both cases, tenants had to bear all input costs. Fixed-rent contracts were more prevalent in this village than sharecropping arrangements.

The major crops grown in the village were paddy (kharif) and wheat (rabi). These two crops together accounted for about 88 per cent of the gross cropped area. Sugarcane, fodder and vegetables accounted for the remaining 12 per cent of cropped area in the village. Mustard was sometimes inter-

---

[1] According to the AIDIS, 2002–03, among all the four regions of Uttar Pradesh, the average size of operational holding was the smallest in eastern Uttar Pradesh (1.3 acres), while the southern region had the largest average size of operational holding (3.5 acres). The small size of landholdings in eastern Uttar Pradesh has been noted in other studies as well; see, for example, Singh (1987).

cropped with wheat. Other than sugarcane, cultivation of all other crops was primarily for household consumption.

Non-agricultural occupations, both within and outside the village, were of major significance to the economy of Mahatwar. Many people migrated seasonally or for longer periods of time in search of non-agricultural employment. As a result, many households in the village received remittance incomes. A number of persons from Mahatwar were also engaged in different types of non-agricultural occupations within the village and in neighbouring areas. The most important of these were sinking tube-wells, construction work and bidi-making. A group of Dalit men in the village specialized in boring tube-wells and received substantial employment through this. Small shops in Mahatwar, particularly along the road, provided self-employment.

Asset Poverty in the Study Villages

All goods owned by households that had money value were considered as household assets. Information was collected under the following broad categories of assets: land, buildings, animal resources, other means of agricultural production, means of transport, electrical equipment, furniture and other assets. Within each of these broad categories, a list of particular assets was used. Under the category of land, agricultural land was the most important. The category also included orchard, homestead land, cattle-shed land and other types of land. Buildings comprised residential houses, cattle-sheds, shops and other commercial establishments. Other means of agricultural production included hand- and animal-driven implements like hand-hoes, sickles, ploughs, spades, harrows and sprayers; and machine implements including tractors and accessories, diesel pumps, electric pumps, trailers, threshers, disc ploughs and power tillers. The value of draught animals was also recorded. The most commonly owned means of transport was bicycles, followed by bullock carts. A few households owned mechanized means of transport such as scooters and motorcycles. Other assets referred to household durables. All such assets owned by a household on the date of the survey were included in the record.

All the assets were valued at prices prevalent in the locality, based on their existing condition (sale value and not replacement cost). Needless to say, there was no single price for a particular asset and prices varied across respondents. As far as possible, the prices quoted by respondents have been used in this analysis. However, in a few cases, where the prices reported varied widely and inexplicably from the prices quoted by the majority of respondents, median values for the specific item were used.

The data exclude two types of assets: financial assets, and gold and other ornaments. Financial assets, according to the AIDIS, constitute a very small proportion of total assets in rural India. Gold and jewellery made of gold are important assets. However, since it is very difficult to collect accurate data on gold owned, particularly by better-off households, this was not attempted.

Intrinsic Value of Asset Ownership:
Assets as Wealth and a Measure of Socio-Economic Status

In both Harevli and Mahatwar, considerable disparity in terms of asset ownership as between Dalit and caste Hindu households was observed (Table 1). In Harevli, the average value of assets owned by Other Caste households, Rs 16.88 lakhs, was eleven times the average value of assets owned by Dalit households, Rs 1.56 lakhs. In Mahatwar, the average value of assets owned by all households was lower, on average, in comparison to Harevli (Rs 4.4 lakhs versus Rs 8.9 lakhs). The gap between Dalit households and Other Caste households was also smaller in Mahatwar, which is a Dalit-majority village.

In Mahatwar, the least wealthy household was that of a landless agricultural labour, owning Rs 4,250 worth of assets. In Harevli, there was a Brahman priest (Jogi Baba) living singly who did not possess any assets (asset value of Rs 550). This was not, of course, a typical household, and excluding this household, the lowest value of asset ownership among Other Castes in Harevli was Rs 8,300 (or twice as much as the poorest in Mahatwar).

Next, we examined a simple distribution of households by the value of assets owned. The highest asset category comprised households with more than 300 times the wealth of the lowest asset category (Table 2). In Harevli, almost one-fifth of the households owned assets worth not more than Rs 30,000. Such households did not own any agricultural land. They possessed some homestead land, some small livestock, simple hand implements used for agricultural operations and a few household utensils. They lived in small huts with thatched roofs, with hardly any household amenities. Among Dalits, 26 per cent of households belonged to this category of extreme asset poverty, that is, households owning less than Rs 30,000 worth of assets.

When households were distributed by size-class of ownership of assets, it was observed that considerable disparity existed across social groups. On the one hand, 50 per cent of Dalit households and 54 per cent of Muslim households owned assets worth less than Rs 60,000, and on the other, 47 per cent of caste Hindu households owned assets worth more than Rs 1,000,000. There were no Dalit or Muslim households in the two highest size classes of asset ownership.

In Mahatwar, 7 per cent of households owned assets worth less than

TABLE 1 *Level of asset ownership per household* in Rs

	Harevli			Mahatwar		
	Dalit	*Other Caste*	*All*	*Dalit*	*Other Caste*	*All*
Mean	156300	1688000	897300	152300	904600	447300
Median	62220	953800	128800	100300	541600	167000
Minimum	550	540	540	4250	24220	4250
Maximum	1502000	12120000	12120000	931300	11670000	11670000

Source: Survey data.

TABLE 2 *Distribution of households, by size-category of asset-holding and by social group, Harevli, 2006* in numbers and per cent

Asset categories (Rs)	Dalit		Muslim		Other Caste		All social groups	
A ≤ 15,000	8	(17)	4	(31)	2	(4)	14	(13)
15,000 < A ≤ 30,000	4	(9)	2	(15)	1	(2)	7	(6)
30,000 < A ≤ 60,000	11	(24)	1	(8)	2	(4)	14	(13)
60,000 < A ≤ 100,000	7	(15)	1	(8)	2	(4)	10	(9)
100,000 < A ≤ 200,000	8	(17)	0	(0)	10	(19)	18	(16)
200,000 < A ≤ 500,000	5	(11)	2	(15)	4	(8)	11	(10)
500,000 < A ≤ 1,000,000	2	(4)	1	(8)	7	(13)	10	(9)
1,000,000 < A ≤ 2,000,000	1	(2)	2	(15)	11	(21)	14	(13)
2,000,000 < A ≤ 5,000,000	0	(0)	0	(0)	11	(21)	11	(10)
A > 5,000,000	0	(0)	0	(0)	3	(6)	3	(3)
All size-classes	46	(100)	13	(100)	53	(100)	112	(100)

Note: 'A' implies total value of assets. Figures in parentheses represent percentages.
Source: Survey data.

TABLE 3 *Distribution of households, by size-category of asset-holding and by social group, Mahatwar, 2006* in numbers and per cent

Asset categories (Rs)	Dalit		Other Caste		All social groups	
A ≤ 15,000	3	(3)	0	(0)	3	(2)
15,000 < A ≤ 30,000	6	(6)	1	(2)	7	(5)
30,000 < A ≤ 60,000	18	(19)	3	(5)	21	(14)
60,000 < A ≤ 100,000	19	(20)	2	(3)	21	(14)
100,000 < A ≤ 200,000	28	(30)	10	(17)	38	(25)
200,000 < A ≤ 500,000	14	(15)	12	(20)	26	(17)
500,000 < A ≤ 1,000,000	5	(5)	16	(27)	21	(14)
1,000,000 < A ≤ 2,000,000	0	(0)	11	(18)	11	(7)
2,000,000 < A ≤ 5,000,000	0	(0)	4	(7)	4	(3)
A > 5,000,000	0	(0)	1	(2)	1	(1)
All size-classes	93	(100)	60	(100)	153	(100)

Note: 'A' implies total value of assets. Figures in parentheses represent percentages.
Source: Survey data.

Rs 30,000, whereas 21 per cent owned assets worth not more than Rs 60,000 (Table 3). The proportion of landless households in Mahatwar was only 20 per cent, and this explains the fact that households were not as asset-poor in absolute terms in Mahatwar as compared to Harevli. However, households in the lowest asset group did not own much agricultural land; also, they owned only a few hand implements and household utensils.

The pattern of asset ownership across size-classes was also character-ized by a concentration of Dalit households in the lower size-classes and Other Caste households in the higher size-classes. The majority of Dalit households

(80 per cent) owned assets worth less than Rs 200,000. By contrast, in the case of Other Caste households, 73 per cent owned assets worth more than Rs 200,000.

Composition of Assets

Across all social groups, land was by far the most important form of asset owned by households in both the study villages. Land alone constituted 79 per cent and 73 per cent, respectively, of the total value of assets in Harevli and Mahatwar (Tables 4 and 5). Other than Muslim households in Harevli, the share of buildings in the total value of assets was the second highest among all asset types for households in both the villages. In every category of asset, the average value owned by a Dalit household was less than the average value owned by an Other Caste household in both villages. To put it differently, landlessness among Dalits was not compensated by higher ownership of any other type of asset.

Next, we have computed a measure of relative access to assets (the access index), defined as the ratio of the proportion of assets owned by a caste group to the proportion of households belonging to that caste group (Tables 6 and 7).

The value of the access index in the case of Dalit households for all categories of assets was less than one, which means that the proportion of

TABLE 4 *Percentage share of different items of assets in the total value of assets and their average value, by social group, Harevli, 2006* in per cent and Rs

Items of assets	Type of estimate	Dalit	Muslim	Caste Hindu	All social groups
Land	P	66.3	79.8	78.4	79.0
	A	102816	236158	1336135	701917
Building	P	17.4	4.8	10.4	10.4
	A	27715	14331	176294	96471
Animal resources	P	3.5	2.3	1.3	1.5
	A	5572	6767	22884	13903
Other means of agricultural production	P	7.4	7.9	5.2	5.3
	A	11719	23425	87368	48876
Means of transport	P	0.8	0.6	1.0	1
	A	1274	1831	17230	8889
Furniture	P	0.6	0.6	0.6	0.4
	A	960	1915	9596	5157
Electrical equipment	P	0.2	0.3	0.3	0.3
	A	343	925	5467	2835
Others	P	3.8	3.6	2.8	2.1
	A	5916	10722	69122	19223
All assets	P	100	100	100	100
	A	156315	296073	1687836	897274

Note: P = percentage share of item of asset in total value of assets. A= average value in Rs.
Source: Survey data.

TABLE 5   *Percentage share of different items of assets in the total value of assets and their average value, by social group, Mahatwar, 2006* in per cent and Rs

Items of assets	Type of estimate	Dalit	Other Caste	All social groups
Land	P	61.1	76.4	73.1
	A	90610	687524	324694
Building	P	29.7	17.9	20.4
	A	46238	161620	91486
Animal resources	P	3.5	1.2	1.7
	A	5373	11412	7741
Other means of agricultural production	P	0.4	1	0.9
	A	495	9588	4061
Means of transport	P	0.9	1.7	1.5
	A	1381	15167	6787
Furniture	P	1	0.3	0.4
	A	1463	2669	1936
Electrical equipment	P	0.5	0.2	0.2
	A	812	1570	1109
Others	P	2.9	1.3	1.8
	A	5781	15085	9429
All assets	P	100	100	100
	A	156056	913994	448332

Note: P = percentage share of item of asset in total value of assets. A = average value in Rs.
Source: Survey data.

TABLE 6   *Access index of different social groups, by item of asset, Harevli, 2006*

Items of assets	Dalit	Muslim	Other Caste
Land	0.15	0.34	1.94
Building	0.29	0.15	1.83
Animal resources	0.40	0.48	1.65
Other means of agricultural production	0.24	0.48	1.79
Means of transport	0.14	0.21	1.94
Furniture	0.18	0.37	1.86
Electrical equipment	0.12	0.33	1.93
Others	0.16	0.29	1.90
All assets	0.17	0.33	1.89

Source: Survey data.

assets owned by Dalit households was always less than the proportion of Dalit households in the population. Therefore, in both the villages, Dalit households were in a much more disadvantageous position vis-a-vis Other Caste households in terms of ownership of assets. In Harevli, the access index was highest for Dalit households with respect to animal resources whereas in Mahatwar, it was high with respect to furniture and electrical equipment.

Ownership of assets in both the study villages was characterized on

TABLE 7   *Access index of different social groups, by item of asset, Mahatwar, 2006*

Items of assets	Dalit	Other Castes
Land	0.28	2.13
Building	0.50	1.77
Animal resources	0.69	1.47
Other means of agricultural production	0.12	2.36
Means of transport	0.20	2.23
Furniture	0.75	1.38
Electrical equipment	0.73	1.42
Others	0.61	1.60
All assets	0.34	2.04

Source: Survey data.

the one hand by a concentration of ownership among Other Caste households, and on the other, by an absence of assets among Dalit households.

In both Harevli and Mahatwar, wealth in respect of assets and social–political power were closely intertwined. In Harevli, Tyagi households were both rich, and politically and socially dominant in the society. They were simultaneously dominant lessors in the tenancy market and dominant employers in the labour market. In Mahatwar, the dominance of caste Hindu households was mostly expressed in the spheres of the economy and social hierarchy.

Assets as a Source of Income Generation

Household income refers to the total net income accruing to a household and the aggregate earnings of all members of the household.[2] In addition to income earned through physical labour, ownership of assets, in particular ownership of productive assets, was an important source of income. Productive assets owned by households in the two study villages included agricultural land, orchards, other means of agricultural production (including machinery, draught animals and animal resources) and assets related to non-farm businesses.

In this section, we measure asset poverty in terms of the income-generating potential of productive assets (other than labour power). Generation of income from owned productive assets requires that households command access to a basket of complementary assets, to other inputs required in the production process, to services required for production, and to markets where the value of production can be realized. Whether or not, and the cost at which, households gain access to complementary assets, other inputs and services, and the nature of markets for the products, determine the extent of income generated on the basis of owned assets. Apart from generating incomes through

---

[2] For further definitions and descriptions of the method of income calculation, see Rawal (2008).

TABLE 8   *Proportion of households with income from ownership of assets less than the official consumption poverty line, by social group, 2006*

Social Group	Harevli	Mahatwar
Dalit	93.0	95.7
Muslim	76.9	–
Other Caste	50.0	85.0
All social groups	69.6	91.5

Note: Owned assets here do not include the labour power of household members.
Source: Survey data.

their use in household enterprises, productive assets may also be rented out.

In both the study villages, income earned by virtue of ownership of productive assets (other than labour power) was much lower for Dalit households (owing to their lower asset base) than for caste Hindu households, and therefore, income from productive assets was insufficient to come out of poverty for a vast majority of Dalit households (Table 8).[3]

It may be noted here that Mahatwar was characterized by a high incidence of asset poverty even among Other Caste households. This implies that even social groups with a substantial asset base were unable to productively utilize it because of lack of ownership of complementary assets and, most importantly, lack of access to irrigation. Therefore, while in Harevli a lower asset base resulted in very high occurrence of income poverty among Dalits, in Mahatwar, lack of access to complementary inputs was an important determinant of income poverty.

Assets as Cushion against Vulnerability

One way of assessing the vulnerability of households to adverse income shocks is to measure the amount of assets the households own. Assets act as a cushion when a household experiences adverse income shocks; that is, when sources of earnings dry up, the household can fulfil its subsistence needs by selling assets.

In the literature on the role of assets as a safety net or cushion against adverse income shocks, scholars have attempted to identify fungible assets that are readily marketable. Carney and Gale (2000) examined patterns and correlates of asset accumulation among low-income households in the United States using cross-section data from the Survey of Income and Programme Participation (SIPP). Among the various types of assets that figured in the SIPP data, the authors considered only financial assets. Their argument was that it was this category of assets that acted as a cushion against economic shocks, and thus the focus of their paper was on the process of accumulation of financial assets among low-income households. The data on wealth distribution showed that 16 per cent of households had zero or negative financial

---

[3] For details of the methodology used in calculating income, see Rawal (2008).

assets. The ratio of net financial assets (gross financial assets – consumer debts) to non-asset income for more than 50 per cent of the households was either zero or of very low positive value, implying a very limited fall-back option in the case of adverse income shocks. Moreover, in the case of 75 per cent of households, net financial assets accounted for half a year's household income. Thus, in the event of an adverse income shock, 75 per cent of the households had just enough financial assets to sustain themselves for half a year. These findings were based on the assumption that the returns from such financial assets would remain unchanged. The situation would have been much worse had the returns from such financial assets deteriorated in the wake of any unfavourable shock to the economy. Regression analysis showed that accumulation of financial assets was positively related with income, age and educational level of the head of a household. Non-financial assets were not considered because of the difficulty of converting them to cash to meet daily expenses, or, in other words, the problem of liquidity.

Torche and Spilerman (2007) argued that very few Latin American households had access to social safety nets to protect themselves from economic distress, and a very common practice among poor households was to withdraw their children from school during periods of economic distress and send them to work. Even though attempts were made to tackle this problem through cash transfers, the problem persisted and 'deeply implicated the lack of material assets'.

Carter and May (1999) pointed out that '20 per cent of rural African households have no fungible assets of any kind that could be converted to cash in case of need'. Therefore, those households were identified as the most vulnerable.

Haveman and Wolff (2004) developed the concept of asset poverty in a more formal way, as a measure of economic hardship. The authors analysed whether or not the asset ownership of a household could sustain it at the minimum level of consumption during the period in which incomes in the form of wage employment were unavailable to the household. A household that did not own adequate assets in this regard was categorized as being asset-poor. Clearly, such a concept of poverty requires a precise definition regarding basic needs (to address the sustenance issue), period of time (how long assets were able to provide a safety net) and wealth (what kind of assets were to be considered). The authors calculated a minimum threshold requirement based on United States Consumer Expenditure data. For a family of two adults and two children, the threshold arrived at was $17,653 per annum. As for the time period, the authors proposed that the 'asset cushion' should allow a family to meet basic needs for a period of three months. So, at any point of time, if a household owned less than $4,413 (25 per cent of $17,653) worth of assets, then that household would be declared asset-poor.

The poverty estimates arrived at were based on two alternative definitions of wealth, namely net worth (current value of marketable assets – current value of debts) and liquid assets (cash or financial assets, which can be easily monetized). The number of items of assets that were included in the net worth definition of wealth was higher than for the liquid assets definition of wealth, and, accordingly, asset poverty estimates based on the net worth definition were lower than poverty estimates based on the liquid assets definition of wealth. The extent of asset poverty for different sub-groups of the population based on ethnicity, age of head of the household and housing status was also calculated. It was found that the asset poverty rates for the period 1983–2001 for African-Americans were more than twice the rate for whites. Asset poverty rates declined with increases in the age and education level of the head of the household. For home owners the asset poverty rate was 6 per cent, while for tenants it was 60 per cent.

When asset poverty was compared with income poverty, it was found that while income poverty declined by 11 per cent during the period 1983–2001, asset poverty rose by more than 10 per cent (irrespective of the definition of wealth considered). On combining both the concepts of poverty (income and asset) it was found that in 1983, 7.6 per cent of households in the United States were both income-poor and asset-poor. In 2001, the number rose to 7.9 per cent.

In most studies of this type, fungible assets were identified, and the incidence of asset poverty was estimated on the basis of a household's ownership of such fungible assets. Studies based in the advanced economies have identified housing equities and other forms of financial assets as fungible assets, and arrived at estimates of asset poverty on the basis of calculation of per capita ownership of such assets. In rural India as a whole, financial assets constituted 2.2 per cent of total household assets; and in rural Uttar Pradesh, they constituted less than 1 per cent of total household assets.[4] In rural India, the wealth of a household consisted primarily of the material assets, most importantly land, that it owned. As a result, it would be misleading to analyse asset poverty here on the basis of ownership of financial assets. Further, as mentioned earlier, getting reliable and verifiable information on ownership of financial assets in rural India is almost impossible.

The alternative conceptualization of poverty based on assets has nevertheless provided a new method of understanding poverty and vulnerability. In view of this, I have attempted to assess the extent of economic security provided to a household by the physical assets it owns. In this analysis, all assets (productive as well as others) that have a market and whose sale price is non-zero are considered. The vulnerability of households is measured in terms of the period of time they can survive at the poverty-line level of consumption, using funds obtained from selling assets that they own.

Table 9 shows that in Harevli, 16.9 per cent of households would have been unable to subsist at the poverty-line level for one year even if they

---

[4] NSS 59th Round, AIDIS, 2002–03.

sold all their assets. The extent of asset poverty was particularly high among Muslims and Dalits in this village. About 38.5 per cent of Muslims would not have been able to subsist at the poverty-line level for even one year were they to sell all their assets. On the other hand, the majority of Other Caste households would have been able to subsist at the poverty line for over three years.

In terms of the value of assets, asset poverty was considerably lower in Mahatwar than in Harevli. This was on account of the higher price of land. In Mahatwar, 6.6 per cent of households would have been unable to subsist at the poverty-line level for less than a year on the basis of funds mobilized from sale of all their assets (Table 10). In terms of disparities across social groups, the familiar pattern of deprivation is seen in Mahatwar too: asset poverty was much higher here among Dalits than among Other Caste households.

Harriss (1992), based on village studies, reported evidence of seasonal depletion of assets (such as inventories of grain, livestock, trees and gold) that performed the role of savings, and of seasonal protection of income-generating assets (most importantly land, the sale of which would have jeopardized chances of economic recovery for a household). It is not the case that in periods of acute dearth a household sells all its assets at a single point

TABLE 9 *Proportion of households by categories of months of poverty-line consumption that can be sustained by selling assets, by social group, Harevli, 2006*

Number of months	Proportion of households			
	Dalit	Muslim	Other Caste	All households
Less than 6 months	15.2	23.1	3.8	10.7
Between 6 months and 12 months	8.7	15.4	1.9	6.2
Between 12 months and 18 months	6.5	15.4	0.0	4.5
Between 18 months and 24 months	13.0	0.0	0.0	5.3
Between 24 months and 36 months	8.7	0.0	9.4	8.0
36 months or more	47.8	46.1	84.9	65.2

Source: Survey data.

TABLE 10 *Proportion of households by categories of months of poverty-line consumption that can be sustained by selling assets, by social group, Mahatwar, 2006*

Number of months	Proportion of households		
	Dalit	Other Caste	All households
Less than 6 months	3.2	0.0	2.0
Between 6 months and 12 months	7.5	0.0	4.6
Between 12 months and 18 months	7.5	1.7	5.2
Between 18 months and 24 months	14.0	5.0	10.4
Between 24 months and 36 months	10.7	3.3	7.8
36 months or more	57.1	90.0	69.9

Source: Survey data.

of time. The most likely tactic of a household is to sell assets sequentially so as to keep the chances of recovery alive for as long as possible.[5] The sequence reported in several village studies was as follows: sale of unproductive assets like household durables, then of jewellery, followed by trees and other low-productive assets. When the acute dearth continued over a prolonged period of time, protected productive assets had to be sold in order to ensure sustenance. According to Harriss (1992), 'when protected assets are no longer protectable, first domestic assets and possessions, then land are mortgaged and then sold'. Following this line of argument, we examine the value of assets other than land and buildings, and evaluate the cushion that such assets provide against economic shocks. Such an analysis shows that about 44.6 per cent of households in Harevli (Table 11) and about 71.2 per cent households in Mahatwar (Table 12) would not have been able to survive at

TABLE 11 *Proportion of households by categories of months of poverty-line consumption that can be sustained by selling assets other than land and buildings, by social group, Harevli, 2006*

Number of months	Proportion of households			
	Dalit	*Muslim*	*Other Caste*	*All households*
Less than 6 months	50.0	61.5	7.5	31.2
Between 6 months and 12 months	21.7	0.0	9.4	13.4
Between 12 months and 18 months	17.4	7.7	17.0	16.1
Between 18 months and 24 months	4.3	0.0	3.8	3.6
Between 24 months and 36 months	2.2	15.4	11.3	8.0
36 months or more	4.3	15.4	50.9	27.7

Source: Survey data.

TABLE 12 *Proportion of households by categories of months of poverty-line consumption that can be sustained by selling assets other than land and buildings, by social group, Mahatwar, 2006*

Number of months	Proportion of households		
	Dalit	*Other Caste*	*All households*
Less than 6 months	61.3	15	43.1
Between 6 months and 12 months	25.8	31.7	28.1
Between 12 months and 18 months	9.7	18.3	13.1
Between 18 months and 24 months	0	13.3	5.2
Between 24 months and 36 months	2.1	8.3	4.6
36 months or more	1.1	13.3	5.9

Source: Survey data.

[5] Carter and Barrett (2006) looked into the issue of recovery in a dynamic asset-based poverty approach; they argued that when households experienced a loss of productive assets and were pushed below a threshold level, they fell into a poverty trap from which the chances of escape or recovery were minimal.

262

DALIT HOUSEHOLDS IN VILLAGE ECONOMIES

the level of the poverty line for even one year by selling off assets other than land and buildings. It is noteworthy that although land prices in Mahatwar were high, assets other than land and buildings provided very little cushion for households in Mahatwar.

Comparative Analysis of Different Measures of Economic Poverty

This section attempts a comparative analysis of income poverty and asset poverty measured using different methods.

Estimates of incomes of households in Harevli and Mahatwar show that the incidence of income poverty was very high in both the villages. A comparison of per capita income with the consumption poverty line shows that 46.4 per cent of households in Harevli (Table 13) and 73.2 per cent of households in Mahatwar (Table 14) were below the poverty line.

A comparison of asset poverty measured by two different approaches, and income poverty measured as the proportion of households with incomes below the poverty line brings out some interesting points.

First, there was a substantial difference in the measurement of asset poverty between the two approaches. In the first approach, which was based on the income-generating potential of productive assets, the incidence of poverty was much higher in Mahatwar (91.5 per cent) than in Harevli (69.6 per cent). As already seen, generation of income from owned productive assets requires that households command access to a basket of complementary assets and inputs. Agricultural land was by far the most important productive asset owned by households in both the study villages. The productive

TABLE 13 *Incidence of income poverty, by social group, Harevli, 2006* in per cent

Social group	Proportion of households with income below the poverty line	Proportion of persons with income below the poverty line
Dalit	54.3	63.6
Muslim	53.8	58.8
Other Caste	37.7	31.3
All social groups	46.4	45.9

Source: Survey data.

TABLE 14 *Incidence of income poverty, by social group, Mahatwar, 2006* in per cent

Social Group	Proportion of households with income below the poverty line	Proportion of persons with income below the poverty line (%)
Dalit	73.1	77.5
Other Caste	73.3	74.0
All social groups	73.2	76.7

Source: Survey data.

potential of agricultural land crucially depends on availability of irrigation. In Mahatwar, with no public irrigation available and only a small part of the land having access to privately owned sources of groundwater irrigation, crop failures due to insufficient rain were a common occurrence. In contrast, most of the land in Harevli received plentiful canal irrigation, and was used for cultivating the highly profitable crop of sugarcane. The income-generating potential of agricultural land in Harevli, therefore, was much higher than that in Mahatwar. As a result, despite more unequal distribution of land in Harevli than in Mahatwar, incidence of asset poverty measured in terms of the income-generating potential of owned productive assets was lower in Harevli than in Mahatwar.

In the second approach to the measurement of asset poverty, in which ownership of assets was viewed as a cushion against adverse economic shocks, it was observed that the incidence of poverty was higher in Harevli than in Mahatwar. This was because the price of land was higher in Mahatwar than in Harevli – primarily on account of the fact that unlike Harevli, Mahatwar was situated close to a highway. As a result, there was a disjuncture between

TABLE 15 *Correlation matrix for different types of poverty measures, Harevli, 2006*

	Poverty in terms of income from ownership of productive assets	Poverty in terms of ownership of all assets	Poverty in terms of total income
Poverty in terms of income from ownership of productive assets	1.00	0.91 (2.2e–16)	0.88 (2.2e–16)
Poverty in terms of ownership of all assets	0.91 (2.2e–16)	1.00	0.92 (2.2e–16)
Poverty in terms of total income	0.88 (2.2e–16)	0.92 (2.2e–16)	1.00

Note: Figures in parentheses are p-values.
Source: Survey data.

TABLE 16 *Correlation matrix for different types of poverty measures, Mahatwar, 2006*

	Poverty in terms of income from ownership of productive assets	Poverty in terms of ownership of all assets	Poverty in terms of total income
Poverty in terms of income from ownership of productive assets	1.00	0.28 (0.0004)	0.66 (2.2e–16)
Poverty in terms of ownership of all assets	0.28 (0.0004)	1.00	0.36 (0.000005)
Poverty in terms of total income	0.66 (2.2e–16)	0.36 (0.000005)	1.00

Note: Figures in parentheses are p-values.
Source: Survey data.

the productive potential of land and its market price in Mahatwar. The dis-juncture between the productive potential of land and its market price was seen in a low correlation between the income from owned assets and the value of assets in Mahatwar. In contrast, income from owned assets and value of assets were strongly correlated in Harevli (Table 15). This disjuncture was also reflected in the low degree of association between total household income and value of total assets in Mahatwar (Table 16).

The two alternative measures of asset poverty looked into asset dep-rivation from two different perspectives. In the first approach, based on the income-generating potential of productive assets, access to complementary inputs and assets was important in determining the productive potential of assets. In the second approach, where ownership of assets was viewed as a cushion against adverse economic shocks, the value of the asset base itself determined the extent to which households could withstand economic shocks. The analysis showed that while the levels of poverty measured on the basis of the two approaches could be very different, a common feature was that asset poverty among Dalits and Muslims was considerably higher than among caste Hindus. This conclusion was also confirmed by estimates of asset poverty for rural Uttar Pradesh on the basis of AIDIS data.

Concluding Remarks

In both Harevli and Mahatwar, Dalit households were characterized by lack of ownership of assets, and, in particular, lack of ownership of produc-tive assets (other than labour power). Assets were concentrated among Other Caste households, who were the dominant group in the social hierarchy of the villages, and whose supremacy extended over the social and economic spheres. In Harevli, Tyagi households enjoyed absolute dominance over the rest of village society. They were not only the dominant lessors, leasing out land to Dalit and Muslim households, but also the dominant employers, employing their tenants as wage labourers on their own operational holdings, primar-ily in sugarcane cultivation. In Mahatwar, the dominance of Other Caste households was mostly expressed in the spheres of customs and traditions.

The lack of ownership of assets, and in particular productive assets, resulted in higher levels of income poverty among Dalit households than Oth-ers in both the study villages. Further, the low asset base of Dalit households meant that the role played by assets as a cushion against adverse income shocks was weak among them, and was limited to a short duration.

The two approaches used for measuring asset poverty (assets as a source of income and assets as a cushion against vulnerability) brought out an interesting point. In the first approach, which was based on the income-generating potential of productive assets, the incidence of poverty was much higher in Mahatwar than in Harevli, and this was on account of lack of access to complementary inputs in Mahatwar. In the second approach to the measurement of asset poverty, in which ownership of assets was viewed as a cushion against adverse economic shocks, the incidence of poverty appeared lower in Mahatwar. This was on account of high land prices in Mahatwar, owing to its locational advantage of being situated close to a highway. There was thus a clear disjuncture between the productive (agricultural) potential of land and its market price in Mahatwar.

Therefore, poverty measurement depends not only on the choice of variable (consumption, or income or asset), but also on the type of role we assign to that variable. The outcome of the assigned role will, of course, be influenced by local conditions and the socio-economic characteristics of the region.

References

Ajakaiye, D.O. and Adeyeye, V.A. (2002), 'Concepts, Measurement and Causes of Poverty', *CBN Economic and Financial Review*, vol. 39, no. 4, available at http://www.cen-bank.org/OUT/PUBLICATIONS/EFR/RD/2002/EFRVOL39-4-5.PDF, viewed on 1 October 2013.

Attwood, D.W. (1979), 'Why Some of the People Get Richer: Economic Change and Mobility in Rural West India', *Current Anthropology*, vol. 20, no. 3, pp. 495–516.

Carter, Michael R. and May, Julian (1999), 'Poverty, Livelihood and Class in Rural South Africa', *World Development*, vol. 27, no. 1, pp. 1–20.

Carter, Michael R. and May, Julian (2001), 'One Kind of Freedom: Poverty Dynamics in Post-apartheid South Africa', *World Development*, vol. 29, no. 12, pp. 1987–2006.

Carter, Michael R. and Barrett, Christopher B. (2006), 'The Economics of Poverty Traps and Persistent Poverty: An Asset Based Approach', *Journal of Development Studies*, vol. 42, no. 2, pp. 178–99.

Dreze, Jean and Gazdar, Haris (1996), 'Uttar Pradesh: The Burden of Inertia', in Jean Dreze and Amartya Sen, eds, *Indian Development: Selected Regional Perspectives,* Oxford University Press, New Delhi.

Ellis, Frank (1998), 'Household Strategies and Rural Livelihood Diversification', *Journal of Development Studies*, vol. 35, no. 1, pp. 1–38.

Finan, Frederico, Sadoulet, Elisabeth and Janvry, Alain de (2005), 'Measuring the Poverty Reduction Potential of Land in Rural Mexico', *Journal of Development Economics*, vol. 77, no. 1, pp. 27–51.

Harriss, Barbara (1992), 'Rural Poverty in India: Micro Level Evidence', in Barbara Harriss, Sanjivi Guhan and R.H. Cassen, eds, *Poverty in India: Research and Policy*, Oxford University Press, New Delhi.

Harriss, John (1991), 'The Green Revolution in North Arcot: Economic Trends, Household Mobility, and the Politics of an Awkward Class', in Peter B.R. Hazell and C. Ramasamy, eds, *The Green Revolution Reconsidered*, Oxford University Press, New Delhi.

Haveman, Robert H. and Wolff, Edward Nathan (2004), 'The Concept and Measurement of Asset Poverty: Levels, Trends and Composition for the U.S.,1983–2001', *Journal of Economic Inequality*, vol. 2, no. 2, pp. 145–69.

Jalan, Jyotsna and Murgai, Rinku (2007), 'An Effective Targeting Shortcut? An Assessment of the 2002 Below-Poverty Line Census Method', Working Paper no. 8, Economics Working Paper Series, Centre for Studies in Social Sciences, Calcutta, available at http://www.cssscal.org/pdf/WP-2012-8.pdf, viewed on 1 October 2013.

Kozel, Valerie and Parker, Barbara (2003), 'A Profile and Diagnostic of Poverty in Uttar Pradesh', *Economic and Political Weekly*, vol. 38, no. 4, January, pp. 385–403.

Kurien, C.T. (1980), 'Dynamics of Rural Transformation: A Case Study of Tamil Nadu', *Economic and Political Weekly*, vol. 15, no. 5/7, Annual Number, February, pp. 365–90.

Lanjouw, Peter and Shariff, A. (2004), 'Rural Non-Farm Employment in India: Access, Incomes and Poverty Impact', *Economic and Political Weekly*, vol. 39, no. 40, October, pp. 4429–46.

Lanjouw, Peter and Stern, Nicholas (1991), 'Poverty in Palanpur', *World Bank Economic Review*, vol. 5, no. 1, pp. 23–55.

May, J., Carter, M.R. and Posel, D. (1995), 'The Composition and Persistence of Rural Poverty in South Africa: An Entitlements Approach', LAPC Policy Paper No. 15, Land and Agricultural Policy Centre, Johannesburg.

McKenzie, David J. (2005), 'Measuring Inequality with Asset Indicators', *Journal of Population Economics*, vol. 18, no. 2, pp. 229–60.

Meenakshi, J.V. and Viswanathan, Brinda (2005), 'Calorie Deprivation in Rural India Between 1983 and 1999/2000: Evidence from Unit Record Data', in Angus Deaton and Valerie Kozel, eds, *The Great Indian Poverty Debate*, Macmillan India.

Oliver, M.L. and Shapiro, T.M. (1990), 'Wealth of a Nation: A Reassessment of Asset Inequality in America Shows at Least One Third of Households are Asset-Poor', *American Journal of Economics and Sociology*, vol. 49, no. 2, pp. 129–51.

Planning Commission (2006), *Report of the XI Plan Working Group on Poverty Elimination Programmes*, Government of India, New Delhi.

Ramachandran, V.K. (1990), *Wage Labour and Unfreedom in Agriculture: An Indian Case Study*, Clarendon Press, Oxford.

Rawal, Vikas (2001), 'Irrigation Statistics in West Bengal-1', *Economic and Political Weekly*, vol. 36, no. 27, July, pp. 2537–44.

Rawal, Vikas (2008), 'Estimation of Rural Household Incomes in India: Selected Methodological Issues', paper presented at *Studying Village Economies in India: A Colloquium on Methodology*, Kolkata, 21–24 December.

Reardon, Thomas and Vosti, Stephan A. (1995), 'Links between Rural Poverty and the Environment in Developing Countries: Asset Categories and Investment Poverty', *World Development*, vol. 23, no. 9, pp. 1495–506.

Rodgers, Gerry and Rodgers, Janine (1984), 'Incomes and Work among the Poor of Rural Bihar, 1971–81', *Economic and Political Weekly*, vol. 19, no. 13, pp. A17–A28.

Sherraden, Michael (2001), 'Assets and the Poor: Implications for Individual Accounts and Social Security', Invited Testimony to the President's Commission on Social Security, Washington, D.C., available at http://ssa.gov/history/reports/pcsss/Sherraden_Testimony.pdf, viewed on 1 October 2013.

Spilerman, Seymour (2000), 'Wealth and Stratification Processes', *Annual Review of Sociology*, vol. 26, pp. 497–524.

Sundaram, K. (2003), 'On Identification of Households below Poverty Line in BPL Census 2002: Some Comments on the Proposed Methodology', *Economic and Political Weekly*, vol. 38, no. 9, March, pp. 896–901.

Torche, Florencia and Spilerman, Seymour (2007), 'Household Wealth in Latin America', in James B. Davies, ed., *Personal Assets from a Global Perspective*, Cambridge University Press, Cambridge.

Vaidyanathan, A. (1993), 'Asset Holdings and Consumption of Rural Households in India: A Study of Spatial and Temporal Variations', in *Agricultural Development Policy: Adjustments and Reorientation, Indian Society of Agricultural Economics*, Oxford and IBH Publications, New Delhi.

Wolff, Edward N. and Zacharias, Ajit (2006), 'Household Wealth and the Measurement of Economic Well-Being in the United States', Working Paper No. 447, The Levy Economics Institute of Bard College, New York, available at http://www.levyinstitute.org/pubs/wp_447.pdf, viewed on 1 October 2013.

Zezza, Alberto, Winters, Paul, Davis, Benjamin, Carletto, Gero, Covarrubias, Katia, Quinones, Esteban, Stamoulis, Kostas, Karfakis, Takis, Tasciotti, Luca, DiGiuseppe, Stefania and Bonomi, Genny (2007), 'Rural Household Access to Assets and Agrarian Institutions: A Cross Country Comparison', ESA Working Paper No. 07–17, Agricultural Development Economics Division, FAO, available at ftp://ftp.fao.org/docrep/fao/011/aj303e/aj303e.pdf, viewed on 1 October 2013.

Appendix Tables

TABLE A1 *Proportion of households by categories of months of poverty-line consumption that can be sustained by selling assets, by social group, western Uttar Pradesh, 2002–03*

Number of months	Proportion of households			
	Dalit	*OBC*	*Others*	*All households*
Less than 6 months	1.7	1.3	0.5	1.2
Between 6 months and 12 months	4.1	1.7	1	2.1
Between 12 months and 18 months	7	3.7	5.1	4.8
Between 18 months and 24 months	5.7	4.8	3.7	4.8
Between 24 months and 36 months	12.3	7.9	5.8	8.5
36 months or more	69.2	80.6	83.9	78.6

Note: ST households are not included in all households.
Source: NSS 59th round, unit-level data.

TABLE A2 *Proportion of households by categories of months of poverty-line consumption that can be sustained by selling assets, by social group, central Uttar Pradesh, 2002–03*

Number of months	Proportion of households			
	Dalit	*OBC*	*Others*	*All households*
Less than 6 months	3.3	1.8	1.3	2.3
Between 6 months and 12 months	4.6	4.9	1.8	4.2
Between 12 months and 18 months	5.2	4.8	3.0	4.6
Between 18 months and 24 months	5.9	5.6	0.8	4.8
Between 24 months and 36 months	14.2	10.9	6.9	11.3
36 months or more	66.8	72.1	86.3	72.8

Note: ST households are not included in all households.
Source: NSS 59th round, unit-level data.

TABLE A3 *Proportion of households by categories of months of poverty-line consumption that can be sustained by selling assets, by social group, eastern Uttar Pradesh, 2002–03*

Number of months	Proportion of households			
	Dalit	*OBC*	*Others*	*All households*
Less than 6 months	2.4	1.5	0.9	1.8
Between 6 months and 12 months	6.5	2.8	1.2	3.6
Between 12 months and 18 months	6.1	3.1	1.8	3.7
Between 18 months and 24 months	8.9	3.7	1.2	4.7
Between 24 months and 36 months	12.9	7.5	5.2	8.4
36 months or more	63.1	81.5	89.7	77.7

Note: ST households are not included in all households.
Source: NSS 59th round, unit-level data.

TABLE A4 *Proportion of households by categories of months of poverty-line consumption that can be sustained by selling assets, by social group, southern Uttar Pradesh, 2002–03*

Number of months	Proportion of households			
	Dalit	OBC	Others	All households
Less than 6 months	2.6	1.5	0.4	2.0
Between 6 months and 12 months	7.0	1.3	0.7	2.8
Between 12 months and 18 months	3.7	1.3	2.1	2.3
Between 18 months and 24 months	8.4	4.3	0.7	4.6
Between 24 months and 36 months	10.2	3.2	0.7	4.5
36 months or more	68.1	88.5	95.5	83.8

Note: ST households are not included in all households.
Source: NSS 59th round, unit-level data.

TABLE A5 *Proportion of households by categories of months of poverty-line consumption that can be sustained by selling assets other than land and buildings, by social group, western Uttar Pradesh, 2002–03*

Number of months	Proportion of households			
	Dalit	OBC	Others	All households
Less than 6 months	58.7	39.2	25.5	41.0
Between 6 months and 12 months	26.2	28.1	26.3	27.2
Between 12 months and 18 months	9.2	11.7	11.6	11.0
Between 18 months and 24 months	1.6	6.5	9.1	5.9
Between 24 months and 36 months	1.7	4.2	7.2	4.3
36 months or more	2.7	10.2	20.3	10.5

Note: ST households are not included in all households.
Source: NSS 59th round, unit-level data.

TABLE A6 *Proportion of households by categories of months of poverty-line consumption that can be sustained by selling assets other than land and buildings, by social group, central Uttar Pradesh, 2002–03*

Number of months	Proportion of households			
	Dalit	OBC	Others	All households
Less than 6 months	60.1	50.4	31.0	50.8
Between 6 months and 12 months	25.9	25.1	24.9	25.2
Between 12 months and 18 months	6.5	12.1	17.5	10.9
Between 18 months and 24 months	3.2	4.8	7.0	4.6
Between 24 months and 36 months	2.1	3.7	4.6	3.3
36 months or more	2.3	3.8	15.0	5.2

Note: ST households are not included in all households.
Source: NSS 59th round, unit-level data.

TABLE A7 *Proportion of households by categories of months of poverty-line consumption that can be sustained by selling assets other than land and buildings, by social group, eastern Uttar Pradesh, 2002–03*

Number of months	Proportion of households			
	Dalit	OBC	Others	All households
Less than 6 months	72.5	51.6	33.7	54.0
Between 6 months and 12 months	18.5	25.0	20.3	22.2
Between 12 months and 18 months	4.3	11.3	14.7	9.9
Between 18 months and 24 months	2.4	4.1	8.3	4.4
Between 24 months and 36 months	1.2	3.5	6.3	3.5
36 months or more	1.1	4.5	16.7	6.0

Note: ST households are not included in all households.
Source: NSS 59th round, unit-level data.

TABLE A8 *Proportion of households by categories of months of poverty-line consumption that can be sustained by selling assets other than land and buildings, by social group, southern Uttar Pradesh, 2002–03*

Number of months	Proportion of households			
	Dalit	OBC	Others	All households
Less than 6 months	49.3	23.1	12.9	28.5
Between 6 months and 12 months	30.2	32.3	33.1	31.8
Between 12 months and 18 months	7.7	18.6	19.5	15.7
Between 18 months and 24 months	3.4	10.4	16.2	9.6
Between 24 months and 36 months	3.3	6.8	8.9	6.2
36 months or more	6.2	8.7	9.4	8.1

Note: ST households are not included in all households.
Source: NSS 59th round, unit-level data.

Income Inequality in Village India and the Role of Caste

Vikas Rawal and Madhura Swaminathan

In recent years, the rate of economic growth in India has accelerated: per capita income grew at 10.7 per cent per annum at current prices and 6 per cent per annum at constant prices during the Tenth Plan period (2002–07), as compared to 3 per cent during the Ninth Plan period (1997–2002). Studies of the nature of this growth, and whether it is equalizing or unequalizing, are seriously lacking, however, due to lack of data on income distribution.

There is a very thin literature on income inequality in India, since most studies of so-called income inequality actually deal with expenditure inequality. The few available studies, of which only a handful look at income inequality in rural India, indicate that levels of inequality are quite high in rural India. Most of these studies draw upon multi-State sample surveys conducted by the National Council of Applied Economic Research (NCAER). Based on the NCAER data, Azam and Shariff (2009) estimate that the Gini coefficient for rural incomes rose from 0.46 in 1993–94 to 0.5 in 2004–05. Using the same dataset, Vanneman and Dubey (2010) indicate that the Gini coefficient for rural incomes was 0.54 in 2004–05 (see also, Desai *et al.* 2010; Borooah 2005). There are some problems with the quality and reliability of the data on household incomes in the NCAER surveys, particularly the 1993 survey. Nevertheless, these studies give us a rough order of magnitude of income inequality at the national level. In addition, village surveys indicate extremely high levels of income inequality (Swaminathan and Rawal 2011).

We also know that caste continues to play a significant role in the economic life of village India, and, specifically, that persons belonging to the Scheduled Castes (also termed Dalits) face discrimination, and are disadvantaged in respect of social and economic attainments. There is both theoretical and empirical work on the discrimination of Dalit households relative to other caste and social groups (Thorat 2009; Deshpande 2011).

In terms of economic status, however, most of the literature focuses on differences in consumption expenditure (from National Sample Surveys), and poverty is defined on the basis of per capita consumption expenditure as between Dalits or Scheduled Castes (SCs), Scheduled Tribes (STs), and all 'Others' (that is, neither Scheduled Caste nor Scheduled Tribe). It is well established that per capita monthly expenditure among Dalits (and STs) is lower than among Others in rural India (Thorat 2007).[1] Further, and not surprisingly, the incidence of poverty is higher among SCs than Others. Even after taking account of population shares, the disparity ratio is less than 1, indicating that SC households accounted for a less than proportionate share of total consumption expenditure, and the disparity ratios rose between 1983 and 2000 at the all-India level and in all States (Thorat and Mahamallik 2007).

In this essay, we examine the role of caste in observed inequality in incomes in rural India, using a unique dataset comprising household data from a cross-section of eight villages across four States. The specific focus of this paper is on Dalit households. The only similar analysis is a recent paper based on panel data for two villages, Palanpur in Uttar Pradesh and Sugao in Maharashtra (Lanjouw and Rao 2011).[2]

Dataset

The income data used in this essay come from the Project on Agrarian Relations in India (PARI), a project to study village economies in different agro-ecological regions of India.[3] Between 2005 and 2007, household surveys were undertaken in eight villages: three in Andhra Pradesh, two in Uttar Pradesh, two in Maharashtra and one in Rajasthan (Table 1). In 2005–06, in-depth census and sample surveys were conducted in three villages of Andhra Pradesh: Ananthavaram, a village in the paddy-growing region of Guntur district; Bukkacherla, a village in the dry and drought-prone district of Anantapur; and Kothapalle village in Karimnagar district, a groundwater-irrigated region of north Telengana. This was followed in June 2006 by census-type surveys in two villages of Uttar Pradesh: Harevli, in the canal-irrigated, wheat-growing district of Bijnor; and Mahatwar in Ballia district, selected from a groundwater-irrigated, wheat and paddy-growing belt in eastern Uttar Pradesh. In 2007, surveys were conducted in two villages of Maharashtra. Nimshirgaon is located in Kolhapur district, and has relatively prosperous agriculture based on irrigated sugarcane, and a variety of vegetable and fruit crops. By contrast, Warwat Khanderao is a village in the unirrigated cotton-growing tracts of Vidarbha, in Buldhana district. A census survey was also completed in 25 F Gulabewala village of Sri Ganganagar district, Rajasthan, in 2007. With irrigation from the Gang Canal project, the main crops cultivated in this village were wheat, rapeseed, cotton, cluster beans and fodder crops.

---

[1] See also, Saggar and Pan (1994), Kijima (2006), Deshpande (2000) and Thorat (2009). In the literature, it is quite common for expenditure inequality to be termed income inequality.

[2] In this paper, income inequality is decomposed by caste sub-group using conventional measures as well as the ELMO (Elbers, Lanjouw, Mistiaen and Ozler 2008) approach. The paper is not exclusively focused on Scheduled Castes, but it shows that in Palanpur, Jatabs (belonging to a Scheduled Caste) did not share in the rise in prosperity of the village population.

[3] For the objectives of PARI and design of the surveys, see www.agrarianstudies.org.

Brief descriptions of the eight villages surveyed under PARI are given below.[4]

Ananthavaram

Ananthavaram village is located in Kollur *mandal* (taluk), Guntur district, Andhra Pradesh. At the Census of 2001, the population of Ananthavaram was 3,100 persons (1,559 males and 1,541 females). The PARI survey of 2005 covered 2,424 persons in 667 households. Ananthavaram is a multi-caste village with a significant Dalit population (Malas and Madigas together constitute 45 per cent of the population).

The village is irrigated by the waters of the Krishna river. Supplementary irrigation from groundwater was almost the norm on land officially classified as under the canal irrigation system. In the kharif (monsoon) season, paddy cultivation dominated the agriculture of the village (96.9 per cent of the cropped area was sown to paddy). The two most important crops of the rabi (winter) season were maize and black gram. Land hunger was acute in Ananthavaram: 65 per cent of the households did not own any agricultural land, and 65 per cent did not operate any land. The Gini coefficients for ownership of land and operational holding of land were 0.89 and 0.83.

Bukkacherla

Bukkacherla village is located in Raptadu *mandal* of Anantapur district, Andhra Pradesh. The *mandal* headquarters, Raptadu, is 8–9 kilometres away, and Anantapur, the nearest town and railhead, is at a distance of 14–15 kilometres. The approach road to the village is not an all-weather road and is difficult to travel during the monsoon.

The PARI census survey of 2005 covered 1,220 persons in 292 households. At the Census of 2001, the village had 296 households and a population of 1,383 persons. Households of the dominant landholding Kapu caste constituted 40 per cent of the households, and Dalit (Mala and Madiga) households constituted 20 per cent.

Typically, there is a single agricultural season in the village with cultivation occurring mainly in the kharif season. Cultivation of oilseeds and pulses predominated in Bukkacherla: the two main crops were groundnut and red gram. Incidence of landlessness in Bukkacherla was not as high as in Ananthavaram. In Bukkacherla, only 15 per cent of households did not own land and 18 per cent did not operate land. The Gini coefficient for both ownership of land and operational holding of land was 0.58.

Kothapalle

Kothapalle P.N. (Post Nustlapur) village is located in Thimmapur (Lower Maner Dam Colony) *mandal* of Karimnagar district, in the south Tel-

---

[4] For further details, see www.fas.org.in

angana region of Andhra Pradesh. The village is at a distance of 5 kilometres from the *mandal* headquarters of Thimmapur (which is also the nearest police station). The nearest town is Karimnagar, at a distance of 16 kilometres on a State highway. The PARI village census survey covered 1,430 persons in 372 households. This is a multi-caste village. Dalit households accounted for 30 per cent of the population. In Kothapalle, there has been a clear movement out of agriculture, especially among male workers.

Typically, there is a single agricultural season in the village, the kharif season. The construction of the Lower Maner Dam, however, has raised the water table in the village by improved recharge of groundwater. The irrigated area of the village increased by 232 acres between 1991 and 2001 on account of increased groundwater. The village data reveal a complex cropping system. The two most important crops were maize and paddy. There were mango orchards and other fruit trees (lime, mango, coconut and pomegranate), accounting for almost 5 per cent of the gross cropped area. Tapping toddy from palmyra trees was an important occupation. Almost one-half of the households in the village have neither ownership nor operational holdings of agricultural land.

Harevli

Harevli village is located in Najibabad block of Bijnor district in western Uttar Pradesh. There is no all-weather road leading to the village, and the main mode of transport from the village to Mandavli, the nearest town, is by horse and bullock-cart. Harevli is a small village in terms of population (not in area): the population was 668 persons at the Census of 2001. At the time of the PARI survey, 115 households and 674 persons were resident in the village. The dominant caste was Tyagi. However, in population terms, Dalit households (Chamars and Valmikis) comprised 38 per cent of total households.

Agriculture is the mainstay of the economy of Harevli. Sugarcane was the most important crop; wheat, paddy and fodder crops were also cultivated. Irrigation from a public canal, part of the Eastern Ganga Canal project, provides water during the kharif season, and tubewells (with both diesel and electric pumpsets) provided water for irrigation throughout the year. Most of the tubewells were owned by landowning Tyagi households. There was a high degree of inequality in land ownership in the village. In aggregate, 33 per cent of households in Harevli were landless.

Mahatwar

Mahatwar village belongs to Rasra block of Ballia district in eastern Uttar Pradesh. The village is located just off the highway linking Rasra to Mau, and has access through bus and jeep services to nearby towns as well as larger cities like Varanasi. At the time of the PARI survey, there were 160 households and 1,150 persons resident in the village. Mahatwar is a multi-caste village with ten different castes. Dalit (Chamar and Dusad) households constituted the majority – 94 households or 59 per cent of all households in the village.

The major crops grown in Mahatwar were paddy during the kharif season and wheat (sometimes intercropped with mustard) during the rabi season. Irrigation was from groundwater, using tubewells energized by diesel or electricity. The pattern of land ownership was such that about 20 per cent of households had no land and 71 per cent owned less than 1 acre of land. Non-agricultural occupations, both within and outside the village, were an important source of income to the resident households.

Warwat Khanderao

Warwat Khanderao belongs to Sangrampur tehsil of Buldhana district, in the Vidarbha region of Maharashtra. The nearest town is Shegaon, at a distance of 20 kilometres from the village, linked by a regular concrete road. At the PARI survey, there were 250 households in the village with a population of 1,308 persons (at the Census of 2001, the population was 1,447). The major caste in the village was Kunbi (43 per cent of all households).

The major crop cultivated in 2007 was cotton, using both Bt (GM) and non-Bt seeds. Other crops included groundnut, sunflower, green gram, sesamum, jowar, maize, pulses, wheat, red gram and black gram. The village had no irrigation facility. The pattern of ownership of land revealed that only 26 per cent of all households did not own any agricultural land. The median extent of land ownership was 3.5 acres (excluding the landless), which is not high given that it is mainly dry land.

Nimshirgaon

Nimshirgaon is a village in Shirol taluk of Kolhapur district, in the sugarcane-growing region of western Maharashtra. It is connected by an all-weather road to the highway. The number of households in the PARI survey listing was 768 with a population of 3,515 persons (the Census 2001 population of the village was 4,515). Nimshirgaon is a multi-caste village with almost one-third of the households belonging to the Jain community and another one-third to Scheduled Castes (mainly Mahars and Chamars).

Agriculture in Kolhapur district is relatively modern and dynamic. Sugarcane was the major crop in the village; soyabean, pulses and millets were also cultivated, as were a variety of vegetables and fruit (including grape and mango). Irrigation was from a water supply system linked to the Krishna river. There were also hundreds of open wells, borewells and tubewells in the fields belonging to the village residents. The majority of cultivators had marginal (28 per cent) or small holdings (24 per cent) of land. Under irrigated conditions, the scale of operation of a cultivator with, say, 2 acres, was very different in Nimshirgaon from that in Warwat Khanderao. The landless comprised 28 per cent of all households. Among Dalits, the proportion of landless was 57 per cent.

25 F Gulabewala

25 F Gulabewala is a village in Sri Ganganagar district in Rajasthan. The village is about 25 kilometres from Sri Ganganagar town and is connected by an all-weather road. In 2007, 204 households lived in the village, and the main castes were Jat Sikh, Mazhabi (Dalit) and Nayak (Dalit).

The village is irrigated by the Gang Canal project. The main crops cultivated in Gulabewala were wheat, rapeseed, cotton, cluster beans and fodder crops. Land distribution in the village was extremely unequal. About 65 per cent of all households were landless. At the other end of the distribution, the largest landowning household had about 287 acres of land, and thirty-one households had more than 30 acres of land each. Agricultural land was owned primarily by Jat Sikh households; only three Dalit households, out of a total of 123 resident Dalit households, owned any agricultural land. Another important feature of agriculture in the village was the widespread employment of long-term Dalit workers by large landowners.

TABLE 1 *Location and agro-ecology of villages surveyed, 2005 to 2007*

Village	Block	District	State	Agro-ecological type
Ananthavaram	Kollur	Guntur	Andhra Pradesh	Canal-irrigated, paddy
Bukkacherla	Raptadu	Anantapur	Andhra Pradesh	Dry and drought-prone, groundnut
Kothapalle	Thimmapur	Karimnagar	Andhra Pradesh	Groundwater-irrigated, multicrop system
Harevli	Najibabad	Bijnor	Uttar Pradesh	100% canal-irrigated with supplementary groundwater, wheat and sugarcane
Mahatwar	Rasra	Ballia	Uttar Pradesh	Groundwater-irrigated, wheat–paddy rotation
Warwat Khanderao	Sangrampur	Buldhana	Maharashtra	Rainfed, cotton
Nimshirgaon	Shirol	Kolhapur	Maharashtra	Irrigated, sugarcane and multicrop system
25 F Gulabewala	Karanpur	Sri Ganga-nagar	Rajasthan	Canal and groundwater-irrigated, cotton, wheat and mustard

Source: Survey data.

Table 2 shows the caste/social group composition of households in each of the survey villages. Dalit households accounted for a sizeable proportion of all households in six villages. Dalit households comprised less than one-fifth of all resident households in Bukkacherla and Warwat Khanderao, both rainfed villages. Dalit households comprised the majority in two villages: Mahatwar in eastern Uttar Pradesh and 25 F Gulabewala in canal-irrigated western Rajasthan. Muslim households were few in number in most of the villages, and were a significant presence only in Warwat Khanderao (where they accounted for 21 per cent of households). Adivasis or Scheduled Tribes

TABLE 2 *Number of households by social group, study villages*

Village	Dalit	Adivasi	Muslim	OBC	Other Caste Hindu	All Other house- holds	Total house- holds	Dalit households as % of all households
Ananthavaram	283	44	18	131	190		667	42.4
Bukkacherla	58		8	98	128		292	19.8
Kothapalle	118	11	5	150	87		372	43.3
Harevli	41		14	25	32		112	36.6
Mahatwar	94			53	13		160	58.8
Nimshirgaon	247		47	61	118	285 *	757	32.6
Warwat Khanderao	25		53	122		50 **	250	10.0
25 F Gulabewala	123			78	3		204	60.2

Notes: * These include 245 Jain households and 40 households belonging to Nomadic Tribes.
         ** These households belong to Nomadic Tribes.
Source: Survey data.

were present in two of the villages of Andhra Pradesh, but we have data on their household incomes for only one village – Ananthavaram.

Methodology

There is a growing literature on inter-group inequality that extends beyond the traditional decomposition of inequality into within-group and between-group components.[5] Specifically, there is an interest in looking at not just inequality, but also polarization (understood as separation or absence of middleness).

In this essay, we begin with very simple measures of differences between groups, such as proportional representation in different quintiles, which is termed representational inequality in a recent paper by Jayadev and Reddy 2011). We also look at the frequency distribution of households across income levels in different social groups to assess the degree of non-overlap between them (termed sequential inequality by Jayadev and Reddy 2011). We then estimate a standard GE (2) inequality index (or half the squared coefficient of variation) along with its decomposition by caste.

In most studies attempting a decomposition of inequality by sub-group, it has been found that the between-group component is small and does not exceed 15 per cent of overall inequality (Kanbur 2006). Elbers, Lanjouw, Mistiaen and Ozler (ELMO 2008) point out that the value of the between-group component is affected by the number of sub-groups, their relative sizes and the difference in means across sub-groups. They argue that the existing measure compares observed between-group inequality with an

---

[5] Jayadev and Reddy (2011), Lanjouw and Rao (2011) and other papers in *World Development*, February 2011.

extreme benchmark, namely the inequality that would occur if each individual constituted a separate group. They suggest an alternative benchmark termed maximum between-group inequality, which occurs in a situation 'where sub-group incomes occupy non-overlapping intervals'.[6] We have computed this alternative benchmark as proposed in ELMO (2008).

The estimates of income here include all cash and kind incomes; they account for all cash and kind receipts other than from borrowing and from sale of assets (including cash transfers). All incomes are net of costs incurred by households in the process of production and income generation. Our calculation is based on the understanding that the majority of rural households are self-employed in crop production or other non-agricultural occupations, and unable to report their total household income as such. Income is thus a derived variable, derived on the basis of a detailed accounting of outputs and costs of all economic activities. The derivation is complex, given that markets are thin or even absent for many outputs and inputs. We also argue that the household has to be considered as the basic unit for estimation of incomes, even though this poses challenges such as accurate estimation of remittances of household members who are not regularly resident, or apportioning of incomes in the case of joint cultivation (say, by brothers residing in two separate households). The surveys used a comprehensive definition of income, and included detailed modules on incomes from crop cultivation, from animal husbandry and from wage labour, as well as from salaried employment, non-agricultural self-employment, rent and other transfers. A total of twenty sources of income were used to construct the final income variable.

For most of this essay, we have focused on two social groups: Scheduled Castes or Dalits (combined with Scheduled Tribes in the case of one village, Ananthavaram), and 'Others' or all non-Scheduled Caste, non-Scheduled Tribe and non-Muslim households. There are only a few Muslim households in our survey villages, but as they are also relatively deprived, we have excluded them from the analysis. As the data come from two agricultural years, 2005–06 (for five villages) and 2006–07 (for three villages), we have reported all incomes at constant (2005–06) prices.[7]

Before proceeding to the results, we would like to underline that we see each village as a case study, and that our attempt is to explore and explain income inequality across castes in each village, and not to draw conclusions about the districts or States to which these villages belong. While the data for all villages are reported for convenience in a table, each village must be read

---

[6] If {y} is an income distribution for which inequality between sub-groups *g* and *h* is maximized, then, either all incomes in *g* are higher than all incomes in *h*, or vice versa (ELMO 2008: 236). To illustrate, if there is a village of 100 persons with two groups (Dalits and Others), and if group 1, Dalits, comprises 25 persons, then, between-group inequality would be 'maximum' if the lowest-ranked 25 persons are all Dalits.

[7] We use the State-level Consumer Price Index for Agricultural Labour (CPIAL) as the deflator.

separately. At the same time, since these villages are drawn from different agro-economic zones, we can draw some contrasts between patterns of inequality in a village in a certain type of region with that in another type of region. The essay attempts to describe and comment on patterns of inequality across the big caste divide – Dalit versus Other Castes – in each of the eight villages.

Patterns of Inequality

Before turning our attention to the role of caste in income inequality, we briefly report some of the features of aggregate income inequality in the eight survey villages (see Swaminathan and Rawal 2011 for further details).

First, while income inequality is high in general, there are important differences across villages (Table 3). The lowest estimated Gini coefficient is 0.491, for Nimshirgaon (western Maharashtra), and the highest is 0.686, for 25 F Gulabewala (western Rajasthan) – a difference of 19.5 Gini points. The three villages with the highest Gini coefficients (above 0.6) are Ananthavaram in coastal Andhra Pradesh, Harevli in western Uttar Pradesh, and 25 F Gulabewala in north-west Rajasthan. All three are canal-irrigated villages.

Secondly, there is extreme concentration of income at the top. The income share of the top 10 per cent is highest in 25 F Gulabewala (53.93), followed by Ananthavaram (49.7) and Harevli (48.58). As mentioned above, these three villages are characterized by relatively high-productivity, canal-irrigated agriculture.

The top decile has the lowest income shares in Nimshirgaon (37.5) and Bukkacherla (39.95). Bukkacherla is a rainfed village with unirrigated crop cultivation and a predominance of smallholder cultivation (and could be referred to as a 'dry village'). The fact that Nimshirgaon does not have the same degree of income concentration as the other three villages that are characterized by relatively advanced agriculture may be because it is located

TABLE 3 *Gini coefficients of household and per capita income, study villages*

Village	State	Gini coefficient	
		Households	Persons
Ananthavaram	Andhra Pradesh	0.656	0.602
Bukkacherla	Andhra Pradesh	0.607	0.542
Kothapalle	Andhra Pradesh	0.577	0.565
Harevli	Uttar Pradesh	0.671	0.602
Mahatwar	Uttar Pradesh	0.555	0.509
Warwat Khanderao	Maharashtra	0.586	0.531
Nimshirgaon	Maharashtra	0.549	0.491
25 F Gulabewala	Rajasathan	0.740	0.686

Note: These are Gini coefficients adjusted for negative incomes, following Chen, Tsaur and Rhai (1982).
Source: Swaminathan and Rawal (2011).

close to urban and semi-urban areas that provide opportunities for non-agricultural employment.

Thirdly, income inequality appears to be of the Latin American 'winner takes all' model (Palma 2006), that is, extreme concentration in the tenth decile, with even the ninth decile not gaining a significant share of the income. The share of the ninth decile is barely above 10 per cent in the survey villages (for example, 12 per cent in Kothapalle and 15 per cent in Mahatwar). In all the villages, there is a clear divide between deciles 10 and 9 in the level and share of income.

Thus there appears to be a very small 'middle class' in village India. In all eight villages, households in the middle deciles, say, deciles 5 to 7, do not receive an income share corresponding to their population share.

We now turn to differences in incomes across caste groups.

Absolute Disadvantage

Estimates of mean per capita income for Scheduled Caste or Dalit households and Other households establish that Dalit households are at a disadvantage in terms of income in each of the eight villages (Table 4).

The distance between the mean incomes of Dalit households and Other households varies across villages: it is lowest in Kothapalle village of Andhra Pradesh (where mean incomes of Dalit households are 67 per cent of mean incomes of Other households) and highest in 25 F Guabewala village of Rajasthan.

The two Dalit-majority villages are strikingly different. In the eastern

TABLE 4 *Mean household income by social group, study villages* in Rs per annum at 2005–06 prices

Village (State)	Year of survey	1	2	Col. 1 / Col. 2
		Dalit	Other households	Ratio of Dalit to Other households
Ananthavaram (AP)	2005–06	30,690	93,727	33
Bukkacherla (AP)	2005–06	19,829	40,596	49
Kothapalle (AP)	2005–06	26,197	38,962	67
Harevli (UP)	2005–06	27,540	118,951	23
Mahatwar (UP)	2005–06	25,077	53,530	47
Warwat Khanderao (MAH)	2006–07	24,843	68,400	36
Nimshirgaon (MAH)	2006–07	41,647	87,393	48
25 F Gulabewala (RAJ)	2006–07	25,111	339,078	7

Notes: Figures for villages surveyed in 2006–07 were deflated to 2005–06 prices using State-level CPIAL.

Other households include all non-Dalit, non-Scheduled Tribe and non-Muslim households.

AP = Andhra Pradesh; UP = Uttar Pradesh; MAH = Maharashtra; RAJ = Rajasthan.

Source: Survey data.

TABLE 5 *Median household incomes by social group, study villages* in Rs per annum at 2005–06 prices

Villages (State)	Year of survey	1	2	Col. 1 / Col. 2
		Dalit	Other households	Ratio of Dalit to Other households
Ananthavaram (AP)	2005–06	18,008	34,800	52
Bukkacherla (AP)	2005–06	18,545	19,584	95
Kothapalle (AP)	2005–06	17,608	25,219	70
Harevli (UP)	2005–06	19,223	53,432	36
Mahatwar (UP)	2005–06	19,834	22,882	87
Warwat Khanderao (MAH)	2006–07	15,140	34,479	44
Nimshirgaon (MAH)	2006–07	30,998	47,014	66
25 F Gulabewala (RAJ)	2006–07	19,941	180,785	11

Notes: Figures for villages surveyed in 2006–07 were deflated to 2005–06 prices using State-level CPIAL.
Other households include all non-Dalit, non-Scheduled Tribe and non-Muslim households.
AP = Andhra Pradesh; UP = Uttar Pradesh; MAH = Maharashtra; RAJ = Rajasthan.
Source: Survey data.

Uttar Pradesh village of Mahatwar, on average, a Dalit household receives 47 per cent of the income of a non-Dalit household. By contrast, in Gulabewala village, a Dalit household receives only 7 per cent of the average income of a non-Dalit (in this case, Jat Sikh) household.

When income distribution is highly unequal, we know that mean incomes will be affected by extreme values. We have therefore shown the value of median annual household income for the two social groups in Table 5.

As expected, median incomes are lower than mean incomes in all eight villages for both social groups. Further, in each village, the income of the median Dalit household is lower than the income of the median Other household. The gap between Dalits and Other households, however, is lower in terms of median incomes than it is in terms of mean incomes. The gap is relatively narrow in Bukkacherla, indicating that incomes are low for a substantial number of non-Dalit households in this village.[8]

Income disparities across caste groups are clearly related to disparities in ownership of means of production. Table 6 shows the proportion of Dalit and Other Caste households that own land, and the average value of land owned by households belonging to these caste groups. The table shows that in all the villages, the proportion of households owning land and the average value of land owned are substantially lower for Dalit households than for Other Caste households. Further, it can be seen from the table that villages

---

[8] Note that Dalits account for less than 20 per cent of all village households in Bukkacherla.

TABLE 6   *Proportion of households that own agricultural land and average value of agricultural land owned, Dalit and Other Caste households, study villages* in per cent and Rs

Village	Proportion of households that own agricultural land		Average value of agricultural land owned	
	Dalit	Other households	Dalit	Other households
Ananthavaram	24	58	83,234	1,220,425
Bukkacherla	88	90	29,502	235,441
Kothapalle	58	59	67,149	377,275
Harevli	55	68	162,625	341,794
Mahatwar	73	92	88,135	364,869
Warwat Khanderao	58	78	96,828	477,899
Nimshirgaon	56	85	624,172	1,202,394
25 F Gulabewala	3	85	156,773	5,663,971

Note: Other households include all non-Dalit, non-Scheduled Tribe and non-Muslim households.
Source: Survey data.

with high income disparities across castes, for example 25 F Gulabewala in Sri Ganganagar district, are villages with very high disparities in ownership of land.

Representational Inequality

We now turn to the first of our distributional measures of inter-group inequality. Tables 7, 8 and 9 show the distribution of households from Dalit and other social groups across income quintiles. Equal representation would imply that each quintile has the same proportion of Dalit households as the population proportion (as shown in the last row). The tables have to be read as follows. In Table 8, for example, the first row shows that in Harevli, of

TABLE 7   *Proportion of households belonging to different social groups in each quantile of per capita income, Andhra Pradesh villages*

Quintiles of per capita income	Ananthavaram				Bukkacherla			Kothapalle			
	Dalit	Adivasi	Muslim	Other households	Dalit	Muslim	Other households	Dalit	Adivasi	Muslim	Other households
1	45	15	6	33	16	0	84	43	5	5	46
2	64	0	6	30	25	0	75	39	0	0	61
3	30	12	6	52	35	0	65	37	0	0	63
4	54	3	0	43	16	5	79	11	0	0	89
5	23	0	0	77	5	5	90	37	0	0	63
All	43	6	4	47	19	2	79	33	1	1	65

Note: Other households include all non-Dalit, non-Scheduled Tribe and non-Muslim households.
Source: Survey data.

TABLE 8   *Proportion of households belonging to different social groups in each quintile of per capita income, Uttar Pradesh villages*

Quintiles of per capita income	Harevli			Mahatwar	
	Dalit	Muslim	Other households	Dalit	Other households
1	62	10	29	67	33
2	55	14	32	52	48
3	36	18	45	73	27
4	27	9	64	61	39
5	5	9	86	52	48
All	37	12.5	50.5	59	41

Note: Other households include all non-Dalit, non-Scheduled Tribe and non-Muslim households.
Source: Survey data.

TABLE 9   *Proportion of households belonging to different social groups in each quintile of per capita income, Maharashtra and Rajasthan villages*

Quintiles of per capita income	Warwat Khanderao			Nimshiragon			25 F Gulabewala	
	Dalit	Muslim	Other households	Dalit	Muslim	Other households	Dalit	Other households
1	22	20	58	53	6	41	100	0
2	16	22	62	33	10	57	95	5
3	6	30	64	40	13	47	83	17
4	2	22	76	25	1	74	24	76
5	4	12	84	13	0	87	0	100
All	10	21	69	33	6	61	60	40

Note: Other households include all non-Dalit, non-Scheduled Tribe and non-Muslim households.
Source: Survey data.

all households in the first income quintile, 62 per cent are Dalit households, 10 per cent are Muslim households and the remaining 29 per cent, Other households. (The rows add up to 100 for each village.) The fifth row shows that Dalits comprise only 5 per cent of the top income quintile although they constitute 37 per cent of all households (last row).

With only one exception, in every village, Dalit households are under-represented in the top income quintile (Q5). In three villages (Bukkacherla, Harevli and Warwat Khanderao), Dalits comprise at most 5 per cent of the top quintile. Dalits have no representation in the top income quintile in 25 F Gulabewala village. In Kothapalle, the sole exception, Dalit households comprise 33 per cent of the population and 37 per cent of Q5, but even here the picture changes if we take the top 5 per cent (see Table 10). At the same time, Other households (non-Scheduled Caste, non-Scheduled Tribe and non-Muslim) are over-represented in Q5. In five villages, more than 84 per cent of households in Q5 belong to Other social groups.

Sequential Inequality

We have observed that representation across quintiles (and other income groupings like deciles) is different for Dalit households as compared to Other households. To assess the extent to which Dalit households are over-represented at one end of the income distribution, we look at the frequency distribution of per capita income for the two groups separately (Tables 10, 11, 12, 13). Table 10 shows the distribution of Dalit and Other households across different per capita income categories in the three villages of Andhra Pradesh.

TABLE 10 *Distribution of households by per capita income and social group, Andhra Pradesh villages, 2005–06*

Per capita income category (Rs per annum)	Ananthavaram		Bukkacherla		Kothapalle	
	Dalit	Other households	Dalit	Other households	Dalit	Other households
Less than 5500	39.5	26.3	63.2	46.6	61.4	37.2
5500–10000	26.1	14.6	21.1	22.0	16.2	38.6
10000–20000	23.6	29.3	15.8	18.1	12.7	16.5
20000–30000	10.8	11.8	0.0	6.5	9.7	4.9
30000–40000	0.0	4.4	0.0	3.9	0.0	0.0
40000–50000	0.0	2.2	0.0	2.6	0.0	0.0
> 50000	0.0	11.5	0.0	0.4	0.0	2.8
All households	100.0	100.0	100.0	100.0	100	100.0

Notes: Households are ranked by per capita annual household income at constant prices. The first income category corresponds roughly to the official poverty line.
Other households include all non-Dalit, non-Scheduled Tribe and non-Muslim households.

Source: Survey data.

TABLE 11 *Distribution of households by per capita income per annum, Harevli and Mahatwar, 2005–06*

Per capita income category (Rs per annum)	Harevli		Mahatwar	
	Dalit	Other households	Dalit	Other households
Less than 5500	80.0	37.7	79.8	72.6
5500–10000	12.5	26.1	13.8	11.1
10000–20000	7.5	11.6	4.3	11.3
20000–30000	0.0	10.1	2.1	0.0
30000–40000	0.0	4.3	0.0	1.6
40000–50000	0.0	0.0	0.0	3.2
> 50000	0.0	10.1	0.0	8.1
All households	100.0	100.0	100.0	100.0

Notes: Households are ranked by per capita annual household income at constant prices. The first income category corresponds roughly to the official poverty line.
Other households include all non-Dalit, non-Scheduled Tribe and non-Muslim households.

Source: Survey data.

TABLE 12 *Distribution of households by per capita income per annum, Nimshirgaon and Warwat Khanderao, 2006–07*

Per capita income category	Warwat Khanderao		Nimshirgaon	
(Rs per annum)	Dalit	Other households	Dalit	Other households
Less than 5500	64.0	35.5	49.4	20.5
5500–10000	20.0	25.6	27.3	28.2
10000–20000	12.0	24.4	16.1	31.4
20000–30000	0.0	11.0	1.2	12.1
30000–40000	4.0	2.3	5.9	0.0
40000–50000	0.0	0.6	0.0	3.1
>50000	0.0	0.6	0.0	4.7
All households	100.0	100.0	100.0	100.0

Notes: Households are ranked by per capita annual household income at constant prices. The first income category corresponds roughly to the official poverty line.
Other households include all non-Dalit, non-Scheduled Tribe and non-Muslim households.
Source: Survey data.

TABLE 13 *Distribution of households by per capita income per annum, 25 F Gulabewala, 2006–07*

Per capita income category	25 F Gulabewala	
(Rs per annum)	Dalit	Other households
Less than 5500	63.4	3.7
5500–10000	28.5	6.2
10000–20000	8.1	22.2
20000–30000	0.0	16.0
30000–40000	0.0	9.9
40000–50000	0.0	11.1
>50000	0.0	30.9
All households	100.0	100.0

Notes: Households are ranked by per capita annual household income at constant prices. The first income category corresponds roughly to the official poverty line.
Other households include all non-Dalit, non-Scheduled Tribe and non-Muslim households.
Source: Survey data.

The corresponding data for the other villages are in Tables 11, 12 and 13.

The data in these tables again underline the fact that the incomes of Dalits and Others diverge significantly. For example, there is no Dalit household in any of the eight villages with a per capita income over Rs 40,000 a year.

The extent to which the frequency distributions are non-overlapping is a measure of the degree of sequential inequality or clustering. There is some overlap at lower incomes in all the villages, indicating that there are low-income households among Other Castes as well, although the lowest income category (less than Rs 5,500 per annum) inevitably has a higher proportion of

Dalit households than Other households. However, there is a discernible non-overlapping section in every village at the upper end of income distribution. In other words, the ceiling for incomes among Dalit households is well below the maximum per capita income in each village. The non-overlapping section is largest in 25 F Gulabewala village: here, 68 per cent of Other households reported a per capita income above Rs 20,000, whereas no Dalit household reported an income above Rs 20,000.

The graphic representation of the frequency distribution of per capita incomes (using kernel density plots) of Dalits and Others in Appendix Figures A1 to A8 makes the inter-group differences in income distribution very obvious. The kernel density plots of per capita income of Dalits and Others show the most overlap in Kothapalle and the least overlap in 25 F Gulabewala.

Between-Group Inequality

To identify the role of inter-group inequality in observed total inequality, we have attempted a standard decomposition of inequality by population sub-group using the generalized entropy measure GE (α) with $\alpha = 2$, which corresponds to half of the squared coefficient of variation (Litchfield 1999). With this measure, total observed inequality can be decomposed into a sum of within-group (I_w) and between-group inequality (I_b) components:

$$I = I_w + I_b$$

The within-group inequality measure is the weighted sum of inequality of income within each sub-group, the weights being relative population shares and income shares. The between-group inequality measure is calculated by assigning the mean income of each sub-group to all members of that sub-

TABLE 14 *Estimates of inequality decomposition (within-group and between-group components of inequality) by caste group using GE (2) measure of inequality, Andhra Pradesh villages*

	Ananthavaram	Bukkacherla	Kothapalle
Dalit	0.0539	0.0186	0.1096
Scheduled Tribe	0.0009	–	0.0000
Muslim	0.0008	0.0005	0.0000
OBC	0.0376	0.0981	0.0616
Other Caste Hindu	2.4478	1.6676	7.7464
(a) Total within-group inequality	2.5412	1.7847	7.9176
(b) Between-group inequality	0.3177	0.0606	0.1456
Total inequality (a+b)	2.8589	1.8453	8.0632
Maximum between-group inequality (ELMO)	0.5918	0.3579	0.4836
Between-group inequality as a percentage of maximum between-group inequality	53.7	16.9	30.1
Between-group inequality as a percentage of total inequality	11.1	3.3	1.8

TABLE 15 *Estimates of inequality decomposition (within-group and between-group components of inequality) by caste group using GE (2) measure of inequality, Uttar Pradesh villages*

	Harevli	Mahatwar
Dalit	0.0808	0.1148
Muslim	0.0084	
OBC	0.1752	0.9282
Other Caste Hindu	1.7383	0.4077
(a) Total within-group inequality	2.0026	1.4507
(b) Between-group inequality	0.3169	0.2612
Total inequality (a+b)	2.3195	1.7119
Maximum between-group inequality (ELMO)	0.6337	0.9163
Between-group inequality as a percentage of ELMO between- group inequality	50.0	28.5
Between-group inequality as a percentage of total inequality	13.7	15.3

TABLE 16 *Estimates of inequality decomposition (within-group and between-group components of inequality) by caste group using GE (2) measure of inequality, Maharashtra and Rajasthan villages*

	Warwat Khanderao	Nimshirgaon	25 F Gulabewala
Dalit	0.0125	0.0913	0.0049
Muslim	0.0764	0.0009	–
Nomadic Tribe	0.0507	0.0118	–
OBC	4.2799	0.0036	4.2271
Jain	–	1.1672	–
Other Caste Hindu	–	0.2907	0.0049
(a) Total within-group inequality	4.4195	1.5654	4.2370
(b) Between-group inequality	0.0648	0.0986	0.5361
Total inequality (a+b)	4.4843	1.6640	4.7730
Maximum between-group inequality (ELMO)	0.2700	0.3763	0.5815
Between-group inequality as a percentage of ELMO between-group inequality	24.0	26.2	92.2
Between-group inequality as a percentage of total inequality	1.4	5.9	11.2

group and then computing a measure of inequality (ibid.). We have followed this decomposition method to calculate between-group and within-group inequality for each village. We have also calculated maximum between-group inequality as recommended by ELMO (2008) and identified observed between-group inequality as a share of the estimated maximum value. For the decomposition exercise, we have not used individual castes but social (caste-cum-religion) groups specific to each village. The results are reported in Tables 14, 15 and 16.

For Ananthavaram village, we used five sub-groups: Scheduled Castes (SCs) or Dalits, Scheduled Tribes (STs), Muslims, Other Backward Classes (OBCs) and Other Caste Hindus. The decomposition exercise shows that within-group inequality was least among ST and Muslim households (only a few of the latter were present), followed by OBC and Dalit households. Not surprisingly, within-group inequality was highest among Other Caste Hindu households. The between-group component amounted to 11 per cent of total inequality in the village. However, using the ELMO approach, it is observed that within-group inequality was 53.7 per cent of maximum between-group inequality.

In both Bukkacherla and Kothapalle villages, within-group inequality was highest for Other Caste Hindus. In Kothapalle, between-group inequality accounted for less than 2 per cent of inequality using the conventional approach, but as much as 30 per cent of maximum between-group inequality.

In Mahatwar village, within-group inequality was higher among OBCs than Other Caste Hindus (few in number) and SC households. In Harevli, within-group inequality was very low among Muslims, followed by Dalits, and highest among Other Caste Hindus.

By contrast, between-group inequality was as high as 92 per cent of the maximum value in 25 F Gulabewala village. As discussed earlier, the income distribution of Dalit households and Others (mainly Jat Sikhs, classified as OBCs) in this village had a large non-overlapping section. While within-group inequality among OBCs was undoubtedly the biggest contributor to aggregate income inequality here, nevertheless, the ELMO criterion indicates that between-group inequality should be a matter of serious concern. There was both high income inequality and close overlap between social and economic status in this village: the Dalit households were landless and survived on low incomes from agricultural labour, whereas the OBC (Jat Sikh) households were cultivators with sizeable landholdings and high incomes.

Nimshirgaon village in Maharashtra had the highest number of sub-groups (Dalits, Muslims, Nomadic Tribes, OBCs, Jains and Other Caste Hindus), with within-group inequality being highest among Jain households, followed by Other Caste Hindus. In Warwat Khanderao, the biggest contribution to aggregate inequality was made by within-group inequality among OBCs. In both Warwat Khanderao and Nimshirgaon, the between-group component was around a quarter of the maximum value.

Concluding Remarks

The literature on income inequality in India is thin as there are very few household income surveys. An earlier study by us of income inequality across households in eight villages in India showed extremely high levels of inequality, with the Gini coefficient for per capita income ranging from 0.491 in Nimshirgaon village in Maharashtra, to 0.686 in 25 F Gulabewala village in Rajasthan. There is also a growing body of evidence on the persistence of caste discrimination in rural India. In this context, in this essay, we have used data on household incomes from a set of eight village studies to examine the nature of between-group income inequality, focusing on differences between Scheduled Caste or Dalit households and Others.

The analysis shows that, first, Dalit households are under-represented in the top income quintile in all villages but one, and over-represented in the lower quintiles. Secondly, the frequency distribution of incomes for Dalits versus Others reveals distinct non-overlapping segments. Thirdly, the contribution of between-group inequality to total inequality ranges from 1 to 14 per cent, using the conventional decomposition of GE (2). However, using the ELMO method, between-group inequality is more than 50 per cent of its maximum value in three villages.

While the story of each village is different, there are two general observations we wish to make. First, the three villages with the highest levels of aggregate income inequality – Harevli in western Uttar Pradesh, Ananthavaram in coastal Andhra Pradesh and 25 F Gulabewala in western Rajasthan – are also the villages with the highest contribution of between-group inequality; and all three are canal-irrigated villages of relatively high agricultural productivity. In other words, the more prosperous agricultural villages are characterized by high income inequality as well as marked caste segregation.

Secondly, the size of the Dalit population (or population dominance) in a village does not show any simple relation with the degree of inter-group inequality. Of the two Dalit-majority villages, one, 25 F Gulabewala, shows the highest between-group inequality (using the ELMO approach), and the other, Mahatwar, shows relatively low between-group inequality.

Our research suggests that not only is income inequality very high in village India, but that caste still matters. We need further research on the specific ways in which caste discrimination affects income generation in contemporary rural India.

This article first appeared in *Review of Agrarian Studies*, vol. 1, no. 2, 2011.

References

Azam, M. and Shariff, A. (2009), 'Income Inequality in Rural India: Decomposing the Gini by Incomes Sources', available at http://papers.ssrn.com/sol3/papers.cfm?abstract_id=1433105, viewed on 12 April 2010.

Bakshi, Aparajita (2010), 'Household Incomes in Rural India', unpublished Ph.D. thesis submitted to University of Calcutta, Kolkata.

Borooah, Vani K. (2005), 'Caste, Inequality, and Poverty in India', *Review of Development Economics*, vol. 9, no. 3, pp. 399–414.

Chen, Chau-Nan, Tsaur, Tien-Wang and Rhai, Tong-Shieng (1982), 'The Gini Coefficient and Negative Income', *Oxford Economic Papers*, vol. 34, no. 3, pp. 473–78.

Desai, S., Dubey, A., Joshi, B.L., Sen, M., Sharif, A. and Vanneman, R. (2010), *Human Development in India: Challenges for a Society in Transition*, Oxford University Press, Delhi.

Deshpande, Ashwini (2000), 'Does Caste Still Define Disparity? A Look at Inequality in Kerala, India', *American Economic Review*, vol. 90, no. 2, May.

Deshpande, Ashwini (2011), *The Grammar of Caste*, Oxford University Press, Delhi.

Elbers, C., Lanjouw, P., Mistiaen, J. A. and Ozler, B. (ELMO) (2008), 'Reinterpreting Between-Group Inequality', *Journal of Economic Inequality*, 6, pp. 231–45.

Foundation for Agrarian Studies, *Project on Agrarian Relations in India (PARI)*, available at www.agrarianstudies.org.

Jayadev, Arjun and Reddy, Sanjay G. (2011), 'Inequalities Between Groups: Theory and Empirics', *World Development*, vol. 39, no. 2, pp. 159–73.

Kanbur, Ravi (2006), 'The Policy Significance of Inequality Decompositions', *Journal of Economic Inequality*, vol. 4, no. 3, pp. 367–74.

Kijima, Y. (2006), 'Caste and Tribe Inequality: Evidence from India 1983–1999', *Economic Development and Cultural Change*, vol. 54, no. 2, pp. 369–404.

Lanjouw, Peter and Rao, V. (2011), 'Revisiting Between Group Inequality Measurement: An Application to the Dynamics of Caste in Two Indian Villages', *World Development*, vol. 39, no. 2, pp. 173–87.

Litchfield, Julie A. (1999), 'Inequality: Methods and Tools', available at www.worldbank.org/poverty/inequal/index.htm.

Milanovic, Branko (2002), 'True World Income Distribution, 1988 and 1993: First Calculation Based on Household Surveys Alone', *The Economic Journal*, vol. 112, no. 476, pp. 51–92.

Palma, Jose Gabriel (2006), 'Globalizing Inequality: "Centrifugal" and "Centripetal" Forces at Work', UN DESA working paper no. 35, September; available at http://secint24.un.org/esa/desa/papers/2006/wp35_2006.pdf, viewed on 30 June 2009.

Ramachandran, V.K., Rawal, Vikas and Swaminathan, Madhura (2010), *Socio-Economic Survey of Three Villages in Andhra Pradesh: A Study of Agrarian Relations*, Tulika Books, New Delhi.

Saggar, M. and Pan, I. (1994), 'SCs and STs in Eastern India: Poverty and Inequality Estimates', *Economic and Political Weekly*, vol. 29, no. 10, 5 March.

Swaminathan, Madhura and Rawal, Vikas (2011), 'Is India Really a Country of Low Income-Inequality? Observations from Eight Villages', *Review of Agrarian Studies,* vol. 1, no. 1; available at www.ras.org.in.

Thorat, S. (2007), 'Human Poverty and Socially Disadvantaged Groups', UNDP India Discussion Paper Series, January.

Thorat, S. (2009), *Dalits in India: Search for a Common Destiny*, Sage Publications, New Delhi.

Thorat, S. and Mahamallik, M. (2007), 'Chronic Poverty and Socially Disadvantaged Groups: Analysis of Causes and Remedies', Chronic Poverty Research Centre working paper 33; available at http://www.chronicpoverty.org/uploads/publication_files/CPRC-IIPA_33.pdf.

Vanneman, R. and Dubey, A. (2010), 'Horizontal and Vertical Inequalities in India', paper prepared for the Luxembourg Income Study, Luxembourg, 28–30 June; available at http://www.lisproject.org/conference/papers/vanneman-dubey.pdf.

FIGURE A1 *Kernel density plots of per capita incomes for persons belonging to Dalit and Other households, Ananthavaram, Andhra Pradesh*

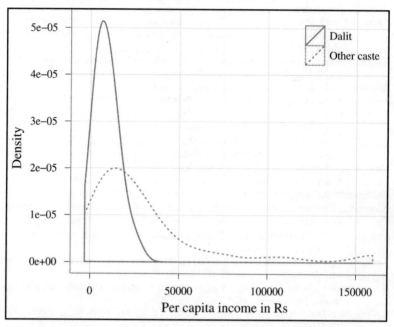

FIGURE A2 *Kernel density plots of per capita incomes for persons belonging to Dalit and Other households, Bukkacherla, Andhra Pradesh*

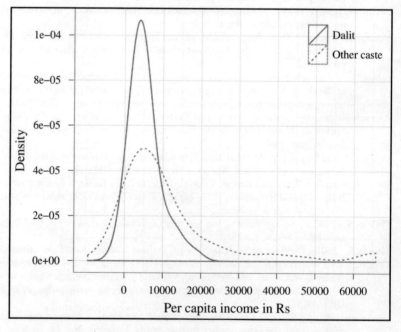

FIGURE A3   *Kernel density plots of per capita incomes for persons belonging to Dalit and Other households, Kothapalle, Andhra Pradesh*

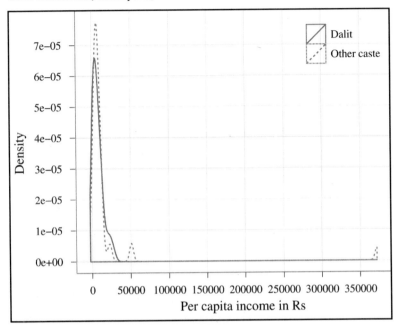

FIGURE A4   *Kernel density plots of per capita incomes for persons belonging to Dalit and Other households, Harevli, Uttar Pradesh*

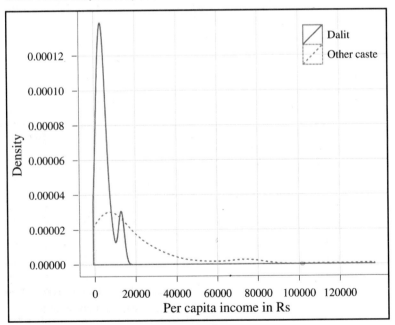

FIGURE A5   *Kernel density plots of per capita incomes for persons belonging to Dalit and Other households, Mahatwar, Uttar Pradesh*

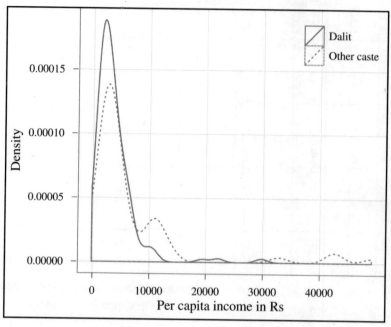

FIGURE A6   *Kernel density plots of per capita incomes for persons belonging to Dalit and Other households, Warwat Khanderao, Maharashtra*

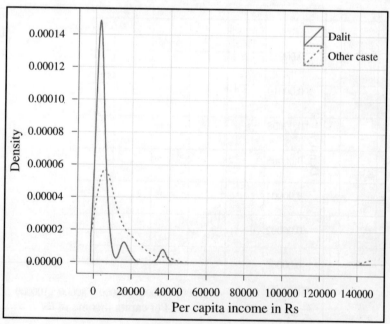

FIGURE A7 *Kernel density plots of per capita incomes for persons belonging to Dalit and Other households, Nimshirgaon, Maharashtra*

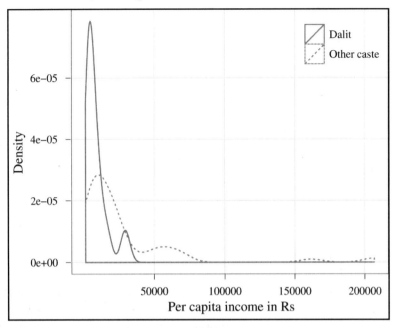

FIGURE A8 *Kernel density plots of per capita incomes for persons belonging to Dalit and Other households, 25 F Gulabewala, Rajasthan*

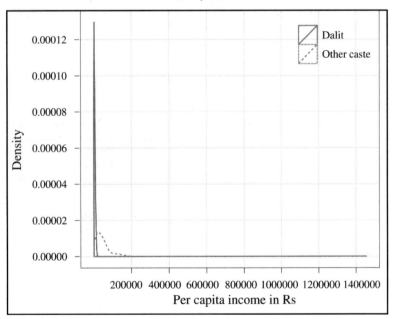

Hired Manual Workers

A Note

V.K. Ramachandran, Niladri Sekhar Dhar, Navpreet Kaur

This note deals with aspects of the employment gained by Dalit manual worker households. Its objectives are, first, to provide some aggregates from household-level data collected through village surveys and from unit-level data collected through the National Sample Survey (as part of the Rural Labour Enquiry); and, secondly, to report some initial results from an examination of these aggregates.

For purposes of this note, a manual worker household is defined as one that derives at least 50 per cent of its income from earnings from hired labour.

In general, manual workers constitute the largest single class in any village, generally over a quarter of all households and often over 40 per cent of all households (see Table 1). In villages where differentiation (in respect of de-peasantization) is relatively low, all classes of the peasantry taken together may outnumber manual workers, while in others, where differentiation is high, manual workers may well outnumber the whole peasantry. In both such cases, manual workers are the largest single class in the village. In our experience, the only villages in which we can envisage a systematic outnumbering

TABLE 1 *Number and proportion of manual worker households, study villages, 2006–08*

Village (State)	Total number of households	Number of manual worker households	(3) as a proportion of (2) (in per cent)
(1)	(2)	(3)	(4)
Ananthavaram (Andhra Pradesh)	665	208	31
Bukkacherla (Andhra Pradesh)	292	71	24
Kothapalle (Andhra Pradesh)	370	95	26
Harevli (Uttar Pradesh)	115	46	40
Mahatwar (Uttar Pradesh)	157	60	38
Nimshirgaon (Maharashtra)	757	340	45
Warwat Khanderao (Maharashtra)	250	72	29
25 F Gulabewala (Rajasthan)	204	100	49

Source: Survey data.

of manual workers by an impoverished small peasantry appear to be Adivasi villages in different parts of the country.

Agricultural and non-agricultural manual labour tasks are traditional village occupations, historically dominated by Dalit and other oppressed castes. In addition, hired manual work is the occupation of last resort within the village for those who have lost all other means of subsistence. For this reason, manual labour is most often the most caste-heterogeneous of all occupations in rural India (although, of course, the share of Other Castes among manual labour households is almost unfailingly lower than the share of Adivasis, Dalits or Backward Class households).

The representation of different castes in the class of manual workers can be seen in the all-India data (Tables 2 and 3) and in the village-level data (Table 4). The all-India data are very interesting in this respect. First, in the Rural Labour Enquiry data, the share of male Dalit workers in all male workers in rural labour households was consistently higher than 25 per cent (other than in Maharashtra, where it was still high, at 23 per cent). The combined share of Scheduled Tribe (ST) and Scheduled Caste (SC) workers was higher still, particularly in States such as Madhya Pradesh, Chhattisgarh,

TABLE 2 *Distribution of male workers in rural labour households, by social group, States of India, 2004–05* in per cent

State	Adivasi	Dalit	OBC	Other
Andhra Pradesh	9	35	41	15
Assam	10	14	26	50
Bihar	1	45	48	7
Chhattisgarh	30	24	45	1
Gujarat	26	26	37	11
Haryana	0	77	18	5
Himachal Pradesh	3	60	0	37
Jharkhand	34	30	27	9
Karnataka	11	29	37	22
Kerala	9	29	41	21
Madhya Pradesh	38	27	30	5
Maharashtra	19	23	38	21
Orissa	33	31	29	7
Punjab	0	74	19	6
Rajasthan	16	47	30	7
Tamil Nadu	1	40	59	0
Uttar Pradesh	1	48	42	10
Uttaranchal	1	50	34	15
West Bengal	13	38	3	46
All India	14	35	35	16

Source: Calculated from unit-level data, NSSO (2004–05).

TABLE 3 *Distribution of female workers in rural labour households, by social group, States of India, 2004–05* in per cent

State	Adivasi	Dalit	OBC	Other
Andhra Pradesh	11	34	44	11
Assam	9	18	39	35
Bihar	1	53	44	3
Chhattisgarh	29	22	48	1
Gujarat	34	28	30	8
Haryana	0	63	24	13
Himachal Pradesh	6	43	0	51
Jharkhand	42	16	32	10
Karnataka	13	30	38	20
Kerala	9	38	33	21
Madhya Pradesh	46	25	27	3
Maharashtra	18	24	38	20
Orissa	41	24	33	3
Punjab	0	67	28	4
Rajasthan	24	48	21	7
Tamil Nadu	1	42	56	0
Uttar Pradesh	1	61	32	7
Uttaranchal	0	61	26	14
West Bengal	31	37	2	30
All India	18	33	38	12

Source: Calculated from unit-level data, NSSO (2004–05).

Orissa, Gujarat, Maharashtra, Jharkhand and Rajasthan. Secondly, the share of male Dalit workers was highest, to the near-exclusion of others, in Punjab, Haryana and Himachal Pradesh (which collectively constitute the old Punjab, and where the representation of STs among male workers in rural labour households was almost negligible). Thirdly, in Bihar, Rajasthan, Uttar Pradesh, Uttaranchal and Tamil Nadu, the share of male Dalit workers was similarly high, between 45 and 50 per cent, though not as high as in the 'old Punjab' States. A striking feature of the data from these States is that – unlike the 'old Punjab' States – the share of male Other Backward Class (OBC) workers as a proportion of all male workers in rural labour households was also very high. This is an aspect of agrarian relations in these States that has important socio-political implications, particularly in a situation of declining opportunities for agricultural employment.

The foregoing conclusions broadly apply to the Rural Labour Enquiry data on women workers in rural labour households as well.

Manual worker households constitute a larger share of Dalit households than of Other Castes (Table 5). In the study villages, the proportion of Dalit manual worker households to all Dalit households ranged from 38

TABLE 4 *Manual worker households in specific social groups as a proportion of all manual worker households, study villages, 2005–08* in per cent

Village (State)	Dalit house-holds	Adivasi house-holds	Muslim house-holds	Nomadic tribe households	OBC house-holds	Other caste households
Ananthavaram (Andhra Pradesh)	53	19	8	0	17	4
Bukkacherla (Andhra Pradesh)	42	0	0	0	29	29
Kothapalle (Andhra Pradesh)	50	0	0	0	42	8
Harevli (Uttar Pradesh)	59	0	11	0	28	2
Mahatwar (Uttar Pradesh)	87	0	0	0	13	0
Nimshirgaon (Maharashtra)	49	0	13	1	8	28
Warwat Khanderao (Maharashtra)	19	0	28	22	31	0
25 F Gulabewala (Rajasthan)	98	0	0	0	2	0

Source: Survey data.

TABLE 5 *Manual worker households as a proportion of all households, Dalit and non-Dalit, study villages, 2005–08* in per cent

Village (State)	Non-Dalit manual worker households as a proportion of all non-Dalit households	Dalit manual worker households as a proportion of all Dalit households
Ananthavaram (Andhra Pradesh)	26	38
Bukkacherla (Andhra Pradesh)	18	53
Kothapalle (Andhra Pradesh)	19	39
Harevli (Uttar Pradesh)	28	68
Mahatwar (Uttar Pradesh)	13	56
Nimshirgaon (Maharashtra)	34	68
Warwat Khanderao (Maharashtra)	26	56
25 F Gulabewala (Rajasthan)	2	80

Source: Survey data.

per cent in Ananthavaram – where a substantial section of landless Dalit households, who would otherwise have worked as hired workers, leased in land and constituted a rack-rented poor peasantry – to 80 per cent in 25 F Gulabewala. Among non-Dalit households, the corresponding range was 2 per cent in 25 F Gulabewala to 34 per cent in the southern Maharashtra village, Nimshirgaon.

The representation of the Dalit rural masses in the class of manual workers far outstrips their representation in the population (Table 6). The data show that the share of Dalit manual worker households is always greater than the share of Dalit households in the population. In fact, in all but two villages, their representation in the class is more than 1.5 times their representation in the population.

Dalit workers are more than proportionately represented in the class of manual workers as a result both of traditional rural divisions of labour and modern processes of differentiation.

Perhaps the most salient indicator of the part played by labouring-out in the lives of Dalit households compared to Others emerges from a comparison of the income that Dalit households earn from wage-paid work as a proportion of total household income (Table 7). The income from wage work earned by Dalit households as a proportion of the total income of all Dalit households varied from 23 per cent (which is not low in absolute terms) in Kothapalle – a village beside a highway where there were opportunities for off-farm employment – to 62 per cent in 25 F Gulabewala in Sri Ganganagar district, Rajasthan – where economic inequality between Dalit households and Others was greatest. In very stark contrast, the corresponding figures for all Other (i.e. non-Dalit) households in the villages varied from 0 in 25 F Gulabewala to a 'high' of only 7 per cent in Warwat Khanderao in the Vidarbha region of Maharashtra. The figures reflect, of course, the very high incomes earned by a small section of the socially privileged rich (super-rich, in village terms).

A fuller understanding of employment patterns in the village requires that we examine data on how caste intervenes in determining the division of labour, and the actual deployment of labour time in agricultural and non-

TABLE 6 *Dalit households in the population and in the class of manual workers, study villages, 2005–08* in per cent

Village (State)	Dalit households as a proportion of all households	Dalit manual worker households as a proportion of all manual worker households	(3) / (2)
(1)	(2)	(3)	(4)
Ananthavaram (Andhra Pradesh)	43	53	1.2
Bukkacherla (Andhra Pradesh)	19	42	2.6
Kothapalle (Andhra Pradesh)	33	50	1.5
Harevli (Uttar Pradesh)	37	59	1.6
Mahatwar (Uttar Pradesh)	61	87	1.4
Nimshirgaon (Maharashtra)	33	49	1.5
Warwat Khanderao (Maharashtra)	10	19	1.9
25 F Gulabewala (Rajasthan)	60	98	1.6

Source: Survey data.

TABLE 7   *Income from manual work as proportion of total household income, by caste, study villages, 2006–08* in per cent

Village (State)	Income from manual work in agriculture as proportion of total income		Income from all manual work as proportion of total income	
	Dalit	Other households	Dalit	Other households
Ananthavaram (Andhra Pradesh)	31	0	38	2
Bukkacherla (Andhra Pradesh)	33	3	52	5
Kothapalle (Andhra Pradesh)	9	2	23	3
Harevli (Uttar Pradesh)	26	0	39	0
Mahatwar (Uttar Pradesh)	6	0	46	1
Nimshirgaon (Maharashtra)*	31	2	24	3
Warwat Khanderao (Maharashtra)**	28	5	32	7
25 F Gulabewala (Rajasthan)	26	0	62	0

Notes: * Other includes Jain and Other Caste Hindus.
  ** Other includes OBC.
Source: Survey data.

agricultural tasks. This is a task in which we are currently engaged.

It is a feature of the data that the share of Dalit manual worker households in all manual worker households and the share of person-days worked by Dalit workers in the total number of person-days worked in the village in agricultural tasks often differed. Aspects of the social division of labour in each village could, in general, explain this difference. We take, as example, the three Andhra Pradesh villages. In Ananthavaram in Guntur district (south coastal Andhra), where opportunities for non-agricultural employment were limited, Dalit households constituted 53 per cent of all manual labour households, but worked for about 68 per cent of the days worked by all manual worker households for wages in the village. In Bukkacherla in Anantapur district (Rayalaseema), Dalit manual worker households constituted about 42 per cent of all manual labour households, and worked for about 34 per cent of the labour days worked by all manual worker households for wages in the village. Drought conditions prevailed in this village and, as a result, opportunities for agricultural work were low, and many Dalit manual worker households worked in occupations such as prospecting for wells. In Kothapalle in Karimnagar district (north Telangana), the corresponding figures were 50 per cent and 45 per cent. This village was on a main highway, thus opening up the possibility of non-agricultural employment. It was also a village in which one significant village occupation, tapping toddy, was generally performed only by members of a specific (non-Dalit) caste.

Tables 8 and 9 show the number of days of paid employment obtained by male and female workers in manual worker households as computed from our village surveys. A caveat has to be entered here. The tables do not refer to the total number of days of all types of work undertaken by manual workers,

TABLE 8 *Average number of days of wage employment per male worker in agricultural and non-agricultural sectors, by social group, study villages, 2006–08*

Village	Agriculture				Non-agriculture				All tasks			
	Dalit	OBC	Other Caste	All	Dalit	OBC	Other Caste	All	Dalit	OBC	Other Caste	All
Ananthavaram (Andhra Pradesh)	69	64	32	63	23	26	35	34	92	90	67	97
Bukkacherla (Andhra Pradesh)	65	85	57	70	53	3	71	40	118	88	128	110
Kothapalle (Andhra Pradesh)	18	26	10	22	30	71	91	54	48	97	101	76
Harevli (Uttar Pradesh)	108	122	NA	108	15	17	NA	22	123	139	NA	130
Mahatwar (Uttar Pradesh)	5	2	NA	4	148	137	NA	147	153	139	NA	151
Nimshirgaon (Maharashtra)*	56	NA	105	67	47	NA	32	37	103	NA	137	104
Warwat Khanderao (Maharashtra)	74	67	NA	66	13	9	NA	19	87	76	NA	85
25 F Gulabewala (Rajasthan)**	103	NA	NA	103	8	NA	NA	8	111	NA	NA	111

Notes: * Jain households are included in Other Caste households.
** Jat Sikhs are included in OBC households.

Source: Survey data.

TABLE 9   *Average number of days of wage employment per female worker in agricultural and non-agricultural sectors, by social group, study villages, 2006–08*

Village	Agriculture				Non-agriculture				All tasks			
	Dalit	OBC	Other Caste	All	Dalit	OBC	Other Caste	All	Dalit	OBC	Other Caste	All
Ananthavaram (Andhra Pradesh)	74	74	0	69	0	0	300	4	74	74	300	73
Bukkacherla (Andhra Pradesh)	68	85	78	78	4	1	0	2	72	86	78	80
Kothapalle (Andhra Pradesh)	71	96	55	84	16	20	0	17	87	116	55	101
Harevli (Uttar Pradesh)	85	55	NA	70	9	0	NA	5	94	55	NA	75
Mahatwar (Uttar Pradesh)	26	10	NA	25	14	120	NA	21	40	130	NA	46
Nimshirgaon (Maharashtra)*	113	NA	98	113	0	NA	1	0	113	NA	99	113
Warwat Khanderao (Maharashtra)	94	91	NA	99	2	0	NA	4	96	91	NA	103
25 F Gulabewala (Rajasthan)**	52	NA	NA	52	0	NA	NA	0	52	NA	NA	52

Notes: * Jain households are included in Other Caste households.
      ** Jat Sikhs are included in OBC households.

Source: Survey data.

but only to the days of work for which a worker receives a wage or wage-like payment. In particular, it does not include the time spent on self-employment in animal husbandry, in forms of other small-scale non-farm employment, in fuel or water collection, in collecting forest produce, in productive activity on homesteads, or other such activity.

Tables 10 and 11 show the corresponding official data from the Rural Labour Enquiry on the number of days of wage employment obtained by male and female workers in rural labour households.

The first conclusion from the data is that the number of days of wage-paid employment actually available to manual workers in the study villages is very low. The average number of days of employment available to a male worker in a manual worker family in the villages we surveyed was about 104 days, and for a woman, 87 days. In each village the proportion of workers who received more than 180 days of employment in a year was also low, with an average of 14 per cent. This figure was much lower for women, ranging from 0 in one village to a high of only 10 per cent.

The second observation is that the official data on the number of days

TABLE 10 *Average number of days of wage employment of male workers of rural labour households, by land ownership status and social group, 2004–05* 8-hour days

State	Landless		With owned land	
	Dalit	*Other*	*Dalit*	*Other*
Andhra Pradesh	240	250	166	145
Assam	251	259	243	254
Bihar	294	317	254	199
Chhattisgarh	301	73	179	294
Gujarat	241	207	296	153
Haryana	258	217	193	46
Himachal Pradesh	225	232	190	152
Jharkhand	300	309	203	234
Karnataka	289	291	210	196
Kerala	190	163	182	131
Madhya Pradesh	226	266	169	137
Maharashtra	222	200	165	158
Orissa	269	229	227	182
Punjab	224	203	143	83
Rajasthan	242	178	246	210
Tamil Nadu	205	15	144	265
Uttar Pradesh	239	202	192	124
Uttaranchal	287	251	241	228
West Bengal	236	255	200	204
All India	250	217	203	179

Source: Calculated from unit-level data, NSSO (2004–05).

TABLE 11 *Average number of days of wage employment of female workers of rural labour households, by land ownership status and social group, 2004–05* 8-hour days

State	Landless		With owned land	
	Dalit	Other	Dalit	Other
Andhra Pradesh	228	207	195	157
Assam	289	262	154	221
Bihar	243	309	270	
Chhattisgarh	282	287	140	240
Gujarat	240	205	201	134
Haryana	154	169		
Himachal Pradesh	143	90	29	9
Jharkhand	243	186	90	205
Karnataka	245	238	216	177
Kerala	159	190	123	105
Madhya Pradesh	203	207	147	53
Maharashtra	230	218	169	179
Orissa	234	293	202	212
Punjab	142	67		
Rajasthan	170	209	156	101
Tamil Nadu	201	214	131	313
Uttar Pradesh	232	180	123	
Uttaranchal	165	209	55	20
West Bengal	182	140	197	98
All India	210	205	154	150

Source: Calculated from unit-level data, NSSO (2004–05).

of paid employment obtained by workers constitutes an almost ludicrous exaggeration. Recent work on employment in rural India has noted that

> there are not good enough macro-data on the number of days of employment, agricultural and non-agricultural, per worker per year in India. Not only do the data from the Rural Labour Enquiries appear intuitively to be incorrect, but it is also well recognized that employment data from micro-studies show consistently lower volumes of employment than Rural Labour Enquiry data. There remain major conceptual, definitional and methodological reasons for this divergence; such divergence is also caused by the simple distortion of official statistical information.[1]

A third observation is that while Dalits are, as we have seen, the caste group most represented in the class of manual workers, within this class, Dalits do not necessarily get fewer days of employment per person in a year than workers of Other Castes (Tables 8 and 9).

[1] A more recent critique of the sources of data on agricultural employment is in Dhar (2012).

TABLE 12 *Proportion of Dalit female workers in manual worker households who worked solely at agricultural wage employment, non-agricultural wage employment and both, study villages, 2006–08* in per cent

Village (State)	Only agriculture	Only non-agriculture	Both	Total
Ananthavaram (Andhra Pradesh)	100	0	0	100
Bukkacherla (Andhra Pradesh)	87	7	7	100
Kothapalle (Andhra Pradesh)	89	5	5	100
Harevli (Uttar Pradesh)	94	0	6	100
Mahatwar (Uttar Pradesh)	95	4	1	100
Nimshirgaon (Maharashtra)	100	0	0	100
Warwat Khanderao (Maharashtra)	89	0	12	100
25 F Gulabewala (Rajasthan)	100	0	0	100

Source: Survey data.

TABLE 13 *Proportion of Dalit male workers in manual worker households who worked solely at agricultural wage employment, non-agricultural wage employment and both, study villages, 2006–08* in per cent

Village	Only agriculture	Only non-agriculture	Both	Total
Ananthavaram (Andhra Pradesh)	76	9	15	100
Bukkacherla (Andhra Pradesh)	42	18	42	100
Kothapalle (Andhra Pradesh)	54	27	20	100
Harevli (Uttar Pradesh)	74	4	22	100
Mahatwar (Uttar Pradesh)	5	77	18	100
Nimshirgaon (Maharashtra)	63	26	10	100
Warwat Khanderao (Maharashtra)	44	8	48	100
25 F Gulabewala (Rajasthan)	69	0	31	100

Source: Survey data.

An extraordinary feature of our village data is the extent to which *agriculture* dominates the wage-work done by Dalit women workers in manual labour households (Table 12). In the eight villages described in the table, the proportion of Dalit women workers in manual worker households who worked solely at agricultural tasks ranged between 87 and 100 per cent. For Dalit men workers, the picture was mixed (Table 13), and dependent on the opportunities for non-agricultural work in each village. The share varied from a high of 76 per cent in Ananthavaram village in south coastal Andhra Pradesh, where opportunities for non-farm employment were few, to 5 per cent in Mahatwar (an outlier), where Dalit men workers were engaged in digging wells and in road construction.

The village-level data serve to support the conclusion that while the class of hired manual workers in rural India is relatively caste-heterogeneous, Dalit workers are the foremost and most characteristic members of this class.

Exclusion in Access to Basic Civic Amenities

Evidence from Fourteen Villages

Madhura Swaminathan and Shamsher Singh

It is well established that proper housing, sanitation and access to safe water are universal basic needs. In this essay, we examine deprivation in rural India in respect of some of these basic amenities, including housing, electricity, lavatories and drinking water. The data come from fourteen PARI (Project on Agrarian Relations in India) survey villages: three from Andhra Pradesh, two each from Uttar Pradesh, Maharashtra, Rajasthan and Madhya Pradesh, and three from Karnataka, all surveyed between 2005 and 2009.

In addition to deprivation, there can be *discrimination* in the access to basic amenities. Deprivation is experienced by specific individuals or households, but when several members of a group all experience similar deprivation, it is likely to be on account of some form of group discrimination or exclusion. Discrimination can take many forms (see Thorat 2010). It can be direct or active, such as when a Dalit woman is prevented from taking water from a particular source. It can also be passive or indirect, as for example if the street lights in a Dalit settlement are left broken. Indirect discrimination is often not recognized as such and is attributed to other factors, such as low income. For example, it may be argued that a house-to-house piped water system is not provided to Dalit households on account of their incapacity to pay a fee and not on account of their caste position. There are clearly problems with such an argument, one of which is that it begs the question as to why Dalit households have systematically lower incomes than other social groups. Secondly, it has to explain the obverse, that is, why members of another caste are able to enjoy better amenities at the same income level on account of belonging to a different group (living in an upper-caste neighbourhood with piped water, for example). In other words, if households at similar income levels belonging to different groups experience dissimilar deprivations, then there is very likely some form of group discrimination. Different types of direct and indirect discrimination – in the access to water, for example – have been at the core of Dalit struggles against untouchability.

Although our focus here is on contemporary deprivation, cumulative discrimination undoubtedly plays a role in a person's current economic and social status. To put it differently, it would be misleading to explain current outcomes based only on current incomes or current opportunities, as discrimination can leave an imprint on successive generations. This is very central to the discussion of housing and household amenities among Dalit households in rural India, given the historical (and continuing) separation of Dalit house-sites and homes from the main village.

This essay examines deprivation in respect of housing, and access to electricity, toilets and drinking water, across households in fourteen villages, with a special focus on deprivation among Scheduled Caste (SC) households. We also examine the relation between household incomes and observed deprivations in basic amenities, as well as the role of public intervention in mitigating group deprivation.

The specific variables examined are ownership of dwelling places, the condition or type of housing (as indicated by the material used for construction), limitation of living space (measured by the number of rooms and availability of homestead land), the existence of a separate cooking area or kitchen, the availability of electricity for domestic use, access to toilets, and access to a source of drinking water (the quality of the source and distance of the source from the dwelling).

Our discussion is based on data for Dalit households in relation to Other Caste households – that is, households other than Dalit, Adivasi or Muslim households – in each village. Of the survey villages for which data have been used here, two villages were predominantly Scheduled Tribe (ST) villages (Dungariya in Rajasthan and Badhar in Madhya Pradesh), and data for them were processed separately. Of the remaining twelve villages, ST households were present in four villages and Muslims in eight villages. It may be noted that since information was missing in some instances (especially on the question of separate kitchens), the number of responses is not the same in all the tables.

Extent of Deprivation
Housing
Ownership

In general, the large majority of households owned their dwelling places. Further, other than in three villages, the proportion of Dalit households that owned their dwellings was higher than the corresponding proportion among Other Caste households.[1] For example, in Ananthavaram, 88 per cent of Dalits owned their homes as compared to 80 per cent among Other households. In Siresandra, all Dalits owned their homes as compared to 96 per cent of Other households. As has been noted, these results reflect the near-absence of rented accommodation in the villages in general, and direct discrimination in respect of renting out houses to Dalits in particular (see Thorat 2009).

[1] This also shows up in data from the Census of India (2001).

TABLE 1 *Number and proportion of households that owned their houses, study villages, Dalit households and Other Caste Households*

Village (State)	Dalit households			Other Caste households			All households*	
	HHs	%	Total HHs	HHs	%	Total HHs	No.	%
Ananthavaram (Andhra Pradesh)	247	88	280	256	80	319	550	83
Bukkacherla (Andhra Pradesh)	54	93	58	181	80	226	241	83
Kothapalle (Andhra Pradesh)	104	88	118	193	81	237	308	83
Harevli (Uttar Pradesh)	38	95	40	54	95	57	105	95
Mahatwar (Uttar Pradesh)	95	100	95	63	100	63	158	100
Nimshirgaon (Maharashtra)	226	92	247	438	93	473	701	91
Warwat Khanderao (Maharashtra)	24	96	25	162	95	171	237	95
25 F Gulabewala (Rajasthan)	103	84	123	76	94	81	179	88
Gharsondi (Madhya Pradesh)	27	100	27	184	96	191	251	95
Alabujanahalli (Karnataka)	30	91	33	197	98	202	227	97
Siresandra (Karnataka)	26	100	26	49	96	51	75	97
Zhapur (Karnataka)	39	87	45	39	93	42	96	91
All	1013	91	1117	1892	90	2113	3128	90

Note: *All refers to all households in the village, not just Scheduled Caste and Other Caste households. In Alabujanahalli and Zhapur, the number of Dalit households without their own houses was small (three and six households, respectively).
HHs refer to households in all the tables.

Source: Survey data.

An exception to this pattern was the village of 25 F Gulabewala in the Gang Canal region of Rajasthan, where only 84 per cent of Dalit (Majhabi Sikh) households owned their homes. These Majhabi households were mainly tenant-labourer (*siri*) households that lived on land and in houses provided by their landlord-employers. In most cases, these houses were non-permanent and old, and abandoned by the landlords, who had shifted to new houses.

Quality of Housing

Different aspects of housing together determine its overall quality. These include, among other things, the space per person or family; appropriate protection against heat, cold, damp, noise, fire, and disease-carrying animals and insects; adequate sanitary and washing facilities; ventilation, cooking and storage facilities; and a minimum degree of privacy (ILO 1961).

In India, both the Census and National Sample Survey Organization (NSSO) identify types of housing based on the construction material used. The Census distinguishes between permanent, semi-permanent and temporary (serviceable temporary and non-serviceable temporary) housing, whereas the NSSO classifies houses as *pucca*, *katcha* (unserviceable *katcha* and serviceable *katcha*) and semi-*pucca* structures. In addition to this, both agencies record observations about the condition of the structure (such as 'good', 'satisfactory/liveable' and 'bad/dilapidated'). Both the Census and NSSO classifications are based on the material used for construction of the house. Specifically, a house with roof and walls made of permanent or *pucca* materials is defined as a *pucca* house;[2] a house with either roof or walls made of temporary material is termed a semi-*pucca* house;[3] and a house with both roof and walls made of temporary materials is termed a *katcha* house. All structures made with thatch, grass, leaves, bamboo, plastic or polythene are termed 'unserviceable temporary'.

These definitions are such that all *pucca* or permanent houses do not meet all the health and safety norms as per the requirements of the International Labour Organization (ILO). Nevertheless, for purposes of this essay, we have used norms for housing based on the Census and NSSO definitions.

The proportion of Dalit households with *katcha* huts was above 20 per cent in five of the study villages, and above 50 per cent in two villages (Ananthavaram and 25 F Gulabewala). Only in Zhapur there was no Dalit household living in a *katcha* house. In contrast, the proportion of Other households with *katcha* homes ranged from 0 in Zhapur and Siresandra, to 8 per cent in Ananthavaram and Gharsondi. Thus, in no village did more than 8 per cent of Other households live in *katcha* structures.

More than 80 per cent of Dalit households lived in *pucca* structures in only four villages: Bukkacherla, Kothapalle, Siresandra and Zhapur. In Zhapur village in Gulbarga district of Karnataka, where almost 100 per cent of Dalit houses were *pucca*, 60 per cent of Dalit households received government aid for the houses in which they lived. Another factor contributing to *pucca* housing in Zhapur was the easy availability of stone in the area. In Kothapalle village, where 90 per cent of Dalit households owned *pucca* structures, one-third had benefited from a government scheme. A similar situation prevailed in Siresandra and Alabujanahalli, where almost 50 per cent of Dalit households with *pucca* houses had received some government aid

---

[2] *Pucca* materials include cement, concrete, oven-burnt bricks, hollow cement or ash bricks, stone, stone blocks, jack boards (cement-plastered reeds), iron, zinc or other metal sheets, timber, tiles, slate, corrugated iron, asbestos cement sheet, veneer, plywood, artificial wood of synthetic material, and polyvinyl chloride (PVC) material.

[3] Non-*pucca* materials include unburnt bricks, bamboo, mud, grass, leaves, reeds thatch, polythene and plastic.

TABLE 2 *Number and proportion of households by type of house, study villages, Dalit households and Other Caste households*

Village (State)	Dalit households								Other Caste households								All households					
	Katcha		Pucca		Semi-pucca		Total HHs		Katcha		Pucca		Semi-pucca		Total HHs		Katcha		Pucca		Semi-pucca	
	HHs	%	HHs	%	HHs	%			HHs	%	HHs	%	HHs	%			HHs	%	HHs	%	HHs	%
Ananthavaram (Andhra Pradesh)	140	50	65	23	77	27	282		27	8	282	88	10	3	319		204	31	365	55	94	14
Bukkacherla (Andhra Pradesh)	3	5	52	90	3	5	58		8	4	108	49	105	48	221		11	4	165	57	111	39
Kothapalle (Andhra Pradesh)	6	5	106	90	6	5	118		4	2	207	88	25	11	236		19	5	319	86	32	9
Harevli (Uttar Pradesh)	12	31	20	51	7	18	39		3	5	42	75	11	20	56		21	20	64	60	22	21
Mahatwar (Uttar Pradesh)	23	24	55	59	16	17	94		1	2	57	90	5	8	63		24	15	112	71	21	13
Nimshirgaon (Maharashtra)	15	6	167	68	62	25	247		19	5	384	82	57	13	473		34	4	579	76	138	18
Warwat Khanderao (Maharashtra)	2	8	9	36	14	56	25		2	1	89	53	76	46	167		9	4	117	48	118	48
25F Gulabewala (Rajasthan)	66	54	34	28	23	19	123		2	3	73	91	5	6	80		68	33	107	53	28	14
Gharsondi (Madhya Pradesh)	6	22	18	67	3	11	27		16	8	148	77	28	15	192		53	20	178	67	34	13
Alabujanahalli (Karnataka)	5	14	25	69	6	17	36		9	4	180	87	19	9	208		14	6	205	84	25	10
Siresandra (Karnataka)	1	4	23	88	2	8	26		0	0	46	90	5	10	51		1	1	69	90	7	9
Zhapur (Karnataka)	0	0	45	100	0	0	45		0	0	41	98	1	2	42		0	0	108	99	1	1
All	279	25	619	55	219	20	1120		91	4	1657	79	347	16	2108		458	13	2388	68	631	18

Source: Survey data.

for construction. Even in villages where the majority of Dalit households did not have *pucca* structures, it is clear that those who did have *pucca* houses had gained from government intervention. In 25 F Gulabewala, for example, of the thirty-four Dalit households with *pucca* houses, thirty had received government assistance for construction.

Availability of Space

The quality of housing is not only a function of the durability of material used in construction, but also of living space available to its residents. Crowding not only hampers the health of residents, especially children, but also provides no privacy (Thorat 2009). As we do not have data on floor area of houses, to get some idea of cramped housing space, we report here the proportion of households living in single-room structures (excluding storeroom and lavatory, if any).

Table 3 shows that the proportion of Dalit households living in single-

TABLE 3   *Number and proportion of households living in single-room structures, study villages, Dalit households and Other Caste households*

Village (State)	Dalit households			Other Caste households			All households	
	HHs	%	Total HHs	No.	%	Total HHs	HHs	%
Ananthavaram (Andhra Pradesh)	151	54	280	93	30	311	295	45
Bukkacherla (Andhra Pradesh)	16	28	58	62	28	219	80	28
Kothapalle (Andhra Pradesh)	46	39	117	68	29	236	122	34
Harevli (Uttar Pradesh)	25	68	37	7	13	54	40	39
Mahatwar (Uttar Pradesh)	11	12	90	12	20	60	23	15
Nimshirgaon (Maharashtra)	72	29	247	121	26	473	203	26
Warwat Khanderao (Maharashtra)	14	58	24	46	28	166	70	29
25F Gulabewala (Rajasthan)	33	27	123	2	3	78	35	17
Gharsondi (Madhya Pradesh)	2	7	27	16	8	192	32	12
Alabujanahalli (Karnataka)	13	38	34	31	15	207	44	18
Siresandra (Karnataka)	9	41	22	14	29	49	23	32
Zhapur (Karnataka)	24	55	44	13	33	39	50	48
All	416	38	1103	485	23	2084	1017	30

Source: Survey data.

room structures was very high, ranging from 27 per cent in 25 F Gulabewala to 68 per cent in Harevli. The sharpest contrast was in Harevli: 13 per cent of Other Caste households lived in single-room houses and 68 per cent of Dalits lived in single-room houses. By contrast, among Other Caste households, the proportion of households with single-room structures ranged from 3 per cent in 25 F Gulabewala to 33 per cent in Zhapur.

As shown in Table 3, 38 per cent of Dalit households across twelve villages lived in single-room, congested houses, often accommodating newly married couples, parents, small children and old persons in the same room. There is clearly a problem of adequate living space among all households, but more so among Dalit households.

Homestead Land

Availability of homestead land is a critical issue in planning for better housing. It plays a crucial role in deciding a household's access to proper housing with all the basic household amenities within the homestead (including an adequate number of rooms, a separate kitchen or cooking space, space for storage, toilet and bathing facility). If a household has sufficient homestead land, it can potentially add to the living space and make provision for amenities such as toilets.

The village-level data show that in almost all the villages, Dalit households owned tiny plots of homestead land, and that the extent of homestead land owned by Dalits was much lower than the extent owned by Other Caste households.

Among Dalit households, the mean extent of homestead land ranged from 1,137 square feet in Siresandra, in Kolar district, Karnataka, to 3,292

TABLE 4 *Availability of homestead land, study villages, Dalit households and Other Caste households* in square feet

Village (State)	Dalit households	Other Caste households	All households
Ananthavaram (Andhra Pradesh)	1490	3652	2568
Bukkacherla (Andhra Pradesh)	2309	2803	2650
Kothapalle (Andhra Pradesh)	2674	4933	4092
Harevli (Uttar Pradesh)	1603	11252	6732
Mahatwar (Uttar Pradesh)	3292	6143	4402
Nimshirgaon (Maharshtra)	1784	2697	2270
Warwat Khanderao (Maharashtra)	1971	2398	2088
25F Gulabewala (Rajasthan)	1851	22426	10587
Alabujnahalli (Karnataka)	2649	3991	3787
Siresandra (Karnataka)	1137	3433	2709
Zhapur (Karnataka)	2134	1732	2245

Note: The area reported here is the actual extent of land, and not floor space.
Source: Survey data.

square feet in Mahatwar, in Ballia district, eastern Uttar Pradesh. In Mahatwar, Dalit households lived in an area that was separate from the main village settlement. The corresponding range for Other Caste households was 1,732 square feet in Zhapur village, Gulbarga district, Karnataka, to 22,426 square feet in 25 F Gulabewala, in the Gang Canal region of Rajasthan. Of the eleven villages for which data are provided in Table 4, it was only in Zhapur village that the average extent of homestead land for Dalit households exceeded the figure for Other Caste households.[4] This is because one Dalit household is an outlier and reported that it owned 21,780 sq feet of homestead land. If we exclude this household, the average extent of homestead land among Dalit households of Zhapur falls to 1,617 sq feet, which is lower than the average for Other Caste households.

Inequality in the ownership of homestead land was high in 25 F Gulabewala and Harevli. In 25 F Gulabewala, a Dalit household had, on average, 1,851 sq feet, as compared to 22,426 sq feet among Other Caste (Jat Sikh, in this case) households. Similarly, in Harevli village of western Uttar Pradesh, the average Dalit household had a total of 1,603 sq feet available as homestead land, while the average Other Caste household had 11,252 square feet. On a per person basis, this implies that a Dalit person lived within 272 sq feet in Harevli and 362 sq feet in 25 F Gulabewala. Dalit households in these two villages were extremely deprived in both absolute and relative terms.

Even in villages such as Bukkacherla in Anantapur district, Andhra Pradesh and Warwat Khanderao in Buldhana district, Maharashtra, where the gap in ownership of homestead land was not large as between Dalits and Other Castes, Dalit houses were segregated from other residences. Thus the problem for Dalit households remains one of acute shortage of space as well as continued segregation from the rest of the village population.

Separate Cooking Space or Kitchen

Separation of the cooking area from the living and sleeping areas is vital for avoiding health hazards. Taking eleven villages together, 61 per cent of Other Caste households reported a separate kitchen, whereas only 37 per cent of Dalit households reported the same (Table 5).[5] Alabujanahalli was an exception, both in respect of having the highest proportion of Dalit households living in houses that had separate kitchens among the eleven villages, and also in this proportion exceeding the corresponding proportion among Other Caste households. The latter may be explained by the fact that most Dalit houses in the village were newly constructed, while the Other Caste households lived in older constructions.

Our field experience indicates that, in practice, many households use the room termed as kitchen only to store utensils and other cooking material, and actually cook their meals in the open (in a courtyard or verandah), because

---

[4] Data on homestead land have not been processed for Gharsondi village.
[5] Data on this variable were not available for Ananthavaram village.

TABLE 5 *Number and proportion of households with separate kitchen, study villages, Dalit households and Other Caste households*

Village (State)	Dalit households			Other Caste households			All households	
	HHs	%	Total HHs	HHs	%	Total HHs	HHs	%
Bukkacherla (Andhra Pradesh)	16	30	54	103	51	201	123	47
Kothapalle (Andhra Pradesh)	16	28	58	70	34	205	88	32
Harevli (Uttar Pradesh)	8	22	37	36	67	54	48	47
Mahatwar (Uttar Pradesh)	28	31	91	29	48	61	57	38
Nimshirgaon (Maharashtra)	82	36	230	267	59	451	351	48
Warwat Khanderao (Maharashtra)	15	60	25	115	67	171	170	68
25F Gulabewala (Rajasthan)	21	18	117	68	87	78	89	46
Gharsondi (Madhya Pradesh)	14	52	27	109	59	186	134	53
Alabujanahalli (Karnataka)	30	91	33	174	84	208	204	85
Siresandra (Karnataka)	17	65	26	44	86	51	61	79
Zhapur (Karnataka)	25	56	45	19	49	39	51	49
All	272	37	743	1034	61	1705	1376	52

Note: Information on this variable was not collected in Ananthavaram.
Source: Survey data.

the main source of fuel for cooking is still either dung-cake or firewood, and these 'kitchens' lack proper ventilation. In other words, even households that have a separate kitchen do not use that space for cooking unless they use gas for cooking. As a result, the majority of households faced all the health hazards deriving from the absence of clean cooking fuel and lack of hygienic cooking space.

Electricity
The data show that, among Other Caste households, with the exception of the two villages in Uttar Pradesh, the large majority of households had electricity connections at home. Nevertheless, the coverage was not universal in even a single village (Table 6). Secondly, the proportion of Dalit households with no electricity in their homes generally exceeded the corresponding proportion among Other Caste households. Deprivation on this count was highest among Dalits in Harevli and Mahatwar (Uttar Pradesh), and 25 F Gulabewala village (Rajasthan). Thirdly, in villages such as Bukkacherla

TABLE 6   *Number and proportion of households with domestic electricity connection, study villages, Dalit households and Other Caste households*

Village (State)	Dalit households			Other Caste households			All households	
	HHs	%	Total HHs	HHs	%	Total HHs	HHs	%
Ananthavaram (Andhra Pradesh)	224	79	283	300	94	320	568	85
Bukkacherla (Andhra Pradesh)	55	95	58	199	88	226	261	89
Kothapalle (Andhra Pradesh)	100	85	118	221	93	237	333	90
Harevli (Uttar Pradesh)	4	10	40	32	56	57	39	35
Mahatwar (Uttar Pradesh)	43	45	95	39	62	63	82	52
Nimshirgaon (Maharashtra)	161	65	247	374	79	473	573	75
Warwat Khanderao (Maharashtra)	16	64	25	126	73	172	188	75
25 F Gulabewala (Rajasthan)	79	64	123	78	96	81	157	77
Gharsondi (Madhya Pradesh)	25	96	26	172	92	186	231	90
Alabujanahalli (Karnataka)	30	83	36	191	93	205	221	92
Siresandra (Karnataka)	26	100	26	50	98	51	76	99
Zhapur (Karnataka)	37	82	45	38	90	42	96	88
All	800	71	1122	1820	86	2113	2825	81

Note: All electricity connections, whether authorized or unauthorized, are included.
Source: Survey data.

and Gharsondi, where more than 90 per cent of Dalit households reported the use of electricity, the proportion of unauthorized electricity connections was as high as 50 per cent. In other words, even where the majority of Dalit households had electricity connections, a large section of them did not have regular, authorized connections. Lastly, a heartening exception was Siresandra village in Kolar district, where electricity had reached all Dalit homes and where all connections were authorized.

Toilets

India performs abominably in respect of the availability of toilets and proper sanitation in rural areas. Lack of proper sanitation is both an individual deprivation and one that affects entire communities or neighbourhoods, in terms of the hazard to public health. The absence of lavatories places a special burden on women, children and old people.

TABLE 7   *Number and proportion of households with access to toilet facilities, study villages, Dalit households and Other Caste households*

Village (State)	Dalit households			Other Caste households			All	
	HHs	%	Total HHs	HHs	%	Total HHs	HHs	%
Ananthavaram (Andhra Pradesh)	64	23	283	245	77	320	319	48
Bukkacherla (Andhra Pradesh)	12	21	58	34	15	226	47	16
Kothapalle (Andhra Pradesh)	47	40	117	106	45	237	157	42
Harevli (Uttar Pradesh)	2	5	40	33	58	57	38	34
Mahatwar (Uttar Pradesh)	3	3	95	9	14	63	12	8
Nimshirgaon (Maharashtra)	157	63	247	339	72	473	533	69
Warwat Khanderao (Maharashtra)	7	28	25	77	45	172	116	46
25F Gulabewala (Rajasthan)	95	77	123	78	96	81	173	85
Gharsondi (Madhya Pradesh)	6	22	27	108	57	189	117	45
Alabujanahalli (Karnataka)	7	19	36	117	57	206	124	51
Siresandra (Karnataka)	0	0	26	6	12	49	6	8
Zhapur (Karnataka)	0	0	45	0	0	42	1	1
All	400	36	1122	1152	54	2115	1643	47

Source: Survey data.

First, of all twelve villages, there was not one village where all the households had access to lavatories or toilets (whether public or private). Secondly, in all the villages, the use of toilets was lower among Dalit households than Other Caste households. In Siresandra and Zhapur villages of Karnataka, open defecation was the norm for all households. Of the two villages of Uttar Pradesh, open defecation was reported by 95 per cent of Dalit households in Harevli and 97 per cent in Mahatwar. In ten of the twelve villages surveyed, two-thirds or more of Dalit households had to defecate in the open. The only better performing village in this respect was 25 F Gulabewala: 77 per cent of Dalit households and 96 per cent of Jat Sikh households in this village reported using private toilets (even though many of the toilets in the houses of Dalits were *katcha* constructions).

Thirdly, as revealed in our interviews, members of landless Dalit households, women in particular, faced severe restrictions in going to the fields for open defecation, as the waste and crop land in most villages were generally under the control of non-Dalit households and policed by these households.

Fourthly, government intervention has contributed to a change in recent times. In 1999, the Central government initiated a Total Sanitation Campaign (TSC), which accelerated the construction of sanitary toilets, both in individual houses and as public toilets (in schools, *anganwadis*, etc). The village survey data show that a majority of households that reported having a toilet had received some government help for constructing it, either in cash or kind or both. For example, only five Dalit households in Harevli had toilets in their houses, but all of them had availed of government aid for constructing toilets. In Kothapalle, of 47 Dalit households who reported having toilets in their houses, twenty-eight had received some form of government assistance for building them. Nimshirgaon was the only village among those surveyed where public toilets had been constructed by the panchayat.

In practice, the use of sanitary toilets depends on the availability of adequate water within a short distance. The better performance of 25 F Gulabewala and Nimshirgaon villages in terms of use of toilets can be linked to the fact that the gram panchayats in these villages had installed an improved water supply system. By contrast, in villages such as Bukkacherla and Gharsondi, people reported not using their toilets because of inadequate water supply. Another important factor is the availability of land for construction of toilets in individual homesteads.

Drinking Water
Quality
In the United Nations' Millennium Development Goals, the indicator for drinking water is 'the proportion of population with sustainable access to an improved water source', where 'improved' includes piped water in dwellings, public taps, tubewells or borewells, protected dug wells, protected springs, and rainwater collection.[6] In the Census of India and surveys of the NSSO, an improved or safe source of drinking water is defined as water from a tap, hand-pump, borewell or tubewell, that is, from a covered source of water. This definition is only a partial approximation to safe water since there could be open wells with clean water and closed sources with contaminated water. Large sections of the population of Kerala, for example, draw water from wells and then boil it, and the problems of quality are consequently less in the State than elsewhere. Nevertheless, we too have used 'covered source' as a proxy for a safe or improved source of drinking water.

In nine of the study villages – Ananthavaram, Bukkacherla, Warwat Khanderao, Harevli, Mahatwar, 25 F Gulabewala, Alabujanahalli, Siresandra and Zhapur – almost all Dalit households (96 to 100 per cent) had access to a covered source of water. The outliers were Gharsondi and Nimshirgaon,

---

[6] See Millennium Development Goals Indicators at http://unstats.un.org/unsd/mdg/ Metadata.aspx?IndicatorId=0&SeriesId=711.

where only 48 and 58 per cent of Dalit households, respectively, had access to a covered source of drinking water.

A new water supply system under the 'Jal Swaraj Yojana' was under construction in Nimshirgaon during our survey. A follow-up visit showed that the water supply scheme has been implemented and that the village panchayat had laid pipelines to various parts of the village. In order to extend the pipeline to their homesteads, households had to pay an initial fixed cost as well as an annual fee of Rs 1,200. In principle, water was to be provided through public taps for those not willing or able to extend the pipeline to their house. In practice, however, we found that there was no provision of public water taps for poor households, and every household that wanted access to water had to pay for a private connection.

In Gharsondi, Dalit households had to fetch drinking water from open wells built on the agricultural land of large cultivator households.

TABLE 8 *Number and proportion of households having access to covered sources of drinking water, study villages, Dalit households and Other Caste households*

Village (State)	Dalit households			Other Caste households			All	
	HHs	%	Total HHs	HHs	%	Total HHs	HHs	%
Ananthavaram (Andhra Pradesh)	283	100	283	317	99	320	661	100
Bukkacherla (Andhra Pradesh)	58	100	58	222	99	224	288	99
Kothapalle (Andhra Pradesh)	100	85	117	177	76	234	290	80
Harevli (Uttar Pradesh)	40	100	40	57	100	57	110	100
Mahatwar (Uttar Pradesh)	94	100	94	61	100	61	155	100
Nimshirgaon (Maharashtra)	144	58	247	332	70	473	487	63
Warwat Khanderao (Maharashtra)	25	100	25	167	99	168	245	100
25F Gulabewala (Rajasthan)	121	98	123	81	100	81	202	99
Gharsondi (Madhya Pradesh)	13	48	27	181	94	192	239	90
Alabujanahalli (Karnataka)	36	100	36	203	97	210	239	97
Siresandra (Karnataka)	26	100	26	51	100	51	77	100
Zhapur (Karnataka)	43	96	45	27	64	42	81	74
All	983	88	1121	1876	89	2113	3074	88

Note: The data here refer to the primary source (used for the major part of the year) in cases where there was more than one source of drinking water.

Source: Survey data.

The data in Table 8 pertain to the primary source of drinking water. In many villages (Harevli, Nimshirgaon, Kothapalle and Gharsondi), households depended on more than one source of water, particularly during the dry summer months. The problem of shortages in summer months was more acute for Dalit households than Others, as the alternative sources of drinking water were usually not owned by Dalits, and they could gain access to such sources only after the Other Caste households.

Location of Source of Drinking Water

In rural areas, many households do not have a source of drinking water within their home or homestead, as the system of distribution of water

TABLE 9 *Proportion of households having primary source of drinking water within or just outside the homestead, study villages, Dalit households and Other Caste households*

Village (State)	Dalit households			Other Caste households			All	
	HHs	%	Total HHs	HHs	%	Total HHs	HHs	%
Ananthavaram (Andhra Pradesh)	86	30	282	244	76	320	340	51
Bukkacherla (Andhra Pradesh)	1	2	58	47	21	226	48	16
Kothapalle (Andhra Pradesh)	58	50	117	86	37	235	147	40
Harevli (Uttar Pradesh)	23	58	40	50	89	56	82	75
Mahatwar (Uttar Pradesh)	27	29	94	39	64	61	66	43
Nimshirgaon (Maharashtra)	105	43	247	282	60	473	398	52
Warwat Khanderao (Maharashtra)	0	0	25	10	6	168	11	4
25F Gulabewala (Rajasthan)	50	41	123	80	99	81	130	64
Gharsondi (Madhya Pradesh)	7	26	27	53	28	190	63	24
Alabujanahalli (Karnataka)*	3 (32)	9 (94)	34	90 (198)	43 (95)	208	93 (230)	38 (95)
Siresandra (Karnataka)*	0 (21)	0 (84)	25	3 (46)	6 (92)	50	3 (67)	4 (89)
Zhapur (Karnataka)*	0 (39)	0 (87)	45	1 (33)	2 (80)	41	1 (88)	1 (81)
All	360	32	1117	985	47	2109	1382	40

Note: * As the norms for distance of source of water from the house were different from earlier rounds of the survey for Karnataka, we have given two numbers for the Karnataka villages: figures outside parentheses refer to households having a source of water within the homestead, and the figures within parentheses refer to households having a source of water within 200 metres of the homestead.

Source: Survey data.

through private taps is uncommon. Among Other Caste households, a large majority reported a source of water within the homestead in Ananthavaram, Harevli, Mahatwar and 25 F Gulabewala (Table 9). The proportion of Dalit households with a source of drinking water within the homestead was lower than the corresponding proportion among Other Caste households in all the study villages except Kothapalle. In Kothapalle, since the quality of water supplied through taps was bad, Other Caste households turned to alternative sources for drinking water, but Dalit households lacked access to alternate sources and so depended on tap water for their drinking water needs.

In absolute terms, the worst-performing village (other than the three Karnataka villages) in respect of access to drinking water within the homestead was Warwat Khanderao in Maharashtra, where only 6 per cent of Other Caste households reported a source of drinking water within the homestead (the proportion was 0 among Dalits). In the Dalit settlement within Warwat Khanderao, however, there was a panchayat-owned water tank, which was the main source of drinking water for all households.

A very small proportion of Dalit households in all the villages had a source of drinking water within their homestead. While we found panchayat-operated water supply projects in most villages, not all households – Dalits in particular – had been provided with water connections within their homesteads. One reason for this was the cost involved: for a tap in the house, there was a fixed charge at the time of installation, as well as a monthly or annual fee. Many Dalit households were unable to afford these payments.

Understanding Deprivation: Role of Caste, Income and Public Action

The quantitative and qualitative data from our village surveys show that there was a clear difference between Dalits and Other Caste households (that is, those belonging to non-Adivasi, non-Muslim communities) in respect of deprivation in basic amenities. Although most of the data reported above are from village census surveys, for which tests of significance are not relevant in the same way as they are for sample surveys, nevertheless, we have combined

TABLE 10 *Pearson's chi-square test for association between caste and access to specified basic amenities, pooled data from seven study villages*

Type of amenity	Value of Pearson's chi-square	Degrees of freedom	P value	Significance level
Pucca house (Yes/No)	81.95	1	2.2e–16	< 1 %
Katcha house (Yes/No)	174.2	1	2.2e–16	< 1 %
House with toilet (Yes/No)	35.6	1	2.32e–09	< 1 %
Water source within homestead (Yes/No)	20.3	1	6.59e–06	< 1 %

Note: Only two caste/social categories are considered: Scheduled Caste and Other Castes. We have only taken data for seven villages (surveyed in 2006 and 2007) for which income data are also available.

Source: Survey data.

the data from all the villages and undertaken a test for statistical association.

The results of the chi-square test, reported in Table 10, establish a highly significant association between caste status and access to selected amenities. For example, the chi-square value for the two-way contingency table of households by caste status and access to a toilet was 35.6, and this was significant at less than 1 per cent level of significance.

The question that arises is whether the observed difference between Scheduled Castes and Other households in access to specified amenities is related to the social characteristics of the household or to some other factor such as income. In the following section, we examine the relation between level of income and access to amenities.

Role of Income

To illustrate the relation between income and access to basic amenities, we first cross-tabulated income levels with access to amenities. In Appendix Tables A1 to A6, we have classified households in seven survey villages into three income groups, based on total household income.[7] The first and lowest income category is made up of households with total incomes of less than Rs 30,000 a year, which roughly corresponds to the official rural poverty line for 2004–05.[8] The second category is of households with incomes from Rs 30,000 to Rs 100,000 per year, and the third category is households with incomes over Rs 100,000. For the three villages of Karnataka, as data on incomes have not been computed, we have used an asset-based categorization (Appendix Tables A3 and A6). We focus here only on access to toilets and drinking water.

Access to Toilets

In Ananthavaram, among all low-income Other Caste households, 68 per cent had toilets; the proportion rose to 100 per cent in the highest income category. However, among Dalits, only 16 per cent of low-income households had toilets, and even among those with Rs 100,000 a year, only two-thirds had a toilet facility. In other words, the chances of having a toilet rose at higher income levels, but differentially for Dalits and Other Caste households. The pattern was similar in Harevli. In Mahatwar and Warwat Khanderao, among Dalits, a shift to higher income categories was not associated with better access to toilets. In Bukkacherla there was no Dalit household with a reported income of over Rs 100,000. In the lowest income category, however, 27 per cent of Dalit households had a lavatory; the corresponding proportion among Other Caste households was only 11 per cent. As discussed below, external intervention has improved housing for some Dalit households in this village.

Overall deprivation in access to lavatories was high in the two vil-

---

[7] Household incomes have not been computed for the two Adivasi villages.

[8] This is based on the assumption of Rs 456 per capita per month at 2004–05 prices and a five-member family.

lages of Uttar Pradesh. Nevertheless, it is surprising to find that the only Dalit household in Harevli, which had an income of over Rs 100,000 per year, did not have a toilet. In the Maharashtra villages, the data indicate that access to lavatories rose with incomes, although in absolute terms, deprivation was higher among Dalit households at all income levels (with one exception). The village of 25 F Gulabewala offers an interesting contrast. Irrespective of income levels, almost all Other Caste households and a high proportion of Dalit households reported access to a lavatory.

The situation in the three villages of Karnataka was appalling. In Zhapur, only one household had a lavatory (this was a Muslim household). In Siresandra, only six Other Caste households (15 per cent) had a lavatory. In Alabujanahalli the situation was a little better, and access to toilets rose with the level of asset ownership.

Access to Water within the Homestead

Access to a source of drinking water within the homestead rose with incomes, though differentially for Dalits and Other Caste households in Ananthavaram, Harevli, Mahatwar, Nimshirgaon and 25 F Gulabewala villages. The situation was remarkably different in Bukkacherla and Warwat Khanderao.

In Bukkacherla village, 90 per cent of Dalit households lived in *pucca* houses. Of all Dalit households, 71 per cent had received some aid for housing (for house or toilet construction). In addition to government support, Dalit households had benefited from a local NGO called Rural Development Trust, which assisted in house construction. From 2002–03, households in this village had access to a panchayat-operated tubewell but this became defunct in 2009, after which all the households had to rely on one hand-pump for supply of drinking water.

In Warwat Khanderao, the data show that no household, irrespective of income level, had a water source within the homestead. These data are somewhat misleading, since the gram panchayat had installed a public water facility in the Dalit settlement and the source of water was within 200 meters for almost all households in the settlement. The fact remains, however, that no household had access to water within the homestead, and that all Dalit households continued to have a separate source of water.

Discussion

Our data on the pattern of access to amenities for households at different income levels indicate that incomes alone do not ensure an improved standard of living, unless, of course, the incomes are very high. There are households below the official poverty line that have certain amenities which households with incomes above the poverty line lack. Although there is a tendency in all the study villages, with a few exceptions, for the proportion of households with a specified amenity to increase as we move from a lower to a higher income level, there are big variations in the extent of improvement at different levels of income. For example, in Harevli, 42 per cent of Other Caste households in the lowest income group and 60 per cent of Other Caste households in the second income group had toilets within the homestead. In respect of access water within the homestead, however, 92 per cent of households in the lowest income had such a facility and the corresponding proportion was 71 per cent among those in the next highest income group. Thus, in terms of both aggregate attainment and extent of improvement at higher income levels, there are big variations even within the same village, in the relationship between access to different amenities and income levels.

Secondly, the relation between income and access to basic amenities is dissimilar for Scheduled Caste and Other Caste households. In many of our survey villages, even the richest Dalit households did not have access to all the basic amenities, while this was not so among Other Caste households. In Ananthavaram, the highest-income Dalit family did not have a *pucca* house. In Warwat Khanderao, the highest-income Dalit family did not have water within the homestead. In Bukkacherla, Harevli, Mahatwar and Warwat Khanderao, the highest-income Dalit household did not have a toilet.

Thirdly, the public-good nature of certain basic amenities implies that access depends not just on individual income but on common facilities. Take the case of piped water, for instance. A house can have provision for piped water indoors only if there is access to piped water in the neighbourhood. The new international literature on social exclusion recognizes the importance of a neighbourhood dimension – that is, the presence or absence of community resources in the neighbourhood – in the prevalence of social exclusion (EC 2008). It is well known that on account of historical deprivation, Dalit households face specific problems with respect to availability and access to public infrastructure and common resources. The location of Dalit hamlets at a distance from the main village, for example, affects access to amenities like drinking water.

Settlement Pattern

In almost all the study villages, Dalit settlements were separate from the 'main' village settlement, and the Dalit area lacked basic infrastructure, such as all-weather *pucca* roads, street lights, open spaces for common use and educational institutions. The Dalit settlements were prone to flooding during the monsoon in all the villages. The Dalit settlement in Ananthavaram was flooded in 2007, and all the families had to abandon their homes for a period of time on account of this. In Harevli, the part of the village where the Dalits lived had no *pucca* roads – only narrow streets without lighting – and few open spaces. In Mahatwar, which is a predominantly Dalit village, the Dalits lived in a separate settlement (though it was the largest settlement of the village) and the area got a *pucca* road only after a Dalit was elected as *sarpanch* (this was just before our survey in 2006).

Thus far, we have documented and discussed deprivation and exclusion. There can also be direct or active discrimination, as for example, separate queues for Dalit households for collecting water from a common source (Tiwary and Phansalkar 2007).

Deprivation and Association with Caste and Income

We now test if the association between caste and access to amenities remains significant after adjusting for incomes (Table 11). The modified chi-square test is highly significant, implying that caste status and availability of basic amenities are related even after separating households by broad income group (approximately below and above poverty line categories). To put it differently, caste differences in access to amenities persist even after accounting for income differences.

TABLE 11 *Mantel-Haenszel chi-square test for association between caste and access to specified basic amenities, given income category, combined data for seven study villages*

Type of amenity	Value of chi square	Degrees of freedom	P value	Significance level
Pucca house (Yes/No)	54.78	1	1.34e–13	< 1 %
Katcha house (Yes/No)	144.82	1	2.2e–16	< 1 %
House with toilet (Yes/No)	11.452	1	0.0007	< 1 %
Water source within homestead (Yes/No)	6.334	1	0.0118	< 2 %

Note: Only two caste/social categories are considered: Scheduled Caste and Other Caste households. Household income is categorized as low (less than Rs 30,000 per annum) and high.

Role of Public Intervention

There is no doubt that public intervention is essential to reverse historical discrimination and to provide public goods. Public policy in India has recognized this and attempted to address the issue by designing schemes to provide better amenities to Dalit houses and settlements (e.g., source of drinking water, special housing programmes). In this section, we do not attempt to evaluate specific public policies, but we provide a picture from the village data of the extent to which external interventions have altered deprivation and discrimination in access to basic amenities.

Respondents in our villages reported three types of government benefits: for house construction and maintenance, for construction of toilets, and for assistance to get an electricity connection.[9] The benefits were in cash or kind or both. With regard to housing, in some cases, the government built the houses directly, but in most cases, households were given financial or material assistance. In aggregate terms the proportion of households that received some benefit was lowest in the two villages in Uttar Pradesh, Mahatwar and

[9] Data on electricity connections were collected only in Karnataka.

Harevli, and highest in Zhapur in Gulbarga district, Karnataka (41 out of 111 households, or 37 per cent, had received some government aid for housing).

A consistent finding from all the study villages was that a higher proportion of Dalit households than Other Caste households received government benefits. In Nimshirgaon, for example, 7 per cent of Other Caste households and 29 per cent of Dalit households got some aid for house improvement. Similarly, in Harevli, 9 per cent of Other Caste households and 16 per cent of Dalit households received some government benefits. The data indicate that government aid is biased – as it should be – in favour of Dalit households, although they also show that Dalit households are worse off in respect of outcomes.[10]

It is clear that the scale and coverage of government assistance remains grossly inadequate. (See box on Dr Ambedkar Gram Vikas Yojana.) For example, some households that received support for housing had to also take loans from other sources in order to construct a house. Some households continued to live in *katcha* or semi-*pucca* houses despite getting government aid. In such cases, clearly, the scale of assistance had been too low. In Ananthavaram, for instance, of the eighteen Dalit households that received assistance for house construction, two lived in *katcha* constructions.

An example of the inadequacy of government schemes comes from the 'Indiramma' housing scheme in Ananthavaram.

> In 2007–08, the Government sanctioned the construction of 23 houses for Scheduled Tribe families under the 'Indiramma' rural housing scheme. The scheme envisages assistance in cash and kind (in the form of bags of cement) for the construction of a house. However, the payment is on an instalment basis. According to the panchayat office, all four instalments are to be paid in cash and according to the following schedule: Rs 4,000 after construction of the foundation, Rs 12,000 after door-level construction, Rs 6,000 after roof-level construction and Rs 10,000 after completion. In short, each household invests in construction and then is reimbursed as per this schedule of payments.
>
> Since all the Adivasi households are too poor to invest the money themselves, the construction of most of these houses has now (that is, in December 2009) been abandoned at the door-level. (Ramachandran, Rawal and Swaminathan, eds 2010: 189)

Our field experience suggests that government schemes also fail if implemented mechanically without taking local needs into consideration. The case of toilets and water supply in Bukkacherla is one example. The water supply system has been abandoned by the local administration, and households that were provided assistance for sanitary toilets could not use them

---

[10] The Indira Awas Yojana was started in 1985–86 as a scheme for construction of houses for SCs, STs and bonded labourers in rural areas, and extended to households from Other groups below the poverty line only in 1993–94.

Dr Ambedkar Gram Vikas Yojana: A Note on Mahatwar's Experience

In 1991, to commemorate the birth centenary of Dr B.R. Ambedkar, the government of Uttar Pradesh inaugurated the Dr Ambedkar Gram Vikas Yojana (Dr Ambedkar Village Development Scheme). The scheme was initially implemented by the Rural Development Department, but in 1995, a new department called the Dr Ambedkar Gram Vikas Vibhag (later renamed Dr Ambedkar Grameen Samagra Vikas Vibhag) was created whose sole function was to implement this scheme.

The main objective of the scheme is to develop rural infrastructure and improve the condition of basic amenities such as housing, drinking water, sanitation facilities, *pucca* roads, primary schools and electrification in Scheduled Caste (SC) and Scheduled Tribe (ST) dominated villages on a priority basis. Villages in which more than one half of the population was Dalit or Adivasi were to be declared 'Dr Ambedkar Villages'. Within selected villages, priority was to be given to SC and ST households over Others.

The scheme also envisaged all-round development of the beneficiary households. The scheme was formed by amalgamating various pre-existing State and central government programmes across departments. These included schemes for drinking water, housing and rural infrastructure (under the Rural Development Department); for sanitation and construction of latrines, and drainage (under the Panchayati Raj Department); and for diverse programmes that were hitherto the responsibility of the School Education, Public Works, Minor Irrigation, Social Welfare, Energy and Women's Welfare Departments.

Mahatwar was selected as a Dr Ambedkar Village in 1995–96, that is, in the very first phase of the scheme. Nevertheless (as reported in the article by Madhura Swaminathan and Shamsher Singh in this volume), evidence from our village survey of 2006, conducted more than a decade after the implementation of the scheme began, shows that basic amenities like *pucca* housing, electricity, sanitation and *pucca* roads were absent in the Dalit settlement of the village.[1] This suggests that the scheme did not result in any significant improvement of social infrastructure in the Dalit settlement of Mahatwar. In 2009–10, Mahatwar was selected for a second time as a Dr Ambedkar Village. Although Mahatwar has been selected twice as an Ambedkar Village, housing and other amenities continue to be severely inadequate in the village (see Table 1).

RS was a 'beneficiary' of the housing scheme in Mahatwar in 2009–10. He was to receive Rs 35,000 for the construction of a *pucca* house. RS

---

[1] Even a board declaring that the village has been selected as a Dr Ambedkar Village was not put up in the village until December 2010, despite an office order of the State government that declared it compulsory.

TABLE 1   *Selected indicators of housing and amenities, Dalit households, Mahatwar village, 2006* in per cent

Indicator	Dalit households that had access to the amenity as a proportion of all Dalit households
House with pucca roof, walls and floor	9
House with two rooms	88
House with authorized electricity connection	2
House with water connection inside or immediately outside the house	29
House with working latrine	3
House with all the above five indicators	1

had to first pay Rs 10,000 to local officials (both government officers and elected representatives) to have his name included in the list of beneficiaries and get all the instalments of the amount due to him. The remaining Rs 25,000 was not sufficient to construct a *pucca* house. RS is a landless manual labourer and did not have any savings to invest in the construction of a house; he also did not want to borrow money from informal moneylenders (at a local rate of interest of 120 per cent per annum). As a result, the construction of his house remained unfinished. The walls of one *pucca* room were constructed, and RS used thatch-and-bamboo to cover the walls. The house has a second *katcha* room (with walls made of mud and thatch, a thatch and polythene roof, and a mud floor). These two rooms house the eight members of RS's household, which includes his elderly parents and four children aged between 2 to 16. The total constructed area of this house is approximately 15 feet by 7 feet. The household does not have a separate kitchen or cooking space. There is no electricity connection. According to RS, low-voltage electricity is supplied for just 7 to 8 hours a day (with day and night supply on alternate weeks). He said it was not worth taking an authorized electricity connection and adding two to three hundred rupees a month to the household expenditure for such erratic supply of electricity. Most households in the village have unauthorized electricity connections. Of RS's four children, two are in school; they cannot study in the evening or nights as there is no electricity and their parents deem it unsafe to leave kerosene lamps burning for very long at night, given the risk of fire in a thatch-covered room. In late 2010, the local administration financed the construction of a latrine for RS's household (as it did for several other households in the Dalit settlement). This is a source of amusement, however, as the latrine does not even have a pit, but only three walls with a tin sheet as the roof. According to RS, his and several other such incomplete latrines were constructed in haste just before a visit of the Chief Minister to the district headquarters six months prior to our interview with him.

for lack of water. Inadequate financial assistance for housing for Scheduled Tribes in Ananthavaram, the poor quality of water supply in Kothapalle, erratic functioning of the water supply system in Gharsondi on account of shortage of electricity – these are some examples of the incompleteness and inadequacy of government intervention. Also, as discussed in the literature, even publicly constructed housing for Dalits has not addressed the problem of segregation (see Sivagnanam and Sivaraj 2002).

Multiple Deprivations

We used our village data to derive another measure of the adequacy of basic housing (see also, Singh, Swaminathan and Ramachandran 2013). Although the criteria we used fell far short of international norms in respect of adequate housing, we recorded the number of households that lived in houses that had at least all of the following: (1) *pucca* roofs, walls and floors; (2) two rooms; (3) a source of water inside or immediately outside the house; (4) an electricity connection; and (5) a functioning latrine. The data on the proportion of households living in houses that fulfilled these criteria in our survey villages are shown in Table 12.

The results are very telling indeed. In five villages – Bukkacherla, Harevli, Warwat Khanderao, Siresandra and Zhapur – *no* Dalit household lived in a house with adequate amenities. In the other villages, the proportion of Dalit households with adequate housing was very small: 1 per cent in Mahatwar, 3 per cent in Alabujanahalli and 8 per cent in Ananthavaram. The peak achievement among Dalit households was 13 per cent in Nimshirgaon.

The overall situation is one where a large majority of households

TABLE 12 *Households with adequate housing as a proportion of all households, by social group, study villages* in per cent

Village	Dalit households	Adivasi households	Muslim households	Other Caste households	All households
Ananthavaram	8	0	12	44	25
Bukkacherla	0	Na	0	2	2
Kothapalle	9	0	0	14	12
Harevli	0	Na	0	15	8
Mahatwar	1	Na	Na	0	1
Nimshirgaon	11	Na	17	39	28
Warwat Khanderao	0	Na	2	3	3
25F Gulabewala	3	Na	Na	76	32
Gharsondi	12	0	0	18	14
Alabujanahalli	3	Na	Na	32	28
Siresandra	0	Na	Na	2	1
Zhapur	0	0	0	0	0
All villages combined	6	0	4	22	15

in all the survey villages have sub-standard housing. Nevertheless, there is a clear difference between Dalit households and Other Caste households in terms of adequate housing.

Taking the combined figure for all twelve villages, only 6 per cent of all Dalit households had adequate housing; the corresponding figure was 0 for Adivasis, 4 per cent for Muslims and 22 per cent for Other Caste households.

No Adivasi household in our survey had a *pucca* house with two rooms, electricity, a toilet and drinking water facilities. The situation of Adivasis in the two Adivasi-majority villages – Dungariya in Udaipur district of Rajasthan and Badhar in Anuppur district of Madhya Pradesh – was as bad as that of Adivasis in multi-caste villages.

Concluding Remarks

Using data from fourteen villages that were surveyed as part of the ongoing Project on Agrarian Relations in India, we explored deprivation and discrimination experienced by Dalit households in access to basic amenities. Amidst a situation of overall inadequacy in the availability of proper housing, water and toilets, there was severe deprivation among Dalit households. The proportion of Dalit households living in *katcha* houses – houses with both walls and roof made of temporary materials such as mud, grass or polythene – was over 50 per cent in Ananthavaram and 25 F Gulabewala, and over 20 per cent in five other villages. Zhapur was the sole exception: the availability of stone locally ensured that all residents could live in *pucca* structures. By contrast, in no village did more than 8 per cent of Other Caste households live in *katcha* houses.

Turning to other amenities, in the majority of cases, deprivation among Dalit households was worse than among Other Caste households. For example, only 37 per cent of Dalit households reported a separate kitchen (across eleven villages), as compared to 61 per cent of Other Caste households. Similarly, 36 per cent of Dalit households had access to a toilet as compared to 54 per cent of Other Caste households. The situation was better in respect of availability of electricity and covered source of water for drinking purposes. However, in villages such as Gharsondi in Madhya Pradesh and Bukkacherla in Andhra Pradesh, where 90 per cent or more of Dalit households reported having an electricity connection in their houses, the proportion of unauthorized connections was high. Similarly, while 88 per cent of Dalit households across twelve villages had access to a covered ('safe') source of water, water was available within or just outside the homestead among only 32 per cent of Dalit households.

Internationally, detailed specifications are available as to what constitutes adequate housing. Taking a simple and far from complete definition of an adequate house as a *pucca* structure with two rooms, a toilet, electricity and water outlet within or just outside the premises, our village data show that deprivation was extremely high among Dalits, Adivasis and Muslims. Across the fourteen villages, no Adivasi household, 4 per cent of Muslim households and 6 per cent of Dalit households had adequate housing.

A distinctive feature of our analysis, thanks to the availability of relevant data from the village surveys, is the examination of the relation between incomes and access to basic amenities. As demonstrated by a simple cross-tabulation, in general, access to amenities tends to rise with income levels; but there were important exceptions, and, more pertinently, there were differences across social groups. For example, in Harevli village of western Uttar Pradesh, among households with annual incomes less than Rs 30,000, only 3 per cent of Dalit households had toilets as compared to 42 per cent of Other households. Further, the sole Dalit household with income above Rs 1 lakh a year did not have a toilet.

The continuation of discrimination is reflected in the fact of a strong association between caste status and access to amenities after adjusting for income levels. The Mantel-Haenszl chi-square test results for the association between caste status and access to selected amenities across income groups were highly significant. The importance of neighbourhood factors was also brought out by our surveys. The location of Dalit homes in separate settlements or hamlets and the lack of public infrastructure in these hamlets affected the living conditions of all households in the settlement irrespective of income level. In other words, segregation in housing imposes additional costs on all Dalit households, irrespective of their economic status.

Our surveys also touched upon the role of public intervention in improving the availability of basic amenities (although we did not focus on this in any detail). Dalit households were more likely to report receipt of government aid for housing or toilet construction than Other households. It is clear, however, that the scale and scope of government intervention has been grossly inadequate.

It is also worth noting that absence of homestead land is a constraint to improvements in housing (especially the construction of toilets, separate kitchens, etc.) for Dalit households. This underlines the importance of basic land reform in improving the living standards of rural households.

In conclusion, our data show that disadvantage and discrimination persist among Dalit households in the sphere of basic amenities. This has to be addressed by public provisioning of basic amenities and public action to end direct discrimination.

We thank V.K. Ramachandran for his detailed comments and suggestions.

References

European Commission (EC) (2008), *Poverty and Social Exclusion in Rural Areas: Final Report*, Directorate-General for Employment, Social Affairs and Equal Opportunities, Unit E2, August, available at http://ec.europa.eu/social/BlobServlet?docId=2087&langId =en, viewed on 26 September 2013.

International Labour Organization (ILO) (1961), 'R115 Workers' Housing Recommendation 1961', ILO, Geneva, available at www.ilo.org, viewed on 18 September 2013.

International Year of Sanitation (IYS) (2008), 'Tackling a Global Crisis: International Year of Sanitation 2008', United Nations, available at www.esa.un.org/iys/docs/IYS_flag-ship_web_small.pdf, viewed on 18 September 2013.

Ramachandran, V.K. (2010), 'Dungariya Village, Southern Rajasthan', *Critical Asian Studies*, vol. 42, no. 2, June, pp. 273–88.

Ramachandran, V.K., Rawal, Vikas and Swaminathan, Madhura, eds (2010), *Socio-Economic Surveys of Three Villages in Andhra Pradesh: A Study of Agrarian Relations*, Tulika Books, New Delhi.

Rawal, Vikas (2008), 'Estimates of Rural Households Incomes in India: Select Methodological Issues', paper presented at *Studying Village Economies in India: A Colloquium on Methodology*, Chalsa, 21–23 December, available at www.agrarianstudies.org, veiwed on 27 December 2010.

Singh, Shamsher, Swaminathan, Madhura and Ramachandran, V.K. (2013), 'Housing Shortages in Rural India', *Review of Agrarian Studies*, vol. 3, no. 2, available at http://www. ras.org.in/housing_shortages_in_rural_india.

Sivagnanam, Jothi K. and Sivaraj, M (2002), 'Tamil Nadu: Samathuvapuram: Towards Spatial Equality', *Economic and Political Weekly*, vol. 28, September, pp. 3990–92; available at http://mpra.ub.uni-muenchen.de/3348/, viewed on 25 January 2011.

Swaminathan, Madhura (1995), 'Aspects of Urban Poverty in Bombay', *Environment and Urbanization*, vol 7, no. 1, April, pp. 133–44.

Thorat, Sukhadeo (2009), *Dalits in India: Search for a Common Destiny*, Sage Publications, New Delhi.

Thorat, Sukhadeo and Newman, Katherine, eds (2010), *Blocked by Caste, Economic Discrimination in Modern India*, Oxford University Press, New Delhi.

Tiwary, R. and Phansalkar, S.J. (2007), 'Dalits' Access to Water: Patterns of Deprivation and Discrimination', *International Journal of Rural Management*, vol. 3, no. 1, pp. 43–67; available at www.irm.sagepub.com, viewed on 18 September 2013.

Appendix Tables

TABLE A1 *Proportion of households with access to lavatory facilities, by income group, study villages in Andhra Pradesh and Uttar Pradesh, 2006* in per cent

Income group (in Rs)	Ananthavaram (Andhra Pradesh)		Bukkacherla (Andhra Pradesh)		Kothapalle (Andhra Pradesh)		Harevli (Uttar Pradesh)		Mahatwar (Uttar Pradesh)	
	Dalits	Others	Dalits	Others	Dalits	Others	Dalits	Others	Dalits	Others
Up to 30000	16	68	27	11	27	45	3	42	3	5
30001–1 lakh	31	67	0	23	56	51	13	60	0	24
Above 1 lakh	67	100	–	86	100 *	35 #	0 *	82	0	50
Richest household	Yes	Yes	No	Yes	Yes	Yes	No	Yes	No	Yes
All	23	77	21	15	37	45	5	58	3	14

Note: * Only one household in this category.
           # This was a sample; only three households were surveyed, of whom one had a toilet.
Source: Survey data.

TABLE A2 *Proportion of households with access to lavatory facilities, by income group, study villages in Maharashtra and Rajasthan, 2007* in per cent

Income group (in Rs)	Warwat Khanderao (Maharashtra)		Nimshirgaon (Maharashtra)		25 F Gulabewala (Rajasthan)	
	Dalits	Others	Dalits	Others	Dalits	Others
Up to 30000	30	30	44	44	71	50
30001–1 lakh	25	51	36	74	90	100
Above 1 lakh	0 *	67	90	84	100	97
Richest household	No	Yes	Yes	Yes	Yes	Yes
All	28	45	63 $	72	77	96

Note: * Only one household in this category.
           $ Households that reported access to a public lavatory have been included.
Source: Survey data.

TABLE A3 *Proportion of households with access to lavatory facilities, by asset group, study villages in Karnataka, 2009* in per cent

Asset group (in Rs)	Alabujanahalli		Siresandra		Zhapur	
	Dalits	Others	Dalits	Others	Dalits	Others
< 100,000	0	13	0 *	0 *	0	0
100,000–500,000	14	25	0	0	0	0
> 500,000	100	70	0	15	0	0
Wealthiest household	Yes	Yes	No	Yes	No	No
All	19	57	0	12	0	0

Note: * Only one household in this category.
Source: Survey data.

TABLE A4 *Proportion of households with source of drinking water within or just outside the homestead, by income group, study villages in Andhra Pradesh and Uttar Pradesh, 2006* in per cent

Income group (in Rs)	Ananthavaram (Andhra Pradesh)		Bukkacherla (Andhra Pradesh)		Kothapalle (Andhra Pradesh)		Harevli (Uttar Pradesh)		Mahatwar (Uttar Pradesh)	
	Dalits	Others	Dalits	Others	Dalits	Others	Dalits	Others	Dalits	Others
Up to 30000	27	62	7	9	51	37	55	92	24	59
30001–1 lakh	35	74	0	15	65	46	64	71	43	76
Above 1 lakh	100	95	–	68	100	35	100	100	50	100
Richest household	Yes	Yes	No	No$	Yes	Yes	Yes	Yes	No	Yes
All	33	76	2	21	50	37	58	89	29	64

Note: $ The household had a tap connection within the homestead but did not use it for drinking water purposes.
Source: Survey data.

TABLE A5 *Proportion of households with source of drinking water within or just outside the homestead, by income group, study villages in Maharashtra and Rajasthan, 2007* in per cent

Income group (in Rs)	Warwat Khanderao (Maharashtra)		Nimshirgaon (Maharashtra)		25 F Gulabewala (Rajasthan)	
	Dalits	Others	Dalits	Others	Dalits	Others
Up to 30000	0	7	38	45	33	100
30001–1 lakh	0	7	40	57	56	100
Above 1 lakh	0 *	0	85	86	100	98 $
Richest household	No	No	Yes	Yes	Yes	Yes
All	0	6	43	60	41	99

Notes: * Only one household in this category.
    $ Only one household did not have water within the homestead.
Source: Survey data.

TABLE A6 *Proportion of households having primary drinking water source less than 200 metres from the house, by asset group, study villages in Karnataka, 2009* in per cent

Asset group (in Rs)	Alabujanahalli		Siresandra		Zhapur	
	Dalits	Others	Dalits	Others	Dalits	Others
< 100,000	100	88	100	100	88	87
100,000–500,000	91	91	86	88	86	95
> 500,000	100	99	80	90	72	67
Wealthiest household	Yes	Yes	Yes	Yes	Yes	Yes
All	94	95	84	92	80	87

Source: Survey data.

Contributors

APARAJITA BAKSHI, Assistant Professor, Tata Institute of Social Sciences, Mumbai.

PALLAVI CHAVAN is the author of *A Study of Rural Credit in Maharashtra: The Resurvey of a Village from Western Maharashtra*.

NILADRI SEKHAR DHAR, Assistant Professor, Tata Institute of Social Sciences, Tuljapur.

JUDITH HEYER, Emeritus Fellow, Somerville College, University of Oxford.

NAVPREET KAUR, Ph.D. student, Jawaharlal Nehru University, New Delhi.

V.K. RAMACHANDRAN, Professor, Indian Statistical Institute, Bangalore Centre.

G. RAMAKRISHNAN, Secretary, Communist Party of India (Marxist), Tamil Nadu State Committee.

R. RAMAKUMAR, Professor, Tata Institute of Social Sciences, Mumbai.

VIKAS RAWAL, Associate Professor, Jawaharlal Nehru University, New Delhi.

NIDHI SADHANA SABHARWAL, Director, Indian Institute of Dalit Studies, New Delhi.

PARTHA SAHA, Assistant Professor, Jindal School of Government and Public Policy, Haryana.

SHAMSHER SINGH, Ph.D. student, Indian Statistical Institute, Bangalore Centre.

V. SURJIT, Agricultural Economist, International Potato Centre, Consultative Group on International Agricultural Research (CGIAR), New Delhi Centre.

MADHURA SWAMINATHAN, Professor, Indian Statistical Institute, Bangalore Centre.

AMIT THORAT, Associate Fellow, National Council of Applied Economic Research, New Delhi.

SUKHADEO THORAT, Professor, Jawaharlal Nehru University and Chairman, Indian Council of Social Science Research, New Delhi.

Index